𝕽𝖎𝖛𝖊𝖗𝖘𝖎𝖉𝖊 𝕰𝖉𝖎𝖙𝖎𝖔𝖓

THE
COMPLETE WORKS OF NATHANIEL
HAWTHORNE, WITH INTRODUCTORY
NOTES BY GEORGE PARSONS
LATHROP

AND ILLUSTRATED WITH

*Etchings by Blum, Church, Dielman, Gifford, Shirlaw,
and Turner*

IN TWELVE VOLUMES
VOLUME XII.

# TALES, SKETCHES, AND OTHER
## PAPERS

BY

## NATHANIEL HAWTHORNE

*WITH A BIOGRAPHICAL SKETCH*

BY

GEORGE PARSONS LATHROP

BOSTON
HOUGHTON, MIFFLIN AND COMPANY
New York: 11 East Seventeenth Street
The Riverside Press, Cambridge
1883

*The Riverside Press, Cambridge:*
Electrotyped and Printed by H. O. Houghton & Co.

# CONTENTS.

                                                                   PAGE
INTRODUCTORY SKETCH . . . . . . . . . . . 7

## TALES AND SKETCHES.

SKETCHES FROM MEMORY.
    I. THE INLAND PORT. . . . . . . . 13
    II. ROCHESTER . . . . . . . . . 17
    III. A NIGHT SCENE . . . . . . . . 21
FRAGMENTS FROM THE JOURNAL OF A SOLITARY MAN.
    I. . . . . . . . . . . . . 23
    II. MY HOME RETURN . . . . . . . 35
MY VISIT TO NIAGARA . . . . . . . . . 42
THE ANTIQUE RING . . . . . . . . . 51
GRAVES AND GOBLINS . . . . . . . . . 68
DR. BULLIVANT . . . . . . . . . 78
A BOOK OF AUTOGRAPHS . . . . . . . . 88
AN OLD WOMAN'S TALE . . . . . . . . 109
TIME'S PORTRAITURE. — ADDRESS . . . . . . 121
"BROWNE'S FOLLY" . . . . . . . . . 131

## BIOGRAPHICAL STORIES.

BENJAMIN WEST . . . . . . . . . 144
SIR ISAAC NEWTON . . . . . . . . . 157
SAMUEL JOHNSON . . . . . . . . . 166
OLIVER CROMWELL . . . . . . . . . 178
BENJAMIN FRANKLIN . . . . . . . . 189
QUEEN CHRISTINA . . . . . . . . . 203

# CONTENTS.

## BIOGRAPHICAL SKETCHES.

Mrs. Hutchinson . . . . . . . . . 217
Sir William Phips . . . . . . . . 227
Sir William Pepperell . . . . . . . 235
Thomas Green Fessenden . . . . . 246
Jonathan Cilley . . . . . . . . . 264

Alice Doane's Appeal . . . . . . . 279
Chiefly about War Matters . . . . . 299
Life of Franklin Pierce . . . . . . 347
Sketch of The Life of Nathaniel Hawthorne . . 441
Index to Hawthorne's Works . . . . . 571

# INTRODUCTORY NOTE.

## TALES, SKETCHES, ETC.

THE first group of short pieces embraced in this volume belongs to Hawthorne's earlier period; excepting "Browne's Folly," which was addressed to the author's cousin, Mr. Richard Manning, of Salem, after the return from Europe. The "Sketches from Memory," like those in the "Mosses," and one in "The Snow-Image," reveal the fact that, at some time in his bachelor life, Hawthorne made a trip through portions of New York; but of this journey no other data have ever come to the editor's knowledge. He took a little tour in 1830 or 1831, or perhaps in both years, in Connecticut, Western Massachusetts, and in New Hampshire; and it was perhaps at this time that he crossed the boundary into New York. The "Journal of a Solitary Man" and "My Home Return" may not improbably be connected with the narrative of "The Story-Teller" which Hawthorne had planned as an accompaniment to the "Twice-Told Tales." [1] All the youthful pieces here preserved had been left in the obscurity of old periodicals, their very existence possibly forgotten by the author himself, and were gradually discovered during the five or six years immediately following his death.

[1] See the editor's Introductory Note to the *Twice-Told Tales*.

In June, 1837, Hawthorne, writing to Longfellow, had observed : "I can turn my attention to all sorts of drudgery, such as children's books, etc." One among several outgrowths of the ability he referred to was the group of " Biographical Stories " in the present volume, hitherto included with " Grandfather's Chair," under the general heading of " True Stories." That he regarded the writing of them as in one sense drudgery, as a performance which would not have been undertaken but for the necessity of earning a livelihood by his pen, appears probable from a letter which he addressed with the MS. of "Queen Christina" to the conductress of a periodical in Northern New York. Of this letter, which has been inaccessible for a long time, the date (according to the editor's remembrance) was about two years after that of the one to Longfellow just mentioned ; and the terms in which it was couched left the impression that Hawthorne was then much in need of employment. We must not, however, forget his own statement in the brief note prefixed to the stories, that " this small volume and others of a similar character . . . have not been composed without a deep sense of responsibility." Indeed, whatever he wrote for children Hawthorne prepared with as much conscientiousness as the matter which he offered to a mature audience ; and, conversely, his stories for older readers were invested with such a refinement of simplicity that they were often well suited for children. A circumstance illustrating this is that " The Lily's Quest," afterwards issued in the second series of " Twice-Told Tales," was first printed (January 19, 1839) in " The Southern Rose," a weekly paper for young readers, published at Charleston, South Carolina.

The "Biographical Sketches," that follow next in the order of contents, appear here as the result of a gleaning from old magazines, which was made after Hawthorne's death. Designed to fulfil purposes of the moment, they are of course not to be placed in the same category with the purely literary work which he acknowledged. Nevertheless, the papers upon Mrs. Hutchinson, Sir William Phips, and Sir William Pepperell, are valuable as evidences of the study which he devoted to passages in the history of New England; study largely instrumental in developing that innate knowledge of his native region which gives perennial force to the picture presented in "The Scarlet Letter." The outline of Jonathan Cilley's career shows how active had been his observation of a classmate in college.

"Alice Doane's Appeal," one of the two remaining contributions, was apparently overlooked until the present editor, coming upon its traces, secured a copy of it in "The Token" for 1835, after a three years' search. Hawthorne's surviving sister, Miss Elizabeth Maria Hawthorne, who died (January 1, 1883) after this edition of the Works had made considerable headway, informed the editor that she retained some recollection of the story; and it seems probable, from an allusion in the opening portion, that the form here preserved embodies a reminiscence of one among those "Seven Tales of my Native Land" which the author burned in manuscript. The chapter entitled "Chiefly about War Matters" was published in the "Atlantic Monthly" soon after a trip to Washington which Hawthorne made in April, 1862. It now first takes its place among his collected writings. The same thing is to be said of the "Life of Franklin Pierce," reprinted in the present volume. It has been thought advisable to include this pamphlet, which accordingly appears in its original form, with the exception of one omitted passage, consisting of extracts from General Pierce's Diary during the Mexican War.

With this Introductory Note the editor's task comes to an end. Slight though the result must appear, no little labor and care have been involved in carrying out the original purpose of the Notes, which was to present, at suitable points and without wearying the general reader by bibliographical details, a brief compend of facts with regard to each work or collection in the series.

G. P. L.

New York, *May* 1, 1883.

# TALES AND SKETCHES.

# SKETCHES FROM MEMORY.[1]

## I.

### THE INLAND PORT.

It was a bright forenoon, when I set foot on the beach at Burlington, and took leave of the two boatmen in whose little skiff I had voyaged since daylight from Peru. Not that we had come that morning from South America, but only from the New York shore of Lake Champlain. The highlands of the coast behind us stretched north and south, in a double range of bold, blue peaks, gazing over each other's shoulders at the Green Mountains of Vermont.

The latter are far the loftiest, and, from the opposite side of the lake, had displayed a more striking outline. We were now almost at their feet, and could see only a sandy beach sweeping beneath a woody bank, around the semicircular Bay of Burlington.

The painted light-house on a small green island, the wharves and warehouses, with sloops and schooners moored alongside, or at anchor, or spreading their canvas to the wind, and boats rowing from point to point, reminded me of some fishing-town on the sea-coast.

But I had no need of tasting the water to convince myself that Lake Champlain was not an arm of the

---

[1] Second series. The first series was added to the revised edition of the *Mosses from an Old Manse.*

sea; its quality was evident, both by its silvery surface, when unruffled, and a faint but unpleasant and
sickly smell, forever steaming up in the sunshine. One
breeze of the Atlantic with its briny fragrance would
be worth more to these inland people than all the per-
fumes of Arabia. On closer inspection the vessels at
the wharves looked hardly seaworthy, — there being
a great lack of tar about the seams and rigging, and
perhaps other deficiencies, quite as much to the purpose.

I observed not a single sailor in the port. There
were men, indeed, in blue jackets and trousers, but not
of the true nautical fashion, such as dangle before slop-
shops; others wore tight pantaloons and coats prepon-
derously long-tailed, — cutting very queer figures at the
masthead; and, in short, these fresh-water fellows had
about the same analogy to the real "old salt" with his
tarpaulin, pea-jacket, and sailor-cloth trousers, as a
lake fish to a Newfoundland cod.

Nothing struck me more in Burlington than the
great number of Irish emigrants. They have filled
the British Provinces to the brim, and still continue to
ascend the St. Lawrence in infinite tribes overflowing
by every outlet into the States. At Burlington, they
swarm in huts and mean dwellings near the lake, lounge
about the wharves, and elbow the native citizens entirely out of competition in their own line. Every
species of mere bodily labor is the prerogative of these
Irish. Such is their multitude in comparison with
any possible demand for their services, that it is difficult to conceive how a third part of them should earn
even a daily glass of whiskey, which is doubtless their
first necessary of life, — daily bread being only the
second.

Some were angling in the lake, but had caught only

a few perch, which little fishes, without a miracle,
would be nothing among so many. A miracle there
certainly must have been, and a daily one, for the subsistence of these wandering hordes. The men exhibit
a lazy strength and careless merriment, as if they had
fed well hitherto, and meant to feed better hereafter;
the women strode about, uncovered in the open air,
with far plumper waists and brawnier limbs as well as
bolder faces, than our shy and slender females; and
their progeny, which was innumerable, had the reddest
and the roundest cheeks of any children in America.

While we stood at the wharf, the bell of a steamboat gave two preliminary peals, and she dashed away
for Plattsburg, leaving a trail of smoky breath behind,
and breaking the glassy surface of the lake before her.
Our next movement brought us into a handsome and
busy square, the sides of which were filled up with
white houses, brick stores, a church, a court-house, and
a bank. Some of these edifices had roofs of tin, in
the fashion of Montreal, and glittered in the sun with
cheerful splendor, imparting a lively effect to the whole
square. One brick building, designated in large letters as the custom house, reminded us that this inland
village is a port of entry, largely concerned in foreign
trade, and holding daily intercourse with the British
empire. In this border country the Canadian bank-
notes circulate as freely as our own, and British and
American coin are jumbled into the same pocket, the
effigies of the King of England being made to kiss
those of the Goddess of Liberty.

Perhaps there was an emblem in the involuntary
contact. There was a pleasant mixture of people in
the square of Burlington, such as cannot be seen elsewhere, at one view; merchants from Montreal, British

officers from the frontier garrisons, French Canadians, wandering Irish, Scotchmen of a better class, gentlemen of the South on a pleasure tour, country squires on business; and a great throng of Green Mountain boys, with their horse-wagons and ox-teams, true Yankees in aspect, and looking more superlatively so, by contrast with such a variety of foreigners.

# II.

## ROCHESTER.

The gray but transparent evening rather shaded than obscured the scene, leaving its stronger features visible, and even improved by the medium through which I beheld them. The volume of water is not very great, nor the roar deep enough to be termed grand, though such praise might have been appropriate before the good people of Rochester had abstracted a part of the unprofitable sublimity of the cascade. The Genesee has contributed so bountifully to their canals and mill-dams, that it approaches the precipice with diminished pomp, and rushes over it in foamy streams of various width, leaving a broad face of the rock insulated and unwashed, between the two main branches of the falling river. Still it was an impressive sight, to one who had not seen Niagara. I confess, however, that my chief interest arose from a legend, connected with these falls, which will become poetical in the lapse of years, and was already so to me as I pictured the catastrophe out of dusk and solitude. It was from a platform, raised over the naked island of the cliff, in the middle of the cataract, that Sam Patch took his last leap, and alighted in the other world. Strange as it may appear, — that any uncertainty should rest upon his fate which was consummated in the sight of thousands, — many will tell you that the illustrious Patch concealed himself in a cave under the falls, and has continued to enjoy post-humous renown, without foregoing the comforts of this present life. But the poor fellow prized the shout of the multitude too much not to have claimed it at the instant, had he survived. He will not be seen again, unless his ghost, in such a twilight as when I was there, should emerge from the foam, and vanish among the shadows that fall from cliff to cliff.

How stern a moral may be drawn from the story of poor Sam Patch! Why do we call him a madman or a fool, when he has left his memory around the falls of the Genesee, more permanently than if the letters of his name had been hewn into the forehead of the precipice?

Was the leaper of cataracts more mad or foolish than other men who throw away life, or misspend it in pursuit of empty fame, and seldom so triumphantly as he? That which he won is as invaluable as any except the unsought glory, spreading like the rich perfume of richer fruit from various and useful deeds.

Thus musing, wise in theory, but practically as great a fool as Sam, I lifted my eyes and beheld the spires, warehouses, and dwellings of Rochester, half a mile distant on both sides of the river, indistinctly cheerful, with the twinkling of many lights amid the fall of the evening. . . .

The town had sprung up like a mushroom, but no presage of decay could be drawn from its hasty growth. Its edifices are of dusky brick, and of stone that will not be grayer in a hundred years than now; its churches are Gothic; it is impossible to look at its worn pavements and conceive how lately the forest leaves have been swept away. The most ancient town in Massachusetts appears quite like an affair of yester-

day, compared with Rochester. Its attributes of youth
are the activity and eager life with which it is redun-
dant. The whole street, sidewalks and centre, was
crowded with pedestrians, horsemen, stage - coaches,
gigs, light wagons, and heavy ox-teams, all hurrying,
trotting, rattling, and rumbling, in a throng that
passed continually, but never passed away. Here, a
country wife was selecting a churn from several gayly
painted ones on the sunny sidewalk; there, a farmer
was bartering his produce; and, in two or three places,
a crowd of people were showering bids on a vocifer-
ous auctioneer. I saw a great wagon and an ox-chain
knocked off to a very pretty woman. Numerous were
the lottery offices, — those true temples of Mammon,
— where red and yellow bills offered splendid fortunes
to the world at large, and banners of painted cloth
gave notice that the "lottery draws next Wednesday."
At the ringing of a bell, judges, jurymen, lawyers,
and clients, elbowed each other to the court-house, to
busy themselves with cases that would doubtless illustrate the state of society, had I the means of re-
porting them. The number of public houses benefited
the flow of temporary population; some were farmer's
taverns, — cheap, homely, and comfortable ; others
were magnificent hotels, with negro waiters, gentle-
manly landlords in black broadcloth, and foppish bar-
keepers in Broadway coats, with chased gold watches
in their waistcoat-pockets. I caught one of these fellows quizzing me through an eye-glass. The porters
were lumbering up the steps with baggage from the
packet boats, while waiters plied the brush on dusty
travellers, who, meanwhile, glanced over the innumerable advertisements in the daily papers.

In short, everybody seemed to be there, and all had

something to do, and were doing it with all their might, except a party of drunken recruits for the Western military posts, principally Irish and Scotch, though they wore Uncle Sam's gray jacket and trousers. I noticed one other idle man. He carried a rifle on his shoulder and a powder-horn across his breast, and appeared to stare about him with confused wonder, as if, while he was listening to the wind among the forest boughs, the hum and bustle of an instantaneous city had surrounded him. . . .

## III.

### A NIGHT SCENE.

THE steamboat in which I was passenger for Detroit had put into the mouth of a small river, where the greater part of the night would be spent in repairing some damages of the machinery.

As the evening was warm, though cloudy and very dark, I stood on deck, watching a scene that would not have attracted a second glance in the daytime, but became picturesque by the magic of strong light and deep shade.

Some wild Irishmen were replenishing our stock of wood, and had kindled a great fire on the bank to illuminate their labors. It was composed of large logs and dry brushwood, heaped together with careless profusion, blazing fiercely, spouting showers of sparks into the darkness, and gleaming wide over Lake Erie, — a beacon for perplexed voyagers leagues from land.

All around and above the furnace there was total obscurity. No trees or other objects caught and reflected any portion of the brightness, which thus wasted itself in the immense void of night, as if it quivered from the expiring embers of the world, after the final conflagration. But the Irishmen were continually emerging from the dense gloom, passing through the lurid glow, and vanishing into the gloom on the other side. Sometimes a whole figure would be made visible, by the shirt-sleeves and light-colored dress; others were but half seen, like imperfect creatures; many flitted, shadow-like, along the skirts of darkness, tempting fancy to a vain pursuit; and often, a face alone was reddened by the fire, and stared strangely distinct, with no traces of a body. In short these wild Irish, distorted and exaggerated by the blaze, now lost in deep shadow, now bursting into sudden splendor, and now struggling between light and darkness, formed a picture which might have been transferred, almost unaltered, to a tale of the supernatural. As they all carried lanterns of wood, and often flung sticks upon the fire, the least imaginative spectator would at once compare them to devils condemned to keep alive the flames of their own torments.

# FRAGMENTS FROM THE JOURNAL OF A SOLITARY MAN.

## I.

.  .  .  .  .  .  .  .  .  .

MY poor friend "Oberon"[1] — for let me be allowed to distinguish him by so quaint a name — sleeps with the silent ages. He died calmly. Though his disease was pulmonary, his life did not flicker out like a wasted lamp, sometimes shooting up into a strange temporary brightness; but the tide of being ebbed away, and the noon of his existence waned till, in the simple phraseology of Scripture, "he was not." The last words he said to me were, " Burn my papers, — all that you can find in yonder escritoire; for I fear there are some there which you may be betrayed into publishing. I have published enough; as for the old disconnected journal in your possession" — But here my poor friend was checked in his utterance by that same hollow cough which would never let him alone. So he coughed himself tired, and sank to slumber. I watched from that midnight hour till high noon on the morrow for his waking. The chamber was dark; till, longing for light, I opened the window-shutter, and the broad day looked in on the marble features of the dead.

I religiously obeyed his instructions with regard to the papers in the escritoire, and burned them in a heap

---

[1] See the sketch or story entitled *The Devil in Manuscript*, in *The Snow-Image, and other Twice-Told Tales*.

without looking into one, though sorely tempted. But the old journal I kept. Perhaps in strict conscience I ought also to have burned that; but casting my eye over some half-torn leaves the other day, I could not resist an impulse to give some fragments of it to the public. To do this satisfactorily, I am obliged to twist this thread, so as to string together into a semblance of order my Oberon's " random pearls."

If anybody that holds any commerce with his fellow-men can be called solitary, Oberon was a " solitary man." He lived in a small village at some distance from the metropolis, and never came up to the city except once in three months for the purpose of looking into a bookstore, and of spending two hours and a half with me. In that space of time I would tell him all that I could remember of interest which had occurred in the interim of his visits. He would join very heartily in the conversation ; but as soon as the time of his usual tarrying had elapsed, he would take up his hat and depart. He was unequivocally the most original person I ever knew. His style of composition was very charming. No tales that have ever appeared in our popular journals have been so generally admired as his. But a sadness was on his spirit ; and this, added to the shrinking sensitiveness of his nature, rendered him not misanthropic, but singularly averse to social intercourse. Of the disease, which was slowly sapping the springs of his life, he first became fully conscious after one of those long abstractions in which he was wont to indulge. It is remarkable, however, that his first idea of this sort, instead of deepening his spirit with a more melancholy hue, restored him to a more natural state of mind.

He had evidently cherished a secret hope that some

impulse would at length be given him, or that he would muster sufficient energy of will to return into the world, and act a wiser and happier part than his former one. But life never called the dreamer forth; it was Death that whispered him. It is to be regretted that this portion of his old journal contains so few passages relative to this interesting period ; since the little which he has recorded, though melancholy enough, breathes the gentleness of a spirit newly restored to communion with its kind. If there be anything bitter in the following reflections, its source is in human sympathy, and its sole object is himself.

"It is hard to die without one's happiness ; to none more so than myself, whose early resolution it had been to partake largely of the joys of life, but never to be burdened with its cares. Vain philosophy ! The very hardships of the poorest laborer, whose whole existence seems one long toil, has something preferable to my best pleasures.

"Merely skimming the surface of life, I know nothing, by my own experience, of its deep and warm realities. I have achieved none of these objects which the instinct of mankind especially prompts them to pursue, and the accomplishment of which must therefore beget a native satisfaction. The truly wise, after all their speculations, will be led into the common path, and, in homage to the human nature that pervades them, will gather gold, and till the earth, and set out trees, and build a house. But I have scorned such wisdom. I have rejected, also, the settled, sober, careful gladness of a man by his own fireside, with those around him whose welfare is committed to his trust, and all their guidance to his fond authority. Without influence among serious affairs, my footsteps were not

imprinted on the earth, but lost in air; and I shall
leave no son to inherit my share of life, with a better sense of its privileges and duties, when his father
should vanish like a bubble; so that few mortals, even
the humblest and the weakest, have been such ineffectual shadows in the world, or die so utterly as I
must. Even a young man's bliss has not been mine.
With a thousand vagrant fantasies, I have never truly
loved, and perhaps shall be doomed to loneliness
throughout the eternal future, because, here on earth,
my soul has never married itself to the soul of woman.

"Such are the repinings of one who feels, too late,
that the sympathies of his nature have avenged themselves upon him. They have prostrated, with a joy-
less life and the prospect of a reluctant death, my selfish purpose to keep aloof from mortal disquietudes,
and be a pleasant idler among care-stricken and laborious men. I have other regrets, too, savoring more of
my old spirit. The time has been when I meant to
visit every region of the earth, except the poles and
Central Africa. I had a strange longing to see the
Pyramids. To Persia and Arabia, and all the gorgeous East, I owed a pilgrimage for the sake of their
magic tales. And England, the land of my ancestors!
Once I had fancied that my sleep would not be quiet
in the grave unless I should return, as it were, to my
home of past ages, and see the very cities, and castles,
and battle-fields of history, and stand within the holy
gloom of its cathedrals, and kneel at the shrines of its
immortal poets, there asserting myself their hereditary
countryman. This feeling lay among the deepest in
my heart. Yet, with this homesickness for the father-
land, and all these plans of remote travel, — which I
yet believe that my peculiar instinct impelled me to

form, and upbraided me for not accomplishing, — the utmost limit of my wanderings has been little more than six hundred miles from my native village. Thus, in whatever way I consider my life, or what must be termed such, I cannot feel as if I had lived at all.

"I am possessed, also, with the thought that I have never yet discovered the real secret of my powers; that there has been a mighty treasure within my reach, a mine of gold beneath my feet, worthless because I have never known how to seek for it; and for want of perhaps one fortunate idea, I am to die

'Unwept, unhonored, and unsung.'

"Once, amid the troubled and tumultuous enjoyment of my life, there was a dreamy thought that haunted me, — the terrible necessity imposed on mortals to grow old, or die. I could not bear the idea of losing one youthful grace. True, I saw other men who had once been young and now were old, enduring their age with equanimity, because each year reconciled them to its own added weight. But for myself, I felt that age would be not less miserable, creeping upon me slowly, than if it fell at once. I sometimes looked in the glass, and endeavored to fancy my cheeks yellow and interlaced with furrows, my forehead wrinkled deeply across, the top of my head bald and polished, my eyebrows and side-locks iron gray, and a grisly beard sprouting on my chin. Shuddering at the picture, I changed it for the dead face of a young man, with dark locks clustering heavily round its pale beauty, which would decay, indeed, but not with years, nor in the sight of men. The latter visage shocked me least.

"Such a repugnance to the hard conditions of long

life is common to all sensitive and thoughtful men,
who minister to the luxury, the refinements, the gayety and lightsomeness, to anything, in short, but the
real necessities of their fellow-creatures. He who has
a part in the serious business of life, though it be only
as a shoemaker, feels himself equally respectable in
youth and in age, and therefore is content to live and
look forward to wrinkles and decrepitude in their due
season. It is far otherwise with the busy idlers of the
world. I was particularly liable to this torment, being
a meditative person in spite of my levity. The truth
could not be concealed, nor the contemplation of it
avoided. With deep inquietude I became aware that
what was graceful now, and seemed appropriate enough
to my age of flowers, would be ridiculous in middle
life; and that the world, so indulgent to the fantastic
youth, would scorn the bearded man, still telling love-
tales, loftily ambitious of a maiden's tears, and squeezing out, as it were, with his brawny strength, the essence of roses. And in his old age the sweet lyrics of
Anacreon made the girls laugh at his white hairs the
more. With such sentiments, conscious that my part
in the drama of life was fit only for a youthful per-
former, I nourished a regretful desire to be summoned
early from the scene. I set a limit to myself, the age
of twenty-five, few years indeed, but too many to be
thrown away. Scarcely had I thus fixed the term of
my mortal pilgrimage, than the thought grew into a
presentiment that, when the space should be completed, the world would have one butterfly the less, by
my far flight.

" Oh, how fond I was of life, even while allotting,
as my proper destiny, an early death! I loved the
world, its cities, its villages, its grassy roadsides, its

wild forests, its quiet scenes, its gay, warm, enlivening bustle; in every aspect, I loved the world so long as I could behold it with young eyes and dance through it with a young heart. The earth had been made so beautiful, that I longed for no brighter sphere, but only an ever-youthful eternity in this. I clung to earth as if my beginning and ending were to be there, unable to imagine any but an earthly happiness, and choosing such, with all its imperfections, rather than perfect bliss, which might be alien from it. Alas! I had not yet known that weariness by which the soul proves itself ethereal."

Turning over the old journal, I open, by chance, upon a passage which affords a signal instance of the morbid fancies to which Oberon frequently yielded himself. Dreams like the following were probably engendered by the deep gloom sometimes thrown over his mind by his reflections on death.

"I dreamed that one bright forenoon I was walking through Broadway, and seeking to cheer myself with the warm and busy life of that far-famed promenade. Here a coach thundered over the pavement, and there an unwieldy omnibus, with spruce gigs rattling past, and horsemen prancing through all the bustle. On the sidewalk people were looking at the rich display of goods, the plate and jewelry, or the latest caricature in the bookseller's windows; while fair ladies and whiskered gentlemen tripped gayly along, nodding mutual recognitions, or shrinking from some rough countryman or sturdy laborer, whose contact might have ruffled their finery. I found myself in this animated scene, with a dim and misty idea that it was not my proper place, or that I had ventured into the crowd with some singularity of dress or aspect which

made me ridiculous. Walking in the sunshine, I was
yet cold as death. By degrees, too, I perceived myself
the object of universal attention, and, as it seemed, of
horror and affright. Every face grew pale; the laugh
was hushed, and the voices died away in broken syl-
lables; the people in the shops crowded to the doors
with a ghastly stare, and the passengers on all sides fled
as from an embodied pestilence. The horses reared
and snorted. An old beggar - woman sat before St.
Paul's Church, with her withered palm stretched out
to all, but drew it back from me, and pointed to the
graves and monuments in that populous churchyard.
Three lovely girls whom I had formerly known, ran
shrieking across the street. A personage in black,
whom I was about to overtake, suddenly turned his
head and showed the features of a long-lost friend.
He gave me a look of horror and was gone.

"I passed not one step farther, but threw my eyes
on a looking-glass which stood deep within the nearest
shop. At first glimpse of my own figure I awoke, with
a horrible sensation of self - terror and self - loathing.
No wonder that the affrighted city fled! I had been
promenading Broadway in my shroud!"

I should be doing injustice to my friend's memory,
were I to publish other extracts even nearer to insanity than this, from the scarcely legible papers before
me. I gather from them — for I do not remember
that he ever related to me the circumstances — that
he once made a journey, chiefly on foot, to Niagara.
Some conduct of the friends among whom he resided
in his native village was constructed by him into oppression. These were the friends to whose care he had
been committed by his parents, who died when Oberon
was about twelve years of age. Though he had always

been treated by them with the most uniform kindness, and though a favorite among the people of the village rather on account of the sympathy which they felt in his situation than from any merit of his own, such was the waywardness of his temper, that on a slight provocation he ran away from the home that sheltered him, expressing openly his determination to die sooner than return to the detested spot. A severe illness overtook him after he had been absent about four months. While ill, he felt how unsoothing were the kindest looks and tones of strangers. He rose from his sick-bed a better man, and determined upon a speedy self-atonement by returning to his native town. There he lived, solitary and sad, but forgiven and cherished by his friends, till the day he died. That part of the journal which contained a description of this journey is mostly destroyed. Here and there is a fragment. I cannot select, for the pages are very scanty; but I do not withhold the following fragments, because they indicate a better and more cheerful frame of mind than the foregoing.

---

"On reaching the ferry-house, a rude structure of boards at the foot of the cliff, I found several of those wretches devoid of poetry, and lost some of my own poetry by contact with them. The hut was crowded by a party of provincials, — a simple and merry set, who had spent the afternoon fishing near the Falls, and were bartering black and white bass and eels for the ferryman's whiskey. A greyhound and three spaniels, brutes of much more grace and decorous demeanor than their masters, sat at the door. A few yards off, yet wholly unnoticed by the dogs, was a beautiful fox,

whose countenance betokened all the sagacity attributed to him in ancient fable.　He had a comfortable
bed of straw in an old barrel, whither he retreated,
flourishing his bushy tail as I made a step towards
him, but soon came forth and surveyed me with a keen
and intelligent eye.　The Canadians bartered their fish
and drank their whiskey, and were loquacious on trifling subjects, and merry at simple jests, with as little
regard to the scenery as they could have to the flattest
part of the Grand Canal.　Nor was I entitled to despise them; for I amused myself with all those foolish matters of fishermen, and dogs, and fox, just as if
Sublimity and Beauty were not married at that place
and moment; as if their nuptial band were not the
brightest of all rainbows on the opposite shore; as if
the gray precipice were not frowning above my head
and Niagara thundering around me.

" The grim ferryman, a black-whiskered giant, half
drunk withal, now thrust the Canadians by main force
out of his door, launched a boat, and bade me sit in
the stern - sheets.　Where we crossed, the river was
white with foam, yet did not offer much resistance to
a straight passage, which brought us close to the outer
edge of the American Falls.　The rainbow vanished
as we neared its misty base, and when I leaped ashore,
the sun had left all Niagara in shadow."

---

" A sound of merriment, sweet voices and girlish
laughter, came dancing through the solemn roar of waters.　In old times, when the French, and afterwards
the English, held garrisons near Niagara, it used to be
deemed a feat worthy of a soldier, a frontier - man, or

an Indian, to cross the rapids to Goat Island. As the country became less rude and warlike, a long space intervened, in which it was but half believed, by a faint and doubtful tradition, that mortal foot had never trod this wild spot of precipice and forest clinging between two cataracts. The island is no longer a tangled forest, but a grove of stately trees, with grassy intervals about their roots and woodland paths among their trunks. There was neither soldier nor Indian here now, but a vision of three lovely girls, running brief races through the broken sunshine of the grove, hiding behind the trees, and pelting each other with the cones of the pine. When their sport had brought them near me, it so happened that one of the party ran up and shook me by the hand, — a greeting which I heartily returned, and would have done the same had it been tenderer. I had known this wild little black-eyed lass in my youth and her childhood, before I had commenced my rambles.

" We met on terms of freedom and kindness, which elder ladies might have thought unsuitable with a gentleman of my description. When I alluded to the two fair strangers, she shouted after them by their Christian names, at which summons, with grave dignity, they drew near, and honored me with a distant courtesy. They were from the upper part of Vermont. Whether sisters, or cousins, or at all related to each other, I cannot tell ; but they are planted in my memory like ' two twin roses on one stem,' with the fresh dew in both their bosoms ; and when I would have pure and pleasant thoughts I think of them. Neither of them could have seen seventeen years. They both were of a height, and that a moderate one. The rose-bloom of the cheeks could hardly be called bright in her who was the rosiest, nor faint, though a shade less deep, in her companion. Both had delicate eyebrows, not strongly defined, yet somewhat darker than their hair; both had small sweet mouths, maiden mouths, of not so warm and deep a tint as ruby, but only red as the reddest rose; each had those gems, the rarest, the most precious, a pair of clear, soft, bright blue eyes. Their style of dress was similar; one had on a black silk gown, with a stomacher of velvet, and scalloped cuffs of the same from the wrist to the elbow; the other wore cuffs and stomacher of the like pattern and material, over a gown of crimson silk. The dress was rather heavy for their slight figures, but suited to September. They and the darker beauty all carried their straw bonnets in their hands."

I cannot better conclude these fragments than with poor Oberon's description of his return to his native village after his slow recovery from his illness. How beautifully does he express his penitential emotions ! A beautiful moral may be indeed drawn from the early death of a sensitive recluse, who had shunned the ordinary avenues of distinction, and with splendid abilities sank to rest into an early grave, almost unknown to mankind, and without any record save what my pen hastily leaves upon these tear-blotted pages.

## II.

### MY HOME RETURN.

WHEN the stage-coach had gained the summit of the hill, I alighted to perform the small remainder of my journey on foot. There had not been a more delicious afternoon than this in all the train of summer, the air being a sunny perfume, made up of balm, and warmth, and gentle brightness. The oak and walnut trees over my head retained their deep masses of foliage, and the grass, though for months the pasturage of stray cattle, had been revived with the freshness of early June by the autumnal rains of the preceding week. The garb of autumn, indeed, resembled that of spring. Dandelions and butterflies were sprinkled along the roadside, like drops of brightest gold in greenest grass, and a star-shaped little flower of blue, with a golden centre. In a rocky spot, and rooted under the stone walk, there was one wild rose-bush bearing three roses, very faintly tinted, but blessed with a spicy fragrance. The same tokens would have announced that the year was brightening into the glow of summer. There were violets too, though few and pale ones. But the breath of September was diffused through the mild air, and became perceptible, too thrillingly for my enfeebled frame, whenever a little breeze shook out the latent coolness.

"I was standing on the hill at the entrance of my native village, whence I had looked back to bid farewell, and forward to the pale mist-bow that overarched my path, and was the omen of my fortunes. How I had misinterpreted that augury, the ghost of hope, with none of hope's bright hues! Nor could I deem that all its portents were yet accomplished, though from the same western sky the declining sun shone brightly in my face. But I was calm and not depressed. Turning to the village, so dim and dreamlike at my last view, I saw the white houses and brick stores, the intermingled trees, the foot-paths with their wide borders of grass, and the dusty road between; all a picture of peaceful gladness in the sunshine.

"'Why have I never loved my home before?' thought I, as my spirit reposed itself on the quiet beauty of the scene.

"On the side of the opposite hill was the graveyard, sloping towards the farther extremity of the village. The sun shone as cheerfully there as on the abodes of the living, and showed all the little hillocks and the burial-stones, white marble or slate, and here and there a tomb, with the pleasant grass about them all. A single tree was tinged with glory from the west, and threw a pensive shade behind. Not far from where it fell was the tomb of my parents, whom I had hardly thought of in bidding adieu to the village, but had remembered them more faithfully among the feelings that drew me homeward. At my departure their tomb had been hidden in the morning mist. Beholding it in the sunshine now, I felt a sensation through my frame as if a breeze had thrown the coolness of September over me, though not a leaf was stirred, nor did the thistle-down take flight. Was I to roam no more through this beautiful world, but only to the other end of the village? Then let me lie down near my parents, but not with them, because I love a green grave better than a tomb.

"Moving slowly forward, I heard shouts and laughter, and perceived a considerable throng of people, who came from behind the meeting-house and made a stand in front of it. Thither all the idlers in the village were congregated to witness the exercises of the engine company, this being the afternoon of their monthly practice. They deluged the roof of the meeting-house, till the water fell from the eaves in a broad cascade; then the stream beat against the dusty windows like a thunder-storm; and sometimes they flung it up beside the steeple, sparkling in an ascending shower about the weathercock. For variety's sake the engineer made it undulate horizontally, like a great serpent flying over the earth. As his last effort, being roguishly inclined, he seemed to take aim at the sky, falling short rather of which, down came the fluid, transformed to drops of silver, on the thickest crowd of the spectators. Then ensued a prodigious rout and mirthful uproar, with no little wrath of the surly ones, whom this is an infallible method of distinguishing. The joke afforded infinite amusement to the ladies at the windows and some old people under the hay-scales. I also laughed at a distance, and was glad to find myself susceptible, as of old, to the simple mirth of such a scene.

"But the thoughts that it excited were not all mirthful. I had witnessed hundreds of such spectacles in my youth, and one precisely similar only a few days before my departure. And now, the aspect of the village being the same, and the crowd composed of my old acquaintances, I could hardly realize that years had passed, or even months, or that the very drops of water were not falling at this moment, which had been flung up then. But I pressed the conviction home, that, brief as the time appeared, it had been long enough for me to wander away and return again, with my fate accomplished, and little more hope in this world. The last throb of an adventurous and wayward spirit kept me from repining. I felt as if it were better or not worse, to have compressed my enjoyments and sufferings into a few wild years, and then to rest myself in an early grave, than to have chosen the untroubled and ungladdened course of the crowd before me, whose days were all alike, and a long lifetime like each day. But the sentiment startled me. For a moment I doubted whether my dear-bought wisdom were anything but the incapacity to pursue fresh follies, and whether, if health and strength could be restored that night, I should be found in the village after to-morrow's dawn.

" Among other novelties, I had noticed that the tavern was now designated as a Temperance House, in letters extending across the whole front, with a smaller sign promising Hot Coffee at all hours, and Spruce Beer to lodgers gratis. There were few new buildings, except a Methodist chapel and a printing-office, with a bookstore in the lower story. The golden mortar still ornamented the apothecary's door, nor had the Indian Chief, with his gilded tobacco stalk, been relieved from doing sentinel's duty before Dominicus Pike's grocery. The gorgeous silks, though of later patterns, were still flaunting like a banner in front of Mr. Nightingale's dry-goods store. Some of the signs introduced me to strangers, whose predecessors had failed, or emigrated to the West, or removed merely to the other end of the village, transferring their names from the sign-boards to slabs of marble or slate. But, on the whole, death and vicissitude had done very little. There were old men, scattered about the street, who had been old in my earliest reminiscences; and, as if their venerable forms were permanent parts of the creation, they appeared to be hale and hearty old men yet. The less elderly were more altered, having generally contracted a stoop, with hair wofully thinned and whitened. Some I could hardly recognize; at my last glance they had been boys and girls, but were young men and women when I looked again; and there were happy little things too, rolling about on the grass, whom God had made since my departure.

"But now, in my lingering course, I had descended the hill, and began to consider, painfully enough, how I should meet my towns-people, and what reception they would give me. Of many an evil prophecy, doubtless, had I been the subject. And would they salute me with a roar of triumph or a low hiss of scorn, on beholding their worst anticipations more than accomplished?

"'No,' said I, 'they will not triumph over me. And should they ask the cause of my return, I will tell them that a man may go far and tarry long away, if his health be good and his hopes high; but that when flesh and spirit begin to fail, he remembers his birthplace and the old burial-ground, and hears a voice calling him to come home to his father and mother. They will know, by my wasted frame and feeble step, that I have heard the summons and obeyed. And, the first greetings over, they will let me walk among them unnoticed, and linger in the sunshine while I may, and steal into my grave in peace.'

"With these reflections I looked kindly at the

crowd, and drew off my glove, ready to give my hand
to the first that should put forth his. It occurred to
me, also, that some youth among them, now at the crisis of his fate, might have felt his bosom thrill at my
example, and be emulous of my wild life and worthless fame. But I would save him.

" ' He shall be taught,' said I, ' by my life, and by
my death, that the world is a sad one for him who
shrinks from its sober duties. My experience shall
warn him to adopt some great and serious aim, such
as manhood will cling to, that he may not feel himself,
too late, a cumberer of this overladen earth, but a
man among men. I will beseech him not to follow
an eccentric path, nor, by stepping aside from the
highway of human affairs, to relinquish his claim
upon human sympathy. And often, as a text of deep
and varied meaning, I will remind him that he is an
American.'

" By this time I had drawn near the meeting-house,
and perceived that the crowd were beginning to recognize me."

These are the last words traced by his hand. Has
not so chastened a spirit found true communion with
the pure in heaven? " Until of late, I never could
believe that I was seriously ill : the past, I thought,
could not extend its misery beyond itself ; life was restored to me, and should not be missed again. I had
day-dreams even of wedded happiness. Still, as the
days wear on, a faintness creeps through my frame
and spirit, recalling the consciousness that a very old
man might as well nourish hope and young desire as
I at twenty-four. Yet the consciousness of my situation does not always make me sad. Sometimes I look
upon the world with a quiet interest, because it cannot

concern me personally, and a loving one for the same reason, because nothing selfish can interfere with the sense of brotherhood. Soon to be all spirit, I have already a spiritual sense of human nature, and see deeply into the hearts of mankind, discovering what is hidden from the wisest. The loves of young men and virgins are known to me, before the first kiss, before the whispered word, with the birth of the first sigh. My glance comprehends the crowd, and penetrates the breast of the solitary man. I think better of the world than formerly, more generously of its virtues, more mercifully of its faults, with a higher estimate of its present happiness, and brighter hopes of its destiny. My mind has put forth a second crop of blossoms, as the trees do in the Indian summer. No winter will destroy their beauty, for they are fanned by the breeze and freshened by the shower that breathes and falls in the gardens of Paradise!"

# MY VISIT TO NIAGARA.

NEVER did a pilgrim approach Niagara with deeper enthusiasm than mine. I had lingered away from it, and wandered to other scenes, because my treasury of anticipated enjoyments, comprising all the wonders of the world, had nothing else so magnificent, and I was loath to exchange the pleasures of hope for those of memory so soon. At length the day came. The stage-coach, with a Frenchman and myself on the back seat, had already left Lewiston, and in less than an hour would set us down in Manchester. I began to listen for the roar of the cataract, and trembled with a sensation like dread, as the moment drew nigh, when its voice of ages must roll, for the first time, on my ear. The French gentleman stretched himself from the window, and expressed loud admiration, while, by a sudden impulse, I threw myself back and closed my eyes. When the scene shut in, I was glad to think, that for me the whole burst of Niagara was yet in futurity. We rolled on, and entered the village of Manchester, bordering on the falls.

I am quite ashamed of myself here. Not that I ran, like a madman to the falls, and plunged into the thickest of the spray, — never stopping to breathe, till breathing was impossible: not that I committed this, or any other suitable extravagance. On the contrary, I alighted with perfect decency and composure, gave my cloak to the black waiter, pointed out my baggage, and inquired, not the nearest way to the cataract, but

about the dinner-hour. The interval was spent in arranging my dress. Within the last fifteen minutes,
my mind had grown strangely benumbed, and my spirits apathetic, with a slight depression, not decided
enough to be termed sadness. My enthusiasm was in
a deathlike slumber. Without aspiring to immortality, as he did, I could have imitated that English traveller, who turned back from the point where he first
heard the thunder of Niagara, after crossing the ocean
to behold it. Many a Western trader, by the by, has
performed a similar act of heroism with more heroic
simplicity, deeming it no such wonderful feat to dine
at the hotel and resume his route to Buffalo or Lewiston, while the cataract was roaring unseen.

Such has often been my apathy, when objects, long
sought, and earnestly desired, were placed within my
reach. After dinner — at which an unwonted and
perverse epicurism detained me longer than usual — I
lighted a cigar and paced the piazza, minutely atten-
tive to the aspect and business of a very ordinary village. Finally, with reluctant step, and the feeling of
an intruder, I walked towards Goat Island. At the
toll-house, there were further excuses for delaying the
inevitable moment. My signature was required in a
huge ledger, containing similar records innumerable,
many of which I read. The skin of a great sturgeon,
and other fishes, beasts, and reptiles; a collection of
minerals, such as lie in heaps near the falls; some Indian moccasons, and other trifles, made of deer-skin
and embroidered with beads; several newspapers from
Montreal, New York, and Boston, — all attracted me
in turn. Out of a number of twisted sticks, the manufacture of a Tuscarora Indian, I selected one of
curled maple, curiously convoluted, and adorned with

the carved images of a snake and a fish. Using this as my pilgrim's staff, I crossed the bridge. Above and below me were the rapids, a river of impetuous snow, with here and there a dark rock amid its whiteness, resisting all the physical fury, as any cold spirit did the moral influences of the scene. On reaching Goat Island, which separates the two great segments of the falls, I chose the right-hand path, and followed it to the edge of the American cascade. There, while the falling sheet was yet invisible, I saw the vapor that never vanishes, and the Eternal Rainbow of Niagara.

It was an afternoon of glorious sunshine, without a cloud, save those of the cataracts. I gained an insulated rock, and beheld a broad sheet of brilliant and unbroken foam, not shooting in a curved line from the top of the precipice, but falling headlong down from height to depth. A narrow stream diverged from the main branch, and hurried over the crag by a channel of its own, leaving a little pine-clad island and a streak of precipice between itself and the larger sheet. Below arose the mist, on which was painted a dazzling sunbow with two concentric shadows, — one, almost as perfect as the original brightness; and the other, drawn faintly round the broken edge of the cloud.

Still I had not half seen Niagara. Following the verge of the island, the path led me to the Horseshoe, where the real, broad St. Lawrence, rushing along on a level with its banks, pours its whole breadth over a concave line of precipice, and thence pursues its course between lofty crags towards Ontario. A sort of bridge, two or three feet wide, stretches out along the edge of the descending sheet, and hangs upon the rising mist, as if that were the foundation of the frail structure. Here I stationed myself in the blast of wind, which the rushing river bore along with it. The bridge was tremulous beneath me, and marked the tremor of the solid earth. I looked along the whitening rapids, and endeavored to distinguish a mass of water far above the falls, to follow it to their verge, and go down with it, in fancy, to the abyss of clouds and storm. Casting my eyes across the river, and every side, I took in the whole scene at a glance, and tried to comprehend it in one vast idea. After an hour thus spent, I left the bridge, and, by a staircase, winding almost interminably round a post, descended to the base of the precipice. From that point, my path lay over slippery stones, and among great fragments of the cliff, to the edge of the cataract, where the wind at once enveloped me in spray, and perhaps dashed the rainbow round me. Were my long desires fulfilled? And had I seen Niagara?

Oh that I had never heard of Niagara till I beheld it! Blessed were the wanderers of old, who heard its deep roar, sounding through the woods, as the summons to an unknown wonder, and approached its awful brink, in all the freshness of native feeling. Had its own mysterious voice been the first to warn me of its existence, then, indeed, I might have knelt down and worshipped. But I had come thither, haunted with a vision of foam and fury, and dizzy cliffs, and an ocean tumbling down out of the sky, — a scene, in short, which nature had too much good taste and calm simplicity to realize. My mind had struggled to adapt these false conceptions to the reality, and finding the effort vain, a wretched sense of disappointment weighed me down. I climbed the precipice, and threw myself on the earth, feeling that I was unworthy to look at the Great Falls, and careless about beholding them again. . . .

All that night, as there has been and will be for ages past and to come, a rushing sound was heard, as if a great tempest were sweeping through the air. It mingled with my dreams, and made them full of storm and whirlwind. Whenever I awoke, and heard this dread sound in the air, and the windows rattling as with a mighty blast, I could not rest again, till looking forth, I saw how bright the stars were, and that every leaf in the garden was motionless. Never was a summer night more calm to the eye, nor a gale of autumn louder to the ear. The rushing sound proceeds from the rapids, and the rattling of the casements is but an effect of the vibration of the whole house, shaken by the jar of the cataract. The noise of the rapids draws the attention from the true voice of Niagara, which is a dull, muffled thunder, resounding between the cliffs. I spent a wakeful hour at midnight, in distinguishing its reverberations, and rejoiced to find that my former awe and enthusiasm were reviving.

Gradually, and after much contemplation, I came to know, by my own feelings, that Niagara is indeed a wonder of the world, and not the less wonderful, because time and thought must be employed in comprehending it. Casting aside all preconceived notions, and preparation to be dire-struck or delighted, the beholder must stand beside it in the simplicity of his heart, suffering the mighty scene to work its own impression. Night after night, I dreamed of it, and was gladdened every morning by the consciousness of a growing capacity to enjoy it. Yet I will not pretend to the all-absorbing enthusiasm of some more fortunate spectators, nor deny that very trifling causes would draw my eyes and thoughts from the cataract.

The last day that I was to spend at Niagara, before my departure for the Far West, I sat upon the Table Rock. This celebrated station did not now, as of old, project fifty feet beyond the line of the precipice, but was shattered by the fall of an immense fragment, which lay distant on the shore below. Still, on the utmost verge of the rock, with my feet hanging over it, I felt as if suspended in the open air. Never before had my mind been in such perfect unison with the scene. There were intervals, when I was conscious of nothing but the great river, rolling calmly into the abyss, rather descending than precipitating itself, and acquiring tenfold majesty from its unhurried motion. It came like the march of Destiny. It was not taken by surprise, but seemed to have anticipated, in all its course through the broad lakes, that it must pour their collected waters down this height. The perfect foam of the river, after its descent, and the ever-varying shapes of mist, rising up, to become clouds in the sky, would be the very picture of confusion, were it merely transient, like the rage of a tempest. But when the beholder has stood awhile, and perceives no lull in the storm, and considers that the vapor and the foam are as everlasting as the rocks which produce them, all this turmoil assumes a sort of calmness. It soothes, while it awes the mind.

Leaning over the cliff, I saw the guide conducting two adventurers behind the falls. It was pleasant, from that high seat in the sunshine, to observe them struggling against the eternal storm of the lower regions, with heads bent down, now faltering, now pressing forward, and finally swallowed up in their victory.

After their disappearance, a blast rushed out with an old hat, which it had swept from one of their heads. The rock, to which they were directing their unseen course, is marked, at a fearful distance on the exterior of the sheet, by a jet of foam. The attempt to reach it appears both poetical and perilous to a looker-on, but may be accomplished without much more difficulty or hazard, than in stemming a violent northeaster. In a few moments, forth came the children of the mist. Dripping and breathless, they crept along the base of the cliff, ascended to the guide's cottage, and received, I presume, a certificate of their achievement, with three verses of sublime poetry on the back.

My contemplations were often interrupted by strangers who came down from Forsyth's to take their first view of the falls. A short, ruddy, middle-aged gentleman, fresh from Old England, peeped over the rock, and evinced his approbation by a broad grin. His spouse, a very robust lady, afforded a sweet example of maternal solicitude, being so intent on the safety of her little boy that she did not even glance at Niagara. As for the child, he gave himself wholly to the enjoyment of a stick of candy. Another traveller, a native American, and no rare character among us, produced a volume of Captain Hall's tour, and labored earnestly to adjust Niagara to the captain's description, departing, at last, without one new idea or sensation of his own. The next comer was provided, not with a printed book, but with a blank sheet of foolscap, from top to bottom of which, by means of an ever-pointed pencil, the cataract was made to thunder. In a little talk, which we had together, he awarded his approbation to the general view, but censured the position of

Goat Island, observing that it should have been thrown farther to the right, so as to widen the American falls, and contract those of the Horseshoe. Next appeared two traders of Michigan, who declared, that, upon the whole, the sight was worth looking at; there certainly was an immense water-power here; but that, after all, they would go twice as far to see the noble stone-works of Lockport, where the Grand Canal is locked down a descent of sixty feet. They were succeeded by a young fellow, in a homespun cotton dress, with a staff in his hand, and a pack over his shoulders. He advanced close to the edge of the rock, where his attention, at first wavering among the different components of the scene, finally became fixed in the angle of the Horseshoe falls, which is, indeed, the central point of interest. His whole soul seemed to go forth and be transported thither, till the staff slipped from his relaxed grasp, and falling down — down — down — struck upon the fragment of the Table Rock.

In this manner I spent some hours, watching the varied impression, made by the cataract, on those who disturbed me, and returning to unwearied contemplation, when left alone. At length my time came to depart. There is a grassy footpath, through the woods, along the summit of the bank, to a point whence a causeway, hewn in the side of the precipice, goes winding down to the Ferry, about half a mile below the Table Rock. The sun was near setting, when I emerged from the shadow of the trees, and began the descent. The indirectness of my downward road continually changed the point of view, and showed me, in rich and repeated succession, now, the whitening rapids and majestic leap of the main river, which appeared more deeply massive as the light departed;

now, the lovelier picture, yet still sublime, of Goat
Island, with its rocks and grove, and the lesser falls,
tumbling over the right bank of the St. Lawrence, like
a tributary stream ; now, the long vista of the river,
as it eddied and whirled between the cliffs, to pass
through Ontario toward the sea, and everywhere to
be wondered at, for this one unrivalled scene.   The
golden sunshine tinged the sheet of the American cascade, and painted on its heaving spray the broken
semicircle of a rainbow, heaven's own beauty crown-
ing earth's sublimity.   My steps were slow, and I paused
long at every turn of the descent, as one lingers and
pauses who discerns a brighter and brightening excellence in what he must soon behold no more.   The solitude of the old wilderness now reigned over the whole
vicinity of the falls.   My enjoyment became the more
rapturous, because no poet shared it, nor wretch devoid of poetry profaned it ; but the spot so famous
through the world was all my own!

# THE ANTIQUE RING.

"Yes, indeed: the gem is as bright as a star, and curiously set," said Clara Pemberton, examining an antique ring, which her betrothed lover had just presented to her, with a very pretty speech. "It needs only one thing to make it perfect."

"And what is that?" asked Mr. Edward Caryl, secretly anxious for the credit of his gift. "A modern setting, perhaps?"

"Oh, no! That would destroy the charm at once," replied Clara. "It needs nothing but a story. I long to know how many times it has been the pledge of faith between two lovers, and whether the vows, of which it was the symbol, were always kept or often broken. Not that I should be too scrupulous about facts. If you happen to be unacquainted with its authentic history, so much the better. May it not have sparkled upon a queen's finger? Or who knows but it is the very ring which Posthumus received from Imogen? In short, you must kindle your imagination at the lustre of this diamond, and make a legend for it."

Now such a task — and doubtless Clara knew it — was the most acceptable that could have been imposed on Edward Caryl. He was one of that multitude of young gentlemen — limbs, or rather twigs, of the law — whose names appear in gilt letters on the front of Tudor's Buildings, and other places in the vicinity of the Court House, which seem to be the haunt of the gentler as well as the severer Muses. Edward, in the dearth of clients, was accustomed to employ his much leisure in assisting the growth of American Literature, to which good cause he had contributed not a few quires of the finest letter-paper, containing some thought, some fancy, some depth of feeling, together with a young writer's abundance of conceits. Sonnets, stanzas of Tennysonian sweetness, tales imbued with German mysticism, versions from Jean Paul, criticisms of the old English poets, and essays smacking of Dialistic philosophy, were among his multifarious productions. The editors of the fashionable periodicals were familiar with his autography, and inscribed his name in those brilliant bead-rolls of ink-stained celebrity which illustrate the first page of their covers. Nor did fame withhold her laurel. Hillard had included him among the lights of the New England metropolis, in his "Boston Book;" Bryant had found room for some of his stanzas, in the "Selections from American Poetry;" and Mr. Griswold, in his recent assemblage of the sons and daughters of song, had introduced Edward Caryl into the inner court of the temple, among his fourscore choicest bards. There was a prospect, indeed, of his assuming a still higher and more independent position. Interviews had been held with Ticknor, and a correspondence with the Harpers, respecting a proposed volume, chiefly to consist of Mr. Caryl's fugitive pieces in the Magazines, but to be accompanied with a poem of some length, never before published. Not improbably, the public may yet be gratified with this collection.

Meanwhile, we sum up our sketch of Edward Caryl, by pronouncing him, though somewhat of a carpet knight in literature, yet no unfavorable specimen of a generation of rising writers, whose spirit is such that we may reasonably expect creditable attempts from all, and good and beautiful results from some. And, it will be observed, Edward was the very man to write pretty legends, at a lady's instance, for an old-fashioned diamond ring. He took the jewel in his hand, and turned it so as to catch its scintillating radiance, as if hoping, in accordance with Clara's suggestion, to light up his fancy with that star-like gleam.

"Shall it be a ballad? — a tale in verse?" he inquired. "Enchanted rings often glisten in old English poetry; I think something may be done with the subject; but it is fitter for rhyme than prose."

"No, no," said Miss Pemberton, "we will have no more rhyme than just enough for a posy to the ring. You must tell the legend in simple prose; and when it is finished, I will make a little party to hear it read."

The young gentleman promised obedience; and going to his pillow, with his head full of the familiar spirits that used to be worn in rings, watches, and sword-hilts, he had the good fortune to possess himself of an available idea in a dream. Connecting this with what he himself chanced to know of the ring's real history, his task was done. Clara Pemberton invited a select few of her friends, all holding the stanchest faith in Edward's genius, and therefore the most genial auditors, if not altogether the fairest critics, that a writer could possibly desire. Blessed be woman for her faculty of admiration, and especially for her tendency to admire with her heart, when man, at most, grants merely a cold approval with his mind!

Drawing his chair beneath the blaze of a solar lamp, Edward Caryl untied a roll of glossy paper, and began as follows: —

### THE LEGEND.

After the death-warrant had been read to the Earl of Essex, and on the evening before his appointed execution, the Countess of Shrewsbury paid his lordship a visit, and found him, as it appeared, toying childishly with a ring. The diamond, that enriched it, glittered like a little star, but with a singular tinge of red. The gloomy prison-chamber in the Tower, with its deep and narrow windows piercing the walls of stone, was now all that the earl possessed of worldly prospect; so that there was the less wonder that he should look steadfastly into the gem, and moralize upon earth's deceitful splendor, as men in darkness and ruin seldom fail to do. But the shrewd observations of the countess, — an artful and unprincipled woman, — the pretended friend of Essex, but who had come to glut her revenge for a deed of scorn which he himself had forgotten, — her keen eye detected a deeper interest attached to this jewel. Even while expressing his gratitude for her remembrance of a ruined favorite, and condemned criminal, the earl's glance reverted to the ring, as if all that remained of time and its affairs were collected within that small golden circlet.

"My dear lord," observed the countess, "there is surely some matter of great moment wherewith this ring is connected, since it so absorbs your mind. A token, it may be, of some fair lady's love, — alas, poor lady, once richest in possessing such a heart! Would you that the jewel be returned to her?"

"The queen! the queen! It was her Majesty's own gift," replied the earl, still gazing into the depths of the gem. "She took it from her finger, and told me,

with a smile, that it was an heirloom from her Tudor
ancestors, and had once been the property of Merlin,
the British wizard, who gave it to the lady of his love.
His art had made this diamond the abiding-place of a
spirit, which, though of fiendish nature, was bound to
work only good, so long as the ring was an unviolated
pledge of love and faith, both with the giver and
receiver. But should love prove false, and faith be
broken, then the evil spirit would work his own devilish will, until the ring were purified by becoming the
medium of some good and holy act, and again the
pledge of faithful love. The gem soon lost its virtue ;
for the wizard was murdered by the very lady to whom
he gave it."

"An idle legend ! " said the countess.

"It is so," answered Essex, with a melancholy
smile. "Yet the queen's favor, of which this ring
was the symbol, has proved my ruin. When death is
nigh, men converse with dreams and shadows. I have
been gazing into the diamond, and fancying — but you
will laugh at me — that I might catch a glimpse of
the evil spirit there. Do you observe this red glow, —
dusky, too, amid all the brightness ? It is the token
of his presence ; and even now, methinks, it grows
redder and duskier, like an angry sunset."

Nevertheless, the earl's manner testified how slight
was his credence in the enchanted properties of the
ring. But there is a kind of playfulness that comes
in moments of despair, when the reality of misfortune,
if entirely felt, would crush the soul at once. He
now, for a brief space, was lost in thought, while the
countess contemplated him with malignant satisfaction.

"This ring," he resumed, in another tone, "alone

remains, of all that my royal mistress's favor lavished upon her servant. My fortune once shone as brightly as the gem. And now, such a darkness has fallen around me, methinks it would be no marvel if its gleam — the sole light of my prison-house — were to be forthwith extinguished; inasmuch as my last earthly hope depends upon it."

"How say you, my lord?" asked the Countess of Shrewsbury. "The stone is bright; but there should be strange magic in it, if it can keep your hopes alive, at this sad hour. Alas! these iron bars and ramparts of the Tower are unlike to yield to such a spell."

Essex raised his head involuntarily; for there was something in the countess's tone that disturbed him, although he could not suspect that an enemy had intruded upon the sacred privacy of a prisoner's dungeon, to exult over so dark a ruin of such once brilliant fortunes. He looked her in the face, but saw nothing to awaken his distrust. It would have required a keener eye than even Cecil's to read the secret of a countenance, which had been worn so long in the false light of a court, that it was now little better than a mask, telling any story save the true one. The condemned nobleman again bent over the ring, and proceeded: —

"It once had power in it, — this bright gem, — the magic that appertains to the talisman of a great queen's favor. She bade me, if hereafter I should fall into her disgrace, — how deep soever, and whatever might be the crime, — to convey this jewel to her sight, and it should plead for me. Doubtless, with her piercing judgment, she had even then detected the rashness of my nature, and foreboded some such deed as has now brought destruction upon my head. And knowing, too, her own hereditary rigor, she designed, it may be, that the memory of gentler and kindlier hours should soften her heart in my behalf, when my need should be the greatest. I have doubted, — I have distrusted, — yet who can tell, even now, what happy influence this ring might have?"

"You have delayed full long to show the ring, and plead her Majesty's gracious promise," remarked the countess, — "your state being what it is."

"True," replied the earl: "but for my honor's sake, I was loath to entreat the queen's mercy, while I might hope for life, at least, from the justice of the laws. If, on a trial by my peers, I had been acquitted of meditating violence against her sacred life, then would I have fallen at her feet, and, presenting the jewel, have prayed no other favor than that my love and zeal should be put to the severest test. But now — it were confessing too much — it were cringing too low — to beg the miserable gift of life, on no other score than the tenderness which her Majesty deems me to have forfeited!"

"Yet it is your only hope," said the countess.

"And besides," continued Essex, pursuing his own reflections, "of what avail will be this token of womanly feeling, when, on the other hand, are arrayed the all-prevailing motives of state policy, and the artifices and intrigues of courtiers, to consummate my downfall? Will Cecil or Raleigh suffer her heart to act for itself, even if the spirit of her father were not in her? It is in vain to hope it."

But still Essex gazed at the ring with an absorbed attention, that proved how much hope his sanguine temperament had concentrated here, when there was none else for him in the wide world, save what lay in

the compass of that hoop of gold. The spark of
brightness within the diamond, which gleamed like an
intenser than earthly fire, was the memorial of his dazzling career. It had not paled with the waning sunshine of his mistress's favor; on the contrary, in spite
of its remarkable tinge of dusky red, he fancied that
it never shone so brightly. The glow of festal torches,
— the blaze of perfumed lamps, — bonfires that had
been kindled for him, when he was the darling of
the people, — the splendor of the royal court, where
he had been the peculiar star, — all seemed to have
collected their moral or material glory into the gem,
and to burn with a radiance caught from the future,
as well as gathered from the past. That radiance
might break forth again. Bursting from the diamond,
into which it was now narrowed, it might beam first
upon the gloomy walls of the Tower, — then wider,
wider, wider, — till all England, and the seas around
her cliffs, should be gladdened with the light. It was
such an ecstasy as often ensues after long depression,
and has been supposed to precede the circumstances
of darkest fate that may befall mortal man. The earl
pressed the ring to his heart as if it were indeed a talisman, the habitation of a spirit, as the queen had
playfully assured him, — but a spirit of happier influences than her legend spake of.

"Oh, could I but make my way to her footstool!"
cried he, waving his hand aloft, while he paced the
stone pavement of his prison-chamber with an impetuous step. "I might kneel down, indeed, a ruined man,
condemned to the block, but how should I rise again?
Once more the favorite of Elizabeth! — England's
proudest noble! — with such prospects as ambition
never aimed at! Why have I tarried so long in this

weary dungeon ? The ring has power to set me free!
The palace wants me! Ho, jailer, unbar the door!"

But then occurred the recollection of the impossibil-
ity of obtaining an interview with his fatally estranged
mistress, and testing the influence over her affections,
which he still flattered himself with possessing. Could
he step beyond the limits of his prison, the world
would be all sunshine; but here was only gloom and
death.

"Alas!" said he, slowly and sadly, letting his head
fall upon his hands. "I die for the lack of one
blessed word."

The Countess of Shrewsbury, herself forgotten amid
the earl's gorgeous visions, had watched him with an
aspect that could have betrayed nothing to the most
suspicious observer; unless that it was too calm for
humanity, while witnessing the flutterings, as it were,
of a generous heart in the death-agony. She now approached him.

"My good lord," she said, "what mean you to do?"

"Nothing, — my deeds are done!" replied he, de-
pondingly; "yet, had a fallen favorite any friends,
I would entreat one of them to lay this ring at her
Majesty's feet; albeit with little hope, save that, hereafter, it might remind her that poor Essex, once far
too highly favored, was at last too severely dealt with."

"I will be that friend," said the countess. "There
is no time to be lost. Trust this precious ring with
me. This very night the queen's eye shall rest upon
it; nor shall the efficacy of my poor words be wanting, to strengthen the impression which it will doubtless make."

The earl's first impulse was to hold out the ring.
But looking at the countess, as she bent forward to

receive it, he fancied that the red glow of the gem
tinged all her face, and gave it an ominous expression.
Many passages of past times recurred to his memory.
A preternatural insight, perchance caught from approaching death, threw its momentary gleam, as from
a meteor, all round his position.

"Countess," he said, "I know not wherefore I hesitate, being in a plight so desperate, and having so little choice of friends.  But have you looked into your
own heart?  Can you perform this office with the
truth — the earnestness — the zeal, even to tears, and
agony of spirit — wherewith the holy gift of human
life should be pleaded for?  Woe be unto you, should
you undertake this task, and deal towards me otherwise than with utmost faith!  For your own soul's
sake, and as you would have peace at your death-hour,
consider well in what spirit you receive this ring!"

The countess did not shrink.

"My lord! — my good lord!" she exclaimed, "wrong
not a woman's heart by these suspicions.  You might
choose another messenger; but who, save a lady of her
bedchamber, can obtain access to the queen at this untimely hour?  It is for your life, — for your life, —
else I would not renew my offer."

"Take the ring," said the earl.

"Believe that it shall be in the queen's hands before the lapse of another hour," replied the countess,
as she received this sacred trust of life and death.
"To-morrow morning look for the result of my inter-
cession."

She departed.  Again the earl's hopes rose high.
Dreams visited his slumber, not of the sable-decked
scaffold in the Tower-yard, but of canopies of state,
obsequious courtiers, pomp, splendor, the smile of the

once more gracious queen, and a light beaming from
the magic gem, which illuminated his whole future.

History records how foully the Countess of Shrewsbury betrayed the trust, which Essex, in his utmost
need, confided to her. She kept the ring, and stood
in the presence of Elizabeth, that night, without one
attempt to soften her stern hereditary temper in behalf of the former favorite. The next day the earl's
noble head rolled upon the scaffold. On her death-
bed, tortured, at last, with a sense of the dreadful
guilt which she had taken upon her soul, the wicked
countess sent for Elizabeth, revealed the story of the
ring, and besought forgiveness for her treachery. But
the queen, still obdurate, even while remorse for past
obduracy was tugging at her heart-strings, shook the
dying woman in her bed, as if struggling with death
for the privilege of wreaking her revenge and spite.
The spirit of the countess passed away, to undergo the
justice, or receive the mercy, of a higher tribunal;
and tradition says, that the fatal ring was found upon
her breast, where it had imprinted a dark red circle,
resembling the effect of the intensest heat. The attendants, who prepared the body for burial, shuddered, whispering one to another, that the ring must
have derived its heat from the glow of infernal fire.
They left it on her breast, in the coffin, and it went
with that guilty woman to the tomb.

Many years afterward, when the church, that contained the monuments of the Shrewsbury family, was
desecrated by Cromwell's soldiers, they broke open the
ancestral vaults, and stole whatever was valuable from
the noble personages who reposed there. Merlin's antique ring passed into the possession of a stout sergeant of the Ironsides, who thus became subject to the

influences of the evil spirit that still kept his abode within the gem's enchanted depths. The sergeant was soon slain in battle, thus transmitting the ring, though without any legal form of testament, to a gay cavalier, who forthwith pawned it, and expended the money in liquor, which speedily brought him to the grave. We next catch the sparkle of the magic diamond at various epochs of the merry reign of Charles the Second. But its sinister fortune still attended it. From whatever hand this ring of portent came, and whatever finger it encircled, ever it was the pledge of deceit between man and man, or man and woman, of faithless vows, and unhallowed passion; and whether to lords and ladies, or to village-maids, — for sometimes it found its way so low, — still it brought nothing but sorrow and disgrace. No purifying deed was done, to drive the fiend from his bright home in this little star. Again, we hear of it at a later period, when Sir Robert Walpole bestowed the ring, among far richer jewels, on the lady of a British legislator, whose political honor he wished to undermine. Many a dismal and unhappy tale might be wrought out of its other adventures. All this while, its ominous tinge of dusky red had been deepening and darkening, until, if laid upon white paper, it cast the mingled hue of night and blood, strangely illuminated with scintillating light, in a circle round about. But this peculiarity only made it the more valuable.

Alas, the fatal ring! When shall its dark secret be discovered, and the doom of ill, inherited from one possessor to another, be finally revoked?

The legend now crosses the Atlantic, and comes down to our own immediate time. In a certain church of our city, not many evenings ago, there was a contribution for a charitable object. A fervid preacher had poured out his whole soul in a rich and tender discourse, which had at least excited the tears, and perhaps the more effectual sympathy, of a numerous audience. While the choristers sang sweetly, and the organ poured forth its melodious thunder, the deacons passed up and down the aisles, and along the galleries, presenting their mahogany boxes, in which each person deposited whatever sum he deemed it safe to lend to the Lord, in aid of human wretchedness. Charity became audible, — chink, chink, chink, — as it fell drop by drop, into the common receptacle. There was a hum, — a stir, — the subdued bustle of people putting their hands into their pockets ; while, ever and anon, a vagrant coin fell upon the floor, and rolled away, with long reverberation, into some inscrutable corner.

At length, all having been favored with an opportunity to be generous, the two deacons placed their boxes on the communion-table, and thence, at the conclusion of the services, removed them into the vestry. Here these good old gentlemen sat down together, to reckon the accumulated treasure.

" Fie, fie, Brother Tilton," said Deacon Trott, peeping into Deacon Tilton's box, " what a heap of copper you have picked up ! Really, for an old man, you must have had a heavy job to lug it along. Copper ! copper ! copper ! Do people expect to get admittance into heaven at the price of a few coppers ? "

" Don't wrong them, brother," answered Deacon Tilton, a simple and kindly old man. " Copper may do more for one person, than gold will for another. In the galleries, where I present my box, we must not expect such a harvest as you gather among the gentry in the broad aisle, and all over the floor of the church.

My people are chiefly poor mechanics and laborers,
sailors, seamstresses, and servant - maids, with a most
uncomfortable intermixture of roguish school-boys."

" Well, well," said Deacon Trott; " but there is a
great deal, Brother Tilton, in the method of presenting
a contribution-box. It is a knack that comes by nature, or not at all."

They now proceeded to sum up the avails of the
evening, beginning with the receipts of Deacon Trott.
In good sooth, that worthy personage had reaped an
abundant harvest, in which he prided himself no less,
apparently, than if every dollar had been contributed
from his own individual pocket. Had the good deacon been meditating a jaunt to Texas, the treasures
of the mahogany box might have sent him on his way
rejoicing. There were bank - notes, mostly, it is true,
of the smallest denomination in the giver's pocket-
book, yet making a goodly average upon the whole.
The most splendid contribution was a check for a hundred dollars, bearing the name of a distinguished merchant, whose liberality was duly celebrated in the
newspapers of the next day. No less than seven half-
eagles, together with an English sovereign, glittered
amidst an indiscriminate heap of silver; the box being polluted with nothing of the copper kind, except a
single bright new cent, wherewith a little boy had performed his first charitable act.

"Very well! very well indeed!" said Deacon Trott,
self-approvingly. "A handsome evening's work! And
now, Brother Tilton, let's see whether you can match
it." Here was a sad contrast! They poured forth
Deacon Tilton's treasure upon the table, and it really
seemed as if the whole copper coinage of the country,
together with an amazing quantity of shop - keeper's

tokens, and English and Irish half-pence, mostly of base metal, had been congregated into the box. There was a very substantial pencil-case, and the semblance of a shilling; but the latter proved to be made of tin, and the former of German-silver. A gilded brass button was doing duty as a gold coin, and a folded shop-bill had assumed the character of a bank-note. But Deacon Tilton's feelings were much revived by the aspect of another bank-note, new and crisp, adorned with beautiful engravings, and stamped with the indubitable word, TWENTY, in large black letters. Alas! it was a counterfeit. In short, the poor old Deacon was no less unfortunate than those who trade with fairies, and whose gains are sure to be transformed into dried leaves, pebbles, and other valuables of that kind.

"I believe the Evil One is in the box," said he, with some vexation.

"Well done, Deacon Tilton!" cried his Brother Trott, with a hearty laugh. "You ought to have a statue in copper."

"Never mind, brother," replied the good Deacon, recovering his temper. "I'll bestow ten dollars from my own pocket, and may Heaven's blessing go along with it. But look! what do you call this?"

Under the copper mountain, which it had cost them so much toil to remove, lay an antique ring! It was enriched with a diamond, which, so soon as it caught the light, began to twinkle and glimmer, emitting the whitest and purest lustre that could possibly be conceived. It was as brilliant as if some magician had condensed the brightest star in heaven into a compass fit to be set in a ring, for a lady's delicate finger.

"How is this?" said Deacon Trott, examining it

carefully, in the expectation of finding it as worthless
as the rest of his colleague's treasure. " Why, upon
my word, this seems to be a real diamond, and of the
purest water. Whence could it have come ? "

" Really, I cannot tell," quoth Deacon Tilton, " for
my spectacles were so misty that all faces looked alike.
But now I remember, there was a flash of light came
from the box, at one moment; but it seemed a dusky
red, instead of a pure white, like the sparkle of this
gem. Well; the ring will make up for the copper ;
but I wish the giver had thrown its history into the
box along with it."

It has been our good luck to recover a portion of
that history. After transmitting misfortune from one
possessor to another, ever since the days of British
Merlin, the identical ring which Queen Elizabeth gave
to the Earl of Essex was finally thrown into the contribution-box of a New England church. The two
deacons deposited it in the glass case of a fashionable
jeweller, of whom it was purchased by the humble
rehearser of this legend, in the hope that it may be
allowed to sparkle on a fair lady's finger. Purified
from the foul fiend, so long its inhabitant, by a deed
of unostentatious charity, and now made the symbol
of faithful and devoted love, the gentle bosom of its
new possessor need fear no sorrow from its influence.

" Very pretty ! — Beautiful ! — How original ! —
How sweetly written ! — What nature ! — What imagination ! — What power ! — What pathos ! — What
exquisite humor ! " — were the exclamations of Edward Caryl's kind and generous auditors, at the conclusion of the legend.

" It is a pretty tale," said Miss Pemberton, who,

conscious that her praise was to that of all others as
a diamond to a pebble, was therefore the less liberal
in awarding it.  " It is really a pretty tale, and very
proper for any of the Annuals.  But, Edward, your
moral does not satisfy me.  What thought did you
embody in the ring ? "

" O Clara, this is too bad ! " replied Edward, with
a half-reproachful smile.  " You know that I can never
separate the idea from the symbol in which it manifests itself.  However, we may suppose the Gem to be
the human heart, and the Evil Spirit to be Falsehood,
which, in one guise or another, is the fiend that causes
all the sorrow and trouble in the world.  I beseech
you to let this suffice."

" It shall," said Clara, kindly.  " And, believe me,
whatever the world may say of the story, I prize it
far above the diamond which enkindled your imagination."

# GRAVES AND GOBLINS.

Now talk we of graves and goblins! Fit themes, — start not! gentle reader, — fit for a ghost like me. Yes; though an earth-clogged fancy is laboring with these conceptions, and an earthly hand will write them down, for mortal eyes to read, still their essence flows from as airy a ghost as ever basked in the pale starlight, at twelve o'clock. Judge them not by the gross and heavy form in which they now appear. They may be gross, indeed, with the earthly pollution contracted from the brain, through which they pass; and heavy with the burden of mortal language, that crushes all the finer intelligences of the soul. This is no fault of mine. But should aught of ethereal spirit be perceptible, yet scarcely so, glimmering along the dull train of words, — should a faint perfume breathe from the mass of clay, — then, gentle reader, thank the ghost, who thus embodies himself for your sake! Will you believe me, if I say that all true and noble thoughts, and elevated imaginations, are but partly the offspring of the intellect which seems to produce them? Sprites, that were poets once, and are now all poetry, hover round the dreaming bard, and become his inspiration; buried statesmen lend their wisdom, gathered on earth and mellowed in the grave, to the historian; and when the preacher rises nearest to the level of his mighty subject, it is because the prophets of old days have communed with him. Who has not been conscious of mysteries within his mind, mysteries of truth and reality, which will not wear the chains of language? Mortal, then the dead were with you! And thus shall the earth-dulled soul, whom I inspire, be conscious of a misty brightness among his thoughts, and strive to make it gleam upon the page, — but all in vain. Poor author! How will he despise what he can grasp, for the sake of the dim glory that eludes him!

So talk we of graves and goblins. But, what have ghosts to do with graves? Mortal man, wearing the dust which shall require a sepulchre, might deem it more a home and resting-place than a spirit can, whose earthly clod has returned to earth. Thus philosophers have reasoned. Yet wiser they who adhere to the ancient sentiment, that a phantom haunts and hallows the marble tomb or grassy hillock where its material form was laid. Till purified from each stain of clay; till the passions of the living world are all forgotten; till it have less brotherhood with the wayfarers of earth than with spirits that never wore mortality, — the ghost must linger round the grave. Oh, it is a long and dreary watch to some of us!

Even in early childhood, I had selected a sweet spot, of shade and glimmering sunshine, for my grave. It was no burial-ground, but a secluded nook of virgin earth, where I used to sit, whole summer afternoons, dreaming about life and death. My fancy ripened prematurely, and taught me secrets which I could not otherwise have known. I pictured the coming years, — they never came to me, indeed; but I pictured them like life, and made this spot the scene of all that should be brightest, in youth, manhood, and old age. There, in a little while, it would be time for me to breathe the bashful and burning vows of first-love;

thither, after gathering fame abroad, I would return
to enjoy the loud plaudit of the world, a vast but unobtrusive sound, like the booming of a distant sea;
and thither, at the far-off close of life, an aged man
would come, to dream, as the boy was dreaming, and
be as happy in the past as he was in futurity. Finally,
when all should be finished, in that spot so hallowed,
in that soil so impregnated with the most precious of
my bliss, there was to be my grave. Methought it
would be the sweetest grave that ever a mortal frame
reposed in, or an ethereal spirit haunted. There, too,
in future times, drawn thither by the spell which I had
breathed around the place, boyhood would sport and
dream, and youth would love, and manhood would enjoy, and age would dream again, and my ghost would
watch but never frighten them. Alas, the vanity of
mortal projects, even when they centre in the grave!
I died in my first youth, before I had been a lover; at
a distance, also, from the grave which fancy had dug
for me; and they buried me in the thronged cemetery
of a town, where my marble slab stands unnoticed
amid a hundred others. And there are coffins on
each side of mine!

"Alas, poor ghost!" will the reader say. Yet I
am a happy ghost enough, and disposed to be contented with my grave, if the sexton will but let it be
my own, and bring no other dead man to dispute my
title. Earth has left few stains upon me, and it will
be but a short time that I need haunt the place. It
is good to die in early youth. Had I lived out three-
score years and ten, or half of them, my spirit would
have been so earth-incrusted, that centuries might not
have purified it for a better home than the dark precincts of the grave. Meantime, there is good choice

of company amongst us. From twilight till near sunrise, we are gliding to and fro, some in the graveyard,
others miles away; and, would we speak with any
friend, we do but knock against his tombstone, and
pronounce the name engraved on it: in an instant,
there the shadow stands!

Some are ghosts of considerable antiquity. There
is an old man, hereabout; he never had a tombstone,
and is often puzzled to distinguish his own grave; but
hereabouts he haunts, and long is doomed to haunt.
He was a miser in his lifetime, and buried a strong
box of ill-gotten gold, almost fresh from the mint, in
the coinage of William and Mary. Scarcely was it
safe, when the sexton buried the old man, and his secret with him. I could point out the place where the
treasure lies; it was at the bottom of the miser's garden; but a paved thoroughfare now passes beside the
spot, and the corner-stone of a market-house presses
right down upon it. Had the workmen dug six inches
deeper, they would have found the hoard. Now
thither must this poor old miser go, whether in starlight, moonshine, or pitch darkness, and brood above
his worthless treasure, recalling all the petty crimes
by which he gained it. Not a coin must he fail to
reckon in his memory, nor forget a pennyworth of the
sin that made up the sum, though his agony is such as
if the pieces of gold, red-hot, were stamped into his
naked soul. Often, while he is in torment there, he
hears the steps of living men, who love the dross of
earth as well as he did. May they never groan over
their miserable wealth like him! Night after night,
for above a hundred years, hath he done this penance,
and still must he do it, till the iron box he brought to
light, and each separate coin be cleansed by grateful

tears of a widow or an orphan. My spirit sighs for his long vigil at the corner of the market-house!

There are ghosts whom I tremble to meet, and cannot think of without a shudder. One has the guilt of blood upon him. The soul which he thrust untimely forth has long since been summoned from our gloomy graveyard, and dwells among the stars of heaven, too far and too high for even the recollection of mortal anguish to ascend thither. Not so the murderer's ghost! It is his doom to spend all the hours of darkness in the spot which he stained with innocent blood, and to feel the hot stream — hot as when it first gushed upon his hand — incorporating itself with his spiritual substance. Thus his horrible crime is ever fresh within him. Two other wretches are condemned to walk arm in arm. They were guilty lovers in their lives, and still, in death, must wear the guise of love, though hatred and loathing have become their very nature and existence. The pollution of their mutual sin remains with them, and makes their souls sick continually. Oh, that I might forget all the dark shadows which haunt about these graves! This passing thought of them has left a stain, and will weigh me down among dust and sorrow, beyond the time that my own transgressions would have kept me here.

There is one shade among us, whose high nature it is good to meditate upon. He lived a patriot, and is a patriot still. Posterity has forgotten him. The simple slab, of red freestone, that bore his name, was broken long ago, and is now covered by the gradual accumulation of the soil. A tuft of thistles is his only monument. This upright spirit came to his grave, after a lengthened life, with so little stain of earth, that he might, almost immediately, have trodden the pathway of the sky. But his strong love of country chained him down, to share its vicissitudes of weal or woe. With such deep yearning in his soul, he was unfit for heaven. That noblest virtue has the effect of sin, and keeps his pure and lofty spirit in a penance, which may not terminate till America be again a wilderness. Not that there is no joy for the dead patriot. Can he fail to experience it, while he contemplates the mighty and increasing power of the land, which he protected in its infancy? No; there is much to gladden him. But sometimes I dread to meet him, as he returns from the bedchambers of rulers and politicians, after diving into their secret motives, and searching out their aims. He looks round him with a stern and awful sadness, and vanishes into his neglected grave. Let nothing sordid or selfish defile your deeds or thoughts, ye great men of the day, lest ye grieve the noble dead.

Few ghosts take such an endearing interest as this, even in their own private affairs. It made me rather sad, at first, to find how soon the flame of love expires amid the chill damps of the tomb; so much the sooner, the more fiercely it may have burned. Forget your dead mistress, youth! She has already forgotten you. Maiden, cease to weep for your buried lover! He will know nothing of your tears, nor value them if he did. Yet it were blasphemy to say that true love is other than immortal. It is an earthly passion, of which I speak, mingled with little that is spiritual, and must therefore perish with the perishing clay. When souls have loved, there is no falsehood or forgetfulness. Maternal affection, too, is strong as adamant. There are mothers here, among us, who might have been in heaven fifty years ago, if they could forbear to cherish

earthly joy and sorrow, reflected from the bosoms of
their children. Husbands and wives have a comfortable gift of oblivion, especially when secure of the
faith of their living halves. Jealousy, it is true, will
play the devil with a ghost, driving him to the bedside
of secondary wedlock, there to scowl, unseen, and gib-
ber inaudible remonstrances. Dead wives, however
jealous in their lifetime, seldom feel this posthumous
torment so acutely.

Many, many things, that appear most important
while we walk the busy street, lose all their interest
the moment we are borne into the quiet graveyard
which borders it. For my own part, my spirit had not
become so mixed up with earthly existence, as to be
now held in an unnatural combination, or tortured
much with retrospective cares. I still love my parents
and a younger sister, who remain among the living,
and often grieve me by their patient sorrow for the
dead. Each separate tear of theirs is an added weight
upon my soul, and lengthens my stay among the
graves. As to other matters, it exceedingly rejoices
me that my summons came before I had time to write
a projected poem, which was highly imaginative in conception, and could not have failed to give me a triumphant rank in the choir of our native bards. Nothing
is so much to be deprecated as posthumous renown.
It keeps the immortal spirit from the proper bliss of
his celestial state, and causes him to feed upon the impure breath of mortal man, till sometimes he forgets
that there are starry realms above him. Few poets —
infatuated that they are ! — soar upward while the
least whisper of their name is heard on earth. On
Sabbath evenings, my sisters sit by the fireside, between our father and mother, and repeat some hymns

of mine, which they have often heard from my own
lips, ere the tremulous voice left them forever. Little
do they think, those dear ones, that the dead stands
listening in the glimmer of the firelight, and is almost
gifted with a visible shape by the fond intensity of
their remembrance.

Now shall the reader know a grief of the poor ghost
that speaks to him ; a grief, but not a helpless one.
Since I have dwelt among the graves, they bore the
corpse of a young maiden hither, and laid her in the
old ancestral vault, which is hollowed in the side of a
grassy bank. It has a door of stone, with rusty iron
hinges, and above it, a rude sculpture of the family
arms, and inscriptions of all their names who have
been buried there, including sire and son, mother and
daughter, of an ancient colonial race. All of her
lineage had gone before, and when the young maiden
followed, the portal was closed forever. The night
after her burial, when the other ghosts were flitting
about their graves, forth came the pale virgin's shadow, with the rest, but knew not whither to go, nor
whom to haunt, so lonesome had she been on earth.
She stood by the ancient sepulchre, looking upward to
the bright stars, as if she would, even then, begin her
flight. Her sadness made me sad. That night and
the next, I stood near her, in the moonshine, but
dared not speak, because she seemed purer than all
the ghosts, and fitter to converse with angels than
with men. But the third bright eve, still gazing upward to the glory of the heavens, she sighed, and said,
" When will my mother come for me ? " Her low,
sweet voice emboldened me to speak, and she was
kind and gentle, though so pure, and answered me
again. From that time, always at the ghostly hour,

I sought the old tomb of her fathers, and either found her standing by the door, or knocked, and she appeared. Blessed creature, that she was; her chaste spirit hallowed mine, and imparted such a celestial buoyancy, that I longed to grasp her hand, and fly, — upward, aloft, aloft! I thought, too, that she only lingered here, till my earthlier soul should be purified for heaven. One night, when the stars threw down the light that shadows love, I stole forth to the accustomed spot, and knocked, with my airy fingers, at her door. She answered not. Again I knocked, and breathed her name. Where was she? At once, the truth fell on my miserable spirit and crushed it to the earth, among dead men's bones and mouldering dust, groaning in cold and desolate agony. Her penance was over! She had taken her trackless flight, and had found a home in the purest radiance of the upper stars, leaving me to knock at the stone portal of the darksome sepulchre. But I know — I know, that angels hurried her away, or surely she would have whispered ere she fled!

She is gone! How could the grave imprison that unspotted one! But her pure, ethereal spirit will not quite forget me, nor soar too high in bliss, till I ascend to join her. Soon, soon be that hour! I am weary of the earth-damps; they burden me; they choke me! Already, I can float in the moonshine; the faint starlight will almost bear up my footsteps; the perfume of flowers, which grosser spirits love, is now too earthly a luxury for me. Grave! Grave! thou art not my home. I must flit a little longer in thy night gloom, and then be gone, — far from the dust of the living and the dead, — far from the corruption that is around me, but no more within!

A few times I have visited the chamber of one who walks, obscure and lonely, on his mortal pilgrimage. He will leave not many living friends, when he goes to join the dead, where his thoughts often stray, and he might better be. I steal into his sleep, and play my part among the figures of his dreams. I glide through the moonlight of his waking fancy, and whisper conceptions, which, with a strange thrill of fear, he writes down as his own. I stand beside him now, at midnight, telling these dreamy truths with a voice so dream-like, that he mistakes them for fictions of a brain too prone to such. Yet he glances behind him and shivers, while the lamp burns pale. Farewell, dreamer, — waking or sleeping! Your brightest dreams are fled; your mind grows too hard and cold for a spiritual guest to enter; you are earthly, too, and have all the sins of earth. The ghost will visit you no more.

But where is the maiden, holy and pure, though wearing a form of clay, that would have me bend over her pillow at midnight, and leave a blessing there? With a silent invocation, let her summon me. Shrink not, maiden, when I come! In life, I was a high-souled youth, meditative, yet seldom sad, full of chaste fancies, and stainless from all grosser sin. And now, in death, I bring no loathsome smell of the grave, nor ghostly terrors, — but gentle, and soothing, and sweetly pensive influences. Perhaps, just fluttering for the skies, my visit may hallow the wellsprings of thy thought, and make thee heavenly here on earth. Then shall pure dreams and holy meditations bless thy life; nor thy sainted spirit linger round the grave, but seek the upper stars, and meet me there!

## DR. BULLIVANT.

THIS person was not eminent enough, either by nature or circumstance, to deserve a public memorial simply for his own sake, after the lapse of a century and a half from the era in which he flourished. His character, in the view which we propose to take of it, may give a species of distinctness and point to some remarks on the tone and composition of New England society, modified as it became by new ingredients from the eastern world, and by the attrition of sixty or seventy years over the rugged peculiarities of the original settlers. We are perhaps accustomed to employ too sombre a pencil in picturing the earlier times among the Puritans, because, at our cold distance, we form our ideas almost wholly from their severest features. It is like gazing on some scenes in the land which we inherit from them; we see the mountains, rising sternly and with frozen summits up to heaven, and the forests, waving in massy depths where sunshine seems a profanation, and we see the gray mist, like the duskiness of years, shedding a chill obscurity over the whole; but the green and pleasant spots in the hollow of the hills, the warm places in the heart of what looks desolate, are hidden from our eyes. Still, however, a prevailing characteristic of the age was gloom, or something which cannot be more accurately expressed than by that term, and its long shadow, falling over all the intervening years, is visible, though not too distinctly, upon ourselves. Without material detriment to a deep and solid happiness, the frolic of the mind was so habitually chastened, that persons have gained a nook in history by the mere possession of animal spirits, too exuberant to be confined within the established bounds. Every vain jest and unprofitable word was deemed an item in the account of criminality, and whatever wit, or semblance thereof, came into existence, its birthplace was generally the pulpit, and its parent some sour old Genevan divine. The specimens of humor and satire, preserved in the sermons and controversial tracts of those days, are occasionally the apt expressions of pungent thoughts ; but oftener they are cruel torturings and twistings of trite ideas, disgusting by the wearisome ingenuity which constitutes their only merit. Among a people where so few possessed, or were allowed to exercise, the art of extracting the mirth which lies hidden like latent caloric in almost everything, a gay apothecary, such as Dr. Bullivant, must have been a phenomenon.

We will suppose ourselves standing in Cornhill, on a pleasant morning of the year 1670, about the hour when the shutters are unclosed, and the dust swept from the doorsteps, and when Business rubs its eyes, and begins to plod sleepily through the town. The street, instead of running between lofty and continuous piles of brick, is but partially lined with wooden buildings of various heights and architecture, in each of which the mercantile department is connected with the domicile, like the gingerbread and candy shops of an after-date. The signs have a singular appearance to a stranger's eye. These are not a barren record of names and occupations, yellow letters on black boards, but images and hieroglyphics, sometimes typifying the principal commodity offered for sale, though generally

intended to give an arbitrary designation to the establishment.    Overlooking the bearded Saracens, the
Indian Queens, and the wooden Bibles, let us direct
our attention to the white post newly erected at the
corner of the street, and surmounted by a gilded countenance which flashes in the early sunbeams like veritable gold.    It is a bust of Æsculapius, evidently of
the latest London manufacture; and from the door
behind it steams forth a mingled smell of musk and
assafœtida, and other drugs of potent perfume, as if an
appropriate sacrifice were just laid upon the altar of
the medical deity.    Five or six idle people are already
collected, peeping curiously in at the glittering array
of galiipots and phials, and deciphering the labels
which tell their contents in the mysterious and imposing nomenclature of ancient physic.    They are next
attracted by the printed advertisement of a Panacea,
promising life but one day short of eternity, and youth
and health commensurate.    An old man, his head as
white as snow, totters in with a hasty clattering of his
staff, and becomes the earliest purchaser, hoping that
his wrinkles will disappear more swiftly than they
gathered.    The Doctor (so styled by courtesy) shows
the upper half of his person behind the counter, and
appears to be a slender and rather tall man; his features are difficult to describe, possessing nothing peculiar, except a flexibility to assume all characters in
turn, while his eye, shrewd, quick, and saucy, remains
the same throughout.    Whenever a customer enters
the shop, if he desire a box of pills, he receives with
them an equal number of hard, round, dry jokes, —
or if a dose of salts, it is mingled with a portion of the
salt of Attica, — or if some hot, Oriental drug, it is
accompanied by a racy word or two that tingle on the

mental palate, — all without the least additional cost. Then there are twistings of mouths which never lost their gravity before. As each purchaser retires, the spectators see a resemblance of his visage pass over that of the apothecary, in which all the ludicrous points are made most prominent, as if a magic looking-glass had caught the reflection, and were making sport with it. Unwonted titterings arise and strengthen into bashful laughter, but are suddenly hushed as some minister, heavy-eyed from his last night's vigil, or magistrate, armed with the terror of the whipping-post and pillory, or perhaps the governor himself, goes by like a dark cloud intercepting the sunshine.

About this period, many causes began to produce an important change on and beneath the surface of colonial society. The early settlers were able to keep within the narrowest limits of their rigid principles, because they had adopted them in mature life, and from their own deep conviction, and were strengthened in them by that species of enthusiasm, which is as sober and as enduring as reason itself. But if their immediate successors followed the same line of conduct, they were confined to it, in a great degree, by habits forced upon them, and by the severe rule under which they were educated, and, in short, more by restraint than by the free exercise of the imagination and understanding. When therefore the old original stock, the men who looked heavenward without a wandering glance to earth, had lost a part of their domestic and public influence, yielding to infirmity or death, a relaxation naturally ensued in their theory and practice of morals and religion, and became more evident with the daily decay of its most strenuous opponents. This gradual but sure operation was assisted by the increas-

ing commercial importance of the colonies, whither a
new set of emigrants followed unworthily in the track
of the pure-hearted Pilgrims. Gain being now the
allurement, and almost the only one, since dissenters
no longer dreaded persecution at home, the people of
New England could not remain entirely uncontami-
nated by an extensive intermixture with worldly men.
The trade carried on by the colonists (in the face of
several inefficient acts of Parliament) with the whole
maritime world, must have had a similar tendency;
nor are the desperate and dissolute visitants of the
country to be forgotten among the agents of a moral
revolution. Freebooters from the West Indies and
the Spanish Main, — state criminals, implicated in the
numerous plots and conspiracies of the period, — fel-
ons, loaded with private guilt, — numbers of these
took refuge in the provinces, where the authority of
the English king was obstructed by a zealous spirit
of independence, and where a boundless wilderness
enabled them to defy pursuit. Thus the new population, temporary and permanent, was exceedingly unlike
the old, and far more apt to disseminate their own
principles than to imbibe those of the Puritans. All
circumstances unfavorable to virtue acquired double
strength by the licentious reign of Charles II.; though
perhaps the example of the monarch and nobility was
less likely to recommend vice to the people of New
England than to those of any other part of the British
Empire.

The clergy and the elder magistrates manifested a
quick sensibility to the decline of godliness, their apprehensions being sharpened in this particular no less
by a holy zeal than because their credit and influence
were intimately connected with the primitive character

of the country. A Synod, convened in the year 1679, gave its opinion that the iniquity of the times had drawn down judgments from Heaven, and proposed methods to assuage the Divine wrath by a renewal of former sanctity. But neither the increased numbers, nor the altered spirit of the people, nor the just sense of a freedom to do wrong, within certain limits, would now have permitted the exercise of that inquisitorial strictness, which had been wont to penetrate to men's firesides and watch their domestic life, recognizing no distinction between private ill conduct and crimes that endanger the community. Accordingly, the tide of worldly principles encroached more and more upon the ancient landmarks, hitherto esteemed the outer boundaries of virtue. Society arranged itself into two classes, marked by strong shades of difference, though separated by an uncertain line : in one were included the small and feeble remnant of the first settlers, many of their immediate descendants, the whole body of the clergy, and all whom a gloomy temperament, or tenderness of conscience, or timidity of thought, kept up to the strictness of their fathers ; the other comprehended the new emigrants, the gay and thoughtless natives, the favorers of Episcopacy, and a various mixture of liberal and enlightened men with most of the evil-doers and unprincipled adventurers in the country. A vivid and rather a pleasant idea of New England manners, when this change had become decided, is given in the journal of John Dunton, a cockney bookseller, who visited Boston and other towns of Massachusetts with a cargo of pious publications, suited to the Puritan market. Making due allowance for the flippancy of the writer, which may have given a livelier tone to his descriptions than

truth precisely warrants, and also for his character,
which led him chiefly among the gayer inhabitants,
there still seems to have been many who loved the
winecup and the song, and all sorts of delightful
naughtiness. But the degeneracy of the times had
made far less progress in the interior of the country
than in the seaports, and until the people lost the elec-
tive privilege, they continued the government in the
hands of those upright old men who had so long possessed their confidence. Uncontrollable events, alone,
gave a temporary ascendency to persons of another
stamp. James II., during the four years of his despotic reign revoked the charters of the American colonies, arrogated the appointment of their magistrates,
and annulled all those legal and prescriptive rights
which had hitherto constituted them nearly independent states. Among the foremost advocates of the
royal usurpations was Dr. Bullivant. Gifted with a
smart and ready intellect, busy and bold, he acquired
great influence in the new government, and assisted
Sir Edmund Andros, Edward Randolph, and five or
six others, to browbeat the council, and misrule the
Northern provinces according to their pleasure. The
strength of the popular hatred against this administration, the actual tyranny that was exercised, and
the innumerable fears and jealousies, well grounded
and fantastic, which harassed the country, may be best
learned from a work of Increase Mather, the " Remarkable Providences of the Earlier Days of American Colonization." The good divine (though writing
when a lapse of nearly forty years should have tamed
the fierceness of party animosity) speaks with the most
bitter and angry scorn of "'Pothecary Bullivant," who
probably indulged his satirical propensities, from the

seat of power, in a manner which rendered him an especial object of public dislike. But the people were about to play off a piece of practical fun on the Doctor and the whole of his coadjutors, and have the laugh all to themselves. By the first faint rumor of the attempt of the Prince of Orange on the throne, the power of James was annihilated in the colonies, and long before the abdication of the latter became known, Sir Edmund Andros, Governor-General of New England and New York, and fifty of the most obnoxious leaders of the court party, were tenants of a prison. We will visit our old acquaintance in his adversity.

The scene now represents a room of ten feet square, the floor of which is sunk a yard or two below the level of the ground; the walls are covered with a dirty and crumbling plaster, on which appear a crowd of ill-favored and lugubrious faces done in charcoal, and the autographs and poetical attempts of a long succession of debtors and petty criminals. Other features of the apartment are a deep fireplace (superfluous in the sultriness of the summer's day), a door of hard-hearted oak, and a narrow window high in the wall, where the glass has long been broken, while the iron bars retain all their original strength. Through this opening come the sound of passing footsteps in the public street, and the voices of children at play. The furniture consists of a bed, or rather an old sack of barley straw, thrown down in the corner farthest from the door, and a chair and table, both aged and infirm, and leaning against the side of the room, besides lending a friendly support to each other. The atmosphere is stifled and of an ill smell, as if it had been kept close prisoner for half a century, and had lost all its pure and elastic nature by feeding the tainted breath of the vicious and the sighs of the unfortunate. Such is the present abode of the man of medicine and politics, and his own appearance forms no contrast to the accompaniments. His wig is unpowdered, out of curl, and put on awry ; the dust of many weeks has worked its way into the web of his coat and small-clothes, and his knees and elbows peep forth to ask why they are so ill clad ; his stockings are ungartered, his shoes down at the heel, his waistcoat is without a button, and discloses a shirt as dingy as the remnant of snow in a showery April day. His shoulders have become rounder, and his whole person is more bent and drawn together, since we last saw him, and his face has exchanged the glory of wit and humor for a sheepish dulness. At intervals, the Doctor walks the room, with an irregular and shuffling pace ; anon he throws himself flat on the sack of barley straw, muttering very reprehensible expressions between his teeth ; then again he starts to his feet, and journeying from corner to corner, finally sinks into the chair, forgetful of its three-legged infirmity till it lets him down upon the floor. The grated window, his only medium of intercourse with the world, serves but to admit additional vexations. Every few moments the steps of the passengers are heard to pause, and some well-known face appears in the free sunshine behind the iron bars, brimful of mirth and drollery, the owner whereof stands on tiptoe to tickle poor Dr. Bullivant with a stinging sarcasm. Then laugh the little boys around the prison door, and the wag goes chuckling away. The apothecary would fain retaliate, but all his quips and repartees, and sharp and facetious fancies, once so abundant, seem to have been transferred from himself to the sluggish brains of his enemies.

While endeavoring to condense his whole intellect into one venomous point, in readiness for the next assailant, he is interrupted by the entrance of the turnkey with the prison fare of Indian bread and water. With these dainties we leave him.

When the turmoil of the Revolution had subsided, and the authority of William and Mary was fixed on a quiet basis throughout the colonies, the deposed governor and some of his partisans were sent home to the new court, and the others released from imprisonment. The New-Englanders, as a people, are not apt to retain a revengeful sense of injury, and nowhere, perhaps, could a politician, however odious in his power, live more peacefully in his nakedness and disgrace. Dr. Bullivant returned to his former occupation, and spent rather a desirable old age. Though he sometimes hit hard with a jest, yet few thought of taking offence; for whenever a man habitually indulges his tongue at the expense of all his associates, they provide against the common annoyance by tacitly agreeing to consider his sarcasms as null and void. Thus for many years, a gray old man with a stoop in his gait, he continued to sweep out his shop at eight o'clock in summer mornings, and nine in the winter, and to waste whole hours in idle talk and irreverent merriment, making it his glory to raise the laughter of silly people, and his delight to sneer at them in his sleeve. At length, one pleasant day, the door and shutters of his establishment kept closed from sunrise till sunset, and his cronies marvelled a moment, and passed on; a week after, the rector of King's Chapel said the death-rite over Dr. Bullivant; and within the month a new apothecary, and a new stock of drugs and medicines, made their appearance at the gilded Head of Æsculapius.

# A BOOK OF AUTOGRAPHS.

WE have before us a volume of autograph letters, chiefly of soldiers and statesmen of the Revolution, and addressed to a good and brave man, General Palmer, who himself drew his sword in the cause. They are profitable reading in a quiet afternoon, and in a mood withdrawn from too intimate relation with the present time; so that we can glide backward some three quarters of a century, and surround ourselves with the ominous sublimity of circumstances that then frowned upon the writers. To give them their full effect, we should imagine that these letters have this moment been brought to town by the splashed and way-worn post-rider, or perhaps by an orderly dragoon, who has ridden in a perilous hurry to deliver his despatches. They are magic scrolls, if read in the right spirit. The roll of the drum and the fanfare of the trumpet is latent in some of them; and in others, an echo of the oratory that resounded in the old halls of the Continental Congress, at Philadelphia; or the words may come to us as with the living utterance of one of those illustrious men, speaking face to face, in friendly communion. Strange, that the mere identity of paper and ink should be so powerful. The same thoughts might look cold and ineffectual, in a printed book. Human nature craves a certain materialism, and clings pertinaciously to what is tangible, as if that were of more importance than the spirit accidentally involved in it. And, in truth, the original manuscript has always something which print itself must inevitably lose. An erasure, even a blot, a casual irregularity of hand, and all such little imperfections of mechanical execution, bring us close to the writer, and perhaps convey some of those subtle intimations for which language has no shape.

There are several letters from John Adams, written in a small, hasty, ungraceful hand, but earnest, and with no unnecessary flourish. The earliest is dated at Philadelphia, September 26, 1774, about twenty days after the first opening of the Continental Congress. We look at this old yellow document, scribbled on half a sheet of foolscap, and ask of it many questions for which words have no response. We would fain know what were their mutual impressions, when all those venerable faces, that have since been traced on steel, or chiselled out of marble, and thus made familiar to posterity, first met one another's gaze! Did one spirit harmonize them, in spite of the dissimilitude of manners between the North and the South, which were now for the first time brought into political relations? Could the Virginian descendant of the Cavaliers, and the New-Englander with his hereditary Puritanism, — the aristocratic Southern planter, and the self-made man from Massachusetts or Connecticut, — at once feel that they were countrymen and brothers? What did John Adams think of Jefferson? — and Samuel Adams of Patrick Henry? Did not North and South combine in their deference for the sage Franklin, so long the defender of the colonies in England, and whose scientific renown was already world-wide? And was there yet any whispered prophecy, any vague conjecture, circulating among the delegates, as to the destiny which might be in reserve for one stately man, who sat, for the most part, silent among them?—what station he was to assume in the world's history?—and how many statues would repeat his form and countenance, and successively crumble beneath his immortality?

The letter before us does not answer these inquiries. Its main feature is the strong expression of the uncertainty and awe that pervaded even the firm hearts of the Old Congress, while anticipating the struggle which was to ensue. "The commencement of hostilities," it says, "is exceedingly dreaded here. It is thought that an attack upon the troops, even should it prove successful, would certainly involve the whole continent in a war. It is generally thought that the Ministry would rejoice at a rupture in Boston, because it would furnish an excuse to the people *at home*" [this was the last time, we suspect, that John Adams spoke of England thus affectionately], "and unite them in an opinion of the necessity of pushing hostilities against us."

His next letter bears on the superscription, "Favored by General Washington." The date is June 20, 1775, three days after the battle of Bunker Hill, the news of which could not yet have arrived at Philadelphia. But the war, so much dreaded, had begun, on the quiet banks of Concord River; an army of twenty thousand men was beleaguering Boston; and here was Washington journeying northward to take the command. It seems to place us in a nearer relation with the hero, to find him performing the little courtesy of bearing a letter between friend and friend, and to hold in our hands the very document intrusted to such a messenger. John Adams says simply, " We send you Generals Washington and Lee for your comfort;" but adds nothing in regard to the character of the Commander-in-Chief. This letter displays much of the writer's ardent temperament; if he had been anywhere but in the hall of Congress, it would have been in the intrenchment before Boston.

" I hope," he writes, " a good account will be given of Gage, Haldiman, Burgoyne, Clinton, and Howe, before winter. Such a wretch as Howe, with a statue in honor of his family in Westminster Abbey, erected by the Massachusetts, to come over with the design to cut the throats of the Massachusetts people, is too much. I most sincerely, coolly, and devoutly wish that a lucky ball or bayonet may make a signal example of him, in warning to all such unprincipled, unsentimental miscreants for the future! "

He goes on in a strain that smacks somewhat of aristocratic feeling: " Our camp will be an illustrious school of military virtue, and will be resorted to and frequented, as such, by gentlemen in great numbers from the other colonies." The term " gentleman " has seldom been used in this sense subsequently to the Revolution. Another letter introduces us to two of these gentlemen, Messrs. Acquilla Hall and Josias Carvill, volunteers, who are recommended as " of the first families in Maryland, and possessing independent fortunes."

After the British had been driven out of Boston, Adams cries out, " Fortify, fortify ; and never let them get in again ! " It is agreeable enough to perceive the filial affection with which John Adams, and the other delegates from the North, regard New England, and especially the good old capital of the Puritans. Their love of country was hardly yet so diluted as to extend over the whole thirteen colonies, which were rather looked upon as allies than as composing one nation. In truth, the patriotism of a citizen of the United States is a sentiment by itself of a peculiar nature, and requiring a lifetime, or at least the custom of many years, to naturalize it among the other possessions of the heart.

The collection is enriched by a letter — dated "Cambridge, August 26, 1775" — from Washington himself. He wrote it in that house, — now so venerable with his memory, — in that very room, where his bust now stands upon a poet's table; from this sheet of paper passed the hand that held the leading-staff! Nothing can be more perfectly in keeping with all other manifestations of Washington than the whole visible aspect and embodiment of this letter. The manuscript is as clear as daylight; the punctuation exact, to a comma. There is a calm accuracy throughout, which seems the production of a species of intelligence that cannot err, and which, if we may so speak, would affect us with a more human warmth, if we could conceive it capable of some slight human error. The chirography is characterized by a plain and easy grace, which, in the signature, is somewhat elaborated, and becomes a type of the personal manner of a gentleman of the old school, but without detriment to the truth and clearness that distinguish the rest of the manuscript. The lines are as straight and equidistant as if ruled; and, from beginning to end, there is no physical symptom — as how should there be? — of a varying mood, of jets of emotion, or any of those fluctuating feelings that pass from the hearts into the fingers of common men. The paper itself (like most of those Revolutionary letters, which are written on fabrics fit to endure the burden of ponderous and earnest thought) is stout, and of excellent quality, and bears the water-mark of Britannia, surmounted by the Crown. The subject of the letter is a statement of reasons for not taking possession of Point Alderton ; a position commanding the entrance of Boston Harbor. After explaining the difficulties of the case, arising from his want of men and munitions for the adequate defence of the lines which he already occupies, Washington proceeds : " To you, sir, who are a well-wisher to the cause, and can reason upon the effects of such conduct, I may open myself with freedom, because no improper disclosures will be made of our situation. But I cannot expose my weakness to the enemy (though I believe they are pretty well informed of everything that passes), by telling this and that man, who are daily pointing out this, and that, and t' other place, of all the motives that govern my actions; notwithstanding I know what will be the consequence of not doing it, — namely, that I shall be accused of inattention to the public service, and perhaps of want of spirit to prosecute it. But this shall have no effect upon my conduct. I will steadily (as far as my judgment will assist me) pursue such measures as I think conducive to the interest of the cause, and rest satisfied under any obloquy that shall be thrown, conscious of having discharged my duty to the best of my abilities."

The above passage, like every other passage that could be quoted from his pen, is characteristic of Washington, and entirely in keeping with the calm elevation of his soul. Yet how imperfect a glimpse do we obtain of him, through the medium of this or any of his letters ! We imagine him writing calmly, with a hand that never falters ; his majestic face

neither darkens nor gleams with any momentary ebul-
lition of feeling, or irregularity of thought; and thus
flows forth an expression precisely to the extent of his
purpose, no more, no less. Thus much we may conceive. But still we have not grasped the man; we
have caught no glimpse of his interior; we have not
detected his personality. It is the same with all the
recorded traits of his daily life. The collection of
them, by different observers, seems sufficiently abundant, and strictly harmonizes with itself, yet never
brings us into intimate relationship with the hero, nor
makes us feel the warmth and the human throb of his
heart. What can be the reason? Is it, that his great
nature was adapted to stand in relation to his country,
as man stands towards man, but could not individual-
ize itself in brotherhood to an individual?

There are two from Franklin, the earliest dated,
" London, August 8, 1767," and addressed to " Mrs.
Franklin, at Philadelphia." He was then in England,
as agent for the colonies in their resistance to the oppressive policy of Mr. Grenville's administration. The
letter, however, makes no reference to political or other
business. It contains only ten or twelve lines, beginning, " My dear child," and conveying an impression
of long and venerable matrimony which has lost all its
romance, but retained a familiar and quiet tenderness.
He speaks of making a little excursion into the country for his health; mentions a larger letter, despatched
by another vessel; alludes with homely affability to
" Mrs. Stevenson," " Sally," and " our dear Polly ";
desires to be remembered to " all inquiring friends ";
and signs himself, " Your ever loving husband." In
this conjugal epistle, brief and unimportant as it is,
there are the elements that summon up the past, and

enable us to create anew the man, his connections and circumstances. We can see the sage in his London lodgings, — with his wig cast aside, and replaced by a velvet cap, — penning this very letter; and then can step across the Atlantic, and behold its reception by the elderly, but still comely, Madam Franklin, who breaks the seal and begins to read, first remembering to put on her spectacles. The seal, by the way, is a pompous one of armorial bearings, rather symbolical of the dignity of the Colonial Agent, and Postmaster General of America, than of the humble origin of the Philadelphia printer. The writing is in the free, quick style of a man with great practice of the pen, and is particularly agreeable to the reader.

Another letter from the same famous hand is addressed to General Palmer, and dated, "Passy, October 27, 1779." By an indorsement on the outside it appears to have been transmitted to the United States through the medium of Lafayette. Franklin was now the ambassador of his country at the Court of Versailles, enjoying an immense celebrity, caressed by the French ladies, and idolized alike by the fashionable and the learned, who saw something sublime and philosophic even in his blue yarn stockings. Still, as before, he writes with the homeliness and simplicity that cause a human face to look forth from the old, yellow sheet of paper, and in words that make our ears re-echo, as with the sound of his long-extinct utterance. Yet this brief epistle, like the former, has so little of tangible matter that we are ashamed to copy it.

Next, we come to the fragment of a letter by Samuel Adams; an autograph more utterly devoid of ornament or flourish than any other in the collection. It would not have been characteristic, had his pen traced so much as a hair-line in tribute to grace, beauty, or the elaborateness of manner; for this earnest-hearted man had been produced out of the past elements of his native land, a real Puritan, with the religion of his forefathers, and likewise with their principles of government, taking the aspect of Revolutionary politics. At heart, Samuel Adams was never so much a citizen of the United States as he was a New-Englander, and a son of the old Bay Province. The following passage has much of the man in it: "I heartily congratulate you," he writes from Philadelphia, after the British have left Boston, "upon the sudden and important change in our affairs, in the removal of the barbarians from the capital. We owe our grateful acknowledgments to Him who is, as he is frequently styled in Sacred Writ, 'The Lord of Hosts.' We have not yet been informed with certainty what course the enemy have steered. I hope we shall be on our guard against future attempts. Will not care be taken to fortify the harbor, and thereby prevent the entrance of ships-of-war hereafter?"

From Hancock, we have only the envelope of a document "on public service," directed to "The Hon. the Assembly, or Council of Safety of New Hampshire," and with the autograph affixed, that stands out so prominently in the Declaration of Independence. As seen in the engraving of that instrument, the signature looks precisely what we should expect and desire in the handwriting of a princely merchant, whose penmanship had been practised in the ledger which he is represented as holding, in Copley's brilliant picture, but to whom his native ability, and the circumstances and customs of his country, had given a place among its rulers. But, on the coarse and dingy paper before us, the effect is very much inferior; the direction, all except the signature, is a scrawl, large and heavy, but not forcible; and even the name itself, while almost identical in its strokes with that of the Declaration, has a strangely different and more vulgar aspect. Perhaps it is all right, and typical of the truth. If we may trust tradition, and unpublished letters, and a few witnesses in point, there was quite as much difference between the actual man and his historical aspect, as between the manuscript signature and the engraved one. One of his associates, both in political life and permanent renown, is said to have characterized him as a "man without a head or heart." We, of an after generation, should hardly be entitled, on whatever evidence, to assume such ungracious liberty with a name that has occupied a lofty position until it has grown almost sacred, and which is associated with memories more sacred than itself, and has thus become a valuable reality to our countrymen, by the aged reverence that clusters round about it. Nevertheless, it may be no impiety to regard Hancock not precisely as a real personage, but as a majestic figure, useful and necessary in its way, but producing its effect far more by an ornamental outside than by any intrinsic force or virtue. The page of all history would be half unpeopled if all such characters were banished from it.

From General Warren we have a letter dated January 14, 1775, only a few months before he attested the sincerity of his patriotism, in his own blood, on Bunker Hill. His handwriting has many ungraceful flourishes. All the small d's spout upward in parabolic curves, and descend at a considerable distance. His pen seems to have had nothing but hair-lines in it; and the whole letter, though perfectly legible, has a look of thin and unpleasant irregularity. The subject is a plan for securing to the colonial party the services of Colonel Gridley the engineer, by an appeal to his private interests. Though writing to General Palmer, an intimate friend, Warren signs himself, most ceremoniously, " Your obedient servant." Indeed, these stately formulas in winding up a letter were scarcely laid aside, whatever might be the familiarity of intercourse : husband and wife were occasionally, on paper at least, the " obedient servants" of one another ; and not improbably, among well-bred people, there was a corresponding ceremonial of bows and courtesies, even in the deepest interior of domestic life. With all the reality that filled men's hearts, and which has stamped its impress on so many of these letters, it was a far more formal age than the present.

It may be remarked that Warren was almost the only man eminently distinguished in the intellectual phase of the Revolution, previous to the breaking out of the war, who actually uplifted his arm to do battle. The legislative patriots were a distinct class from the patriots of the camp, and never laid aside the gown for the sword. It was very different in the great civil war of England, where the leading minds of the age, when argument had done its office, or left it undone, put on their steel breast-plates and appeared as leaders in the field. Educated young men, members of the old colonial families, — gentlemen, as John Adams terms them, — seem not to have sought employment in the Revolutionary army, in such numbers as might have been expected. Respectable as the officers generally were, and great as were the abilities sometimes elicited, the intellect and cultivation of the country was inadequately represented in them, as a body.

Turning another page, we find the frank of a letter from Henry Laurens, President of Congress, — him whose destiny it was, like so many noble men of old, to pass beneath the Traitor's Gate of the Tower of London, — him whose chivalrous son sacrificed as brilliant a future as any young American could have looked forward to, in an obscure skirmish. Likewise, we have the address of a letter to Messrs. Leroy and Bayard, in the handwriting of Jefferson; too slender a material to serve as a talisman for summoning up the writer; a most unsatisfactory fragment, affecting us like a glimpse of the retreating form of the sage of Monticello, turning the distant corner of a street. There is a scrap from Robert Morris, the financier; a letter or two from Judge Jay; and one from General Lincoln, written, apparently, on the gallop, but without any of those characteristic sparks that sometimes fly out in a hurry, when all the leisure in the world would fail to elicit them. Lincoln was the type of a New England soldier; a man of fair abilities, not especially of a warlike cast, without much chivalry, but faithful and bold, and carrying a kind of decency and restraint into the wild and ruthless business of arms.

From good old Baron Steuben, we find not a manuscript essay on the method of arranging a battle, but a commercial draft, in a small, neat hand, as plain as print, elegant without flourish, except a very complicated one on the signature. On the whole, the specimen is sufficiently characteristic, as well of the Baron's soldierlike and German simplicity, as of the polish of the Great Frederick's aid-de-camp, a man of courts and of the world. How singular and picturesque an effect is produced, in the array of our Revolutionary army, by the intermingling of these titled personages from the Continent of Europe, with feudal associations clinging about them, — Steuben, De Kalb, Pulaski, Lafayette ! — the German veteran, who had written from one famous battle - field to another for thirty years; and the young French noble, who had come hither, though yet unconscious of his high office, to light the torch that should set fire to the antiquated trumpery of his native institutions.  Among these autographs, there is one from Lafayette, written long after our Revolution, but while that of his own country was in full progress.  The note is merely as follows : " Enclosed you will find, my dear Sir, two tickets for the sittings of this day.  One part of the debate will be on the Honors of the Pantheon, agreeably to what has been decreed by the Constitutional Assembly."

It is a pleasant and comfortable thought, that we have no such classic folly as is here indicated, to lay to the charge of our Revolutionary fathers.  Both in their acts, and in the drapery of those acts, they were true to their several and simple selves, and thus left nothing behind them for a fastidious taste to sneer at. But it must be considered that our Revolution did not, like that of France, go so deep as to disturb the common-sense of the country.

General Schuyler writes a letter, under date of February 22, 1780, relating not to military affairs, from which the prejudices of his countrymen had almost disconnected him, but to the Salt Springs of Onondaga.  The expression is peculiarly direct, and the hand that of a man of business, free and flowing.  The uncertainty, the vague, hearsay evidence respecting these springs, then gushing into dim daylight beneath the shadow of a remote wilderness, is such as might

now be quoted in reference to the quality of the water
that supplies the fountains of the Nile. The following
sentence shows us an Indian woman and her son, practising their simple process in the manufacture of salt,
at a fire of wind-strewn boughs, the flame of which
gleams duskily through the arches of the forest :
" From a variety of information, I find the smallest
quantity made by a squaw, with the assistance of one
boy, with a kettle of about ten gallons' capacity, is
half a bushel per day ; the greatest, with the same kettle, about two bushels." It is particularly interesting
to find out anything as to the embryo, yet stationary
arts of life among the red people, their manufactures,
their agriculture, their domestic labors. It is partly
the lack of this knowledge — the possession of which
would establish a ground of sympathy on the part of
civilized men — that makes the Indian race so shadow-
like and unreal to our conception.

We could not select a greater contrast to the upright and unselfish patriot whom we have just spoken
of, than the traitor Arnold, from whom there is a
brief note, dated, "Crown Point, January 19, 1775,"
addressed to an officer under his command. The three
lines of which it consists can prove bad spelling, erroneous grammar, and misplaced and superfluous punctuation ; but, with all this complication of iniquity,
the ruffian General contrives to express his meaning
as briefly and clearly as if the rules of correct composition had been ever so scrupulously observed. This
autograph, impressed with the foulest name in our history, has somewhat of the interest that would attach
to a document on which a fiend-devoted wretch had
signed away his salvation. But there was not substance enough in the man — a mere cross between the

bull-dog and the fox — to justify much feeling of any sort about him personally. The interest, such as it is, attaches but little to the man, and far more to the circumstances amid which he acted, rendering the villany almost sublime, which, exercised in petty affairs, would only have been vulgar.

We turn another leaf, and find a memorial of Hamilton. It is but a letter of introduction, addressed to Governor Jay in favor of Mr. Davies, of Kentucky; but it gives an impression of high breeding and courtesy, as little to be mistaken as if we could see the writer's manner and hear his cultivated accents, while personally making one gentleman known to another. There is likewise a rare vigor of expression and pregnancy of meaning, such as only a man of habitual energy of thought could have conveyed into so commonplace a thing as an introductory letter. This autograph is a graceful one, with an easy and picturesque flourish beneath the signature, symbolical of a courteous bow at the conclusion of the social ceremony so admirably performed. Hamilton might well be the leader and idol of the Federalists; for he was preëminent in all the high qualities that characterized the great men of that party, and which should make even a Democrat feel proud that his country had produced such a noble old band of aristocrats; and he shared all the distrust of the people, which so inevitably and so righteously brought about their ruin. With his autograph we associate that of another Federalist, his friend in life; a man far narrower than Hamilton, but endowed with a native vigor, that caused many partisans to grapple to him for support; upright, sternly inflexible, and of a simplicity of manner that might have befitted the sturdiest republican among us. In our boyhood we used to see a thin, severe figure of an ancient man, time-worn, but apparently indestructible, moving with a step of vigorous decay along the street, and knew him as "Old Tim Pickering."

Side by side, too, with the autograph of Hamilton, we would place one from the hand that shed his blood. It is a few lines of Aaron Burr, written in 1823 ; when all his ambitious schemes, whatever they once were, had been so long shattered that even the fragments had crumbled away, leaving him to exert his withered energies on petty law cases, to one of which the present note refers. The hand is a little tremulous with age, yet small and fastidiously elegant, as became a man who was in the habit of writing billet-doux on scented note-paper, as well as documents of war and state. This is to us a deeply interesting autograph. Remembering what has been said of the power of Burr's personal influence, his art to tempt men, his might to subdue them, and the fascination that enabled him, though cold at heart, to win the love of woman, we gaze at this production of his pen as into his own inscrutable eyes, seeking for the mystery of his nature. How singular that a character imperfect, ruined, blasted, as this man's was, excites a stronger interest than if it had reached the highest earthly perfection of which its original elements would admit! It is by the diabolical part of Burr's character that he produces his effect on the imagination. Had he been a better man, we doubt, after all, whether the present age would not already have suffered him to wax dusty, and fade out of sight, among the mere respectable mediocrities of his own epoch. But, certainly, he was a strange, wild off-shoot to have sprung from the united stock of those two singular Christians, President Burr of Princeton College, and Jonathan Edwards !

Omitting many, we have come almost to the end of these memorials of historical men. We observe one other autograph of a distinguished soldier of the Revolution, Henry Knox, but written in 1791, when he was Secretary of War. In its physical aspect, it is well worthy to be a soldier's letter. The hand is large, round, and legible at a glance ; the lines far apart, and accurately equidistant ; and the whole affair looks not unlike a company of regular troops in marching order. The signature has a point-like firmness and simplicity. It is a curious observation, sustained by these autographs, though we know not how generally correct, that Southern gentlemen are more addicted to a flourish of the pen beneath their names, than those of the North.

And now we come to the men of a later generation, whose active life reaches almost within the verge of present affairs ; people of dignity, no doubt, but whose characters have not acquired, either from time or circumstances, the interest that can make their autographs valuable to any but the collector. Those whom we have hitherto noticed were the men of an heroic age. They are departed, and now so utterly departed, as not even to touch upon the passing generation through the medium of persons still in life, who can claim to have known them familiarly. Their letters, therefore, come to us like material things out of the hands of mighty shadows, long historical, and traditionary, and fit companions for the sages and warriors of a thousand years ago. In spite of the proverb, it is not in a single day, or in a very few years, that a man can be reckoned " as dead as Julius Cæsar." We feel little interest in scraps from the pens of old gentlemen, ambassadors, governors, senators, heads of de-

partments, even presidents though they were, who
lived lives of praiseworthy respectability, and whose
powdered heads and black knee-breeches have but just
vanished out of the drawing-room. Still less do we
value the blotted paper of those whose reputations are
dusty, not with oblivious time, but with present political turmoil and newspaper vogue. Really great men,
however, seem, as to their effect on the imagination,
to take their place amongst past worthies, even while
walking in the very sunshine that illuminates the autumnal day in which we write. We look, not without
curiosity, at the small, neat hand of Henry Clay, who,
as he remarks with his habitual deference to the wishes
of the fair, responds to a young lady's request for his
seal; and we dwell longer over the torn-off conclusion
of a note from Mr. Calhoun, whose words are strangely
dashed off without letters, and whose name, were it
less illustrious, would be unrecognizable in his own
autograph. But of all hands that can still grasp a
pen, we know not the one, belonging to a soldier or a
statesman, which could interest us more than the hand
that wrote the following: " Sir, your note of the 6th
inst. is received. I hasten to answer that there was
no man 'in the station of colonel, by the name of J.
T. Smith,' under my command, at the battle of New
Orleans; and am, respectfully,

" Yours,    ANDREW JACKSON.

*Oct.* 19*th,* 1833."

The old general, we suspect, has been insnared by
a pardonable little stratagem on the part of the autograph collector. The battle of New Orleans would
hardly have been won, without better aid than this
problematical Colonel J. T. Smith.

Intermixed with and appended to these historical autographs, there are a few literary ones. Timothy Dwight — the "old Timotheus" who sang the Conquest of Canaan, instead of choosing a more popular subject, in the British Conquest of Canada — is of eldest date. Colonel Trumbull, whose hand, at various epochs of his life, was familiar with sword, pen, and pencil, contributes two letters, which lack the picturesqueness of execution that should distinguish the chirography of an artist. The value of Trumbull's pictures is of the same nature with that of daguerreotypes, depending not upon the ideal but the actual. The beautiful signature of Washington Irving appears as the indorsement of a draft, dated in 1814, when, if we may take this document as evidence, his individuality seems to have been merged into the firm of " P. E. Irving & Co." Never was anything less mercantile than this autograph, though as legible as the writing of a bank-clerk. Without apparently aiming at artistic beauty, it has all the "Sketch Book" in it. We find the signature and seal of Pierpont, the latter stamped with the poet's almost living countenance. What a pleasant device for a seal is one's own face, which he may thus multiply at pleasure, and send letters to his friends, — the Head without, and the Heart within! There are a few lines in the schoolgirl hand of Margaret Davidson, at nine years old ; and a scrap of a letter from Washington Allston, a gentle and delicate autograph, in which we catch a glimpse of thanks to his correspondent for the loan of a volume of poetry. Nothing remains, save a letter from Noah Webster, whose early toils were manifested in a spelling-book, and those of his later age in a ponderous dictionary. Under date of February

10, 1843, he writes in a sturdy, awkward hand, very fit for a lexicographer, an epistle of old man's reminiscences, from which we extract the following anecdote of Washington, presenting the patriot in a festive light: —

"When I was travelling to the South, in the year 1785, I called on General Washington at Mount Vernon. At dinner, the last course of dishes was a species of pancakes, which were handed round to each guest, accompanied with a bowl of sugar and another of molasses for seasoning them, that each guest might suit himself. When the dish came to me, I pushed by me the bowl of molasses, observing to the gentlemen present, that I had enough of *that* in my own country. The General burst out with a *loud laugh*, a thing very unusual with him. 'Ah,' said he, 'there is nothing in that story about your eating molasses in New England.' There was a gentleman from Maryland at the table; and the General immediately told a story, stating that, during the Revolution, a hogshead of molasses was stove in, in West Chester, by the oversetting of a wagon; and a body of Maryland troops being near, the soldiers ran hastily, and saved all they could by filling their hats or caps with molasses."

There are said to be temperaments endowed with sympathies so exquisite, that, by merely handling an autograph, they can detect the writer's character with unerring accuracy, and read his inmost heart as easily as a less-gifted eye would peruse the written page. Our faith in this power, be it a spiritual one, or only a refinement of the physical nature, is not unlimited, in spite of evidence. God has imparted to the human soul a marvellous strength in guarding its secrets, and he keeps at least the deepest and most inward record for his own perusal. But if there be such sympathies as we have alluded to, in how many instances would History be put to the blush by a volume of autograph letters, like this which we now close!

# AN OLD WOMAN'S TALE.

In the house where I was born, there used to be an old woman crouching all day long over the kitchen fire, with her elbows on her knees and her feet in the ashes. Once in a while she took a turn at the spit, and she never lacked a coarse gray stocking in her lap, the foot about half finished; it tapered away with her own waning life, and she knit the toe-stitch on the day of her death. She made it her serious business and sole amusement to tell me stories at any time from morning till night, in a mumbling, toothless voice, as I sat on a log of wood, grasping her check-apron in both my hands. Her personal memory included the better part of a hundred years, and she had strangely jumbled her own experience and observation with those of many old people who died in her young days; so that she might have been taken for a contemporary of Queen Elizabeth, or of John Rogers in the Primer. There are a thousand of her traditions lurking in the corners and by-places of my mind, some more marvellous than what is to follow, some less so, and a few not marvellous in the least, all of which I should like to repeat, if I were as happy as she in having a listener. But I am humble enough to own, that I do not deserve a listener half so well as that old toothless woman, whose narratives possessed an excellence attributable neither to herself, nor to any single individual. Her ground-plots, seldom within the widest scope of probability, were filled up with homely and natural incidents, the gradual accretions of a long course of years, and fiction hid its grotesque extravagance in this garb of truth, like the Devil (an appropriate simile, for the old woman supplies it) disguising himself, cloven-foot and all, in mortal attire. These tales generally referred to her birthplace, a village in the valley of the Connecticut, the aspect of which she impressed with great vividness on my fancy. The houses in that tract of country, long a wild and dangerous frontier, were rendered defensible by a strength of architecture that has preserved many of them till our own times, and I cannot describe the sort of pleasure with which, two summers since, I rode through the little town in question, while one object after another rose familiarly to my eye, like successive portions of a dream becoming realized. Among other things equally probable, she was wont to assert that all the inhabitants of this village (at certain intervals, but whether of twenty-five or fifty years, or a whole century, remained a disputable point) were subject to a simultaneous slumber, continuing one hour's space. When that mysterious time arrived, the parson snored over his half-written sermon, though it were Saturday night and no provision made for the morrow, — the mother's eyelids closed as she bent over her infant, and no childish cry awakened, — the watcher at the bed of mortal sickness slumbered upon the death-pillow, — and the dying man anticipated his sleep of ages by one as deep and dreamless. To speak emphatically, there was a soporific influence throughout the village, stronger than if every mother's son and daughter were reading a dull story ; notwithstanding which the old woman professed to hold the substance of the ensuing account from one of those principally concerned in it.

One moonlight summer evening, a young man and a girl sat down together in the open air. They were distant relatives, sprung from a stock once wealthy, but of late years so poverty-stricken, that David had not a penny to pay the marriage fee, if Esther should consent to wed. The seat they had chosen was in an open grove of elm and walnut-trees, at a right angle of the road; a spring of diamond water just bubbled into the moonlight beside them, and then whimpered away through the bushes and long grass, in search of a neighboring mill-stream. The nearest house (situate within twenty yards of them, and the residence of their great-grandfather in his lifetime) was a venerable old edifice, crowned with many high and narrow peaks, all overrun by innumerable creeping plants, which hung curling about the roof like a nice young wig on an elderly gentleman's head. Opposite to this establishment was a tavern, with a well and horse-trough before it, and a low green bank running along the left side of the door. Thence, the road went onward, curving scarce perceptibly, through the village, divided in the midst by a narrow lane of verdure, and bounded on each side by a grassy strip of twice its own breadth. The houses had generally an odd look. Here, the moonlight tried to get a glimpse of one, a rough old heap of ponderous timber, which, ashamed of its dilapidated aspect, was hiding behind a great thick tree; the lower story of the next had sunk almost under ground, as if the poor little house were a-weary of the world, and retiring into the seclusion of its own cellar; farther on stood one of the few recent structures, thrusting its painted face conspicuously into the street, with an evident idea that it was the fairest thing there. About midway in the village was a grist - mill, partly concealed by the descent of the ground towards the stream which turned its wheel. At the southern extremity, just so far distant that the window-panes dazzled into each other, rose the meeting-house, a dingy old barnlike building, with an enormously disproportioned steeple sticking up straight into heaven, as high as the Tower of Babel, and the cause of nearly as much confusion in its day. This steeple, it must be understood, was an afterthought, and its addition to the main edifice, when the latter had already begun to decay, had excited a vehement quarrel, and almost a schism in the church, some fifty years before. Here the road wound down a hill, and was seen no more, the remotest object in view being the graveyard gate, beyond the meeting-house. The youthful pair sat hand in hand beneath the trees, and for several moments they had not spoken, because the breeze was hushed, the brook scarce tinkled, the leaves had ceased their rustling, and everything lay motionless and silent as if Nature were composing herself to slumber.

" What a beautiful night it is, Esther ! " remarked David, somewhat drowsily.

" Very beautiful," answered the girl, in the same tone.

" But how still ! " continued David.

" Ah, too still ! " said Esther, with a faint shudder, like a modest leaf when the wind kisses it.

Perhaps they fell asleep together, and, united as their spirits were by close and tender sympathies, the same strange dream might have wrapped them in its shadowy arms. But they conceived, at the time, that they still remained wakeful by the spring of bubbling water, looking down through the village, and all along the moon-lighted road, and at the queer old houses, and at the trees, which thrust their great twisted branches almost into the windows. There was only a sort of mistiness over their minds like the smoky air of an early autumn night. At length, without any vivid astonishment, they became conscious that a great many people were either entering the village or already in the street, but whether they came from the meeting-house, or from a little beyond it, or where the devil they came from, was more than could be determined. Certainly a crowd of people seemed to be there, men, women, and children, all of whom were yawning and rubbing their eyes, stretching their limbs, and stagger-ing from side to side of the road, as if but partially awakened from a sound slumber. Sometimes they stood stock-still, with their hands over their brows to shade their sight from the moonbeams. As they drew near, most of their countenances appeared familiar to Esther and David, possessing the peculiar features of families in the village, and that general air and aspect by which a person would recognize his own townsmen in the remotest ends of the earth. But though the whole multitude might have been taken, in the mass, for neighbors and acquaintances, there was not a single individual whose exact likeness they had ever before seen. It was a noticeable circumstance, also, that the newest fashioned garment on the backs of these people might have been worn by the great-grandparents of the existing generation. There was one figure behind all the rest, and not yet near enough to be perfectly distinguished.

"Where on earth, David, do all these odd people come from?" said Esther, with a lazy inclination to laugh.

"Nowhere on earth, Esther," replied David, un-knowing why he said so.

As they spoke, the strangers showed some symptoms of disquietude, and looked towards the fountain for an instant, but immediately appeared to assume their own trains of thought and previous purposes. They now separated to different parts of the village, with a readi-ness that implied intimate local knowledge, and it may be worthy of remark, that, though they were evidently loquacious among themselves, neither their footsteps nor their voices reached the ears of the beholders. Wherever there was a venerable old house, of fifty years' standing and upwards, surrounded by its elm or walnut-trees, with its dark and weather-beaten barn, its well, its orchard and stone-walls, all ancient and all in good repair around it, there a little group of these people assembled. Such parties were mostly composed of an aged man and woman, with the younger mem-bers of a family; their faces were full of joy, so deep that it assumed the shade of melancholy; they pointed to each other the minutest objects about the home-steads, things in their hearts, and were now compar-ing them with the originals. But where hollow places by the wayside, grass-grown, and uneven, with un-sightly chimneys rising ruinous in the midst, gave indications of a fallen dwelling and of hearths long cold, there did a few of the strangers sit them down on the mouldering beams, and on the yellow moss that had overspread the door-stone. The men folded their arms, sad and speechless; the women wrung their hands with a more vivid expression of grief; and the little children tottered to their knees, shrinking away from the open grave of domestic love. And wherever a re-cent edifice reared its white and flashy front on the foundation of an old one, there a gray-haired man might be seen to shake his staff in anger at it, while his aged dame and their offspring appeared to join in their maledictions, forming a fearful picture in the ghostly moonlight. While these scenes were passing, the one figure in the rear of all the rest was descending the hollow towards the mill, and the eyes of David and Esther were drawn thence to a pair with whom they could fully sympathize. It was a youth in a sailor's dress and a pale slender maiden, who met each other with a sweet embrace in the middle of the street.

"How long it must be since they parted," observed David.

"Fifty years at least," said Esther.

They continued to gaze with wondering calmness and quiet interest, as the dream (if such it were) unrolled its quaint and motley semblance before them, and their notice was now attracted by several little knots of people apparently engaged in conversation. Of these one of the earliest collected and most characteristic was near the tavern, the persons who composed it being seated on the low green bank along the left side of the door. A conspicuous figure here was a fine corpulent old fellow in his shirt-sleeves and flame-colored breeches, and with a stained white apron over his paunch, beneath which he held his hands, and wherewith at times he wiped his ruddy face. The stately decrepitude of one of his companions, the scar of an Indian tomahawk on his crown, and especially his worn buff-coat, were appropriate marks of a veteran belonging to an old Provincial garrison, now deaf to the roll-call. Another showed his rough face under a tarry hat and wore a pair of wide trousers, like an ancient mariner who had tossed away his youth upon the sea,

and was returned, hoary and weather-beaten, to his
inland home. There was also a thin young man, carelessly dressed, who ever and anon cast a sad look towards the pale maiden above mentioned. With these
there sat a hunter, and one or two others, and they
were soon joined by a miller, who came upward from
the dusty mill, his coat as white as if besprinkled with
powdered starlight. All these (by the aid of jests,
which might indeed be old, but had not been recently
repeated) waxed very merry, and it was rather strange,
that just as their sides shook with the heartiest laughter, they appeared greatly like a group of shadows
flickering in the moonshine. Four personages, very
different from these, stood in front of the large house
with its periwig of creeping plants. One was a little
elderly figure, distinguished by the gold on his three-
cornered hat and sky-blue coat, and by the seal of
arms annexed to his great gold watch-chain; his air and
aspect befitted a Justice of Peace and County Major,
and all earth's pride and pomposity were squeezed
into this small gentleman of five feet high. The next
in importance was a grave person of sixty or seventy
years, whose black suit and band sufficiently indicated
his character, and the polished baldness of whose head
was worthy of a famous preacher in the village, half a
century before, who had made wigs a subject of pulpit denunciation. The two other figures, both clad in
dark gray, showed the sobriety of Deacons; one was
ridiculously tall and thin, like a man of ordinary bulk
infinitely produced, as the mathematicians say; while
the brevity and thickness of his colleague seemed a
compression of the same man. These four talked with
great earnestness, and their gestures intimated that
they had revived the ancient dispute about the meet-

ing-house steeple. The grave person in black spoke
with composed solemnity, as if he were addressing a
Synod; the short deacon grunted out occasional sen-
tences, as brief as himself; his tall brother drew the
long thread of his argument through the whole discussion, and (reasoning from analogy) his voice must
indubitably have been small and squeaking. But the
little old man in gold-lace was evidently scorched by
his own red-hot eloquence; he bounced from one to
another, shook his cane at the steeple, at the two deacons, and almost in the parson's face, stamping with
his foot fiercely enough to break a hole through the
very earth; though, indeed, it could not exactly be
said that the green grass bent beneath him. The figure, noticed as coming behind all the rest, had now
surmounted the ascent from the mill, and proved to
be an elderly lady with something in her hand.

"Why does she walk so slow?" asked David.

"Don't you see she is lame?" said Esther.

This gentlewoman, whose infirmity had kept her so
far in the rear of the crowd, now came hobbling on,
glided unobserved by the polemic group, and paused
on the left brink of the fountain, within a few feet of
the two spectators. She was a magnificent old dame,
as ever mortal eye beheld. Her spangled shoes and
gold - clocked stockings shone gloriously within the
spacious circle of a red hoop-petticoat, which swelled
to the very point of explosion, and was bedecked all
over with embroidery a little tarnished. Above the
petticoat, and parting in front so as to display it to
the best advantage, was a figured blue damask gown.
A wide and stiff ruff encircled her neck, a cap of the
finest muslin, though rather dingy, covered her head,
and her nose was bestridden by a pair of gold-bowed

spectacles with enormous glasses. But the old lady's
face was pinched, sharp, and sallow, wearing a nig-
gardly and avaricious expression, and forming an odd
contrast to the splendor of her attire, as did likewise
the implement which she held in her hand. It was a
sort of iron shovel (by housewives termed a "slice"),
such as is used in clearing the oven, and with this,
selecting a spot between a walnut-tree and the fountain, the good dame made an earnest attempt to dig.
The tender sods, however, possessed a strange impen-
etrability. They resisted her efforts like a quarry of
living granite, and, losing her breath, she cast down
the shovel and seemed to bemoan herself most pit-
eously, gnashing her teeth (what few she had) and
wringing her thin yellow hands. Then, apparently
with new hope, she resumed her toil, which still had
the same result, — a circumstance the less surprising
to David and Esther, because at times they would
catch the moonlight shining through the old woman,
and dancing in the fountain beyond. The little man
in gold-lace now happened to see her, and made his
approach on tiptoe.

"How hard this elderly lady works!" remarked
David.

"Go and help her, David," said Esther, compas-
sionately.

As their drowsy voices spoke, both the old woman
and the pompous little figure behind her lifted their
eyes, and for a moment they regarded the youth and
damsel with something like kindness and affection;
which, however, were dim and uncertain, and passed
away almost immediately. The old woman again betook herself to the shovel, but was startled by a hand
suddenly laid upon her shoulder; she turned round in

great trepidation, and beheld the dignitary in the blue
coat; then followed an embrace of such closeness as
would indicate no remoter connection than matrimony
between these two decorous persons. The gentleman
next pointed to the shovel, appearing to inquire the
purpose of his lady's occupation; while she as evidently parried his interrogatories, maintaining a de-
mure and sanctified visage as every good woman ought,
in similar cases. Howbeit, she could not forbear looking askew, behind her spectacles, towards the spot of
stubborn turf. All the while, their figures had a
strangeness in them, and it seemed as if some cunning jeweller had made their golden ornaments of the
yellowest of the setting sunbeams, and that the blue
of their garments was brought from the dark sky near
the moon, and that the gentleman's silk waistcoat was
the bright side of a fiery cloud, and the lady's scarlet
petticoat a remnant of the blush of morning, — and
that they both were two unrealities of colored air.
But now there was a sudden movement throughout the
multitude. The Squire drew forth a watch as large
as the dial on the famous steeple, looked at the warning hands and got him gone, nor could his lady tarry;
the party at the tavern door took to their heels, headed
by the fat man in the flaming breeches; the tall deacon
stalked away immediately, and the short deacon wad-
dled after, making four steps to the yard; the mothers called their children about them and set forth,
with a gentle and sad glance behind. Like cloudy
fantasies that hurry by a viewless impulse from the
sky, they all were fled, and the wind rose up and followed them with a strange moaning down the lonely
street. Now whither these people went is more than
may be told; only David and Esther seemed to see the

shadowy splendor of the ancient dame, as she lingered in the moonshine at the graveyard gate, gazing backward to the fountain.

"O Esther! I have had such a dream!" cried David, starting up, and rubbing his eyes.

"And I such another!" answered Esther, gaping till her pretty red lips formed a circle.

"About an old woman with gold-bowed spectacles," continued David.

"And a scarlet hoop-petticoat," added Esther. They now stared in each other's eyes, with great astonishment and some little fear. After a thoughtful moment or two, David drew a long breath and stood upright.

"If I live till to-morrow morning," said he, "I'll see what may be buried between that tree and the spring of water."

"And why not to-night, David?" asked Esther; for she was a sensible little girl, and bethought herself that the matter might as well be done in secrecy.

David felt the propriety of the remark, and looked round for the means of following her advice. The moon shone brightly on something that rested against the side of the old house, and, on a nearer view, it proved to be an iron shovel, bearing a singular resemblance to that which they had seen in their dreams. He used it with better success than the old woman, the soil giving way so freely to his efforts, that he had soon scooped a hole as large as the basin of the spring. Suddenly, he poked his head down to the very bottom of this cavity. "Oho! — what have we here?" cried David.

# TIME'S PORTRAITURE.

BEING THE CARRIER'S ADDRESS TO THE PATRONS OF "THE SALEM
GAZETTE" FOR THE 1ST OF JANUARY, 1838.

## ADDRESS.

KIND PATRONS: We newspaper carriers are Time's
errand-boys; and all the year round the old gentleman sends us from one of your doors to another, to let
you know what he is talking about and what he is doing. We are a strange set of urchins; for, punctually
on New Year's morning, one and all of us are seized
with a fit of rhyme, and break forth in such hideous
strains, that it would be no wonder if the infant Year,
with her step upon the threshold, were frightened
away by the discord with which we strive to welcome
her. On these occasions, most generous patrons, you
never fail to give us a taste of your bounty; but
whether as a reward for our verses, or to purchase a
respite from further infliction of them, is best known
to your worshipful selves. Moreover, we, Time's errand-boys as aforesaid, feel it incumbent upon us,
on the first day of every year, to present a sort of
summary of our master's dealings with the world,
throughout the whole of the preceding twelvemonth.
Now it had so chanced, by a misfortune heretofore unheard of, that I, your present petitioner, have been
altogether forgotten by the Muse. Instead of being

able (as I naturally expected) to measure my ideas into six-foot lines, and tack a rhyme at each of their tails, I find myself, this blessed morning, the same simple proser that I was yesterday, and shall probably be to-morrow. And to my further mortification, being a humble-minded little sinner, I feel nowise capable of talking to your worships with the customary wisdom of my brethren, and giving sage opinions as to what Time has done right, and what he has done wrong, and what of right or wrong he means to do hereafter. Such being my unhappy predicament, it is with no small confusion of face that I make bold to present myself at your doors. Yet it were surely a pity that my non-appearance should defeat your bountiful designs for the replenishing of my pockets. Wherefore I have bethought me, that it might not displease your worships to hear a few particulars about the person and habits of Father Time, with whom, as being one of his errand-boys, I have more acquaintance than most lads of my years.

For a great many years past, there has been a woodcut on the cover of the " Farmer's Almanac," pretending to be a portrait of Father Time. It represents that respectable personage as almost in a state of nudity, with a single lock of hair on his forehead, wings on his shoulders, and accoutred with a scythe and an hourglass. These two latter symbols appear to betoken that the old fellow works in haying time, by the hour. But, within my recollection, Time has never carried a scythe and an hour-glass, nor worn a pair of wings, nor shown himself in the half-naked condition that the almanac would make us believe. Nowadays, he is the most fashionably dressed figure about town; and I take it to be his natural disposition, old as he is, to adopt every fashion of the day and of the hour. Just at the present period, you may meet him in a furred surtout, with pantaloons strapped under his narrow-toed boots ; on his head, instead of a single forelock, he wears a smart auburn wig, with bushy whiskers of the same hue, the whole surmounted by a German - lustre hat. He has exchanged his hour-glass for a gold patent-lever watch, which he carries in his vest-pocket ; and as for his scythe, he has either thrown it aside altogether, or converted its handle into a cane not much stouter than a riding-switch. If you stare him full in the face, you will perhaps detect a few wrinkles ; but, on a hasty glance, you might suppose him to be in the very heyday of life, as fresh as he was in the garden of Eden. So much for the present aspect of Time ; but I by no means insure that the description shall suit him a month hence, or even at this hour to-morrow.

It is another very common mistake to suppose that Time wanders among old ruins, and sits on mouldering walls and moss-grown stones, meditating about matters which everybody else has forgotten. Some people, perhaps, would expect to find him at the burial-ground in Broad Street, poring over the half-illegible inscriptions on the tombs of the Higginsons, the Hathornes,[1] the Holyokes, the Brownes, the Olivers, the Pickmans, the Pickerings, and other worthies with whom he kept company of old. Some would look for him on the ridge of Gallows Hill, where, in one of his darkest moods, he and Cotton Mather hung

---

[1] Not "Hawthorne," as one of the present representatives of the family has seen fit to transmogrify a good old name. However, Time has seldom occasion to mention the gentleman's name, so that it is no great matter how he spells or pronounces it.

the witches. But they need not seek him there. Time
is invariably the first to forget his own deeds, his own
history, and his own former associates. His place is
in the busiest bustle of the world. If you would meet
Time face to face, you have only to promenade in
Essex Street, between the hours of twelve and one;
and there, among beaux and belles, you will see old
Father Time, apparently the gayest of the gay. He
walks arm in arm with the young men, talking about
balls and theatres, and afternoon rides, and midnight
merry-makings; he recommends such and such a fashionable tailor, and sneers at every garment of six
months' antiquity; and, generally, before parting, he
invites his friends to drink champagne, — a wine in
which Time delights, on account of its rapid efferves-
cence. And Time treads lightly beside the fair girls,
whispering to them (the old deceiver!) that they are
the sweetest angels he ever was acquainted with. He
tells them that they have nothing to do but dance and
sing, and twine roses in their hair, and gather a train
of lovers, and that the world will always be like an
illuminated ball-room. And Time goes to the Commercial News - Room, and visits the insurance - offices,
and stands at the corner of Essex and St. Peter's
Streets, talking with the merchants about the arrival
of ships, the rise and fall of stocks, the price of cotton
and breadstuffs, the prospects of the whaling-business,
and the cod - fishery, and all other news of the day.
And the young gentlemen, and the pretty girls, and
the merchants, and all others with whom he makes acquaintance, are apt to think that there is nobody like
Time, and that Time is all in all.

But Time is not near so good a fellow as they take
him for. He is continually on the watch for mischief,

and often seizes a sly opportunity to lay his cane over
the shoulders of some middle-aged gentleman; and lo
and behold! the poor man's back is bent, his hair
turns gray, and his face looks like a shrivelled apple.
This is what is meant by being "time-stricken." It
is the worst feature in Time's character that he always inflicts the greatest injuries on his oldest friends.
Yet, shamefully as he treats them, they evince no desire to cut his acquaintance, and can seldom bear to
think of a final separation.

Again, there is a very prevalent idea that Time
loves to sit by the fireside, telling stories of the Puritans, the witch persecutors, and the heroes of the old
French War and the Revolution; and that he has no
memory for anything more recent than the days of the
first President Adams. This is another great mistake.
Time is so eager to talk of novelties, that he never
fails to give circulation to the most incredible rumors
of the day, though at the hazard of being compelled to
eat his own words to-morrow. He shows numberless
instances of this propensity while the national elections
are in progress. A month ago, his mouth was full of
the wonderful Whig victories; and to do him justice, he
really seems to have told the truth for once. Whether
the same story will hold good another year, we must
leave Time himself to show. He has a good deal to
say, at the present juncture, concerning the revolutionary movements in Canada; he blusters a little about
the northeastern boundary question; he expresses
great impatience at the sluggishness of our commanders in the Florida War; he gets considerably excited
whenever the subject of abolition is brought forward,
and so much the more, as he appears hardly to have
made up his mind on one side or the other. When-

ever this happens to be the case, — as it often does, — Time works himself into such a rage, that you would think he were going to tear the universe to pieces; but I never yet knew him to proceed, in good earnest, to such terrible extremities. During the last six or seven months, he has been seized with intolerable sulkiness at the slightest mention of the currency; for nothing vexes Time so much as to be refused cash upon the nail. The above are the chief topics of general interest which Time is just now in the habit of discussing. For his more private gossip he has rumors of new matches, of old ones broken off, with now and then a whisper of good-natured scandal; sometimes, too, he condescends to criticise a sermon, or a lyceum lecture, or performance of the glee-club; and, to be brief, catch the volatile essence of present talk and transitory opinions, and you will have Time's gossip, word for word. I may as well add, that he expresses great approbation of Mr. Russell's vocal abilities, and means to be present from beginning to end of his next concert. It is not every singer that could *keep Time* with his voice and instrument, for a whole evening.

Perhaps you will inquire, " What are Time's literary tastes ? " And here again there is a general mistake. It is conceived by many, that Time spends his leisure hours at the Athenæum, turning over the musty leaves of those large worm-eaten folios, which nobody else has disturbed since the death of the venerable Dr. Oliver. So far from this being the case, Time's profoundest studies are the new novels from Messrs. Ives and Jewett's Circulating Library. He skims over the lighter articles in the periodicals of the day, glances at the newspapers, and then throws them aside for-

ever, all except " The Salem Gazette," of which he
preserves a file, for his amusement a century or two
hence.

We will now consider Time as a man of business.
In this capacity, our citizens are in the habit of com-
plaining, not wholly without reason, that Time is sluggish and dull. You may see him occasionally at the
end of Derby Wharf, leaning against a post, or sitting
on the breech of an iron cannon, staring listlessly at
an unrigged East-Indiaman. Or, if you look through
the windows of the Union Marine Insurance Office,
you may get a glimpse of him there, nodding over a
newspaper, among the old weather-beaten sea-captains
who recollect when Time was quite a different sort of
fellow. If you enter any of the dry-goods stores along
Essex Street, you will be likely to find him with his
elbows on the counter, bargaining for a yard of tape
or a paper of pins. To catch him in his idlest mood,
you must visit the office of some young lawyer. Still,
however, Time does contrive to do a little business
among us, and should not be denied the credit of it.
During the past season, he has worked pretty dili-
gently upon the railroad, and promises to start the
cars by the middle of next summer. Then we may fly
from Essex Street to State Street, and be back again
before Time misses us. In conjunction with our
worthy mayor (with whose ancestor, the Lord Mayor
of London, Time was well acquainted more than two
hundred years ago) he has laid the corner-stone of a
new city hall, the granite front of which is already an
ornament to Court Street. But besides these public
affairs, Time busies himself a good deal in private.
Just at this season of the year, he is engaged in collecting bills, and may be seen at almost any hour per-

egrinating from street to street, and knocking at half
the doors in town, with a great bundle of these infernal documents.  On such errands he appears in the
likeness of an undersized, portly old gentleman, with
gray hair, a bluff red face, and a loud tone of voice ;
and many people mistake him for the penny-post.

Never does a marriage take place, but Time is present among the wedding-guests ; for marriage is an affair in which Time takes more interest than in almost
any other.  He generally gives away the bride, and
leads the bridegroom by the hand to the threshold of
the bridal chamber.  Although Time pretends to be
very merry on these occasions, yet, if you watch him
well, you may often detect a sigh.  Whenever a babe
is born into this weary world, Time is in attendance,
and receives the wailing infant in his arms.  And the
poor babe shudders instinctively at his embrace, and
sets up a feeble cry.  Then again, from the birth-
chamber, he must hurry to the bedside of some old acquaintance, whose business with Time is ended forever,
though their accounts remain to be settled at a future
day.  It is terrible, sometimes, to perceive the lingering reluctance, the shivering agony, with which the
poor souls bid Time farewell, if they have gained no
other friend to supply the gray deceiver's place.  How
do they cling to Time, and steal another and yet another glance at his familiar aspect !  But Time, the
hard-hearted old fellow !  goes through such scenes
with infinite composure, and dismisses his best friends
from memory the moment they are out of sight.
Others, who have not been too intimate with Time,
as knowing him to be a dangerous character, and
apt to ruin his associates, — these take leave of him
with joy, and pass away with a look of triumph on

their features. They know that, in spite of all his flattering promises, he could not make them happy, but that now they shall be so, long after Time is dead and buried.

For Time is not immortal. Time must die, and be buried in the deep grave of eternity. And let him die. From the hour when he passed forth through the gate of Eden, till this very moment, he has gone to and fro about the earth, staining his hands with blood, committing crimes innumerable, and bringing misery on himself and all mankind. Sometimes he has been a pagan; sometimes a persecutor. Sometimes he has spent centuries in darkness, where he could neither read nor write. These were called the Dark Ages. There has hardly been a single year, when he has not stirred up strife among the nations. Sometimes, as in France less than fifty years ago, he has been seized with fits of frenzy, and murdered thousands of innocent people at noonday. He pretends, indeed, that he has grown wiser and better now. Trust him who will; for my part, I rejoice that Time shall not live forever. He hath an appointed office to perform. Let him do his task, and die. Fresh and young as he would make himself appear, he is already hoary with age; and the very garments that he wears about the town were put on thousands of years ago, and have been patched and pieced to suit the present fashion. There is nothing new in him nor about him. Were he to die while I am speaking, we could not pronounce it an untimely death. Methinks, with his heavy heart and weary brain, Time should himself be glad to die.

Meanwhile, gentle patrons, as Time has brought round another New Year, pray remember your poor petitioner. For so small a lad, you will agree that I talk pretty passably well, and have fairly earned whatever spare specie Time has left in your pockets. Be kind to me; and I have good hope that Time will be kind to you. After all the hard things which I have said about him, he is really, — that is, if you take him for neither more nor less than he is worth, and use him as not abusing him, — Time is really a very tolerable old fellow, and may be endured for a little while that we are to keep him company. Be generous, kind patrons, to Time's errand-boy. So may he bring to the merchant his ship safe from the Indies; to the lawyer, a goodly number of new suits; to the doctor, a crowd of patients with the dyspepsia and fat purses; to the farmer, a golden crop and a ready market; to the mechanic, steady employment and good wages; to the idle gentleman some honest business; to the rich, kind hearts and liberal hands; to the poor, warm firesides and food enough, patient spirits, and the hope of better days; to our country, a return of specie payments; and to you, sweet maid, the youth who stole into your dream last night! And next New Year's Day (if I find nothing better to do in the mean while) may Time again bring to your doors your loving little friend,

THE CARRIER.

## "BROWNE'S FOLLY."

THE WAYSIDE, *August* 28, 1860.

MY DEAR COUSIN : I should be very glad to write a story, as you request, for the benefit of the Essex Institute, or for any other purpose that might be deemed desirable by my native towns-people. But it is now many years since the epoch of the "Twice-Told Tales," and the "Mosses from an Old Manse"; and my mind seems to have lost the plan and measure of those little narratives, in which it was once so unprofitably fertile. I can write no story, therefore; but (rather than be entirely wanting to the occasion) I will endeavor to describe a spot near Salem, on which it was once my purpose to locate such a dreamy fiction as you now demand of me.

It is no other than that conspicuous hill (I really know not whether it lies in Salem, Danvers, or Beverly) which used in my younger days to be known by the name of "Browne's Folly." This eminence is a long ridge rising out of the level country around, like a whale's back out of a calm sea, with the head and tail beneath the surface. Along its base ran a green and seldom - trodden lane, with which I was very familiar in my boyhood ; and there was a little brook, which I remember to have dammed up till its overflow made a mimic ocean. When I last looked for this tiny streamlet, which was still rippling freshly through my memory, I found it strangely shrunken; a mere ditch indeed, and almost a dry one. But the green

lane was still there, precisely as I remembered it ; two
wheel-tracks, and the beaten path of the horses' feet,
and grassy strips between ; the whole overshadowed
by tall locust-trees, and the prevalent barberry-bushes,
which are rooted so fondly into the recollections of
every Essex man.

From this lane there is a steep ascent up the side of
the hill, the ridge of which affords two views of very
wide extent and variety. On one side is the ocean,
and Salem and Beverly on its shores ; on the other a
rural scene, almost perfectly level, so that each man's
metes and bounds can be traced out as on a map. The
beholder takes in at a glance the estates on which different families have long been situated, and the houses
where they have dwelt, and cherished their various interests, intermarrying, agreeing together, or quarrelling, going to live, annexing little bits of real estate,
acting out their petty parts in life, and sleeping quietly
under the sod at last. A man's individual affairs look
not so very important, when we can climb high enough
to get the idea of a complicated neighborhood.

But what made the hill particularly interesting to
me were the traces of an old and long-vanished edifice
midway on the curving ridge, and at its highest point.
A pre-revolutionary magnate, the representative of a
famous old Salem family, had here built himself a
pleasure-house, on a scale of magnificence, which, combined with it airy site and difficult approach, obtained
for it, and for the entire hill on which it stood, the traditionary title of " Browne's Folly." Whether a folly
or no, the house was certainly an unfortunate one.
While still in its glory, it was so tremendously shaken
by the earthquake of 1755 that the owner dared no
longer reside in it ; and, practically acknowledging

that its ambitious site rendered it indeed a Folly, he
proceeded to locate it on humbler ground. The great
house actually took up its march along the declining
ridge of the hill, and came safely to the bottom,
where it stood till within the memory of men now
alive.

The proprietor, meanwhile, had adhered to the Roy-
alist side, and fled to England during the Revolution.
The mansion was left under the care of Richard Derby
(an ancestor of the present Derby family), who had a
claim to the Browne property through his wife, but
seems to have held the premises precisely as the refu-
gee left them, for a long term of years, in the expectation of his eventual return. The house remained,
with all its furniture in its spacious rooms and chambers, ready for the exile's occupancy, as soon as he
should reappear. As time went on, however, it began to be neglected, and was accessible to whatever
vagrant or idle school-boy, or berrying party, might
choose to enter through its ill-secured windows.

But there was one closet in the house which everybody was afraid to enter, it being supposed that an evil
spirit — perhaps a domestic Demon of the Browne
family — was confined in it. One day, three or four
score years ago, some school-boys happened to be playing in the deserted chambers, and took it into their
heads to develop the secrets of this mysterious closet.
With great difficulty and tremor they succeeded in
forcing the door. As it flew open, there was a vision
of people in garments of antique magnificence, — gentlemen in curled wigs and tarnished gold-lace, and
ladies in brocade and quaint head-dresses, rushing tu-
multuously forth and tumbling upon the floor. The

urchins took to their heels, in huge dismay, but crept back, after a while, and discovered that the apparition was composed of a mighty pile of family portraits. I had the story, the better part of a hundred years afterwards, from the very school-boy who pried open the closet door.

After standing many years at the foot of the hill, the house was again removed in three portions, and was fashioned into three separate dwellings, which, for aught I know, are yet extant in Danvers.

The ancient site of this proud mansion may still be traced (or could have been ten years ago) upon the summit of the hill. It consisted of two spacious wings, connected by an intermediate hall of entrance, which fronted likewise upon the ridge. Two shallow and grass-grown cavities remain, of what were once the deep and richly stored cellars under the two wings; and between them is the outline of the connecting hall, about as deep as a plough furrow, and somewhat greener than the surrounding sod. The two cellars are still deep enough to shelter a visitor from the fresh breezes that haunt the summit of the hill; and barberry-bushes clustering within them offer the harsh acidity of their fruits, instead of the rich wines which the colonial magnate was wont to store there for his guests. There I have sometimes sat and tried to rebuild, in my imagination, the stately house, or to fancy what a splendid show it must have made even so far off as in the streets of Salem, when the old proprietor illuminated his many windows to celebrate the King's birthday.

I have quite forgotten what story I once purposed writing about " Browne's Folly," and I freely offer the theme and site to any of my young townsmen who may be afflicted with the same tendency towards fanciful narratives which haunted me in my youth and long afterwards.     Truly yours,

NATHANIEL HAWTHORNE.

# BIOGRAPHICAL STORIES.

This small volume and others of a similar character, from the same hand, have not been composed without a deep sense of responsibility. The author regards children as sacred, and would not, for the world, cast anything into the fountain of a young heart that might embitter and pollute its waters. And, even in point of the reputation to be aimed at, juvenile literature is as well worth cultivating as any other. The writer, if he succeed in pleasing his little readers, may hope to be remembered by them till their own old age, — a far longer period of literary existence than is generally attained by those who seek immortality from the judgments of full-grown men.

# BIOGRAPHICAL STORIES.

## CHAPTER I.

WHEN Edward Temple was about eight or nine years old he was afflicted with a disorder of the eyes. It was so severe, and his sight was naturally so delicate, that the surgeon felt some apprehensions lest the boy should become totally blind. He therefore gave strict directions to keep him in a darkened chamber, with a bandage over his eyes. Not a ray of the blessed light of heaven could be suffered to visit the poor lad.

This was a sad thing for Edward. It was just the same as if there were to be no more sunshine, nor moonlight, nor glow of the cheerful fire, nor light of lamps. A night had begun which was to continue perhaps for months, — a longer and drearier night than that which voyagers are compelled to endure when their ship is ice-bound, throughout the winter, in the Arctic Ocean. His dear father and mother, his brother George, and the sweet face of little Emily Robinson, must all vanish and leave him in utter darkness and solitude. Their voices and footsteps, it is true, would be heard around him; he would feel his mother's embrace and the kind pressure of all their hands; but still it would seem as if they were a thousand miles away.

And then his studies, — they were to be entirely

given up. This was another grievous trial; for Edward's memory hardly went back to the period when he had not known how to read. Many and many a holiday had he spent at his book, poring over its pages until the deepening twilight confused the print and made all the letters run into long words. Then would he press his hands across his eyes and wonder why they pained him so; and when the candles were lighted, what was the reason that they burned so dimly, like the moon in a foggy night? Poor little fellow! So far as his eyes were concerned he was already an old man, and needed a pair of spectacles almost as much as his own grandfather did.

And now, alas! the time was come, when even grandfather's spectacles could not have assisted Edward to read. After a few bitter tears, which only pained his eyes the more, the poor boy submitted to the surgeon's orders. His eyes were bandaged, and, with his mother on one side and his little friend Emily on the other, he was led into a darkened chamber.

"Mother, I shall be very miserable!" said Edward, sobbing.

"Oh no, my dear child!" replied his mother, cheerfully. "Your eyesight was a precious gift of Heaven, it is true; but you would do wrong to be miserable for its loss, even if there were no hope of regaining it. There are other enjoyments besides what come to us through our eyes."

"None that are worth having," said Edward.

"Ah, but you will not think so long," rejoined Mrs. Temple, with tenderness. "All of us — your father, and myself, and George, and our sweet Emily — will try to find occupation and amusement for you. We will use all our eyes to make you happy. Will they not be better than a single pair?"

" I will sit by you all day long," said Emily, in her low, sweet voice, putting her hand into that of Edward.

"And so will I, Ned," said George, his elder brother, " school time and all, if my father will permit me."

Edward's brother George was three or four years older than himself, — a fine, hardy lad, of a bold and ardent temper. He was the leader of his comrades in all their enterprises and amusements. As to his proficiency at study there was not much to be said. He had sense and ability enough to have made himself a scholar, but found so many pleasanter things to do that he seldom took hold of a book with his whole heart. So fond was George of boisterous sports and exercises that it was really a great token of affection and sympathy, when he offered to sit all day long in a dark chamber with his poor brother Edward.

As for little Emily Robinson, she was the daughter of one of Mr. Temple's dearest friends. Ever since her mother went to heaven (which was soon after Emily's birth) the little girl had dwelt in the household where we now find her. Mr. and Mrs. Temple seemed to love her as well as their own children; for they had no daughter except Emily; nor would the boys have known the blessing of a sister had not this gentle stranger come to teach them what it was. If I could show you Emily's face, with her dark hair smoothed away from her forehead, you would be pleased with her look of simplicity and loving kindness, but might think that she was somewhat too grave for a child of seven years old. But you would not love her the less for that.

So brother George and this loving little girl were to be Edward's companions and playmates while he should be kept prisoner in the dark chamber. When the first bitterness of his grief was over, he began to feel that there might be some comforts and enjoyments in life even for a boy whose eyes were covered with a bandage.

"I thank you, dear mother," said he, with only a few sobs; "and you, Emily ; and you, too, George. You will all be very kind to me I know. And my father, — will not he come and see me every day?"

"Yes, my dear boy," said Mr. Temple; for, though invisible to Edward, he was standing close beside him. "I will spend some hours of every day with you. And as I have often amused you by relating stories and adventures while you had the use of your eyes, I can do the same now that you are unable to read. Will this please you, Edward?"

"Oh, very much," replied Edward.

"Well, then," said his father, "this evening we will begin the series of Biographical Stories which I promised you some time ago."

## CHAPTER II.

WHEN evening came, Mr. Temple found Edward considerably revived in spirits, and disposed to be resigned to his misfortune. Indeed, the figure of the boy, as it was dimly seen by the firelight, reclining in a well-stuffed easy chair, looked so very comfortable that many people might have envied him. When a man's eyes have grown old with gazing at the ways of the world, it does not seem such a terrible misfortune to have them bandaged.

Little Emily Robinson sat by Edward's side with the air of an accomplished nurse. As well as the duskiness of the chamber would permit, she watched all his motions and each varying expression of his face, and tried to anticipate her patient's wishes before his tongue could utter them. Yet it was noticeable that the child manifested an indescribable awe and disquietude whenever she fixed her eyes on the bandage; for, to her simple and affectionate heart, it seemed as if her dear friend Edward was separated from her because she could not see his eyes. A friend's eyes tell us many things which could never be spoken by the tongue.

George, likewise, looked awkward and confused, as stout and healthy boys are accustomed to do in the society of the sick or afflicted. Never having felt pain or sorrow, they are abashed, from not knowing how to sympathize with the sufferings of others.

" Well, my dear Edward," inquired Mrs. Temple,

" is your chair quite comfortable? and has your little nurse provided for all your wants? If so, your father is ready to begin his stories."

" Oh, I am very well now," answered Edward, with a faint smile. " And my ears have not forsaken me, though my eyes are good for nothing. So pray, dear father, begin."

It was Mr. Temple's design to tell the children a series of true stories, the incidents of which should be taken from the childhood and early life of eminent people. Thus he hoped to bring George, and Edward, and Emily into closer acquaintance with the famous persons who have lived in other times by showing that they also had been children once. Although Mr. Temple was scrupulous to relate nothing but what was founded on fact, yet he felt himself at liberty to clothe the incidents of his narrative in a new coloring, so that his auditors might understand them the better.

" My first story," said he, " shall be about a painter of pictures."

" Dear me!" cried Edward, with a sigh. " I am afraid I shall never look at pictures any more."

" We will hope for the best," answered his father. " In the mean time, you must try to see things within your own mind."

Mr. Temple then began the following story: —

### BENJAMIN WEST.

[BORN 1738.   DIED 1820.]

In the year 1738 there came into the world, in the town of Springfield, Pennsylvania, a Quaker infant, from whom his parents and neighbors looked for wonderful things. A famous preacher of the Society of Friends had prophesied about little Ben, and foretold that he would be one of the most remarkable characters that had appeared on the earth since the days of William Penn. On this account, the eyes of many people were fixed upon the boy. Some of his ancestors had won great renown in the old wars of England and France; but it was probably expected that Ben would become a preacher, and would convert multitudes to the peaceful doctrines of the Quakers. Friend West and his wife were thought to be very fortunate in having such a son.

Little Ben lived to the ripe age of six years without doing anything that was worthy to be told in history. But one summer afternoon, in his seventh year, his mother put a fan into his hand and bade him keep the flies away from the face of a little babe who lay fast asleep in the cradle. She then left the room.

The boy waved the fan to and fro, and drove away the buzzing flies whenever they had the impertinence to come near the baby's face. When they had all flown out of the window or into distant parts of the room, he bent over the cradle and delighted himself with gazing at the sleeping infant. It was, indeed, a very pretty sight. The little personage in the cradle slumbered peacefully, with its waxen hands under its chin, looking as full of blissful quiet as if angels were singing lullabies in its ear. Indeed, it must have been dreaming about heaven; for, while Ben stooped over the cradle, the little baby smiled.

"How beautiful she looks!" said Ben to himself. "What a pity it is that such a pretty smile should not last forever!"

Now Ben, at this period of his life, had never heard of that wonderful art by which a look, that appears and vanishes in a moment, may be made to last for hundreds of years. But, though nobody had told him of such an art, he may be said to have invented it for himself. On a table near at hand there were pens and paper, and ink of two colors, black and red. The boy seized a pen and sheet of paper, and, kneeling down beside the cradle, began to draw a likeness of the infant. While he was busied in this manner he heard his mother's step approaching, and hastily tried to conceal the paper.

"Benjamin, my son, what hast thou been doing?" inquired his mother, observing marks of confusion in his face.

At first Ben was unwilling to tell; for he felt as if there might be something wrong in stealing the baby's face and putting it upon a sheet of paper. However, as his mother insisted, he finally put the sketch into her hand, and then hung his head, expecting to be well scolded. But when the good lady saw what was on the paper, in lines of red and black ink, she uttered a scream of surprise and joy.

"Bless me!" cried she. "It is a picture of little Sally!"

And then she threw her arms around our friend Benjamin, and kissed him so tenderly that he never afterwards was afraid to show his performances to his mother.

As Ben grew older, he was observed to take vast delight in looking at the hues and forms of nature. For instance, he was greatly pleased with the blue violets of spring, the wild roses of summer, and the scarlet cardinal-flowers of early autumn. In the decline of the year, when the woods were variegated with all the colors of the rainbow, Ben seemed to desire nothing better than to gaze at them from morn till night. The purple and golden clouds of sunset were a joy to him. And he was continually endeavoring to draw the figures of trees, men, mountains, houses, cattle, geese, ducks, and turkeys, with a piece of chalk, on barn doors or on the floor.

In these old times the Mohawk Indians were still numerous in Pennsylvania. Every year a party of them used to pay a visit to Springfield, because the wigwams of their ancestors had formerly stood there. These wild men grew fond of little Ben, and made him very happy by giving him some of the red and yellow paint with which they were accustomed to adorn their faces. His mother, too, presented him with a piece of indigo. Thus he had now three colors, — red, blue, and yellow, — and could manufacture green by mixing the yellow with the blue. Our friend Ben was overjoyed, and doubtless showed his gratitude to the Indians by taking their likenesses in the strange dresses which they wore, with feathers, tomahawks, and bows and arrows.

But all this time the young artist had no paintbrushes; nor were there any to be bought, unless he had sent to Philadelphia on purpose. However, he was a very ingenious boy, and resolved to manufacture paint-brushes for himself. With this design he laid hold upon — what do you think? Why, upon a respectable old black cat, who was sleeping quietly by the fireside.

" Puss," said little Ben to the cat, " pray give me some of the fur from the tip of thy tail? "

Though he addressed the black cat so civilly, yet Ben was determined to have the fur whether she were willing or not. Puss, who had no great zeal for the fine arts, would have resisted if she could ; but the boy was armed with his mother's scissors, and very dexterously clipped off fur enough to make a paint-brush. This was of so much use to him that he applied to Madam Puss again and again, until her warm coat of fur had become so thin and ragged that she could hardly keep comfortable through the winter. Poor thing! she was forced to creep close into the chimney-corner, and eyed Ben with a very rueful physiognomy. But Ben considered it more necessary that he should have paint-brushes than that puss should be warm.

About this period friend West received a visit from Mr. Pennington, a merchant of Philadelphia, who was likewise a member of the Society of Friends. The visitor, on entering the parlor, was surprised to see it ornamented with drawings of Indian chiefs, and of birds with beautiful plumage, and of the wild flowers of the forest. Nothing of the kind was ever seen before in the habitation of a Quaker farmer.

"Why, Friend West," exclaimed the Philadelphia merchant, "what has possessed thee to cover thy walls with all these pictures? Where on earth didst thou get them?"

Then Friend West explained that all these pictures were painted by little Ben, with no better materials than red and yellow ochre and a piece of indigo, and with brushes made of the black cat's fur.

"Verily," said Mr. Pennington, "the boy hath a wonderful faculty. Some of our friends might look upon these matters as vanity; but little Benjamin appears to have been born a painter; and Providence is wiser than we are."

The good merchant patted Benjamin on the head, and evidently considered him a wonderful boy. When his parents saw how much their son's performances were admired, they, no doubt, remembered the prophecy of the old Quaker preacher respecting Ben's future eminence. Yet they could not understand how he was ever to become a very great and useful man merely by making pictures.

One evening, shortly after Mr. Pennington's return to Philadelphia, a package arrived at Springfield, directed to our little friend Ben.

"What can it possibly be?" thought Ben, when it was put into his hands. "Who can have sent me such a great square package as this?"

On taking off the thick brown paper which enveloped it, behold! there was a paint-box, with a great many cakes of paint, and brushes of various sizes. It was the gift of good Mr. Pennington. There were likewise several squares of canvas such as artists use for painting pictures upon, and, in addition to all these treasures, some beautiful engravings of landscapes. These were the first pictures that Ben had ever seen except those of his own drawing.

What a joyful evening was this for the little artist! At bedtime he put the paint-box under his pillow, and got hardly a wink of sleep; for, all night long, his fancy was painting pictures in the darkness. In the morning he hurried to the garret, and was seen no more till the dinner-hour; nor did he give himself time to eat more than a mouthful or two of food before he hurried back to the garret again. The next day, and the next, he was just as busy as ever; until at last his mother thought it time to ascertain what he was about. She accordingly followed him to the garret.

On opening the door, the first object that presented

itself to her eyes was our friend Benjamin, giving the last touches to a beautiful picture. He had copied portions of two of the engravings, and made one picture out of both, with such admirable skill that it was far more beautiful than the originals. The grass, the trees, the water, the sky, and the houses were all painted in their proper colors. There, too, were the sunshine and the shadow, looking as natural as life.

" My dear child, thou hast done wonders ! " cried his mother.

The good lady was in an ecstasy of delight. And well might she be proud of her boy ; for there were touches in this picture which old artists, who had spent a lifetime in the business, need not have been ashamed of. Many a year afterwards, this wonderful production was exhibited at the Royal Academy in London.

When Benjamin was quite a large lad he was sent to school at Philadelphia. Not long after his arrival he had a slight attack of fever, which confined him to his bed. The light, which would otherwise have disturbed him, was excluded from his chamber by means of closed wooden shutters. At first it appeared so totally dark that Ben could not distinguish any object in the room. By degrees, however, his eyes became accustomed to the scanty light.

He was lying on his back, looking up towards the ceiling, when suddenly he beheld the dim apparition of a white cow moving slowly over his head ! Ben started, and rubbed his eyes in the greatest amazement.

" What can this mean ? " thought he.

The white cow disappeared ; and next came several pigs, which trotted along the ceiling and vanished into the darkness of the chamber. So lifelike did these grunters look that Ben almost seemed to hear them squeak.

"Well, this is very strange!" said Ben to himself.

When the people of the house came to see him, Benjamin told them of the marvellous circumstance which had occurred. But they would not believe him.

"Benjamin, thou art surely out of thy senses!" cried they. "How is it possible that a white cow and a litter of pigs should be visible on the ceiling of a dark chamber?"

Ben, however, had great confidence in his own eye-sight, and was determined to search the mystery to the bottom. For this purpose, when he was again left alone, he got out of bed and examined the window-shutters. He soon perceived a small chink in one of them, through which a ray of light found its passage and rested upon the ceiling. Now, the science of optics will inform us that the pictures of the white cow and the pigs, and of other objects out of doors, came into the dark chamber through this narrow chink, and were painted over Benjamin's head. It is greatly to his credit that he discovered the scientific principle of this phenomenon, and, by means of it, constructed a camera-obscura, or magic-lantern, out of a hollow box. This was of great advantage to him in drawing land-scapes.

Well, time went on, and Benjamin continued to draw and paint pictures until he had now reached the age when it was proper that he should choose a busi-ness for life. His father and mother were in consider-able perplexity about him. According to the ideas of the Quakers, it is not right for people to spend their lives in occupations that are no real and sensible advantage to the world. Now, what advantage could the world expect from Benjamin's pictures? This was a difficult question; and, in order to set their minds at rest, his parents determined to consult the preachers and wise men of their society. Accordingly, they all assembled in the meeting-house, and discussed the matter from beginning to end.

Finally they came to a very wise decision. It seemed so evident that Providence had created Benjamin to be a painter, and had given him abilities which would be thrown away in any other business, that the Quakers resolved not to oppose his inclination. They even acknowledged that the sight of a beautiful picture might convey instruction to the mind, and might benefit the heart as much as a good book or a wise discourse. They therefore committed the youth to the direction of God, being well assured that he best knew what was his proper sphere of usefulness. The old men laid their hands upon Benjamin's head and gave him their blessing, and the women kissed him affectionately. All consented that he should go forth into the world and learn to be a painter by studying the best pictures of ancient and modern times.

So our friend Benjamin left the dwelling of his parents, and his native woods and streams, and the good Quakers of Springfield, and the Indians who had given him his first colors; he left all the places and persons whom he had hitherto known, and returned to them no more. He went first to Philadelphia, and afterwards to Europe. Here he was noticed by many great people, but retained all the sobriety and simplicity which he had learned among the Quakers. It is related of him, that, when he was presented at the court of the Prince of Parma, he kept his hat upon his head even while kissing the Prince's hand.

When he was twenty-five years old he went to London, and established himself there as an artist. In due course of time he acquired great fame by his pictures, and was made chief painter to King George III. and president of the Royal Academy of Arts. When the Quakers of Pennsylvania heard of his success, they felt that the prophecy of the old preacher as to little Ben's future eminence was now accomplished. It is true, they shook their heads at his pictures of battle and bloodshed, such as the Death of Wolfe, thinking that these terrible scenes should not be held up to the admiration of the world.

But they approved of the great paintings in which he represented the miracles and sufferings of the Redeemer of mankind. King George employed him to adorn a large and beautiful chapel at Windsor Castle with pictures of these sacred subjects. He likewise painted a magnificent picture of Christ Healing the Sick, which he gave to the hospital at Philadelphia. It was exhibited to the public, and produced so much profit that the hospital was enlarged so as to accommodate thirty more patients. If Benjamin West had done no other good deed than this, yet it would have been enough to entitle him to an honorable remembrance forever. At this very day there are thirty poor people in the hospital who owe all their comforts to that same picture.

We shall mention only a single incident more. The picture of Christ Healing the Sick was exhibited at the Royal Academy in London, where it covered a vast space, and displayed a multitude of figures as large as life. On the wall, close beside this admirable picture, hung a small and faded landscape. It was the same that little Ben had painted in his father's garret, after receiving the paint-box and engravings from good Mr. Pennington.

He lived many years in peace and honor, and died in 1820, at the age of eighty-two. The story of his life is almost as wonderful as a fairy tale; for there are few stranger transformations than that of a little unknown Quaker boy, in the wilds of America, into the most distinguished English painter of his day. Let us each make the best use of our natural abilities as Benjamin West did; and, with the blessing of Providence, we shall arrive at some good end. As for fame, it is but little matter whether we acquire it or not.

"Thank you for the story, my dear father," said Edward, when it was finished. "Do you know that it seems as if I could see things without the help of my eyes? While you were speaking I have seen little Ben, and the baby in its cradle, and the Indians, and the white cow, and the pigs, and kind Mr. Pennington, and all the good old Quakers, almost as plainly as if they were in this very room."

"It is because your attention was not disturbed by outward objects," replied Mr. Temple. "People, when deprived of sight, often have more vivid ideas than those who possess the perfect use of their eyes. I will venture to say that George has not attended to the story quite so closely."

"No, indeed," said George; "but it was a very pretty story for all that. How I should have laughed to see Ben making a paint-brush out of the black cat's tail! I intend to try the experiment with Emily's kitten."

"Oh no, no, George!" cried Emily, earnestly. "My kitten cannot spare her tail."

Edward being an invalid, it was now time for him to retire to bed. When the family bade him good night he turned his face towards them, looking very loath to part.

"I shall not know when morning comes," said he, sorrowfully. "And, besides, I want to hear your voices all the time; for, when nobody is speaking, it seems as if I were alone in a dark world."

"You must have faith, my dear child," replied his mother. "Faith is the soul's eyesight; and when we possess it the world is never dark nor lonely."

## CHAPTER III.

THE next day Edward began to get accustomed to his new condition of life. Once, indeed, when his parents were out of the way and only Emily was left to take care of him, he could not resist the temptation to thrust aside the bandage, and peep at the anxious face of his little nurse. But, in spite of the dimness of the chamber, the experiment caused him so much pain that he felt no inclination to take another look. So, with a deep sigh, he resigned himself to his fate.

"Emily, pray talk to me!" said he, somewhat impatiently.

Now, Emily was a remarkably silent little girl, and did not possess that liveliness of disposition which renders some children such excellent companions. She seldom laughed, and had not the faculty of making many words about small matters. But the love and earnestness of her heart taught her how to amuse poor Edward in his darkness. She put her knitting-work into his hands.

"You must learn how to knit," said she.

"What! without using my eyes?" cried Edward.

"I can knit with my eyes shut," replied Emily.

Then with her own little hands she guided Edward's fingers while he set about this new occupation. So awkward were his first attempts that any other little girl would have laughed heartily. But Emily preserved her gravity, and showed the utmost patience in taking up the innumerable stitches which he let down.

In the course of an hour or two, his progress was quite encouraging.

When evening came, Edward acknowledged that the day had been far less wearisome than he anticipated. But he was glad, nevertheless, when his father and mother, and George and Emily, all took their seats around his chair. He put out his hand to grasp each of their hands, and smiled with a very bright expression upon his lips.

" Now I can see you all with my mind's eye," said he. " And now, father, pray tell us another story."

So Mr. Temple began.

### SIR ISAAC NEWTON.

[BORN 1642.    DIED 1727.]

On Christmas Day, in the year 1642, Isaac Newton was born at the small village of Woolsthorpe, in England. Little did his mother think, when she beheld her new-born babe, that he was destined to explain many matters which had been a mystery ever since the creation of the world.

Isaac's father being dead, Mrs. Newton was married again to a clergyman, and went to reside at North Witham. Her son was left to the care of his good old grandmother, who was very kind to him and sent him to school. In his early years Isaac did not appear to be a very bright scholar, but was chiefly remarkable for his ingenuity in all mechanical occupations. He had a set of little tools and saws of various sizes manufactured by himself. With the aid of these Isaac contrived to make many curious articles, at which he worked with so much skill that he seemed to have been born with a saw or chisel in hand.

The neighbors looked with vast admiration at the

things which Isaac manufactured.    And his old grand-mother, I suppose, was never weary of talking about him.

" He 'll make a capital workman one of these days," she would probably say.    " No fear but what Isaac will do well in the world and be a rich man before he dies."

It is amusing to conjecture what were the antici-pations of his grandmother and the neighbors about Isaac's future life.    Some of them, perhaps, fancied that he would make beautiful furniture of mahogany, rosewood, or polished oak, inlaid with ivory and ebony, and magnificently gilded.    And then, doubtless, all the rich people would purchase these fine things to adorn their drawing-rooms.    Others probably thought that little Isaac was destined to be an architect, and would build splendid mansions for the nobility and gentry, and churches too, with the tallest steeples that had ever been seen in England.

Some of his friends, no doubt, advised Isaac's grand-mother to apprentice him to a clock-maker; for, be-sides his mechanical skill, the boy seemed to have a taste for mathematics, which would be very useful to him in that profession.    And then, in due time, Isaac would set up for himself, and would manufacture curi-ous clocks, like those that contain sets of dancing fig-ures, which issue from the dial-plate when the hour is struck; or like those where a ship sails across the face of the clock, and is seen tossing up and down on the waves as often as the pendulum vibrates.

Indeed, there was some ground for supposing that Isaac would devote himself to the manufacture of clocks; since he had already made one of a kind which nobody had ever heard of before.    It was set a-going, not by wheels and weights like other clocks, but by the dropping of water. This was an object of great wonderment to all the people round about; and it must be confessed that there are few boys, or men either, who could contrive to tell what o'clock it is by means of a bowl of water.

Besides the water-clock, Isaac made a sundial. Thus his grandmother was never at a loss to know the hour; for the water-clock would tell it in the shade, and the dial in the sunshine. The sundial is said to be still in existence at Woolsthorpe, on the corner of the house where Isaac dwelt. If so, it must have marked the passage of every sunny hour that has elapsed since Isaac Newton was a boy. It marked all the famous moments of his life; it marked the hour of his death; and still the sunshine creeps slowly over it, as regularly as when Isaac first set it up.

Yet we must not say that the sundial has lasted longer than its maker; for Isaac Newton will exist long after the dial — yea, and long after the sun itself — shall have crumbled to decay.

Isaac possessed a wonderful faculty of acquiring knowledge by the simplest means. For instance, what method do you suppose he took to find out the strength of the wind? You will never guess how the boy could compel that unseen, inconstant, and ungovernable wonder, the wind, to tell him the measure of its strength. Yet nothing can be more simple. He jumped against the wind; and by the length of his jump he could calculate the force of a gentle breeze, a brisk gale, or a tempest. Thus, even in his boyish sports, he was continually searching out the secrets of philosophy.

Not far from his grandmother's residence there was a windmill which operated on a new plan. Isaac was in the habit of going thither frequently, and would spend whole hours in examining its various parts. While the mill was at rest he pried into its internal machinery. When its broad sails were set in motion by the wind, he watched the process by which the mill-stones were made to revolve and crush the grain that was put into the hopper. After gaining a thorough knowledge of its construction he was observed to be unusually busy with his tools.

It was not long before his grandmother and all the neighborhood knew what Isaac had been about. He had constructed a model of the windmill, though not so large, I suppose, as one of the box-traps which boys set to catch squirrels, yet every part of the mill and its machinery was complete. Its little sails were neatly made of linen, and whirled round very swiftly when the mill was placed in a draught of air. Even a puff of wind from Isaac's mouth or from a pair of bellows was sufficient to set the sails in motion. And, what was most curious, if a handful of grains of wheat were put into the little hopper, they would soon be converted into snow-white flour.

Isaac's playmates were enchanted with his new windmill. They thought that nothing so pretty and so wonderful had ever been seen in the whole world.

"But, Isaac," said one of them, "you have forgotten one thing that belongs to a mill."

"What is that?" asked Isaac; for he supposed that, from the roof of the mill to its foundation, he had forgotten nothing.

"Why, where is the miller?" said his friend.

"That is true, — I must look out for one," said Isaac; and he set himself to consider how the deficiency should be supplied.

He might easily have made the miniature figure of a man; but then it would not have been able to move about and perform the duties of a miller. As Captain Lemuel Gulliver had not yet discovered the island of Lilliput, Isaac did not know that there were little men in the world whose size was just suited to his windmill. It so happened, however, that a mouse had just been caught in the trap; and, as no other miller could be found, Mr. Mouse was appointed to that important office. The new miller made a very respectable appearance in his dark-gray coat. To be sure, he had not a very good character for honesty, and was suspected of sometimes stealing a portion of the grain which was given him to grind. But perhaps some two-legged millers are quite as dishonest as this small quadruped.

As Isaac grew older, it was found that he had far more important matters in his mind than the manufacture of toys like the little windmill. All day long, if left to himself, he was either absorbed in thought or engaged in some book of mathematics or natural philosophy. At night, I think it probable, he looked up with reverential curiosity to the stars, and wondered whether they were worlds like our own, and how great was their distance from the earth, and what was the power that kept them in their courses. Perhaps, even so early in life, Isaac Newton felt a presentiment that he should be able, hereafter, to answer all these questions.

When Isaac was fourteen years old, his mother's second husband being now dead, she wished her son to leave school and assist her in managing the farm at Woolsthorpe. For a year or two, therefore, he tried to turn his attention to farming. But his mind was so bent on becoming a scholar that his mother sent him back to school, and afterwards to the University of Cambridge.

I have now finished my anecdotes of Isaac Newton's boyhood. My story would be far too long were I to mention all the splendid discoveries which he made after he came to be a man. He was the first that found out the nature of light; for, before his day, nobody could tell what the sunshine was composed of. You remember, I suppose, the story of an apple's falling on his head, and thus leading him to discover the force of gravitation, which keeps the heavenly bodies in their courses. When he had once got hold of this idea, he never permitted his mind to rest until he had searched out all the laws by which the planets are guided through the sky. This he did as thoroughly as if he had gone up among the stars and tracked them in their orbits. The boy had found out the mechanism of a windmill; the man explained to his fellow-men the mechanism of the universe.

While making these researches he was accustomed to spend night after night in a lofty tower, gazing at the heavenly bodies through a telescope. His mind was lifted far above the things of this world. He may be said, indeed, to have spent the greater part of his life in worlds that lie thousands and millions of miles away; for where the thoughts and the heart are, there is our true existence.

Did you never hear the story of Newton and his little dog Diamond? One day, when he was fifty years old, and had been hard at work more than twenty years studying the theory of light, he went out of his chamber, leaving his little dog asleep before the fire. On the table lay a heap of manuscript papers, containing all the discoveries which Newton had made during those twenty years. When his master was gone, up rose little Diamond, jumped upon the table, and over-threw the lighted candle. The papers immediately caught fire.

Just as the destruction was completed Newton opened the chamber door, and perceived that the la-bors of twenty years were reduced to a heap of ashes. There stood little Diamond, the author of all the mis-chief. Almost any other man would have sentenced the dog to immediate death. But Newton patted him on the head with his usual kindness, although grief was at his heart.

"O Diamond, Diamond," exclaimed he, "thou lit-tle knowest the mischief thou hast done!"

This incident affected his health and spirits for some time afterwards; but, from his conduct towards the little dog, you may judge what was the sweetness of his temper.

Newton lived to be a very old man, and acquired great renown, and was made a member of Parliament, and received the honor of knighthood from the king. But he cared little for earthly fame and honors, and felt no pride in the vastness of his knowledge. All that he had learned only made him feel how little he knew in comparison to what remained to be known.

"I seem to myself like a child," observed he, "play-ing on the sea-shore, and picking up here and there a curious shell or a pretty pebble, while the boundless ocean of Truth lies undiscovered before me."

At last, in 1727, when he was forescore and five years old, Sir Isaac Newton died,— or rather he ceased to live on earth. We may be permitted to believe that he is still searching out the infinite wisdom and goodness of the Creator as earnestly, and with even more success, than while his spirit animated a mortal body. He has left a fame behind him which will be as endurable as if his name were written in letters of light formed by the stars upon the midnight sky.

"I love to hear about mechanical contrivances, such as the water-clock and the little windmill," remarked George. "I suppose, if Sir Isaac Newton had only thought of it, he might have found out the steam-engine, and railroads, and all the other famous inventions that have come into use since his day."

"Very possibly he might," replied Mr. Temple; "and no doubt a great many people would think it more useful to manufacture steam-engines than to search out the system of the universe. Other great astronomers besides Newton have been endowed with mechanical genius. There was David Rittenhouse, an American, — he made a perfect little water-mill when he was only seven or eight years old. But this sort of ingenuity is but a mere trifle in comparison with the other talents of such men."

"It must have been beautiful," said Edward, "to spend whole nights in a high tower as Newton did, gazing at the stars, and the comets, and the meteors. But what would Newton have done had he been blind? or if his eyes had been no better than mine?"

"Why, even then, my dear child," observed Mrs. Temple, "he would have found out some way of enlightening his mind and of elevating his soul. But come; little Emily is waiting to bid you good-night. You must go to sleep and dream of seeing all our faces."

"But how sad it will be when I awake!" murmured Edward.

# CHAPTER IV.

In the course of the next day the harmony of our little family was disturbed by something like a quarrel between George and Edward.

The former, though he loved his brother dearly, had found it quite too great a sacrifice of his own enjoyments to spend all his play-time in a darkened chamber. Edward, on the other hand, was inclined to be despotic. He felt as if his bandaged eyes entitled him to demand that everybody who enjoyed the blessing of sight should contribute to his comfort and amusement. He therefore insisted that George, instead of going out to play football, should join with himself and Emily in a game of questions and answers.

George resolutely refused, and ran out of the house. He did not revisit Edward's chamber till the evening, when he stole in, looking confused, yet somewhat sullen, and sat down beside his father's chair. It was evident, by a motion of Edward's head and a slight trembling of his lips, that he was aware of George's entrance, though his footsteps had been almost inaudible. Emily, with her serious and earnest little face, looked from one to the other, as if she longed to be a messenger of peace between them.

Mr. Temple, without seeming to notice any of these circumstances, began a story.

## SAMUEL JOHNSON.

[BORN 1709. DIED 1784.]

" Sam," said Mr. Michael Johnson, of Lichfield, one morning, " I am very feeble and ailing to-day. You must go to Uttoxeter in my stead, and tend the book-stall in the market-place there."

This was spoken above a hundred years ago by an elderly man, who had once been a thriving bookseller at Lichfield, in England. Being now in reduced circumstances, he was forced to go every market-day and sell books at a stall, in the neighboring village of Uttoxeter.

His son, to whom Mr. Johnson spoke, was a great boy, of very singular aspect. He had an intelligent face ; but it was seamed and distorted by a scrofulous humor, which affected his eyes so badly that sometimes he was almost blind. Owing to the same cause his head would often shake with a tremulous motion as if he were afflicted with the palsy. When Sam was an infant, the famous Queen Anne had tried to cure him of this disease by laying her royal hands upon his head. But though the touch of the king or queen was supposed to be a certain remedy for scrofula, it produced no good effect upon Sam Johnson.

At the time which we speak of the poor lad was not very well dressed, and wore shoes from which his toes peeped out ; for his old father had barely the means of supporting his wife and children. But, poor as the family were, young Sam Johnson had as much pride as any nobleman's son in England. The fact was, he felt conscious of uncommon sense and ability, which, in his own opinion, entitled him to great respect from the world. Perhaps he would have been glad if grown

people had treated him as reverentially as his schoolfellows did. Three of them were accustomed to come
for him every morning; and while he sat upon the
back of one, the two others supported him on each
side; and thus he rode to school in triumph.

Being a personage of so much importance, Sam could
not bear the idea of standing all day in Uttoxeter market offering books to the rude and ignorant country
people. Doubtless he felt more reluctant on account
of his shabby clothes, and the disorder of his eyes, and
the tremulous motion of his head.

When Mr. Michael Johnson spoke, Sam pouted and
made an indistinct grumbling in his throat; then he
looked his old father in the face, and answered him
loudly and deliberately.

" Sir," said he, " I will not go to Uttoxeter market ! "

Mr. Johnson had seen a great deal of the lad's obstinacy ever since his birth; and while Sam was
younger, the old gentleman had probably used the rod
whenever occasion seemed to require. But he was
now too feeble and too much out of spirits to contend
with this stubborn and violent - tempered boy. He
therefore gave up the point at once, and prepared
to go to Uttoxeter himself.

" Well, Sam," said Mr. Johnson, as he took his hat
and staff, " if for the sake of your foolish pride you
can suffer your poor sick father to stand all day in the
noise and confusion of the market when he ought to
be in his bed, I have no more to say. But you will
think of this, Sam, when I am dead and gone."

So the poor old man (perhaps with a tear in his
eye, but certainly with sorrow in his heart) set forth
towards Uttoxeter. The gray-haired, feeble, melan-

choly Michael Johnson! How sad a thing it was that
he should be forced to go, in his sickness, and toil for
the support of an ungrateful son who was too proud to
do anything for his father, or his mother, or himself!
Sam looked after Mr. Johnson with a sullen countenance till he was out of sight.

But when the old man's figure, as he went stooping
along the street, was no more to be seen, the boy's
heart began to smite him. He had a vivid imagination, and it tormented him with the image of his
father standing in the market-place of Uttoxeter and
offering his books to the noisy crowd around him.
Sam seemed to behold him arranging his literary merchandise upon the stall in such a way as was best calculated to attract notice. Here was Addison's " Spectator," a long row of little volumes ; here was Pope's
translation of the Iliad and Odyssey ; here were Dry-
den's poems, or those of Prior, Here, likewise, were
" Gulliver's Travels," and a variety of little gilt-cov-
ered children's books, such as " Tom Thumb, " " Jack
the Giant Queller," " Mother Goose's Melodies," and
others which our great-grandparents used to read in
their childhood. And here were sermons for the
pious, and pamphlets for the politicians, and ballads,
some merry and some dismal ones, for the country
people to sing.

Sam, in imagination, saw his father offer these
books, pamphlets, and ballads, now to the rude yeomen, who perhaps could not read a word ; now to the
country squires, who cared for nothing but to hunt
hares and foxes ; now to the children, who chose to
spend their coppers for sugar-plums or gingerbread
rather than for picture-books. And if Mr. Johnson
should sell a book to man, woman, or child, it would

cost him an hour's talk to get a profit of only six-pence.

"My poor father!" thought Sam to himself. "How his head will ache! and how heavy his heart will be! I am almost sorry that I did not do as he bade me."

Then the boy went to his mother, who was busy about the house. She did not know of what had passed between Mr. Johnson and Sam.

"Mother," said he, "did you think father seemed very ill to-day?"

"Yes, Sam," answered his mother, turning with a flushed face from the fire, where she was cooking their scanty dinner. "Your father did look very ill; and it is a pity he did not send you to Uttoxeter in his stead. You are a great boy now, and would rejoice, I am sure, to do something for your poor father, who has done so much for you."

The lad made no reply. But again his imagination set to work and conjured up another picture of poor Michael Johnson. He was standing in the hot sun-shine of the market-place, and looking so weary, sick, and disconsolate, that the eyes of all the crowd were drawn to him. "Had this old man no son," the peo-ple would say among themselves, "who might have taken his place at the book-stall while the father kept his bed?" And perhaps, — but this was a terrible thought for Sam! — perhaps his father would faint away and fall down in the market-place, with his gray hair in the dust and his venerable face as deathlike as that of a corpse. And there would be the by-standers gazing earnestly at Mr. Johnson and whispering, "Is he dead? Is he dead?"

And Sam shuddered as he repeated to himself, "Is he dead?"

"Oh, I have been a cruel son!" thought he within his own heart. "God forgive me! God forgive me!"

But God could not yet forgive him; for he was not truly penitent. Had he been so, he would have hastened away that very moment to Uttoxeter, and have fallen at his father's feet, even in the midst of the crowded market-place. There he would have confessed his fault, and besought Mr. Johnson to go home and leave the rest of the day's work to him. But such was Sam's pride and natural stubbornness that he could not bring himself to this humiliation. Yet he ought to have done so, for his own sake, for his father's sake, and for God's sake.

After sunset old Michael Johnson came slowly home and sat down in his customary chair. He said nothing to Sam; nor do I know that a single word ever passed between them on the subject of the son's disobedience. In a few years his father died, and left Sam to fight his way through the world by himself. It would make our story much too long were I to tell you even a few of the remarkable events of Sam's life. Moreover, there is the less need of this, because many books have been written about that poor boy, and the fame that he acquired, and all that he did or talked of doing after he came to be a man.

But one thing I must not neglect to say. From his boyhood upward until the latest day of his life he never forgot the story of Uttoxeter market. Often when he was a scholar of the University of Oxford, or master of an academy at Edial, or a writer for the London booksellers, — in all his poverty and toil and in all his success, — while he was walking the streets without a shilling to buy food, or when the greatest men of England were proud to feast him at their table, — still that heavy and remorseful thought came back to him, " I was cruel to my poor father in his illness! " Many and many a time, awake or in his dreams, he seemed to see old Michael Johnson standing in the dust and confusion of the market-place, and pressing his withered hand to his forehead as if it ached.

Alas! my dear children, it is a sad thing to have such a thought as this to bear us company through life.

Though the story was but half finished, yet, as it was longer than usual, Mr. Temple here made a short pause. He perceived that Emily was in tears, and Edward turned his half-veiled face towards the speaker with an air of great earnestness and interest. As for George, he had withdrawn into the dusky shadow behind his father's chair.

# CHAPTER V.

In a few moments Mr. Temple resumed the story, as follows: —

## SAMUEL JOHNSON.

[CONTINUED.]

Well, my children, fifty years had passed away since young Sam Johnson had shown himself so hard-hearted towards his father. It was now market-day in the village of Uttoxeter.

In the street of the village you might see cattle-dealers with cows and oxen for sale, and pig-drovers with herds of squeaking swine, and farmers with cart-loads of cabbages, turnips, onions, and all other produce of the soil. Now and then a farmer's red-faced wife trotted along on horseback, with butter and cheese in two large panniers. The people of the village, with country squires, and other visitors from the neighborhood, walked hither and thither, trading, jesting, quarrelling, and making just such a bustle as their fathers and grandfathers had made half a century before.

In one part of the street there was a puppet-show, with a ridiculous merry-andrew, who kept both grown people and children in a roar of laughter. On the opposite side was the old stone church of Uttoxeter, with ivy climbing up its walls and partly obscuring its Gothic windows.

There was a clock in the gray tower of the ancient

church, and the hands on the dial-plate had now almost reached the hour of noon. At this busiest hour of the market a strange old gentleman was seen making his way among the crowd. He was very tall and bulky, and wore a brown coat and small-clothes, with black worsted stockings and buckled shoes. On his head was a three-cornered hat, beneath which a bushy gray wig thrust itself out, all in disorder. The old gentleman elbowed the people aside, and forced his way through the midst of them with a singular kind of gait, rolling his body hither and thither, so that he needed twice as much room as any other person there.

"Make way, sir!" he would cry out, in a loud, harsh voice, when somebody happened to interrupt his progress. "Sir, you intrude your person into the public thoroughfare!"

"What a queer old fellow this is!" muttered the people among themselves, hardly knowing whether to laugh or to be angry.

But when they looked into the venerable stranger's face, not the most thoughtless among them dared to offer him the least impertinence. Though his features were scarred and distorted with the scrofula, and though his eyes were dim and bleared, yet there was something of authority and wisdom in his look, which impressed them all with awe. So they stood aside to let him pass; and the old gentleman made his way across the market-place, and paused near the corner of the ivy-mantled church. Just as he reached it the clock struck twelve.

On the very spot of ground where the stranger now stood some aged people remembered that old Michael Johnson had formerly kept his book-stall. The little children who had once bought picture-books of him were grandfathers now.

"Yes; here is the very spot!" muttered the old gentleman to himself.

There this unknown personage took his stand and removed the three-cornered hat from his head. It was the busiest hour of the day. What with the hum of human voices, the lowing of cattle, the squeaking of pigs, and the laughter caused by the merry-andrew, the market-place was in very great confusion. But the stranger seemed not to notice it any more than if the silence of a desert were around him. He was rapt in his own thoughts. Sometimes he raised his furrowed brow to Heaven, as if in prayer; sometimes he bent his head, as if an insupportable weight of sorrow were upon him. It increased the awfulness of his aspect that there was a motion of his head and an almost continual tremor throughout his frame, with singular twitchings and contortions of his features.

The hot sun blazed upon his unprotected head; but he seemed not to feel its fervor. A dark cloud swept across the sky and rain-drops pattered into the market-place; but the stranger heeded not the shower. The people began to gaze at the mysterious old gentleman with superstitious fear and wonder. Who could he be? Whence did he come? Wherefore was he standing bareheaded in the market-place? Even the school-boys left the merry-andrew and came to gaze, with wide-open eyes, at this tall, strange-looking old man.

There was a cattle-drover in the village who had recently made a journey to the Smithfield Market, in London. No sooner had this man thrust his way through the throng and taken a look at the unknown personage, than he whispered to one of his acquaintances, —

"I say, Neighbor Hutchins, would ye like to know who this old gentleman is?"

" Ay, that I would," replied Neighbor Hutchins, "for a queerer chap I never saw in my life. Somehow it makes me feel small to look at him. He's more than a common man."

" You may well say so," answered the cattle-drover. " Why, that's the famous Doctor Samuel Johnson, who they say is the greatest and learnedest man in England. I saw him in London streets, walking with one Mr. Boswell."

Yes; the poor boy, the friendless Sam, with whom we began our story, had become the famous Doctor Samuel Johnson. He was universally acknowledged as the wisest man and greatest writer in all England. He had given shape and permanence to his native language by his Dictionary. Thousands upon thousands of people had read his "Idler," his "Rambler," and his " Rasselas." Noble and wealthy men and beautiful ladies deemed it their highest privilege to be his companions. Even the King of Great Britain had sought his acquaintance, and told him what an honor he considered it that such a man had been born in his dominions. He was now at the summit of literary renown.

But all his fame could not extinguish the bitter remembrance which had tormented him through life. Never, never had he forgotten his father's sorrowful and upbraiding look. Never, though the old man's troubles had been over so many years, had he forgiven himself for inflicting such a pang upon his heart. And now, in his old age, he had come hither to do penance, by standing at noonday, in the market-place of Uttoxeter, on the very spot where Michael Johnson had once kept his book-stall. The aged and illustrious man had done what the poor boy refused to do. By thus expressing his deep repentance and humiliation of heart, he hoped to gain peace of conscience and the forgiveness of God.

My dear children, if you have grieved (I will not say your parents, but if you have grieved) the heart of any human being who has a claim upon your love, then think of Samuel Johnson's penance. Will it not be better to redeem the error now than to endure the agony of remorse for fifty years? Would you not rather say to a brother, "I have erred; forgive me!" than perhaps to go hereafter and shed bitter tears upon his grave?

Hardly was the story concluded when George hastily arose, and Edward likewise, stretching forth his hands into the darkness that surrounded him to find his brother. Both accused themselves of unkindness; each besought the other's forgiveness; and having done so, the trouble of their hearts vanished away like a dream.

"I am glad! I am so glad!" said Emily, in a low, earnest voice. "Now I shall sleep quietly to-night."

"My sweet child," thought Mrs. Temple as she kissed her, "mayest thou never know how much strife there is on earth! It would cost thee many a night's rest."

## CHAPTER VI.

ABOUT this period Mr. Temple found it necessary to take a journey, which interrupted the series of "Biographical Stories" for several evenings. In the interval, Edward practised various methods of employing and amusing his mind.

Sometimes he meditated upon beautiful objects which he had formerly seen, until the intensity of his recollection seemed to restore him the gift of sight and place everything anew before his eyes. Sometimes he repeated verses of poetry which he did not know to be in his memory until he found them there just at the time of need. Sometimes he attempted to solve arithmetical questions which had perplexed him while at school.

Then, with his mother's assistance, he learned the letters of the string alphabet, which is used in some of the institutions for the blind in Europe. When one of his friends gave him a leaf of St. Mark's Gospel, printed in embossed characters, he endeavored to read it by passing his fingers over the letters as blind children do.

His brother George was now very kind, and spent so much time in the darkened chamber that Edward often insisted upon his going out to play. George told him all about the affairs at school, and related many amusing incidents that happened among his comrades, and informed him what sports were now in fashion, and whose kite soared the highest, and whose little ship sailed fleetest on the Frog Pond. As for Emily, she repeated stories which she had learned from a new book called " The Flower People," in which the snow-drops, the violets, the columbines, the roses, and all that lovely tribe are represented as telling their secrets to a little girl. The flowers talked sweetly, as flowers should ; and Edward almost fancied that he could behold their bloom and smell their fragrant breath.

Thus, in one way or another, the dark days of Edward's confinement passed not unhappily. In due time his father returned ; and the next evening, when the family were assembled, he began a story.

"I must first observe, children," said he, " that some writers deny the truth of the incident which I am about to relate to you. There certainly is but little evidence in favor of it. Other respectable writers, however, tell it for a fact ; and, at all events, it is an interesting story, and has an excellent moral."

So Mr. Temple proceeded to talk about the early days of

### OLIVER CROMWELL.

[BORN 1599.    DIED 1658.]

Not long after King James I. took the place of Queen Elizabeth on the throne of England, there lived an English knight at a place called Hinchinbrooke. His name was Sir Oliver Cromwell. He spent his life, I suppose, pretty much like other English knights and squires in those days, hunting hares and foxes and drinking large quantities of ale and wine. The old house in which he dwelt had been occupied by his ancestors before him for a good many years. In it there was a great hall, hung round with coats of arms and helmets, cuirasses and swords, which his forefathers had used in battle, and with horns of deer and tails of foxes which they or Sir Oliver himself had killed in the chase.

This Sir Oliver Cromwell had a nephew, who had been called Oliver, after himself, but who was generally known in the family by the name of little Noll. His father was a younger brother of Sir Oliver. The child was often sent to visit his uncle, who probably found him a troublesome little fellow to take care of. He was forever in mischief, and always running into some danger or other, from which he seemed to escape only by miracle.

Even while he was an infant in the cradle a strange accident had befallen him. A huge ape, which was kept in the family, snatched up little Noll in his fore paws and clambered with him to the roof of the house. There this ugly beast sat grinning at the affrighted spectators, as if it had done the most praiseworthy thing imaginable. Fortunately, however, he brought the child safe down again ; and the event was afterwards considered an omen that Noll would reach a very elevated station in the world.

One morning, when Noll was five or six years old, a royal messenger arrived at Hinchinbrooke with tidings that King James was coming to dine with Sir Oliver Cromwell. This was a high honor, to be sure, but a very great trouble; for all the lords and ladies, knights, squires, guards, and yeomen, who waited on the king, were to be feasted as well as himself; and more provisions would be eaten and more wine drunk in that one day than generally in a month. However, Sir Oliver expressed much thankfulness for the king's intended visit, and ordered his butler and cook to make the best preparations in their power. So a great fire was kindled in the kitchen; and the neighbors knew, by the smoke which poured out of the chimney, that boiling, baking, stewing, roasting, and frying were going on merrily.

By and by the sound of trumpets was heard approaching nearer and nearer; a heavy, old-fashioned coach, surrounded by guards on horseback, drove up to the house. Sir Oliver, with his hat in his hand, stood at the gate to receive the king. His Majesty was dressed in a suit of green not very new: he had a feather in his hat, and a triple ruff round his neck, and over his shoulder was slung a hunting-horn instead of a sword. Altogether he had not the most dignified aspect in the world; but the spectators gazed at him as if there was something superhuman and divine in his person. They even shaded their eyes with their hands, as if they were dazzled by the glory of his countenance.

"How are ye, man?" cried King James, speaking in a Scotch accent; for Scotland was his native country. "By my crown, Sir Oliver, but I am glad to see ye!"

The good knight thanked the king; at the same time kneeling down while his Majesty alighted. When King James stood on the ground, he directed Sir Oliver's attention to a little boy who had come with him in the coach. He was six or seven years old, and wore a hat and feather, and was more richly dressed than the king himself. Though by no means an ill-looking child, he seemed shy, or even sulky; and his cheeks were rather pale, as if he had been kept moping within doors, instead of being sent out to play in the sun and wind.

"I have brought my son Charlie to see ye," said the

king. "I hope, Sir Oliver, ye have a son of your own to be his playmate."

Sir Oliver Cromwell made a reverential bow to the little prince, whom one of the attendants had now taken out of the coach. It was wonderful to see how all the spectators, even the aged men with their gray beards, humbled themselves before this child. They bent their bodies till their beards almost swept the dust. They looked as if they were ready to kneel down and worship him.

The poor little prince! From his earliest infancy not a soul had dared to contradict him; everybody around him had acted as if he were a superior being; so that, of course, he had imbibed the same opinion of himself. He naturally supposed that the whole kingdom of Great Britain and all its inhabitants had been created solely for his benefit and amusement. This was a sad mistake; and it cost him dear enough after he had ascended his father's throne.

"What a noble little prince he is!" exclaimed Sir Oliver, lifting his hands in admiration. "No, please your Majesty, I have no son to be the playmate of his royal highness; but there is a nephew of mine somewhere about the house. He is near the prince's age, and will be but too happy to wait upon his royal highness."

"Send for him, man! send for him!" said the king.

But, as it happened, there was no need of sending for Master Noll. While King James was speaking, a rugged, bold-faced, sturdy little urchin thrust himself through the throng of courtiers and attendants, and greeted the prince with a broad stare. His doublet and hose (which had been put on new and clean in honor of the king's visit) were already soiled and torn

with the rough play in which he had spent the morning. He looked no more abashed than if King James
were his uncle and the prince one of his customary
playfellows.

This was little Noll himself.

" Here, please your majesty, is my nephew," said
Sir Oliver, somewhat ashamed of Noll's appearance
and demeanor. " Oliver, make your obeisance to the
king's majesty."

The boy made a pretty respectful obeisance to the
king ; for in those days children were taught to pay
reverence to their elders. King James, who prided
himself greatly on his scholarship, asked Noll a few
questions in the Latin grammar, and then introduced
him to his son. The little prince, in a very grave and
dignified manner, extended his hand, not for Noll to
shake, but that he might kneel down and kiss it.

" Nephew," said Sir Oliver, " pay your duty to the
prince."

" I owe him no duty," cried Noll, thrusting aside
the prince's hand with a rude laugh. " Why should I
kiss that boy's hand ? "

All the courtiers were amazed and confounded, and
Sir Oliver the most of all. But the king laughed
heartily, saying that little Noll had a stubborn English spirit, and that it was well for his son to learn betimes what sort of a people he was to rule over.

So King James and his train entered the house ;
and the prince, with Noll and some other children, was
sent to play in a separate room while his Majesty was
at dinner. The young people soon became acquainted ;
for boys, whether the sons of monarchs or of peasants,
all like play, and are pleased with one another's society. What games they diverted themselves with I

cannot tell. Perhaps they played at ball, perhaps at blind-man's-buff, perhaps at leap-frog, perhaps at prison-bars. Such games have been in use for hundreds of years; and princes as well as poor children have spent some of their happiest hours in playing at them.

Meanwhile King James and his nobles were feasting with Sir Oliver in the great hall. The king sat in a gilded chair, under a canopy, at the head of a long table. Whenever any of the company addressed him, it was with the deepest reverence. If the attendants offered him wine, or the various delicacies of the festival, it was upon their bended knees. You would have thought, by these tokens of worship, that the monarch was a supernatural being; only he seemed to have quite as much need of those vulgar matters, food and drink, as any other person at the table. But fate had ordained that good King James should not finish his dinner in peace.

All of a sudden there arose a terrible uproar in the room where the children were at play. Angry shouts and shrill cries of alarm were mixed up together; while the voices of elder persons were likewise heard, trying to restore order among the children. The king and everybody else at table looked aghast; for perhaps the tumult made them think that a general rebellion had broken out.

" Mercy on us ! " muttered Sir Oliver; " that graceless nephew of mine is in some mischief or other. The naughty little whelp ! "

Getting up from table, he ran to see what was the matter, followed by many of the guests, and the king among them. They all crowded to the door of the playroom.

On looking in, they beheld the little Prince Charles,

with his rich dress all torn and covered with the dust of the floor. His royal blood was streaming from his nose in great abundance. He gazed at Noll with a mixture of rage and affright, and at the same time a puzzled expression, as if he could not understand how any mortal boy should dare to give him a beating. As for Noll, there stood his sturdy little figure, bold as a lion, looking as if he were ready to fight, not only the prince, but the king and kingdom too.

" You little villain ! " cried his uncle. " What have you been about ? Down on your knees, this instant, and ask the prince's pardon. How dare you lay your hands on the king's majesty's royal son ? "

" He struck me first," grumbled the valiant little Noll ; " and I 've only given him his due."

Sir Oliver and the guests lifted up their hands in astonishment and horror. No punishment seemed severe enough for this wicked little varlet, who had dared to resent a blow from the king's own son. Some of the courtiers were of opinion that Noll should be sent prisoner to the Tower of London and brought to trial for high treason. Others, in their great zeal for the king's service, were about to lay hands on the boy and chastise him in the royal presence.

But King James, who sometimes showed a good deal of sagacity, ordered them to desist.

" Thou art a bold boy," said he, looking fixedly at little Noll ; " and, if thou live to be a man, my son Charlie would do wisely to be friends with thee."

" I never will ! " cried the little prince, stamping his foot.

" Peace, Charlie, peace ! " said the king ; then addressing Sir Oliver and the attendants, " Harm not the urchin ; for he has taught my son a good lesson,

if Heaven do but give him grace to profit by it. Hereafter, should he be tempted to tyrannize over the stubborn race of Englishmen, let him remember little Noll
Cromwell and his own bloody nose."

So the king finished his dinner and departed; and
for many a long year the childish quarrel between
Prince Charles and Noll Cromwell was forgotten.
The prince, indeed, might have lived a happier life,
and have met a more peaceful death, had he remembered that quarrel and the moral which his father
drew from it. But when old King James was dead,
and Charles sat upon his throne, he seemed to forget
that he was but a man, and that his meanest subjects
were men as well as he. He wished to have the property and lives of the people of England entirely at his
own disposal. But the Puritans, and all who loved
liberty, rose against him and beat him in many battles, and pulled him down from his throne.

Throughout this war between the king and nobles on
one side and the people of England on the other, there
was a famous leader, who did more towards the ruin
of royal authority than all the rest. The contest
seemed like a wrestling-match between King Charles
and this strong man. And the king was overthrown.

When the discrowned monarch was brought to trial,
that warlike leader sat in the judgment hall. Many
judges were present besides himself; but he alone had
the power to save King Charles or to doom him to the
scaffold. After sentence was pronounced, this victorious general was entreated by his own children, on their
knees, to rescue his Majesty from death.

"No!" said he, sternly. "Better that one man
should perish than that the whole country should be
ruined for his sake. It is resolved that he shall die!"

When Charles, no longer a king, was led to the scaffold, his great enemy stood at a window of the royal palace of Whitehall. He beheld the poor victim of pride, and an evil education, and misused power, as he laid his head upon the block. He looked out with a steadfast gaze while a black-veiled executioner lifted the fatal axe and smote off that anointed head at a single blow.

"It is a righteous deed," perhaps he said to himself. "Now Englishmen may enjoy their rights."

At night, when the body of Charles was laid in the coffin, in a gloomy chamber, the general entered, lighting himself with a torch. Its gleam showed that he was now growing old; his visage was scarred with the many battles in which he had led the van; his brow was wrinkled with care and with the continual exercise of stern authority. Probably there was not a single trait, either of aspect or manner, that belonged to the little Noll who had battled so stoutly with Prince Charles. Yet this was he!

He lifted the coffin-lid, and caused the light of his torch to fall upon the dead monarch's face. Then, probably, his mind went back over all the marvellous events that had brought the hereditary King of England to this dishonored coffin, and had raised himself, a humble individual, to the possession of kingly power. He was a king, though without the empty title or the glittering crown.

"Why was it," said Cromwell to himself, or might have said, as he gazed at the pale features in the coffin, — "why was it that this great king fell, and that poor Noll Cromwell has gained all the power of the realm?"

And, indeed, why was it?

King Charles had fallen, because, in his manhood the same as when a child, he disdained to feel that every human creature was his brother. He deemed himself a superior being, and fancied that his subjects were created only for a king to rule over. And Cromwell rose, because, in spite of his many faults, he mainly fought for the rights and freedom of his fellow-men ; and therefore the poor and the oppressed all lent their strength to him.

"Dear father, how I should hate to be a king!" exclaimed Edward.

"And would you like to be a Cromwell?" inquired his father.

"I should like it well," replied George; "only I would not have put the poor old king to death. I would have sent him out of the kingdom, or perhaps have allowed him to live in a small house near the gate of the royal palace. It was too severe to cut off his head."

"Kings are in such an unfortunate position," said Mr. Temple, "that they must either be almost deified by their subjects, or else be dethroned and beheaded. In either case it is a pitiable lot."

"Oh, I had rather be blind than be a king!" said Edward.

"Well, my dear Edward," observed his mother, with a smile, "I am glad you are convinced that your own lot is not the hardest in the world."

## CHAPTER VII.

IT was a pleasant sight, for those who had eyes, to see how patiently the blinded little boy now submitted to what he had at first deemed an intolerable calamity. The beneficent Creator has not allowed our comfort to depend on the enjoyment of any single sense. Though he has made the world so very beautiful, yet it is possible to be happy without ever beholding the blue sky, or the green and flowery earth, or the kind faces of those whom we love. Thus it appears that all the external beauty of the universe is a free gift from God over and above what is necessary to our comfort. How grateful, then, should we be to that divine Benevolence, which showers even superfluous bounties upon us!

One truth, therefore, which Edward's blindness had taught him was, that his mind and soul could dispense with the assistance of his eyes. Doubtless, however, he would have found this lesson far more difficult to learn had it not been for the affection of those around him. His parents, and George and Emily, aided him to bear his misfortune; if possible, they would have lent him their own eyes. And this, too, was a good lesson for him. It taught him how dependent on one another God has ordained us to be, insomuch that all the necessities of mankind should incite them to mutual love.

So Edward loved his friends, and perhaps all the world, better than he ever did before. And he felt grateful towards his father for spending the evenings in telling him stories, — more grateful, probably, than any of my little readers will feel towards me for so carefully writing these same stories down.

"Come, dear father," said he, the next evening, "now tell us about some other little boy who was destined to be a famous man."

"How would you like a story of a Boston boy?" asked his father.

"Oh, pray let us have it!" cried George, eagerly. "It will be all the better if he has been to our schools, and has coasted on the Common, and sailed boats in the Frog Pond. I shall feel acquainted with him then."

"Well, then," said Mr. Temple, "I will introduce you to a Boston boy whom all the world became acquainted with after he grew to be a man."

The story was as follows : —

### BENJAMIN FRANKLIN.

[BORN 1706.  DIED 1790.]

In the year 1716, or about that period, a boy used to be seen in the streets of Boston who was known among his schoolfellows and playmates by the name of Ben Franklin. Ben was born in 1706; so that he was now about ten years old. His father, who had come over from England, was a soap-boiler and tallow-chandler, and resided in Milk Street, not far from the Old South Church.

Ben was a bright boy at his book, and even a brighter one when at play with his comrades. He had some remarkable qualities which always seemed to give him the lead, whether at sport or in more serious matters. I might tell you a number of amusing anecdotes about him. You are acquainted, I suppose, with his famous story of the WHISTLE, and how he bought it with a whole pocketful of coppers and afterwards repented of his bargain. But Ben had grown a great boy since those days, and had gained wisdom by experience ; for it was one of his peculiarities, that no incident ever happened to him without teaching him some valuable lesson. Thus he generally profited more by his misfortunes than many people do by the most favorable events that could befall them.

Ben's face was already pretty well known to the inhabitants of Boston. The selectmen and other people of note often used to visit his father, for the sake of talking about the affairs of the town or province. Mr. Franklin was considered a person of great wisdom and integrity, and was respected by all who knew him, although he supported his family by the humble trade of boiling soap and making tallow candles.

While his father and the visitors were holding deep consultations about public affairs, little Ben would sit on his stool in a corner, listening with the greatest interest, as if he understood every word. Indeed, his features were so full of intelligence that there could be but little doubt, not only that he understood what was said, but that he could have expressed some very sagacious opinions out of his own mind. But in those days boys were expected to be silent in the presence of their elders. However, Ben Franklin was looked upon as a very promising lad, who would talk and act wisely by and by.

"Neighbor Franklin," his father's friends would sometimes say, "you ought to send this boy to college and make a minister of him."

"I have often thought of it," his father would reply; "and my brother Benjamin promises to give him a great many volumes of manuscript sermons, in case he should be educated for the church. But I have a large family to support, and cannot afford the expense."

In fact, Mr. Franklin found it so difficult to provide bread for his family, that, when the boy was ten years old, it became necessary to take him from school. Ben was then employed in cutting candle-wicks into equal lengths and filling the moulds with tallow; and many families in Boston spent their evenings by the light of the candles which he had helped to make. Thus, you see, in his early days, as well as in his manhood, his labors contributed to throw light upon dark matters.

Busy as his life now was, Ben still found time to keep company with his former schoolfellows. He and the other boys were very fond of fishing, and spent many of their leisure hours on the margin of the mill-pond, catching flounders, perch, eels, and tomcod, which came up thither with the tide. The place where they fished is now, probably, covered with stone pavements and brick buildings, and thronged with people and with vehicles of all kinds. But at that period it was a marshy spot on the outskirts of the town, where gulls flitted and screamed overhead and salt-meadow grass grew under foot.

On the edge of the water there was a deep bed of clay, in which the boys were forced to stand while they caught their fish. Here they dabbled in mud and mire like a flock of ducks.

"This is very uncomfortable," said Ben Franklin one day to his comrades, while they were standing mid-leg deep in the quagmire.

"So it is," said the other boys. " What a pity we have no better place to stand ! "

If it had not been for Ben, nothing more would have been done or said about the matter. But it was not in his nature to be sensible of an inconvenience without using his best efforts to find a remedy. So, as he and his comrades were returning from the water-side, Ben suddenly threw down his string of fish with a very determined air.

"Boys," cried he, " I have thought of a scheme which will be greatly for our benefit and for the public benefit."

It was queer enough, to be sure, to hear this little chap — this rosy-cheeked, ten-year-old boy — talking about schemes for the public benefit! Nevertheless, his companions were ready to listen, being assured that Ben's scheme, whatever it was, would be well worth their attention. They remembered how sagaciously he had conducted all their enterprises ever since he had been old enough to wear small-clothes.

They remembered, too, his wonderful contrivance of sailing across the mill-pond by lying flat on his back in the water and allowing himself to be drawn along by a paper kite. If Ben could do that, he might certainly do anything.

"What is your scheme, Ben? — what is it? " cried they all.

It so happened that they had now come to a spot of ground where a new house was to be built. Scattered round about lay a great many large stones which were to be used for the cellar and foundation. Ben mounted upon the highest of these stones, so that he might speak with the more authority.

"You know, lads," said he, " what a plague it is to

be forced to stand in the quagmire yonder, — over shoes and stockings (if we wear any) in mud and water. See! I am bedaubed to the knees of my small-clothes; and you are all in the same pickle. Unless we can find some remedy for this evil, our fishing business must be entirely given up. And, surely, this would be a terrible misfortune!"

"That it would! that it would!" said his comrades sorrowfully.

"Now, I propose," continued Master Benjamin, "that we build a wharf, for the purpose of carrying on our fisheries You see these stones. The workmen mean to use them for the underpinning of a house; but that would be for only one man's advantage. My plan is to take these same stones and carry them to the edge of the water and build a wharf with them. This will not only enable us to carry on the fishing business with comfort and to better advantage, but it will likewise be a great convenience to boats passing up and down the stream. Thus, instead of one man, fifty, or a hundred, or a thousand, besides ourselves, may be benefited by these stones. What say you, lads? Shall we build the wharf?"

Ben's proposal was received with one of those uproarious shouts wherewith boys usually express their delight at whatever completely suits their views. Nobody thought of questioning the right and justice of building a wharf with stones that belonged to another person.

"Hurrah! hurrah!" shouted they. "Let 's set about it."

It was agreed that they should all be on the spot that evening and commence their grand public enterprise by moonlight. Accordingly, at the appointed time, the whole gang of youthful laborers assembled, and eagerly began to remove the stones. They had not calculated how much toil would be requisite in this important part of their undertaking. The very first stone which they laid hold of proved so heavy that it almost seemed to be fastened to the ground. Nothing but Ben Franklin's cheerful and resolute spirit could have induced them to persevere.

Ben, as might be expected, was the soul of the enterprise. By his mechanical genius, he contrived methods to lighten the labor of transporting the stones, so that one boy, under his directions, would perform as much as half a dozen if left to themselves. Whenever their spirits flagged he had some joke ready, which seemed to renew their strength, by setting them all into a roar of laughter. And when, after an hour or two of hard work, the stones were transported to the waterside, Ben Franklin was the engineer to superintend the construction of the wharf.

The boys, like a colony of ants, performed a great deal of labor by their multitude, though the individual strength of each could have accomplished but little. Finally, just as the moon sank below the horizon, the great work was finished.

"Now, boys," cried Ben, "let's give three cheers and go home to bed. To-morrow we may catch fish at our ease."

"Hurrah! hurrah! hurrah!" shouted his comrades.

Then they all went home in such an ecstasy of delight that they could hardly get a wink of sleep.

The story was not yet finished; but George's impatience caused him to interrupt it.

"How I wish that I could have helped to build that wharf!" exclaimed he. "It must have been glorious fun. Ben Franklin forever, say I."

"It was a very pretty piece of work," said Mr. Temple. "But wait till you hear the end of the story."

"Father," inquired Edward, "whereabouts in Boston was the mill-pond on which Ben built his wharf?"

"I do not exactly know," answered Mr. Temple; "but I suppose it to have been on the northern verge of the town, in the vicinity of what are now called Merrimack and Charlestown Streets. That thronged portion of the city was once a marsh. Some of it, in fact, was covered with water."

# CHAPTER VIII.

As the children had no more questions to ask, Mr. Temple proceeded to relate what consequences ensued from the building of Ben Franklin's wharf.

## BENJAMIN FRANKLIN.

### [CONTINUED.]

In the morning, when the early sunbeams were gleaming on the steeples and roofs of the town and gilding the water that surrounded it, the masons came, rubbing their eyes, to begin their work at the foundation of the new house. But, on reaching the spot, they rubbed their eyes so much the harder. What had become of their heap of stones?

" Why, Sam," said one to another, in great perplexity, " here 's been some witchcraft at work while we were asleep. The stones must have flown away through the air ! "

" More likely they have been stolen ! " answered Sam.

" But who on earth would think of stealing a heap of stones ? " cried a third. " Could a man carry them away in his pocket ? "

The master mason, who was a gruff kind of man, stood scratching his head, and said nothing at first. But, looking carefully on the ground, he discerned innumerable tracks of little feet, some with shoes and some barefoot. Following these tracks with his eye, he saw that they formed a beaten path towards the water-side.

" Ah, I see what the mischief is," said he, nodding his head. " Those little rascals, the boys, — they have stolen our stones to build a wharf with ! "

The masons immediately went to examine the new structure. And, to say the truth, it was well worth looking at, so neatly and with such admirable skill had it been planned and finished. These stones were put together so securely that there was no danger of their being loosened by the tide, however swiftly it might sweep along. There was a broad and safe platform to stand upon, whence the little fishermen might cast their lines into deep water and draw up fish in abundance. Indeed, it almost seemed as if Ben and his comrades might be forgiven for taking the stones, because they had done their job in such a workmanlike manner.

" The chaps that built this wharf understood their business pretty well," said one of the masons. " I should not be ashamed of such a piece of work myself."

But the master mason did not seem to enjoy the joke. He was one of those unreasonable people who care a great deal more for their own rights and privileges than for the convenience of all the rest of the world.

" Sam," said he, more gruffly than usual, " go call a constable."

So Sam called a constable, and inquiries were set on foot to discover the perpetrators of the theft. In the course of the day warrants were issued, with the signature of a justice of the peace, to take the bodies of Benjamin Franklin, and other evil-disposed persons, who had stolen a heap of stones. If the owner of the stolen property had not been more merciful than the master mason, it might have gone hard with our friend Benjamin and his fellow-laborers. But, luckily for them, the gentleman had a respect for Ben's father, and, moreover, was amused with the spirit of the whole affair. He therefore let the culprits off pretty easily.

But, when the constables were dismissed, the poor boys had to go through another trial, and receive sentence, and suffer execution, too, from their own fathers. Many a rod, I grieve to say, was worn to the stump on that unlucky night.

As for Ben, he was less afraid of a whipping than of his father's disapprobation. Mr. Franklin, as I have mentioned before, was a sagacious man, and also an inflexibly upright one. He had read much for a person in his rank of life, and had pondered upon the ways of the world, until he had gained more wisdom than a whole library of books could have taught him. Ben had a greater reverence for his father than for any other person in the world, as well on account of his spotless integrity as of his practical sense and deep views of things.

Consequently, after being released from the clutches of the law, Ben came into his father's presence with no small perturbation of mind.

"Benjamin, come hither," began Mr. Franklin, in his customary solemn and weighty tone.

The boy approached and stood before his father's chair, waiting reverently to hear what judgment this good man would pass upon his late offence. He felt that now the right and wrong of the whole matter would be made to appear.

"Benjamin!" said his father, "what could induce you to take property which did not belong to you?"

"Why, father," replied Ben, hanging his head at

first, but then lifting his eyes to Mr. Franklin's face, "if it had been merely for my own benefit, I never should have dreamed of it. But I knew that the wharf would be a public convenience. If the owner of the stones should build a house with them, nobody will enjoy any advantage except himself. Now, I made use of them in a way that was for the advantage of many persons. I thought it right to aim at doing good to the greatest number."

"My son," said Mr. Franklin, solemnly, "so far as it was in your power, you have done a greater harm to the public than to the owner of the stones."

"How can that be, father?" asked Ben.

"Because," answered his father, "in building your wharf with stolen materials, you have committed a moral wrong. There is no more terrible mistake than to violate what is eternally right for the sake of a seeming expediency. Those who act upon such a principle do the utmost in their power to destroy all that is good in the world."

"Heaven forbid!" said Benjamin.

"No act," continued Mr. Franklin, "can possibly be for the benefit of the public generally which involves injustice to any individual. It would be easy to prove this by examples. But, indeed, can we suppose that our all-wise and just Creator would have so ordered the affairs of the world that a wrong act should be the true method of attaining a right end? It is impious to think so. And I do verily believe, Benjamin, that almost all the public and private misery of mankind arises from a neglect of this great truth, — that evil can produce only evil, — that good ends must be wrought out by good means."

"I will never forget it again," said Benjamin, bowing his head.

"Remember," concluded his father, "that, whenever we vary from the highest rule of right, just so far we do an injury to the world. It may seem otherwise for the moment; but, both in time and in eternity, it will be found so."

To the close of his life Ben Franklin never forgot this conversation with his father; and we have reason to suppose that, in most of his public and private career, he endeavored to act upon the principles which that good and wise man had then taught him.

After the great event of building the wharf, Ben continued to cut wick-yarn and fill candle-moulds for about two years. But, as he had no love for that occupation, his father often took him to see various artisans at their work, in order to discover what trade he would prefer. Thus Ben learned the use of a great many tools, the knowledge of which afterwards proved very useful to him. But he seemed much inclined to go to sea. In order to keep him at home, and likewise to gratify his taste for letters, the lad was bound apprentice to his elder brother, who had lately set up a printing-office in Boston.

Here he had many opportunities of reading new books and of hearing instructive conversation. He exercised himself so successfully in writing compositions, that, when no more than thirteen or fourteen years old, he became a contributor to his brother's newspaper. Ben was also a versifier, if not a poet. He made two doleful ballads, — one about the shipwreck of Captain Worthilake; and the other about the pirate Black Beard, who, not long before, infested the American seas.

When Ben's verses were printed, his brother sent him to sell them to the towns-people wet from the press. " Buy my ballads ! " shouted Benjamin, as he trudged through the streets with a basketful on his arm. " Who 'll buy a ballad about Black Beard ? A penny apiece ! a penny apiece ! Who 'll buy my ballads ? "

If one of those roughly composed and rudely printed ballads could be discovered now, it would be worth more than its weight in gold.

In this way our friend Benjamin spent his boyhood and youth, until, on account of some disagreement with his brother, he left his native town and went to Philadelphia. He landed in the latter city, a homeless and hungry young man, and bought threepence worth of bread to satisfy his appetite. Not knowing where else to go, he entered a Quaker meeting-house, sat down, and fell fast asleep. He has not told us whether his slumbers were visited by any dreams. But it would have been a strange dream, indeed, and an incredible one, that should have foretold how great a man he was destined to become, and how much he would be honored in that very city where he was now friendless and unknown.

So here we finish our story of the childhood of Benjamin Franklin. One of these days, if you would know what he was in his manhood, you must read his own works and the history of American independence.

" Do let us hear a little more of him ! " said Edward ; " not that I admire him so much as many other characters ; but he interests me, because he was a Yankee boy."

" My dear son," replied Mr. Temple, " it would require a whole volume of talk to tell you all that is worth knowing about Benjamin Franklin. There is a very pretty anecdote of his flying a kite in the midst of a thunder-storm, and thus drawing down the lightning from the clouds and proving that it was the same thing as electricity. His whole life would be an interesting story, if we had time to tell it."

"But, pray, dear father, tell us what made him so famous," said George. "I have seen his portrait a great many times. There is a wooden bust of him in one of our streets; and marble ones, I suppose, in some other places. And towns, and ships of war, and steamboats, and banks, and academies, and children, are often named after Franklin. Why should he have grown so very famous?"

"Your question is a reasonable one, George," answered his father. "I doubt whether Franklin's philosophical discoveries, important as they were, or even his vast political services, would have given him all the fame which he acquired. It appears to me that "Poor Richard's Almanac" did more than anything else towards making him familiarly known to the public. As the writer of those proverbs which Poor Richard was supposed to utter, Franklin became the counsellor and household friend of almost every family in America. Thus it was the humblest of all his labors that has done the most for his fame."

"I have read some of those proverbs," remarked Edward; "but I do not like them. They are all about getting money or saving it."

"Well," said his father, "they were suited to the condition of the country; and their effect, upon the whole, has doubtless been good, although they teach men but a very small portion of their duties."

# CHAPTER IX.

HITHERTO Mr. Temple's narratives had all been about boys and men. But, the next evening, he bethought himself that the quiet little Emily would perhaps be glad to hear the story of a child of her own sex. He therefore resolved to narrate the youthful adventures of Christina, of Sweden, who began to be a queen at the age of no more than six years. If we have any little girls among our readers, they must not suppose that Christina is set before them as a pattern of what they ought to be. On the contrary, the tale of her life is chiefly profitable as showing the evil effects of a wrong education, which caused this daughter of a king to be both useless and unhappy. Here follows the story.

## QUEEN CHRISTINA.

[BORN 1626.    DIED 1689.]

In the royal palace at Stockholm, the capital city of Sweden, there was born, in 1626, a little princess. The king, her father, gave her the name of Christina, in memory of a Swedish girl with whom he had been in love. His own name was Gustavus Adolphus; and he was also called the Lion of the North, because he had gained greater fame in war than any other prince or general then alive. With this valiant king for their commander, the Swedes had made themselves terrible to the Emperor of Germany and to the King of France, and were looked upon as the chief defence of the Protestant religion.

The little Christina was by no means a beautiful child. To confess the truth, she was remarkably plain. The queen, her mother, did not love her so much as she ought; partly, perhaps, on account of Christina's want of beauty, and also because both the king and queen had wished for a son, who might have gained as great renown in battle as his father had.

The king, however, soon became exceedingly fond of the infant princess. When Christina was very young she was taken violently sick. Gustavus Adolphus, who was several hundred miles from Stockholm, travelled night and day, and never rested until he held the poor child in his arms. On her recovery he made a solemn festival, in order to show his joy to the people of Sweden and express his gratitude to Heaven. After this event he took his daughter with him in all the journeys which he made throughout his kingdom.

Christina soon proved herself a bold and sturdy little girl. When she was two years old, the king and herself, in the course of a journey, came to the strong fortress of Colmar. On the battlements were soldiers clad in steel armor, which glittered in the sunshine. There were likewise great cannons, pointing their black mouths at Gustavus and little Christina, and ready to belch out their smoke and thunder; for, whenever a king enters a fortress, it is customary to receive him with a royal salute of artillery.

But the captain of the fortress met Gustavus and his daughter as they were about to enter the gateway. "May it please your Majesty," said he, taking off his steel cap and bowing profoundly, "I fear that, if we receive you with a salute of cannon, the little princess will be frightened almost to death."

Gustavus looked earnestly at his daughter, and was

indeed apprehensive that the thunder of so many cannon might perhaps throw her into convulsions. He had almost a mind to tell the captain to let them enter the fortress quietly, as common people might have done, without all this head-splitting racket. But no; this would not do.

"Let them fire," said he, waving his hand. "Christina is a soldier's daughter, and must learn to bear the noise of cannon."

So the captain uttered the word of command, and immediately there was a terrible peal of thunder from the cannon, and such a gush of smoke that it enveloped the whole fortress in its volumes. But, amid all the din and confusion, Christina was seen clapping her little hands, and laughing in an ecstasy of delight. Probably nothing ever pleased her father so much as to see that his daughter promised to be fearless as himself. He determined to educate her exactly as if she had been a boy, and to teach her all the knowledge needful to the ruler of a kingdom and the commander of an army.

But Gustavus should have remembered that Providence had created her to be a woman, and that it was not for him to make a man of her.

However, the king derived great happiness from his beloved Christina. It must have been a pleasant sight to see the powerful monarch of Sweden playing in some magnificent hall of the palace with his merry little girl. Then he forgot that the weight of a kingdom rested upon his shoulders. He forgot that the wise Chancellor Oxenstiern was waiting to consult with him how to render Sweden the greatest nation of Europe. He forgot that the Emperor of Germany and the King of France were plotting together how they might pull him down from his throne.

Yes; Gustavus forgot all the perils, and cares, and pompous irksomeness of a royal life; and was as happy, while playing with his child, as the humblest peasant in the realm of Sweden. How gayly did they dance along the marble floor of the palace, this valiant king, with his upright, martial figure, his war-worn visage, and commanding aspect, and the small, round form of Christina, with her rosy face of childish merriment! Her little fingers were clasped in her father's hand, which had held the leading staff in many famous victories. His crown and sceptre were her playthings. She could disarm Gustavus of his sword, which was so terrible to the princes of Europe.

But, alas! the king was not long permitted to enjoy Christina's society. When she was four years old Gustavus was summoned to take command of the allied armies of Germany, which were fighting against the emperor. His greatest affliction was the necessity of parting with his child; but people in such high stations have but little opportunity for domestic happiness. He called an assembly of the senators of Sweden and confided Christina to their care, saying, that each one of them must be a father to her if he himself should fall in battle.

At the moment of his departure Christina ran towards him and began to address him with a speech which somebody had taught her for the occasion. Gustavus was busied with thoughts about the affairs of the kingdom, so that he did not immediately attend to the childish voice of his little girl. Christina, who did not love to be unnoticed, immediately stopped short and pulled him by the coat.

" Father," said she, " why do not you listen to my speech ? "

In a moment the king forgot everything except that he was parting with what he loved best in all the world. He caught the child in his arms, pressed her to his bosom, and burst into tears. Yes; though he was a brave man, and though he wore a steel corselet on his breast, and though armies were waiting for him to lead them to battle, still his heart melted within him, and he wept. Christina, too, was so afflicted that her attendants began to fear that she would actually die of grief. But probably she was soon comforted; for children seldom remember their parents quite so faithfully as their parents remember them.

For two years more Christina remained in the palace at Stockholm. The queen, her mother, had accompanied Gustavus to the wars. The child, therefore, was left to the guardianship of five of the wisest men in the kingdom. But these wise men knew better how to manage the affairs of state than how to govern and educate a little girl so as to render her a good and happy woman.

When two years had passed away, tidings were brought to Stockholm which filled everybody with triumph and sorrow at the same time. The Swedes had won a glorious victory at Lutzen. But, alas! the warlike King of Sweden, the Lion of the North, the father of our little Christina, had been slain at the foot of a great stone, which still marks the spot of that hero's death.

Soon after this sad event, a general assembly, or congress, consisting of deputations from the nobles, the clergy, the burghers, and the peasants of Sweden, was summoned to meet at Stockholm. It was for the purpose of declaring little Christina to be Queen of Sweden, and giving her the crown and sceptre of her deceased father. Silence being proclaimed, the Chancellor Oxenstiern arose.

"We desire to know," said he, "whether the people of Sweden will take the daughter of our dead king, Gustavus Adolphus, to be their queen."

When the chancellor had spoken, an old man, with white hair and in coarse apparel, stood up in the midst of the assembly. He was a peasant, Lars Larrson by name, and had spent most of his life in laboring on a farm.

"Who is this daughter of Gustavus?" asked the old man. "We do not know her. Let her be shown to us."

Then Christina was brought into the hall and placed before the old peasant. It was strange, no doubt, to see a child — a little girl of six years old — offered to the Swedes as their ruler instead of the brave king, her father, who had led them to victory so many times. Could her baby fingers wield a sword in war? Could her childish mind govern the nation wisely in peace?

But the Swedes do not appear to have asked themselves these questions. Old Lars Larrson took Christina up in his arms and gazed earnestly into her face. He had known the great Gustavus well; and his heart was touched when he saw the likeness which the little girl bore to that heroic monarch.

"Yes," cried he, with the tears gushing down his furrowed cheeks; "this is truly the daughter of our Gustavus! Here is her father's brow! — here is his piercing eye! She is his very picture! This child shall be our queen!"

Then all the proud nobles of Sweden, and the reverend clergy, and the burghers, and the peasants, knelt down at the child's feet and kissed her hand.

"Long live Christina, Queen of Sweden!" shouted they.

Even after she was a woman grown Christina remembered the pleasure which she felt in seeing all these men at her feet and hearing them acknowledge her as their supreme ruler. Poor child! she was yet to learn that power does not insure happiness. As yet, however, she had not any real power. All the public business, it is true, was transacted in her name; but the kingdom was governed by a number of the most experienced statesmen, who were called a regency.

But it was considered necessary that the little queen should be present at the public ceremonies, and should behave just as if she were in reality the ruler of the nation. When she was seven years of age, some ambassadors from the Czar of Muscovy came to the Swedish court. They wore long beards, and were clad in a strange fashion, with furs and other outlandish ornaments; and as they were inhabitants of a half-civilized country, they did not behave like other people. The Chancellor Oxenstiern was afraid that the young queen would burst out a laughing at the first sight of these queer ambassadors, or else that she would be frightened by their unusual aspect.

"Why should I be frightened?" said the little queen. "And do you suppose that I have no better manners than to laugh? Only tell me how I must behave, and I will do it."

Accordingly, the Muscovite ambassadors were introduced; and Christina received them and answered their speeches with as much dignity and propriety as if she had been a grown woman.

All this time, though Christina was now a queen,

you must not suppose that she was left to act as she pleased. She had a preceptor, named John Mathias, who was a very learned man and capable of instructing her in all the branches of science. But there was nobody to teach her the delicate graces and gentle virtues of a woman. She was surrounded almost entirely by men, and had learned to despise the society of her own sex. At the age of nine years she was separated from her mother, whom the Swedes did not consider a proper person to be intrusted with the charge of her. No little girl who sits by a New England fireside has cause to envy Christina in the royal palace at Stockholm.

Yet she made great progress in her studies. She learned to read the classical authors of Greece and Rome, and became a great admirer of the heroes and poets of old times. Then, as for active exercises, she could ride on horseback as well as any man in her kingdom. She was fond of hunting, and could shoot at a mark with wonderful skill. But dancing was the only feminine accomplishment with which she had any acquaintance.

She was so restless in her disposition that none of her attendants were sure of a moment's quiet neither day nor night. She grew up, I am sorry to say, a very unamiable person, ill-tempered, proud, stubborn, and, in short, unfit to make those around her happy, or to be happy herself. Let every little girl, who has been taught self-control and a due regard for the rights of others, thank Heaven that she has had better instruction than this poor little Queen of Sweden.

At the age of eighteen Christina was declared free to govern the kingdom by herself without the aid of a regency. At this period of her life she was a young woman of striking aspect, a good figure, and intelligent face, but very strangely dressed. She wore a short habit of gray cloth, with a man's vest over it, and a black scarf around her neck; but no jewels nor ornaments of any kind.

Yet, though Christina was so negligent of her appearance, there was something in her air and manner that proclaimed her as the ruler of a kingdom. Her eyes, it is said, had a very fierce and haughty look. Old General Wrangel, who had often caused the enemies of Sweden to tremble in battle, actually trembled himself when he encountered the eyes of the queen. But it would have been better for Christina if she could have made people love her, by means of soft and gentle looks, instead of affrighting them by such terrible glances.

And now I have told you almost all that is amusing or instructive in the childhood of Christina. Only a few more words need be said about her; for it is neither pleasant nor profitable to think of many things that she did after she grew to be a woman.

When she had worn the crown a few years, she began to consider it beneath her dignity to be called a queen, because the name implied that she belonged to the weaker sex. She therefore caused herself to be proclaimed KING; thus declaring to the world that she despised her own sex and was desirous of being ranked among men. But in the twenty-eighth year of her age Christina grew tired of royalty, and resolved to be neither a king nor a queen any longer. She took the crown from her head with her own hands, and ceased to be the ruler of Sweden. The people did not greatly regret her abdication; for she had governed them ill, and had taken much of their property to supply her extravagance.

Having thus given up her hereditary crown, Christina left Sweden and travelled over many of the countries of Europe. Everywhere she was received with great ceremony, because she was the daughter of the renowned Gustavus, and had herself been a powerful queen. Perhaps you would like to know something about her personal appearance in the latter part of her life. She is described as wearing a man's vest, a short gray petticoat, embroidered with gold and silver, and a black wig, which was thrust awry upon her head. She wore no gloves, and so seldom washed her hands that nobody could tell what had been their original color. In this strange dress, and, I suppose, without washing her hands or face, she visited the magnificent court of Louis XIV.

She died in 1689. None loved her while she lived, nor regretted her death, nor planted a single flower upon her grave. Happy are the little girls of America, who are brought up quietly and tenderly at the domestic hearth, and thus become gentle and delicate women! May none of them ever lose the loveliness of their sex by receiving such an education as that of Queen Christina!

Emily, timid, quiet, and sensitive, was the very reverse of little Christina. She seemed shocked at the idea of such a bold masculine character as has been described in the foregoing story.

"I never could have loved her," whispered she to Mrs. Temple; and then she added, with that love of personal neatness which generally accompanies purity of heart, "It troubles me to think of her unclean hands!"

"Christina was a sad specimen of womankind indeed," said Mrs. Temple. "But it is very possible for a woman to have a strong mind, and to be fitted for the active business of life, without losing any of her natural delicacy. Perhaps some time or other Mr. Temple will tell you a story of such a woman."

It was now time for Edward to be left to repose. His brother George shook him heartily by the hand, and hoped, as he had hoped twenty times before, that to-morrow or the next day Ned's eyes would be strong enough to look the sun right in the face.

"Thank you, George," replied Edward, smiling; "but I am not half so impatient as at first. If my bodily eyesight were as good as yours, perhaps I could not see things so distinctly with my mind's eye. But now there is a light within which shows me the little Quaker artist, Ben West, and Isaac Newton with his windmill, and stubborn Sam Johnson, and stout Noll Cromwell, and shrewd Ben Franklin, and little Queen Christina, with the Swedes kneeling at her feet. It seems as if I really saw these personages face to face. So I can bear the darkness outside of me pretty well."

When Edward ceased speaking, Emily put up her mouth and kissed him as her farewell for the night.

"Ah, I forgot!" said Edward, with a sigh. "I cannot see any of your faces. What would it signify to see all the famous people in the world, if I must be blind to the faces that I love?"

"You must try to see us with your heart, my dear child," said his mother.

Edward went to bed somewhat dispirited; but, quickly falling asleep, was visited with such a pleasant dream of the sunshine and of his dearest friends that he felt the happier for it all the next day. And we hope to find him still happy when we meet again.

# BIOGRAPHICAL SKETCHES.

# BIOGRAPHICAL SKETCHES.

## MRS. HUTCHINSON.

THE character of this female suggests a train of thought which will form as natural an Introduction to her story, as most of the Prefaces to Gay's Fables, or the tales of Prior; besides that, the general soundness of the moral may excuse any want of present applicability. We will not look for a living resemblance of Mrs. Hutchinson, though the search might not be altogether fruitless. But there are portentous indications, changes gradually taking place in the habits and feelings of the gentle sex, which seem to threaten our posterity with many of those public women, whereof one was a burden too grievous for our fathers. The press, however, is now the medium through which feminine ambition chiefly manifests itself; and we will not anticipate the period (trusting to be gone hence ere it arrive) when fair orators shall be as numerous as the fair authors of our own day. The hastiest glance may show how much of the texture and body of cisatlantic literature is the work of those slender fingers from which only a light and fanciful embroidery has heretofore been required, that might sparkle upon the garment without enfeebling the web. Woman's intellect should never give the tone to that of man; and even her morality is not exactly the material for masculine virtue. A false liberality, which mistakes the strong division-lines of Nature for arbitrary distinctions, and a courtesy, which might polish criticism, but should never soften it, have done their best to add a girlish feebleness to the tottering infancy of our literature. The evil is likely to be a growing one. As yet, the great body of American women are a domestic race ; but when a continuance of ill-judged incitements shall have turned their hearts away from the fireside, there are obvious circumstances which will render female pens more numerous and more prolific than those of men, though but equally encouraged; and (limited, of course, by the scanty support of the public, but increasing indefinitely within those limits) the ink-stained Amazons will expel their rivals by actual pressure, and petticoats wave triumphantly over all the field. But, allowing that such forebodings are slightly exaggerated, is it good for woman's self that the path of feverish hope, of tremulous success, of bitter and ignominious disappointment, should be left wide open to her? Is the prize worth her having if she win it? Fame does not increase the peculiar respect which men pay to female excellence, and there is a delicacy (even in rude bosoms, where few would think to find it) that perceives, or fancies, a sort of impropriety in the display of woman's natal mind to the gaze of the world, with indications by which its inmost secrets may be searched out. In fine, criticism should examine with a stricter, instead of a more indulgent eye, the merits of females at its bar, because they are to justify themselves for an irregularity which men do not commit in appearing there ; and woman, when she feels the impulse of genius like a command of Heaven within her, should be aware that she is relinquishing a part of the loveliness of her sex, and obey the inward voice with sorrowing reluctance, like the Arabian maid who bewailed the gift of prophecy. Hinting thus imperfectly at sentiments which may be developed on a future occasion, we proceed to consider the celebrated subject of this sketch.

Mrs. Hutchinson was a woman of extraordinary talent and strong imagination, whom the latter quality, following the general direction taken by the enthusiasm of the times, prompted to stand forth as a reformer in religion. In her native country, she had shown symptoms of irregular and daring thought, but, chiefly by the influence of a favorite pastor, was restrained from open indiscretion. On the removal of this clergyman, becoming dissatisfied with the ministry under which she lived, she was drawn in by the great tide of Puritan emigration, and visited Massachusetts within a few years after its first settlement. But she bore trouble in her own bosom, and could find no peace in this chosen land. She soon began to promulgate strange and dangerous opinions, tending, in the peculiar situation of the colony, and from the principles which were its basis and indispensable for its temporary support, to eat into its very existence. We shall endeavor to give a more practical idea of this part of her course.

It is a summer evening. The dusk has settled heavily upon the woods, the waves, and the Trimountain peninsula, increasing that dismal aspect of the embryo town which was said to have drawn tears of despondency from Mrs. Hutchinson, though she believed that her mission thither was divine. The houses, straw thatched and lowly roofed, stand irregularly along streets that are yet roughened by the roots of the trees, as if the forest, departing at the approach of man, had left its reluctant footprints behind. Most of the dwellings are lonely and silent : from a few we may hear the reading of some sacred text, or the quiet voice of prayer; but nearly all the sombre life of the scene is collected near the extremity of the village. A crowd of hooded women, and of men in steeple-hats and close-cropped hair, are assembled at the door and open windows of a house newly built. An earnest expression glows in every face ; and some press inward, as if the bread of life were to be dealt forth, and they feared to lose their share ; while others would fain hold them back, but enter with them, since they may not be restrained. We, also, will go in, edging through the thronged doorway to an apartment which occupies the whole breadth of the house. At the upper end, behind a table, on which are placed the Scriptures and two glimmering lamps, we see a woman, plainly attired, as befits her ripened years ; her hair, complexion, and eyes are dark, the latter somewhat dull and heavy, but kindling up with a gradual brightness. Let us look round upon the hearers. At her right hand, his countenance suiting well with the gloomy light which discovers it, stands Vane, the youthful governor preferred by a hasty judgment of the people over all the wise and hoary heads that had preceded him to New England. In his mysterious eyes we may read a dark enthusiasm, akin to that of the woman whose cause he has espoused, combined with a shrewd worldly foresight, which tells him that her doctrines will be productive of change and tumult, the elements of his power and delight. On her left, yet slightly drawn back, so as to evince a less decided support, is Cotton, no young and hot enthusiast, but a

mild, grave man in the decline of life, deep in all the
learning of the age, and sanctified in heart, and made
venerable in feature, by the long exercise of his holy
profession. He, also, is deceived by the strange fire
now laid upon the altar; and he alone among his
brethren is excepted in the denunciation of the new
apostle, as sealed and set apart by Heaven to the work
of the ministry. Others of the priesthood stand full
in front of the woman, striving to beat her down with
brows of wrinkled iron, and whispering sternly and
significantly among themselves as she unfolds her se-
ditious doctrines, and grows warm in their support.
Foremost is Hugh Peters, full of holy wrath, and
scarce containing himself from rushing forward to con-
vict her of damnable heresies. There, also, is Ward,
meditating a reply of empty puns, and quaint antith-
eses, and tinkling jests that puzzle us with nothing
but a sound. The audience are variously affected;
but none are indifferent. On the foreheads of the
aged, the mature, and strong-minded, you may generally read steadfast disapprobation, though here and
there is one whose faith seems shaken in those whom
he had trusted for years. The females, on the other
hand, are shuddering and weeping, and at times they
cast a desolate look of fear around them; while the
young men lean forward, fiery and impatient, fit in-
struments for whatever rash deed may be suggested.
And what is the eloquence that gives rise to all these
passions? The woman tells them (and cites texts
from the Holy Book to prove her words) that they
have put their trust in unregenerated and uncommis-
sioned men, and have followed them into the wilderness for nought. Therefore their hearts are turning
from those whom they had chosen to lead them to

heaven ; and they feel like children who have been en-
ticed far from home, and see the features of their
guides change all at once, assuming a fiendish shape
in some frightful solitude.

These proceedings of Mrs. Hutchinson could not
long be endured by the provincial government. The
present was a most remarkable case, in which religious
freedom was wholly inconsistent with public safety,
and where the principles of an illiberal age indicated
the very course which must have been pursued by
worldly policy and enlightened wisdom. Unity of
faith was the star that had guided these people over
the deep ; and a diversity of sects would either have
scattered them from the land to which they had as yet
so few attachments, or, perhaps, have excited a dimin-
utive civil war among those who had come so far to
worship together. The opposition to what may be
termed the Established Church had now lost its chief
support by the removal of Vane from office, and his
departure for England ; and Mr. Cotton began to have
that light in regard to his errors, which will sometimes
break in upon the wisest and most pious men, when
their opinions are unhappily discordant with those of
the powers that be. A synod, the first in New England, was speedily assembled, and pronounced its condemnation of the obnoxious doctrines. Mrs. Hutchinson was next summoned before the supreme civil tribunal, at which, however, the most eminent of the
clergy were present, and appear to have taken a very
active part as witnesses and advisers. We shall here
resume the more picturesque style of narration.

It is a place of humble aspect where the elders of
the people are met, sitting in judgment upon the dis-
turber of Israel. The floor of the low and narrow

hall is laid with planks hewn by the axe; the beams
of the roof still wear the rugged bark with which they
grew up in the forest; and the hearth is formed of
one broad, unhammered stone, heaped with logs that
roll their blaze and smoke up a chimney of wood and
clay. A sleety shower beats fitfully against the windows, driven by the November blast, which comes
howling onward from the northern desert, the boisterous and unwelcome herald of a New England winter.
Rude benches are arranged across the apartment, and
along its sides, occupied by men whose piety and learning might have entitled them to seats in those high
councils of the ancient church, whence opinions were
sent forth to confirm or supersede the gospel in the
belief of the whole world and of posterity. Here
are collected all those blessed fathers of the land, who
rank in our veneration next to the evangelists of Holy
Writ; and here, also, are many, unpurified from the
fiercest errors of the age, and ready to propagate the
religion of peace by violence. In the highest place
sits Winthrop, — a man by whom the innocent and
guilty might alike desire to be judged; the first con-
fiding in his integrity and wisdom, the latter hoping
in his mildness. Next is Endicott, who would stand
with his drawn sword at the gate of heaven, and resist
to the death all pilgrims thither, except they travelled
his own path. The infant eyes of one in this assembly
beheld the fagots blazing round the martyrs in Bloody
Mary's time; in later life he dwelt long at Leyden,
with the first who went from England for conscience'
sake; and now, in his weary age, it matters little
where he lies down to die. There are others whose
hearts were smitten in the high meridian of ambitious
hope, and whose dreams still tempt them with the

pomp of the Old World and the din of its crowded cities, gleaming and echoing over the deep. In the midst, and in the centre of all eyes, we see the woman. She stands loftily before her judges with a determined brow; and, unknown to herself, there is a flash of carnal pride half hidden in her eye, as she surveys the many learned and famous men whom her doctrines have put in fear. They question her; and her answers are ready and acute: she reasons with them shrewdly, and brings Scripture in support of every argument. The deepest controversialists of that scholastic day find here a woman, whom all their trained and sharpened intellects are inadequate to foil. But, by the excitement of the contest, her heart is made to rise and swell within her, and she bursts forth into eloquence. She tells them of the long unquietness which she had endured in England, perceiving the corruption of the Church, and yearning for a purer and more perfect light, and how, in a day of solitary prayer, that light was given. She claims for herself the peculiar power of distinguishing between the chosen of man and the sealed of Heaven, and affirms that her gifted eye can see the glory round the foreheads of saints, sojourning in their mortal state. She declares herself commissioned to separate the true shepherds from the false, and denounces present and future judgments on the land, if she be disturbed in her celestial errand. Thus the accusations are proved from her own mouth. Her judges hesitate, and some speak faintly in her defence; but, with a few dissenting voices, sentence is pronounced, bidding her go out from among them, and trouble the land no more.

Mrs. Hutchinson's adherents throughout the colony were now disarmed; and she proceeded to Rhode Island, an accustomed refuge for the exiles of Massachusetts in all seasons of persecution. Her enemies believed that the anger of Heaven was following her, of which Governor Winthrop does not disdain to record a notable instance, very interesting in a scientific point of view, but fitter for his old and homely narrative than for modern repetition. In a little time, also, she lost her husband, who is mentioned in history only as attending her footsteps, and whom we may conclude to have been (like most husbands of celebrated women) a mere insignificant appendage of his mightier wife. She now grew uneasy away from the Rhode Island colonists, whose liberality towards her, at an era when liberality was not esteemed a Christian virtue, probably arose from a comparative insolicitude on religious matters, more distasteful to Mrs. Hutchinson than even the uncompromising narrowness of the Puritans. Her final movement was to lead her family within the limits of the Dutch jurisdiction, where, having felled the trees of a virgin soil, she became herself the virtual head, civil and ecclesiastical, of a little colony.

Perhaps here she found the repose hitherto so vainly sought. Secluded from all whose faith she could not govern, surrounded by the dependants over whom she held an unlimited influence, agitated by none of the tumultuous billows which were left swelling behind her, we may suppose that, in the stillness of Nature, her heart was stilled. But her impressive story was to have an awful close. Her last scene is as difficult to be described as a shipwreck, where the shrieks of the victims die unheard, along a desolate sea, and a shapeless mass of agony is all that can be brought home to the imagination. The savage foe was on the watch for blood.  Sixteen persons assembled at the evening prayer: in the deep midnight their cry rang through the forest; and daylight dawned upon the lifeless clay of all but one.  It was a circumstance not to be unnoticed by our stern ancestors, in considering the fate of her who had so troubled their religion, that an infant daughter, the sole survivor amid the terrible destruction of her mother's household, was bred in a barbarous faith, and never learned the way to the Christian's heaven.  Yet we will hope that there the mother and child have met.

## SIR WILLIAM PHIPS.

FEW of the personages of past times (except such as have gained renown in fireside legends as well as in written history) are anything more than mere names to their successors. They seldom stand up in our imaginations like men. The knowledge communicated by the historian and biographer is analogous to that which we acquire of a country by the map, — minute, perhaps, and accurate, and available for all necessary purposes, but cold and naked, and wholly destitute of the mimic charm produced by landscape-painting. These defects are partly remediable, and even without an absolute violation of literal truth, although by methods rightfully interdicted to professors of biographical exactness. A license must be assumed in brightening the materials which time has rusted, and in tracing out half-obliterated inscriptions on the columns of antiquity : Fancy must throw her reviving light on the faded incidents that indicate character, whence a ray will be reflected, more or less vividly, on the person to be described. The portrait of the ancient governor whose name stands at the head of this article will owe any interest it may possess, not to his internal self, but to certain peculiarities of his fortune. These must be briefly noticed.

The birth and early life of Sir William Phips were rather an extraordinary prelude to his subsequent distinction. He was one of the twenty-six children of a gunsmith, who exercised his trade — where hunting

and war must have given it a full encouragement—
in a small frontier settlement near the mouth of the
river Kennebec. Within the boundaries of the Puritan provinces, and wherever those governments extended an effectual sway, no depth nor solitude of the
wilderness could exclude youth from all the common
opportunities of moral, and far more than common
ones of religious education. Each settlement of the
Pilgrims was a little piece of the Old World inserted
into the New. It was like Gideon's fleece, unwet with
dew: the desert wind that breathed over it left none
of its wild influences there. But the first settlers of
Maine and New Hampshire were led thither entirely
by carnal motives: their governments were feeble, uncertain, sometimes nominally annexed to their sister
colonies, and sometimes asserting a troubled independence. Their rulers might be deemed, in more than
one instance, lawless adventurers, who found that security in the forest which they had forfeited in Europe. Their clergy (unlike that revered band who
acquired so singular a fame elsewhere in New England) were too often destitute of the religious fervor
which should have kept them in the track of virtue, un-
aided by the restraints of human law and the dread of
worldly dishonor; and there are records of lamentable
lapses on the part of those holy men, which, if we may
argue the disorder of the sheep from the unfitness of
the shepherd, tell a sad tale as to the morality of the
eastern provinces. In this state of society, the future
governor grew up; and many years after, sailing with
a fleet and an army to make war upon the French,
he pointed out the very hills where he had reached
the age of manhood, unskilled even to read and write.
The contrast between the commencement and close of

his life was the effect of casual circumstances. During a considerable time, he was a mariner, at a period when there was much license on the high-seas. After attaining to some rank in the English navy, he heard of an ancient Spanish wreck off the coast of Hispaniola, of such mighty value, that, according to the stories of the day, the sunken gold might be seen to glisten, and the diamonds to flash, as the triumphant billows tossed about their spoil. These treasures of the deep (by the aid of certain noblemen who claimed the lion's share) Sir William Phips sought for, and recovered, and was sufficiently enriched, even after an honest settlement with the partners of his adventure. That the land might give him honor, as the sea had given him wealth, he received knighthood from King James. Returning to New England, he professed repentance of his sins (of which, from the nature both of his early and more recent life, there could scarce fail to be some slight accumulation), was baptized, and, on the accession of the Prince of Orange to the throne, became the first governor under the second charter. And now, having arranged these preliminaries, we shall attempt to picture forth a day of Sir William's life, introducing no very remarkable events, because history supplies us with none such convertible to our purpose.

It is the forenoon of a day in summer, shortly after the governor's arrival; and he stands upon his door-steps, preparatory to a walk through the metropolis. Sir William is a stout man, an inch or two below the middle size, and rather beyond the middle point of life. His dress is of velvet, — a dark purple, broadly embroidered; and his sword-hilt and the lion's head of his cane display specimens of the gold from the

Spanish wreck. On his head, in the fashion of the court of Louis XIV., is a superb, full-bottomed periwig, amid whose heap of ringlets his face shows like a rough pebble in the setting that befits a diamond. Just emerging from the door are two footmen, — one an African slave of shining ebony, the other an English bond-servant, the property of the governor for a term of years. As Sir William comes down the steps, he is met by three elderly gentlemen in black, grave and solemn as three tombstones on a ramble from the burying-ground. These are ministers of the town, among whom we recognize Dr. Increase Mather, the late provincial agent at the English court, the author of the present governor's appointment, and the right arm of his administration. Here follow many bows and a deal of angular politeness on both sides. Sir William professes his anxiety to reënter the house, and give audience to the reverend gentlemen: they, on the other hand, cannot think of interrupting his walk; and the courteous dispute is concluded by a junction of the parties; Sir William and Dr. Mather setting forth side by side, the two other clergymen forming the centre of the column, and the black and white footmen bringing up the rear. The business in hand relates to the dealings of Satan in the town of Salem. Upon this subject, the principal ministers of the province have been consulted; and these three eminent persons are their deputies, commissioned to express a doubtful opinion, implying, upon the whole, an exhortation to speedy and vigorous measures against the accused. To such counsels Sir William, bred in the forest and on the ocean, and tinctured with the superstition of both, is well inclined to listen.

As the dignitaries of Church and State make their

way beneath the overhanging houses, the lattices are thrust ajar, and you may discern, just in the boundaries of light and shade, the prim faces of the little Puritan damsels, eying the magnificent governor, and envious of the bolder curiosity of the men. Another object of almost equal interest now appears in the middle of the way. It is a man clad in a hunting-shirt and Indian stockings, and armed with a long gun. His feet have been wet with the waters of many an inland lake and stream ; and the leaves and twigs of the tangled wilderness are intertwined with his garments : on his head he wears a trophy which we would not venture to record without good evidence of the fact, — a wig made of the long and straight black hair of his slain savage enemies. This grim old heathen stands bewildered in the midst of King Street. The governor regards him attentively, and, recognizing a playmate of his youth, accosts him with a gracious smile, inquires as to the prosperity of their birthplace, and the life or death of their ancient neighbors, and makes appropriate remarks on the different stations allotted by fortune to two individuals born and bred beside the same wild river. Finally he puts into his hand, at parting, a shilling of the Massachusetts coinage, stamped with the figure of a stubbed pine-tree, mistaken by King Charles for the oak, which saved his royal life. Then all the people praise the humility and bountifulness of the good governor, who struts onward flourishing his gold-headed cane ; while the gentleman in the straight black wig is left with a pretty accurate idea of the distance between himself and his old companion.

Meantime, Sir William steers his course towards the town dock. A gallant figure is seen approaching on

the opposite side of the street, in a naval uniform profusely laced, and with a cutlass swinging by his side.
This is Captain Short, the commander of a frigate in
the service of the English king, now lying in the harbor. Sir William bristles up at sight of him, and
crosses the street with a lowering front, unmindful of
the hints of Dr. Mather, who is aware of an unsettled
dispute between the captain and the governor, relative
to the authority of the latter over a king's ship on the
provincial station. Into this thorny subject, Sir William plunges headlong. The captain makes answer
with less deference than the dignity of the potentate
requires : the affair grows hot ; and the clergymen endeavor to interfere in the blessed capacity of peace-
makers. The governor lifts his cane ; and the captain lays his hand upon his sword, but is prevented
from drawing by the zealous exertions of Dr. Mather.
There is a furious stamping of feet, and a mighty uproar from every mouth, in the midst of which his Ex-
cellency inflicts several very sufficient whacks on the
head of the unhappy Short. Having thus avenged
himself by manual force, as befits a woodman and a
mariner, he vindicates the insulted majesty of the governor by committing his antagonist to prison. This
done, Sir William removes his periwig, wipes away
the sweat of the encounter, and gradually composes
himself, giving vent to a few oaths, like the subsiding
ebullitions of a pot that has boiled over.

It being now near twelve o'clock, the three ministers
are bidden to dinner at the governor's table, where the
party is completed by a few Old Charter senators, —
men reared at the feet of the Pilgrims, and who remember the days when Cromwell was a nursing-father
to New England. Sir William presides with com-

mendable decorum till grace is said and the cloth removed. Then, as the grape-juice glides warm into
the ventricles of his heart, it produces a change, like
that of a running stream upon enchanted shapes ; and
the rude man of the sea and wilderness appears in the
very chair where the stately governor sat down. He
overflows with jovial tales of the forecastle and of his
father's hut, and stares to see the gravity of his guests
become more and more portentous in exact proportion
as his own merriment increases. A noise of drum and
fife fortunately breaks up the session.

The governor and his guests go forth, like men
bound upon some grave business, to inspect the train-
bands of the town. A great crowd of people is collected on the Common, composed of whole families,
from the hoary grandsire to the child of three years.
All ages and both sexes look with interest on the array of their defenders ; and here and there stand a
few dark Indians in their blankets, dull spectators of
the strength that has swept away their race. The soldiers wear a proud and martial mien, conscious that
beauty will reward them with her approving glances ;
not to mention that there are a few less influential motives to contribute to keep up an heroic spirit, such as
the dread of being made to " ride the wooden horse "
(a very disagreeable mode of equestrian exercise, —
hard riding, in the strictest sense), or of being " laid
neck and heels," in a position of more compendious-
ness than comfort. Sir William perceives some error
in their tactics, and places himself with drawn sword
at their head. After a variety of weary evolutions,
evening begins to fall, like the veil of gray and misty
years that have rolled betwixt that warlike band and

us. They are drawn into a hollow square, the officers in the centre; and the governor (for John Dunton's authority will bear us out in this particular) leans his hands upon his sword-hilt, and closes the exercises of the day with a prayer.

## SIR WILLIAM PEPPERELL.

THE mighty man of Kittery has a double claim to remembrance. He was a famous general, the most prominent military character in our ante-Revolutionary annals; and he may be taken as the representative of a class of warriors peculiar to their age and country, — true citizen-soldiers, who diversified a life of commerce or agriculture by the episode of a city sacked, or a battle won, and, having stamped their names on the page of history, went back to the routine of peaceful occupation. Sir William Pepperell's letters, written at the most critical period of his career, and his conduct then and at other times, indicate a man of plain good sense, with a large share of quiet resolution, and but little of an enterprising spirit, unless aroused by external circumstances. The Methodistic principles, with which he was slightly tinctured, instead of impelling him to extravagance, assimilated themselves to his orderly habits of thought and action. Thus respectably endowed, we find him, when near the age of fifty, a merchant of weight in foreign and domestic trade, a provincial counsellor, and colonel of the York County militia, filling a large space in the eyes of his generation, but likely to gain no other posthumous memorial than the letters on his tombstone, because undistinguished from the many worshipful gentlemen who had lived prosperously and died peacefully before him. But in the year 1745, an expedition was projected against Louisburg, a walled city of the

French in the island of Cape Breton. The idea of reducing this strong fortress was conceived by William Vaughan, a bold, energetic, and imaginative adventurer, and adopted by Governor Shirley, the most bustling, though not the wisest, ruler, that ever presided over Massachusetts. His influence at its utmost stretch carried the measure by a majority of only one vote in the legislature : the other New England provinces consented to lend their assistance ; and the next point was to select a commander from among the gentlemen of the country, none of whom had the least particle of scientific soldiership, although some were experienced in the irregular warfare of the frontiers. In the absence of the usual qualifications for military rank, the choice was guided by other motives, and fell upon Colonel Pepperell, who, as a landed proprietor in three provinces, and popular with all classes of people, might draw the greatest number of recruits to his banner. When this doubtful speculation was proposed to the prudent merchant, he sought advice from the celebrated Whitefield, then an itinerant preacher in the country, and an object of vast antipathy to many of the settled ministers. The response of the apostle of Methodism, though dark as those of the Oracle of Delphos, intimating that the blood of the slain would be laid to Colonel Pepperell's charge in case of failure, and that the envy of the living would persecute him if victorious, decided him to gird on his armor. That the French might be taken unawares, the legislature had been laid under an oath of secrecy while their deliberations should continue ; this precaution, however, was nullified by the pious perjury of a country member of the lower house, who, in the performance of domestic worship at his lodgings, broke into a fervent and involuntary petition for the success of the enterprise against Louisburg. We of the present generation, whose hearts have never been heated and amalgamated by one universal passion, and who are, perhaps, less excitable in the mass than our fathers, cannot easily conceive the enthusiasm with which the people seized upon the project. A desire to prove in the eyes of England the courage of her provinces; the real necessity for the destruction of this Dunkirk of America; the hope of private advantage; a remnant of the old Puritan detestation of Papist idolatry; a strong hereditary hatred of the French, who, for half a hundred years, had shed the blood of the English settlers in concert with the savages; the natural proneness of the New-Englanders to engage in temporary undertakings, even though doubtful and hazardous, — such were some of the motives which soon drew together a host, comprehending nearly all the effective force of the country. The officers were grave deacons, justices of the peace, and other similar dignitaries; and in the ranks were many warm householders, sons of rich farmers, mechanics in thriving business, husbands weary of their wives, and bachelors disconsolate for want of them. The disciples of Whitefield also turned their excited imaginations in this direction, and increased the resemblance borne by the provincial army to the motley assemblages of the first Crusaders. A part of the peculiarities of the affair may be grouped in one picture, by selecting the moment of General Pepperell's embarkation.

It is a bright and breezy day of March; and about twenty small white clouds are scudding seaward before the wind, airy forerunners of the fleet of privateers and transports that spread their sails to the sunshine in the

harbor. The tide is at its height; and the gunwale of a
barge alternately rises above the wharf, and then sinks
from view, as it lies rocking on the waves in readiness
to convey the general and his suite on board the Shirley galley. In the background, the dark wooden dwellings of the town have poured forth their inhabitants ;
and this way rolls an earnest throng, with the great
man of the day walking in the midst. Before him
struts a guard of honor, selected from the yeomanry
of his own neighborhood, and stout young rustics in
their Sunday clothes; next appear six figures who demand our more minute attention. He in the centre is
the general, a well-proportioned man, with a slight
hoar-frost of age just visible upon him ; he views the
fleet in which he is about to embark with no stronger
expression than a calm anxiety, as if he were sending
a freight of his own merchandise to Europe. A scarlet British uniform, made of the best of broadcloth, because imported by himself, adorns his person ; and in
the left pocket of a large buff waistcoat, near the pommel of his sword, we see the square protuberance of
a small Bible, which certainly may benefit his pious
soul, and, perchance, may keep a bullet from his body.
The middle-aged gentleman at his right hand, to whom
he pays such grave attention, in silk, gold, and velvet,
and with a pair of spectacles thrust above his forehead, is Governor Shirley. The quick motion of his
small eyes in their puckered sockets, his grasp on one
of the general's bright military buttons, the gesticulation of his forefinger, keeping time with the earnest
rapidity of his words, have all something characteristic. His mind is calculated to fill up the wild conceptions of other men with its own minute ingenuities ;
and he seeks, as it were, to climb up to the moon by

piling pebble-stones one upon another. He is now impressing on the general's recollection the voluminous
details of a plan for surprising Louisburg in the depth
of midnight, and thus to finish the campaign within
twelve hours after the arrival of the troops. On the
left, forming a striking contrast with the unruffled deportment of Pepperell, and the fidgety vehemence of
Shirley, is the martial figure of Vaughan : with one
hand he has seized the general's arm ; and he points
the other to the sails of the vessel fluttering in the
breeze, while the fire of his inward enthusiasm glows
through his dark complexion, and flashes in tips of
flame from his eyes. Another pale and emaciated person, in neglected and scarcely decent attire, and distinguished by the abstracted fervor of his manner, presses
through the crowd, and attempts to lay hold of Pepperell's skirt. He has spent years in wild and shadowy studies, and has searched the crucible of the alche-
mist for gold, and wasted the life allotted him, in a
weary effort to render it immortal. The din of warlike preparation has broken in upon his solitude; and
he comes forth with a fancy of his half-maddened
brain, — the model of a flying bridge, — by which the
army is to be transported into the heart of the hostile
fortress with the celerity of magic. But who is this,
of the mild and venerable countenance shaded by locks
of a hallowed whiteness, looking like Peace with its
gentle thoughts in the midst of uproar and stern designs ? It is the minister of an inland parish, who,
after much prayer and fasting, advised by the elders
of the church and the wife of his bosom, has taken
his staff, and journeyed townward. The benevolent
old man would fain solicit the general's attention to
a method of avoiding danger from the explosion of

mines, and of overcoming the city without bloodshed
of friend or enemy. We start as we turn from this
picture of Christian love to the dark enthusiast close
beside him, — a preacher of the new sect, in every
wrinkled line of whose visage we can read the stormy
passions that have chosen religion for their outlet.
Woe to the wretch that shall seek mercy there! At
his back is slung an axe, wherewith he goes to hew
down the carved altars and idolatrous images in the
Popish churches; and over his head he rears a banner, which, as the wind unfolds it, displays the motto
given by Whitefield, — Christo Duce, — in letters red
as blood. But the tide is now ebbing; and the general makes his adieus to the governor, and enters the
boat: it bounds swiftly over the waves, the holy banner fluttering in the bows: a huzza from the fleet
comes riotously to the shore ; and the people thunder
back their many-voiced reply.

When the expedition sailed, the projectors could not
reasonably rely on assistance from the mother-country.
At Canso, however, the fleet was strengthened by a
squadron of British ships-of-the-line and frigates, under Commodore Warren; and this circumstance undoubtedly prevented a discomfiture, although the active
business, and all the dangers of the siege, fell to the
share of the provincials. If we had any confidence
that it could be done with half so much pleasure to
the reader as to ourself, we would present a whole gallery of pictures from these rich and fresh historic
scenes. Never, certainly, since man first indulged his
instinctive appetite for war, did a queerer and less
manageable host sit down before a hostile city. The
officers, drawn from the same class of citizens with the
rank and file, had neither the power to institute an

awful discipline, nor enough of the trained soldier's spirit to attempt it. Of headlong valor, when occasion offered, there was no lack, nor of a readiness to encounter severe fatigue ; but, with few intermissions, the provincial army made the siege one long day of frolic and disorder. Conscious that no military virtues of their own deserved the prosperous result which followed, they insisted that Heaven had fought as manifestly on their side as ever on that of Israel in the battles of the Old Testament. We, however, if we consider the events of after-years, and confine our view to a period short of the Revolution, might doubt whether the victory was granted to our fathers as a blessing or as a judgment. Most of the young men who had left their paternal firesides, sound in constitution, and pure in morals, if they returned at all, returned with ruined health, and with minds so broken up by the interval of riot, that they never after could resume the habits of good citizenship. A lust for military glory was also awakened in the country ; and France and England gratified it with enough of slaughter ; the former seeking to recover what she had lost, the latter to complete the conquest which the colonists had begun. There was a brief season of repose, and then a fiercer contest, raging almost from end to end of North America. Some went forth, and met the red men of the wilderness ; and when years had rolled, and the settler came in peace where they had come in war, there he found their unburied bones among the fallen boughs and withered leaves of many autumns. Others were foremost in the battles of the Canadas, till, in the day that saw the downfall of the French dominion, they poured their blood with Wolfe on the Heights of Abraham. Through all this troubled time, the flower of the youth were cut down by the sword, or died of physical diseases, or became unprofitable citizens—by moral ones contracted in the camp and field. Dr. Douglass, a shrewd Scotch physician of the last century, who died before war had gathered in half its harvest, computes that many thousand blooming damsels, capable and well inclined to serve the state as wives and mothers, were compelled to lead lives of barren celibacy by the consequences of the successful siege of Louisburg. But we will not sadden ourselves with these doleful thoughts, when we are to witness the triumphal entry of the victors into the surrendered town.

The thundering of drums, irregularly beaten, grows more and more distinct, and the shattered strength of the western wall of Louisburg stretches out before the eye, forty feet in height, and far overtopped by a rock-built citadel. In yonder breach the broken timber, fractured stones, and crumbling earth prove the effect of the provincial cannon. The drawbridge is down over the wide moat; the gate is open; and the general and British commodore are received by the French authorities beneath the dark and lofty portal arch. Through the massive gloom of this deep avenue there is a vista of the main street, bordered by high peaked houses, in the fashion of old France; the view is terminated by the centre square of the city, in the midst of which rises a stone cross; and shaven monks, and women with their children, are kneeling at its foot. A confused sobbing and half-stifled shrieks are heard, as the tumultuous advance of the conquering army becomes audible to those within the walls. By the light which falls through the archway, we perceive that a few months have somewhat changed the general's mien, giving it the freedom of one acquainted with peril, and accustomed to command; nor, amid hopes of more solid reward, does he appear insensible to the thought that posterity will remember his name among those renowned in arms. Sir Peter Warren, who receives with him the enemy's submission, is a rough and haughty English seaman, greedy of fame, but despising those who have won it for him. Pressing forward to the portal, sword in hand, comes a comical figure in a brown suit, and blue yarn stockings, with a huge frill sticking forth from his bosom, to which the whole man seems an appendage: this is that famous worthy of Plymouth County, who went to the war with two plain shirts and a ruffled one, and is now about to solicit the post of governor in Louisburg. In close vicinity stands Vaughan, worn down with toil and exposure, the effect of which has fallen upon him at once in the moment of accomplished hope. The group is filled up by several British officers, who fold their arms, and look with scornful merriment at the provincial army, as it stretches far behind in garments of every hue, resembling an immense strip of patchwork carpeting thrown down over the uneven ground. In the nearer ranks we may discern the variety of ingredients that compose the mass. Here advance a row of stern, unmitigable fanatics, each of whom clinches his teeth, and grasps his weapon with a fist of iron, at sight of the temples of the ancient faith, with the sunlight glittering on their cross-crowned spires. Others examine the surrounding country, and send scrutinizing glances through the gateway, anxious to select a spot, whither the good woman and her little ones in the Bay Province may be advantageously transported. Some, who drag their diseased limbs forward in weariness and pain, have made the wretched exchange of health or life for what share of fleeting glory may fall to them among four thousand men. But these are all exceptions, and the exulting feelings of the general host combine in an expression like that of a broad laugh on an honest countenance. They roll onward riotously, flourishing their muskets above their heads, shuffling their heavy heels into an instinctive dance, and roaring out some holy verse from the New England Psalmody, or those harsh old warlike stanzas which tell the story of "Lovell's Fight." Thus they pour along, till the battered town and the rabble of its conquerors, and the shouts, the drums, the singing, and the laughter, grow dim, and die away from Fancy's eye and ear.

The arms of Great Britain were not crowned by a more brilliant achievement during that unprosperous war; and, in adjusting the terms of a subsequent peace, Louisburg was an equivalent for many losses nearer home. The English, with very pardonable vanity, attributed the conquest chiefly to the valor of the naval force. On the Continent of Europe, our fathers met with greater justice, and Voltaire has ranked this enterprise of the husbandmen of New England among the most remarkable events in the reign of Louis XV. The ostensible leaders did not fail of reward. Shirley, originally a lawyer, was commissioned in the regular army, and rose to the supreme military command in America. Warren, also, received honors and professional rank, and arrogated to himself, without scruple, the whole crop of laurels gathered at Louisburg. Pepperell was placed at the head of a royal regiment, and, first of his countrymen, was distinguished by the title of baronet. Vaughan alone, who had been soul of the deed from its adventurous conception till the triumphant close, and in every danger and every hardship had exhibited a rare union of ardor and perseverance, — Vaughan was entirely neglected, and died in London, whither he had gone to make known his claims. After the great era of his life, Sir William Pepperell did not distinguish himself either as a warrior or a statesman. He spent the remainder of his days in all the pomp of a colonial grandee, and laid down his aristocratic head among the humbler ashes of his fathers, just before the commencement of the earliest troubles between England and America.

# THOMAS GREEN FESSENDEN.

THOMAS GREEN FESSENDEN was the eldest of nine children of the Rev. Thomas Fessenden. He was born on the 22d of April, 1771, at Walpole, in New Hampshire, where his father, a man of learning and talent, was long settled in the ministry. On the maternal side, likewise, he was of clerical extraction; his mother, whose piety and amiable qualities are remembered by her descendants, being the daughter of the Rev. Samuel Kendal, of New Salem. The early education of Thomas Green was chiefly at the common school of his native place, under the tuition of students from the college at Hanover; and such was his progress, that he became himself the instructor of a school in New Salem at the age of sixteen. He spent most of his youthful days, however, in bodily labor upon the farm, thus contributing to the support of a numerous family; and the practical knowledge of agriculture which he then obtained was long afterwards applied to the service of the public. Opportunities for cultivating his mind were afforded him, not only in his father's library, but by the more miscellaneous contents of a large bookstore. He had passed the age of twenty-one when his inclination for mental pursuits determined him to become a student at Dartmouth College. His father being able to give but little assistance, his chief resources at college consisted in his wages as teacher of a village school during the vacations. At times, also, he gave instruction to an evening class in psalmody.

From his childhood upward, Mr. Fessenden had shown symptoms of that humorous turn which afterwards so strongly marked his writings; but his first effort in verse, as he himself told me, was made during his residence at college. The themes, or exercises, of his fellow-students in English composition, whether prose or rhyme, were well characterized by the lack of native thought and feeling, the cold pedantry, the mimicry of classic models, common to all such productions. Mr. Fessenden had the good taste to disapprove of these vapid and spiritless performances, and resolved to strike out a new course for himself. On one occasion, when his classmates had gone through with their customary round of verbiage and threadbare sentiment, he electrified them and their instructor, President Wheelock, by reading "Jonathan's Courtship." There has never, to this day, been produced by any of our countrymen a more original and truly Yankee effusion. He had caught the rare art of sketching familiar manners, and of throwing into verse the very spirit of society as it existed around him; and he had imbued each line with a peculiar yet perfectly natural and homely humor. This excellent ballad compels me to regret, that, instead of becoming a satirist in politics and science, and wasting his strength on temporary and evanescent topics, he had not continued to be a rural poet. A volume of such sketches as "Jonathan's Courtship," describing various aspects of life among the yeomanry of New England, could not have failed to gain a permanent place in American literature. The effort in question met with unexampled success: it ran through the newspapers of the day, reappeared on the other side of the Atlantic, and was warmly applauded by the English critics, nor has it yet lost its popularity. New editions may be found every year at the ballad-stalls; and I saw last summer, on the veteran author's table, a broadside copy of his maiden poem, which he had himself bought in the street.

Mr. Fessenden passed through college with a fair reputation for scholarship, and took his degree in 1796. It had been his father's wish that he should imitate the example of some of his ancestors on both sides, by devoting himself to the ministry. He, however, preferred the law, and commenced the study of that profession at Rutland, in Vermont, with Nathaniel Chipman, then the most eminent practitioner in the State. After his admission to the bar, Mr. Chipman received him into partnership. But Mr. Fessenden was ill qualified to succeed in the profession of law, by his simplicity of character, and his utter inability to acquire an ordinary share of shrewdness and worldly wisdom. Moreover, the success of "Jonathan's Courtship," and other poetical effusions, had turned his thoughts from law to literature, and had procured him the acquaintance of several literary luminaries of those days; none of whose names, probably, have survived to our own generation, save that of Joseph Dennie, once esteemed the finest writer in America. His intercourse with these people tempted Mr. Fessenden to spend much time in writing for newspapers and periodicals. A taste for scientific pursuits still further diverted him from his legal studies, and soon engaged him in an affair which influenced the complexion of all his after-life.

A Mr. Langdon had brought forward a newly invented hydraulic machine, which was supposed to possess the power of raising water to a greater height than had hitherto been considered possible. A company of mechanics and others became interested in this machine, and appointed Mr. Fessenden their agent for the purpose of obtaining a patent in London. He was, likewise, a member of the company. Mr. Fessenden was urged to hasten his departure, in consequence of a report that certain persons had acquired the secret of the invention, and were determined to anticipate the proprietors in securing a patent. Scarcely time was allowed for testing the efficacy of the machine by a few hasty experiments, which, however, appeared satisfactory. Taking passage immediately, Mr. Fessenden arrived in London on the 4th of July, 1801, and waited on Mr. King, then our minister, by whom he was introduced to Mr. Nicholson, a gentleman of eminent scientific reputation. After thoroughly examining the invention, Mr. Nicholson gave an opinion unfavorable to its merits; and the question was soon settled by a letter from one of the Vermont proprietors to Mr. Fessenden, informing him that the apparent advantages of the machine had been found altogether deceptive. In short, Mr. Fessenden had been lured from his profession and country by as empty a bubble as that of the perpetual motion. Yet it is creditable both to his ability and energy, that, laying hold of what was really valuable in Langdon's contrivance, he constructed the model of a machine for raising water from coal-mines, and other great depths, by means of what he termed the "renovated pressure of the atmosphere." On communicating this invention to Mr. Nicholson and other eminent mechanicians, they acknowledged its originality and ingenuity, and thought that, in some situations, it might be useful. But the expenses of a patent in England, the difficulty of obtaining patronage for such a project, and the uncertainty of the result, were obstacles too weighty to be overcome. Mr. Fessenden threw aside the scheme, and, after a two months' residence in London, was preparing to return home, when a new and characteristic adventure arrested him.

He received a visit, at his lodging in the Strand, from a person whom he had never before seen, but who introduced himself to his good-will as being likewise an American. His business was of a nature well calculated to excite Mr. Fessenden's interest. He produced the model of an ingenious contrivance for grinding corn. A patent had already been obtained ; and a company, with the Lord Mayor of London at its head, was associated for the construction of mills upon this new principle. The inventor, according to his own story, had disposed of one fourth part of his patent for five hundred pounds, and was willing to accommodate his countryman with another fourth. After some inquiry into the stranger's character and the accuracy of his statements, Mr. Fessenden became a purchaser of the share that was offered him; on what terms is not stated, but probably such as to involve his whole property in the adventure. The result was disastrous. The lord mayor soon withdrew his countenance from the project. It ultimately appeared that Mr. Fessenden was the only real purchaser of any part of the patent ; and, as the original patentee shortly afterwards quitted the concern, the former was left to manage the business as he best could. With a perseverance not less characteristic than his credulity, he associated himself with four partners, and undertook to superintend the construction of one of these patent-mills upon the Thames. But his associates, who were

men of no respectability, thwarted his plans; and after much toil of body, as well as distress of mind, he
found himself utterly ruined, friendless and penniless,
in the midst of London. No other event could have
been anticipated, when a man so devoid of guile was
thrown among a set of crafty adventurers.

Being now in the situation in which many a literary
man before him had been, he remembered the success
of his fugitive poems, and betook himself to the pen
as his most natural resource. A subject was offered
him, in which no other poet would have found a theme
for the Muse. It seemed to be his fatality to form
connections with schemers of all sorts; and he had become acquainted with Benjamin Douglas Perkins, the
patentee of the famous metallic tractors. These im-
plements were then in great vogue for the cure of in-
flammatory diseases, by removing the superfluous electricity. Perkinism, as the doctrine of metallic tractors
was styled, had some converts among scientific men,
and many among the people, but was violently opposed
by the regular corps of physicians and surgeons. Mr.
Fessenden, as might be expected, was a believer in the
efficacy of the tractors, and, at the request of Perkins,
consented to make them the subject of a poem in Hu-
dibrastic verse, the satire of which was to be levelled
against their opponents. "Terrible Tractoration" was
the result. It professes to be a poetical petition from
Dr. Christopher Caustic, a medical gentleman who has
been ruined by the success of the metallic tractors,
and who applies to the Royal College of Physicians
for relief and redress. The wits of the poor doctor
have been somewhat shattered by his misfortunes;
and, with crazy ingenuity, he contrives to heap ridicule on his medical brethren, under pretence of rail-

ing against Perkinism. The poem is in four cantos, the first of which is the best, and the most characteristic of the author. It is occupied with Dr. Caustic's description of his mechanical and scientific contrivances, embracing all sorts of possible and impossible projects; every one of which, however, has a ridiculous plausibility. The inexhaustible variety in which they flow forth proves the author's invention unrivalled in its way. It shows what had been the nature of Mr. Fessenden's mental toil during his residence in London, continually brooding over the miracles of mechanism and science, his enthusiasm for which had cost him so dear. Long afterwards, speaking of the first conception of this poem, the author told me that he had shaped it out during a solitary day's ramble in the outskirts of London; and the character of Dr. Caustic so strongly impressed itself on his mind, that, as he walked homeward through the crowded streets, he burst into frequent fits of laughter. The truth is, that, in the sketch of this wild projector, Mr. Fessenden had caricatured some of his own features; and, when he laughed so heartily, it was at the perception of the resemblance.

"Terrible Tractoration" is a work of strange and grotesque ideas aptly expressed : its rhymes are of a most singular character, yet fitting each to each as accurately as echoes. As in all Mr. Fessenden's productions, there is great exactness in the language ; the author's thoughts being thrown off as distinctly as impressions from a type. In regard to the pleasure to be derived from reading this poem, there is room for diversity of taste ; but that it is an original and remarkable work, no person competent to pass judgment on a literary question will deny. It was first published early in the year 1803, in an octavo pamphlet of above fifty pages. Being highly applauded by the principal reviews, and eagerly purchased by the public, a new edition appeared at the end of two months, in a volume of nearly two hundred pages, illustrated with engravings. It received the praise of Gifford, the severest of English critics. Its continued success encouraged the author to publish a volume of " Original Poems," consisting chiefly of his fugitive pieces from the American newspapers. This, also, was favorably received. He was now, what so few of his countrymen have ever been, a popular author in London ; and, in the midst of his triumphs, he bethought himself of his native land.

Mr. Fessenden returned to America in 1804. He came back poorer than he went, but with an honorable reputation, and with unstained integrity, although his evil fortune had connected him with men far unlike himself. His fame had preceded him across the Atlantic. Shortly before his arrival, an edition of " Terrible Tractoration " had been published at Philadelphia, with a prefatory memoir of the author, the tone of which proves that the American people felt themselves honored in the literary success of their countryman. Another edition appeared in New York, in 1806, considerably enlarged, with a new satire on the topics of the day. It is symptomatic of the course which the author had now adopted, that much of this new satire was directed against Democratic principles and the prominent upholders of them. This was soon followed by " Democracy Unveiled," a more elaborate attack on the same political party.

In "Democracy Unveiled," our friend Dr. Caustic appears as a citizen of the United States, and pours out six cantos of vituperative verse, with copious notes of the same tenor, on the heads of President Jefferson and his supporters. Much of the satire is unpardonably coarse. The literary merits of the work are inferior to those of " Terrible Tractoration ; " but it is no less original and peculiar. Even where the matter is a mere versification of newspaper slander, Dr Caustic's manner gives it an individuality not to be mistaken. The book passed through three editions in the course of a few months. Its most pungent portions were copied into all the opposition prints ; its strange, jog-trot stanzas were familiar to every ear ; and Mr. Fessenden may fairly be allowed the credit of having given expression to the feelings of the great Federal party.

On the 30th of August, 1806, Mr. Fessenden commenced the publication, at New York, of " The Weekly Inspector," a paper at first of eight, and afterwards of sixteen, octavo pages. It appeared every Saturday. The character of this journal was mainly political ; but there are also a few flowers and sweet-scented twigs of literature intermixed among the nettles and burrs, which alone flourish in the arena of party strife. Its columns are profusely enriched with scraps of satirical verse, in which Dr. Caustic, in his capacity of balladmaker to the Federal faction, spared not to celebrate every man or measure of government that was anywise susceptible of ridicule. Many of his prose articles are carefully and ably written, attacking not men so much as principles and measures ; and his deeply felt anxiety for the welfare of his country sometimes gives an impressive dignity to his thoughts and style. The dread of French domination seems to have haunted him like a nightmare. But, in spite of the editor's

satirical reputation, " The Weekly Inspector " was too
conscientious a paper, too sparingly spiced with the
red pepper of personal abuse, to succeed in those out-
rageous times. The publication continued but for a
single year, at the end of which we find Mr. Fessenden's valedictory to his readers. Its tone is despondent both as to the prospects of the country and his
own private fortunes. The next token of his labors
that has come under my notice is a small volume of
verse, published at Philadelphia in 1809, and alliter-
atively entitled " Pills, Poetical, Political, and Philosophical; prescribed for the Purpose of purging the
Public of Piddling Philosophers, Penny Poetasters, of
Paltry Politicians, and Petty Partisans. By Peter
Pepper-Box, Poet and Physician." This satire had
been written during the embargo, but, not making its
appearance till after the repeal of that measure, met
with less success than " Democracy Unveiled."

Everybody who has known Mr. Fessenden must
have wondered how the kindest hearted man in all the
world could have likewise been the most noted satirist
of his day. For my part, I have tried in vain to form
a conception of my venerable and peaceful friend as a
champion in the stormy strife of party, flinging mud
full in the faces of his foes, and shouting forth the
bitter laughter that rang from border to border of the
land; and I can hardly believe, though well assured
of it, that his antagonists should ever have meditated
personal violence against the gentlest of human creatures. I am sure, at least, that Nature never meant
him for a satirist. On careful examination of his
works, I do not find in any of them the ferocity of
the true blood-hound of literature, — such as Swift, or
Churchill, or Cobbett, — which fastens upon the throat

of its victim, and would fain drink his life-blood.  In my opinion, Mr. Fessenden never felt the slightest personal ill-will against the objects of his satire, except, indeed, they had endeavored to detract from his literary reputation, — an offence which he resented with a poet's sensibility, and seldom failed to punish. With such exceptions, his works are not properly satirical, but the offspring of a mind inexhaustibly fertile in ludicrous ideas, which it appended to any topic in hand.  At times, doubtless, the all-pervading frenzy of the times inspired him with a bitterness not his own.  But, in the least defensible of his writings, he was influenced by an honest zeal for the public good. There was nothing mercenary in his connection with politics.  To an antagonist, who had taunted him with being poor, he calmly replied, that he " need not have been accused of the crime of poverty, could he have prostituted his principles to party purposes, and become the hireling assassin of the dominant faction." Nor can there be a doubt that the administration would gladly have purchased the pen of so popular a writer.

I have gained hardly any information of Mr. Fessenden's life between the years 1807 and 1812 ; at which latter period, and probably some time previous, he was settled at the village of Bellows Falls, on Connecticut River, in the practice of the law.  In May of that year, he had the good fortune to become acquainted with Miss Lydia Tuttle, daughter of Mr. John Tuttle, an independent and intelligent farmer at Littleton, Mass.  She was then on a visit in Vermont. After her return home, a correspondence ensued between this lady and Mr. Fessenden, and was continued till their marriage, in September, 1813.  She was considerably younger than himself, but endowed with the

qualities most desirable in the wife of such a man ;
and it would not be easy to overestimate how much his
prosperity and happiness were increased by this union.
Mrs. Fessenden could appreciate what was excellent in
her husband, and supply what was deficient. In her
affectionate good sense he found a substitute for the
worldly sagacity which he did not possess, and could
not learn. To her he intrusted the pecuniary cares,
always so burdensome to a literary man. Her influence restrained him from such imprudent enterprises
as had caused the misfortunes of his earlier years.
She smoothed his path of life, and made it pleasant to
him, and lengthened it; for, as he once told me (I believe it was while advising me to take, betimes, a similar treasure to myself), he would have been in his
grave long ago, but for her care.

Mr. Fessenden continued to practise law at Bellows
Falls till 1815, when he removed to Brattleborough,
and assumed the editorship of " The Brattleborough
Reporter," a political newspaper. The following year,
in compliance with a pressing invitation from the inhabitants, he returned to Bellows Falls, and edited,
with much success, a literary and political paper,
called " The Intelligencer." He held this employment
till the year 1822, at the same time practising law, and
composing a volume of poetry, " The Ladies' Monitor,"
besides compiling several works in law, the arts, and
agriculture. During this part of his life, he usually
spent sixteen hours of the twenty-four in study. In
1822 he came to Boston as editor of " The New England Farmer," a weekly journal, the first established,
and devoted principally to the diffusion of agricultural knowledge.

His management of the " Farmer " met unreserved

approbation. Having been bred upon a farm, and passed much of his later life in the country, and being thoroughly conversant with the writers on rural economy, he was admirably qualified to conduct such a journal. It was extensively circulated throughout New England, and may be said to have fertilized the soil like rain from heaven. Numerous papers on the same plan sprung up in various parts of the country ; but none attained the standard of their prototype. Besides his editorial labors, Mr. Fessenden published, from time to time, various compilations on agricultural subjects, or adaptations of English treatises to the use of the American husbandman. Verse he no longer wrote, except, now and then, an ode or song for some agricultural festivity. His poems, being connected with topics of temporary interest, ceased to be read, now that the metallic tractors were thrown aside, and that the blending and merging of parties had created an entire change of political aspects, since the days of " Democracy Unveiled." The poetic laurel withered among his gray hairs, and dropped away, leaf by leaf. His name, once the most familiar, was forgotten in the list of American bards. I know not that this oblivion was to be regretted. Mr. Fessenden, if my observation of his temperament be correct, was peculiarly sensitive and nervous in regard to the trials of authorship : a little censure did him more harm than much praise could do him good ; and methinks the repose of total neglect was better for him than a feverish notoriety. Were it worth while to imagine any other course for the latter part of his life, which he made so useful and so honorable, it might be wished that he could have devoted himself entirely to scientific research. He had a strong taste for studies of that kind, and sometimes used to lament that his daily drudgery afforded him no leisure to compose a work on caloric, which subject he had thoroughly investigated.

In January, 1836, I became, and continued for a few months, an inmate of Mr. Fessenden's family. It was my first acquaintance with him. His image is before my mind's eye at this moment; slowly approaching me with a lamp in his hand, his hair gray, his face solemn and pale, his tall and portly figure bent with heavier infirmity than befitted his years. His dress, though he had improved in this particular since middle life, was marked by a truly scholastic negligence. He greeted me kindly, and with plain, old-fashioned courtesy; though I fancied that he somewhat regretted the interruption of his evening studies. After a few moments' talk, he invited me to accompany him to his study, and give my opinion on some passages of satirical verse, which were to be inserted in a new edition of "Terrible Tractoration." Years before, I had lighted on an illustrated copy of this poem, bestrewn with venerable dust, in a corner of a college library ; and it seemed strange and whimsical that I should find it still in progress of composition, and be consulted about it by Dr. Caustic himself. While Mr. Fessenden read, I had leisure to glance around at his study, which was very characteristic of the man and his occupations. The table, and great part of the floor, were covered with books and pamphlets on agricultural subjects, newspapers from all quarters, manuscript articles for " The New England Farmer," and manuscript stanzas for " Terrible Tractoration." There was such a litter as always gathers around a literary man. It bespoke, at once, Mr. Fessenden's amiable temper and

his abstracted habits, that several members of the family, old and young, were sitting in the room, and engaged in conversation, apparently without giving him
the least disturbance. A specimen of Dr. Caustic's
inventive genius was seen in the "Patent Steam and
Hot-Water Stove," which heated the apartment, and
kept up a pleasant singing sound, like that of a tea-
kettle, thereby making the fireside more cheerful. It
appears to me, that, having no children of flesh and
blood, Mr. Fessenden had contracted a fatherly fondness for this stove, as being his mental progeny; and
it must be owned that the stove well deserved his affection, and repaid it with much warmth.

The new edition of "Tractoration" came out not
long afterwards. It was noticed with great kindness
by the press, but was not warmly received by the public. Mr. Fessenden imputed the failure, in part, to the
illiberality of the "trade," and avenged himself by a
little poem, in his best style, entitled "Wooden Booksellers"; so that the last blow of his satirical scourge
was given in the good old cause of authors against
publishers.

Notwithstanding a wide difference of age, and many
more points of dissimilarity than of resemblance, Mr.
Fessenden and myself soon became friends. His par-
tiality seemed not to be the result of any nice discrimi-
nation of my good and evil qualities (for he had no
acuteness in that way), but to be given instinctively,
like the affection of a child. On my part, I loved the
old man because his heart was as transparent as a
fountain; and I could see nothing in it but integrity
and purity, and simple faith in his fellow-men, and
good-will towards all the world. His character was
so open, that I did not need to correct my original

conception of it. He never seemed to me like a new acquaintance, but as one with whom I had been familiar from my infancy. Yet he was a rare man, such as few meet with in the course of a lifetime.

It is remarkable, that, with such kindly affections, Mr. Fessenden was so deeply absorbed in thought and study as scarcely to allow himself time for domestic and social enjoyment. During the winter when I first knew him, his mental drudgery was almost continual. Besides "The New England Farmer," he had the editorial charge of two other journals, — "The Horticultural Register," and "The Silk Manual"; in addition to which employment, he was a member of the State Legislature, and took some share in the debates. The new matter of "Terrible Tractoration" likewise cost him intense thought. Sometimes I used to meet him in the street, making his way onward apparently by a sort of instinct; while his eyes took note of nothing, and would, perhaps, pass over my face without sign of recognition. He confessed to me that he was apt to go astray when intent on rhyme. With so much to abstract him from outward life, he could hardly be said to live in the world that was bustling around him. Almost the only relaxation that he allowed himself was an occasional performance on a bass-viol, which stood in the corner of his study, and from which he loved to elicit some old-fashioned tune of soothing potency. At meal-times, however, dragged down and harassed as his spirits were, he brightened up, and generally gladdened the whole table with a flash of Dr. Caustic's humor.

Had I anticipated being Mr. Fessenden's biographer, I might have drawn from him many details that would have been well worth remembering. But he had not the tendency of most men in advanced life, to be copious in personal reminiscences; nor did he often speak of the noted writers and politicians with whom the chances of earlier years had associated him. Indeed, lacking a turn for observation of character, his former companions had passed before him like images in a mirror, giving him little knowledge of their inner nature. Moreover, till his latest day, he was more inclined to form prospects for the future than to dwell upon the past. I remember — the last time, save one, that we ever met — I found him on the bed, suffering with a dizziness of the brain. He roused himself, however, and grew very cheerful; talking, with a youthful glow of fancy, about emigrating to Illinois, where he possessed a farm, and picturing a new life for both of us in that Western region. It has since come to my memory, that, while he spoke, there was a purple flush across his brow, — the harbinger of death.

I saw him but once more alive. On the thirteenth day of November last, while on my way to Boston, expecting shortly to take him by the hand, a letter met me with an invitation to his funeral. He had been struck with apoplexy on Friday evening, three days before, and had lain insensible till Saturday night, when he expired. The burial took place at Mount Auburn on the ensuing Tuesday. It was a gloomy day; for the first snow-storm of the season had been drifting through the air since morning; and the "Garden of Graves" looked the dreariest spot on earth. The snow came down so fast, that it covered the coffin in its passage from the hearse to the sepulchre. The few male friends who had followed to the cemetery descended into the tomb; and it was there that I took my last glance at the features of a man who will hold a place in my remembrance apart from other men. He was like no other. In his long pathway through life, from his cradle to the place where we had now laid him, he had come, a man indeed in intellect and achievement, but, in guileless simplicity, a child. Dark would have been the hour, if, when we closed the door of the tomb upon his perishing mortality, we had believed that our friend was there.

It is contemplated to erect a monument, by subscription, to Mr. Fessenden's memory. It is right that he should be thus honored. Mount Auburn will long remain a desert, barren of consecrated marbles, if worth like his be yielded to oblivion. Let his grave be marked out, that the yeomen of New England may know where he sleeps; for he was their familiar friend, and has visited them at all their firesides. He has toiled for them at seed-time and harvest: he has scattered the good grain in every field; and they have garnered the increase. Mark out his grave as that of one worthy to be remembered both in the literary and political annals of our country, and let the laurel be carved on his memorial stone; for it will cover the ashes of a man of genius.

## JONATHAN CILLEY.

THE subject of this brief memorial had barely begun
to be an actor in the great scenes where his part could
not have failed to be a prominent one. The nation
did not have time to recognize him. His death, aside
from the shock with which the manner of it has thrilled
every bosom, is looked upon merely as causing a vacancy in the delegation of his State, which a new
member may fill as creditably as the departed. It
will, perhaps, be deemed praise enough to say of Cilley,
that he would have proved himself an active and efficient partisan. But those who knew him longest and
most intimately, conscious of his high talents and rare
qualities, his energy of mind and force of character,
must claim much more than such a meed for their lost
friend. They feel that not merely a party nor a section, but our collective country, has lost a man who
had the heart and the ability to serve her well. It
would be doing injustice to the hopes which lie withered upon his untimely grave, if, in paying a farewell
tribute to his memory, we were to ask a narrower sympathy than that of the people at large. May no bitterness of party prejudices influence him who writes,
nor those, of whatever political opinions, who may
read !

Jonathan Cilley was born at Nottingham, N. H., on
the 2d of July, 1802. His grandfather, Colonel Joseph Cilley, commanded a New Hampshire regiment
during the Revolutionary War, and established a char-

acter for energy and intrepidity, of which more than one of his descendants have proved themselves the inheritors. Greenleaf Cilley, son of the preceding, died in 1808, leaving a family of four sons and three daughters. The aged mother of this family, and the three daughters, are still living. Of the sons, the only survivor is Joseph Cilley, who was an officer in the late war, and served with great distinction on the Canadian frontier. Jonathan, being desirous of a liberal education, commenced his studies at Atkinson Academy, at about the age of seventeen, and became a member of the freshman class of Bowdoin College, Brunswick, Me., in 1821. Inheriting but little property from his father, he adopted the usual expedient of a young New-Englander in similar circumstances, and gained a small income by teaching a country school during the winter months, both before and after his entrance at college.

Cilley's character and standing at college afforded high promise of usefulness and distinction in after-life. Though not the foremost scholar of his class, he stood in the front rank, and probably derived all the real benefit from the prescribed course of study that it could bestow on so practical a mind. His true education consisted in the exercise of those faculties which fitted him to be a popular leader. His influence among his fellow-students was probably greater than that of any other individual; and he had already made himself powerful in that limited sphere, by a free and natural eloquence, a flow of pertinent ideas in language of unstudied appropriateness, which seemed always to accomplish precisely the result on which he had calculated. This gift was sometimes displayed in class meetings, when measures important to those concerned were under discussion; sometimes in mock trials at law, when judge, jury, lawyers, prisoner, and witnesses were personated by the students, and Cilley played the part of a fervid and successful advocate; and, besides these exhibitions of power, he regularly trained himself in the forensic debates of a literary society, of which he afterwards became president. Nothing could be less artificial than his style of oratory. After filling his mind with the necessary information, he trusted everything else to his mental warmth and the inspiration of the moment, and poured himself out with an earnest and irresistible simplicity. There was a singular contrast between the flow of thought from his lips, and the coldness and restraint with which he wrote; and though, in maturer life, he acquired a considerable facility in exercising the pen, he always felt the tongue to be his peculiar instrument.

In private intercourse, Cilley possessed a remarkable fascination. It was impossible not to regard him with the kindliest feelings, because his companions were intuitively certain of a like kindliness on his part. He had a power of sympathy which enabled him to understand every character, and hold communion with human nature in all its varieties. He never shrank from the intercourse of man with man; and it was to his freedom in this particular that he owed much of his subsequent popularity among a people who are accustomed to take a personal interest in the men whom they elevate to office. In few words, let us characterize him at the outset of life as a young man of quick and powerful intellect, endowed with sagacity and tact, yet frank and free in his mode of action, ambitious of good influence, earnest, active, and persevering, with an elasticity and cheerful strength of mind which made difficulties easy, and the struggle with them a pleasure. Mingled with the amiable qualities that were like sunshine to his friends, there were harsher and sterner traits, which fitted him to make head against an adverse world; but it was only at the moment of need that the iron framework of his character became perceptible.

Immediately on quitting college, Mr. Cilley took up his residence in Thomaston, and began the study of law in the office of John Ruggles, Esq., now a senator in Congress. Mr. Ruggles being then a prominent member of the Democratic party, it was natural that the pupil should lend his aid to promote the political views of his instructor, especially as he would thus uphold the principles which he had cherished from boyhood. From year to year, the election of Mr. Ruggles to the state legislature was strongly opposed. Cilley's services in overcoming this opposition were too valuable to be dispensed with; and thus, at a period when most young men still stand aloof from the world, he had already taken his post as a leading politician. He afterwards found cause to regret that so much time had been abstracted from his professional studies; nor did the absorbing and exciting nature of his political career afford him any subsequent opportunity to supply the defects of his legal education. He was admitted an attorney-at-law in 1829, and in April of the same year was married to Miss Deborah Prince, daughter of Hon. Hezekiah Prince of Thomaston, where Mr. Cilley continued to reside, and entered upon the practice of his profession.

In 1831, Mr. Ruggles having been appointed a judge of the Court of Common Pleas, it became necessary to send a new representative from Thomaston to the legislature of the State. Mr. Cilley was brought forward as the Democratic candidate, obtained his election, and took his seat in January, 1832. But in the course of this year the friendly relations between Judge Ruggles and Mr. Cilley were broken off. The former gentleman, it appears, had imbibed the idea that his political aspirations (which were then directed towards a seat in the Senate of the United States) did not receive all the aid which he was disposed to claim from the influence of his late pupil. When, therefore, Mr. Cilley was held up as a candidate for reëlection to the legislature, the whole strength of Judge Ruggles and his adherents was exerted against him. This was the first act and declaration of a political hostility, which was too warm and earnest not to become, in some degree, personal, and which rendered Mr. Cilley's subsequent career a continual struggle with those to whom he might naturally have looked for friendship and support. It sets his abilities and force of character in the strongest light, to view him, at the very outset of public life, without the aid of powerful connections, an isolated young man, forced into a position of hostility, not merely with the enemies of his party, but likewise with a large body of its adherents, even accused of treachery to its principles, yet gaining triumph after triumph, and making his way steadily onward. Surely his was a mental and moral energy which death alone could have laid prostrate.

We have the testimony of those who knew Mr. Cilley well, that his own feelings were never so imbittered by those conflicts as to prevent him from interchanging the courtesies of society with his most violent opponents. While their resentments rendered his very presence intolerable to them, he could address them

with as much ease and composure as if their mutual
relations had been those of perfect harmony. There
was no affectation in this; it was the good-natured consciousness of his own strength that enabled him to
keep his temper; it was the same chivalrous sentiment
which impels hostile warriors to shake hands in the
intervals of battle. Mr. Cilley was slow to withdraw
his confidence from any man whom he deemed a friend;
and it has been mentioned as almost his only weak
point, that he was too apt to suffer himself to be betrayed before he would condescend to suspect. His
prejudices, however, when once adopted, partook of
the depth and strength of his character, and could
not be readily overcome. He loved to subdue his
foes; but no man could use a triumph more generously
than he.

Let us resume our narrative. In spite of the opposition of Judge Ruggles and his friends, combined
with that of the Whigs, Mr. Cilley was reëlected to
the legislature of 1833, and was equally successful in
each of the succeeding years, until his election to Congress. He was five successive years the representative
of Thomaston. In 1834, when Mr. Dunlap was nominated as the Democratic candidate for governor, Mr.
Cilley gave his support to Governor Smith, in the belief that the substitution of a new candidate had been
unfairly effected. He considered it a stratagem intended to promote the election of Judge Ruggles to the
Senate of the United States. Early in the legislative
session of the same year, the Ruggles party obtained a
temporary triumph over Mr. Cilley, effected his expulsion from the Democratic caucuses, and attempted to
stigmatize him as a traitor to his political friends. But
Mr. Cilley's high and honorable course was erelong un-

derstood and appreciated by his party and the people. He told them openly and boldly that they might undertake to expel him from their caucuses, but they could not expel him from the Democratic party; they might stigmatize him with any appellation they might choose, but they could not reach the height on which he stood, nor shake his position with the people. But a few weeks had elapsed, and Mr. Cilley was the acknowledged head and leader of that party in the legislature. During the same session, Mr. Speaker Clifford (one of the friends of Judge Ruggles) being appointed attorney-general, the Ruggles party were desirous of securing the election of another of their adherents to the chair; but, as it was obvious that Mr. Cilley's popularity would gain him the place, the incumbent was induced to delay his resignation till the end of the term. At the session of 1835, Messrs. Cilley, Davee, and McCrote being candidates for the chair, Mr. Cilley withdrew in favor of Mr. Davee. That gentleman was accordingly elected; but, being soon afterwards appointed sheriff of Somerset County, Mr. Cilley succeeded him as speaker, and filled the same office during the session of 1836. All parties awarded him the praise of being the best presiding officer that the house ever had.

In 1836, he was nominated by a large portion of the Democratic electors of the Lincoln Congressional District as their candidate for Congress. That district has recently shown itself to possess a decided Whig majority; and this would have been equally the case in 1836, had any other man than Mr. Cilley appeared on the Democratic side. He had likewise to contend, as in all the former scenes of his political life, with that portion of his own party which adhered to Mr.

Ruggles. There was still another formidable obstacle in the high character of Judge Bailey, who then represented the district, and was a candidate for reëlection. All these difficulties, however, served only to protract the contest, but could not snatch the victory from Mr. Cilley, who obtained a majority of votes at the third trial. It was a fatal triumph.

In the summer of 1837, a few months after his election to Congress, I met Mr. Cilley for the first time since early youth, when he had been to me almost as an elder brother. The two or three days which I spent in his neighborhood enabled us to renew our former intimacy. In his person there was very little change, and that little was for the better. He had an impending brow, deep-set eyes, and a thin and thoughtful countenance, which, in his abstracted moments, seemed almost stern; but in the intercourse of society it was brightened with a kindly smile, that will live in the recollection of all who knew him. His manners had not a fastidious polish, but were characterized by the simplicity of one who had dwelt remote from cities, holding free companionship with the yeomen of the land. I thought him as true a representative of the people as ever theory could portray. His earlier and later habits of life, his feelings, partialities, and prejudices, were those of the people: the strong and shrewd sense which constituted so marked a feature of his mind was but a higher degree of the popular intellect. He loved the people and respected them, and was prouder of nothing than of his brotherhood with those who had intrusted their public interests to his care. His continual struggles in the political arena had strengthened his bones and sinews: opposition had kept him ardent; while success had cherished the gen-

erous warmth of his nature, and assisted the growth
both of his powers and sympathies. Disappointment
might have soured and contracted him; but it appeared to me that his triumphant warfare had been no
less beneficial to his heart than to his mind. I was
aware, indeed, that his harsher traits had grown apace
with his milder ones; that he possessed iron resolution,
indomitable perseverance, and an almost terrible energy; but these features had imparted no hardness
to his character in private intercourse. In the hour
of public need, these strong qualities would have shown
themselves the most prominent ones, and would have
encouraged his countrymen to rally round him as one
of their natural leaders.

In his private and domestic relations, Mr. Cilley was
most exemplary; and he enjoyed no less happiness
than he conferred. He had been the father of four
children, two of whom were in the grave, leaving, I
thought, a more abiding impression of tenderness and
regret than the death of infants usually makes on the
masculine mind. Two boys — the elder, seven or
eight years of age; and the younger, two — still remained to him; and the fondness of these children for
their father, their evident enjoyment of his society,
was proof enough of his gentle and amiable character
within the precincts of his family. In that bereaved
household there is now another child, whom the father
never saw. Mr. Cilley's domestic habits were simple
and primitive to a degree unusual, in most parts of
our country, among men of so eminent a station as he
had attained. It made me smile, though with anything but scorn, in contrast to the aristocratic stateliness which I have witnessed elsewhere, to see him
driving home his own cow after a long search for her

through the village. That trait alone would have marked him as a man whose greatness lay within himself. He appeared to take much interest in the cultivation of his garden, and was very fond of flowers. He kept bees, and told me that he loved to sit for whole hours by the hives, watching the labors of the insects, and soothed by the hum with which they filled the air. I glance at these minute particulars of his daily life, because they form so strange a contrast with the circumstances of his death. Who could have believed that, with his thoroughly New England character, in so short a time after I had seen him in that peaceful and happy home, among those simple occupations and pure enjoyments, he would be stretched in his own blood, — slain for an almost impalpable punctilio!

It is not my purpose to dwell upon Mr. Cilley's brief career in Congress. Brief as it was, his character and talents had more than begun to be felt, and would soon have linked his name with the history of every important measure, and have borne it onward with the progress of the principles which he supported. He was not eager to seize opportunities of thrusting himself into notice; but, when time and the occasion summoned him, he came forward, and poured forth his ready and natural eloquence with as much effect in the councils of the nation as he had done in those of his own State. With every effort that he made, the hopes of his party rested more decidedly upon him, as one who would hereafter be found in the vanguard of many a Democratic victory. Let me spare myself the details of the awful catastrophe by which all those proud hopes perished; for I write with a blunted pen and a head benumbed, and am the less able to express my feelings as they lie deep at heart, and inexhaustible.

On the 23d of February last, Mr. Cilley received a challenge from Mr. Graves of Kentucky, through the hands of Mr. Wise of Virginia. This measure, as is declared in the challenge itself, was grounded on Mr. Cilley's refusal to receive a message, of which Mr. Graves had been the bearer, from a person of disputed respectability; although no exception to that person's character had been expressed by Mr. Cilley; nor need such inference have been drawn, unless Mr. Graves were conscious that public opinion held his friend in a doubtful light. The challenge was accepted, and the parties met on the following day. They exchanged two shots with rifles. After each shot, a conference was held between the friends of both parties, and the most generous avowals of respect and kindly feeling were made on the part of Cilley towards his antagonist, but without avail. A third shot was exchanged; and Mr. Cilley fell dead into the arms of one of his friends. While I write, a Committee of Investigation is sitting upon this affair : but the public has not waited for its award ; and the writer, in accordance with the public, has formed his opinion on the official statement of Messrs. Wise and Jones. A challenge was never given on a more shadowy pretext; a duel was never pressed to a fatal close in the face of such open kindness as was expressed by Mr. Cilley; and the conclusion is inevitable, that Mr. Graves and his principal second, Mr. Wise, have gone further than their own dreadful code will warrant them, and overstepped the imaginary distinction, which, on their own principles, separates manslaughter from murder.

Alas that over the grave of a dear friend my sorrow for the bereavement must be mingled with another grief, — that he threw away such a life in so miserable a cause! Why, as he was true to the Northern character in all things else, did he swerve from his Northern principles in this final scene? But his error was a generous one, since he fought for what he deemed the honor of New England; and, now that death has paid the forfeit, the most rigid may forgive him. If that dark pitfall — that bloody grave — had not lain in the midst of his path, whither, whither might it not have led him! It has ended there: yet so strong was my conception of his energies, so like destiny did it appear that he should achieve everything at which he aimed, that even now my fancy will not dwell upon his grave, but pictures him still amid the struggles and triumphs of the present and the future.[1]

1838.

[1] A very subtile and searching description of Cilley's mental and moral qualities is given in Hawthorne's *American Note-Books,* p. 75.

# ALICE DOANE'S APPEAL.

# ALICE DOANE'S APPEAL.

BY THE AUTHOR OF THE GENTLE BOY.

————

On a pleasant afternoon of June, it was my good
fortune to be the companion of two young ladies in a
walk. The direction of our course being left to me,
I led them neither to Legge's Hill, nor to the Cold
Spring, nor to the rude shores and old batteries of the
Neck, nor yet to Paradise; though if the latter place
were rightly named, my fair friends would have been
at home there. We reached the outskirts of the town,
and turning aside from a street of tanners and curriers,
began to ascend a hill, which at a distance, by its dark
slope and the even line of its summit, resembled a
green rampart along the road. It was less steep than
its aspect threatened. The eminence formed part of
an extensive tract of pasture land, and was traversed
by cow paths in various directions; but, strange to
tell, though the whole slope and summit were of a peculiarly deep green, scarce a blade of grass was visible
from the base upward. This deceitful verdure was
occasioned by a plentiful crop of " wood-wax," which
wears the same dark and glossy green throughout the
summer, except at one short period, when it puts forth
a profusion of yellow blossoms. At that season, to a
distant spectator, the hill appears absolutely overlaid
with gold, or covered with a glory of sunshine, even

beneath a clouded sky. Iut the curious wanderer on
the hill will perceive that all the grass, and everything
that should nourish man or beast, has been destroyed
by this vile and ineradicable weed : its tufted roots
make the soil their own, and permit nothing else to
vegetate among them ; so that a physical curse may be
said to have blasted the spot, where guilt and frenzy
consummated the most execrable scene that our 1 s-
tory blushes to record. For this was the field where
superstition won her darkest triumph ; the high place
where our fathers set up their shame, to the mournful
gaze of generations far remote. The dust of martyrs
was beneath our feet. We stood on Gallows Hill.

For my own part, I have often courted the historic
influence of the spot. But it is singular how few
come on pilgrimage to this famous hill; how many
spend their lives almost at its base, and never once
obey the summons of the shadowy past, as it beckons
them to the summit. Till a year or two since, this
portion of our history had been very imperfectly written, and, as we are not a people of legend or tradition,
it was not every citizen of our ancient town that could
tell, within half a century, so much as the date of the
witchcraft delusion. Recently, indeed, an historian
has treated the subject in a manner that will keep his
name alive, in the only desirable connection with the
errors of our ancestry, by converting the hill of their
disgrace into an honorable monument of his own anti-
quarian lore, and of that better wisdom, which draws
the moral while it tells the tale. But we are a people
of the present, and have no heartfelt interest in the
olden time. Every fifth of November, in commemora-
tion of they know not what, or rather without an idea
beyond the momentary blaze, the young men scare the

town with bonfires on this haunted height, but never dream of paying funeral honors to those who died so wrongfully, and, without a coffin or a prayer, were buried here.

Though with feminine susceptibility, my companions caught all the melancholy associations of the scene, yet these could but imperfectly overcome the gayety of girlish spirits. Their emotions came and went with quick vicissitude, and sometimes combined to form a peculiar and delicious excitement, the mirth brightening the gloom into a sunny shower of feeling, and a rainbow in the mind. My own more sombre mood was tinged by theirs. With now a merry word and next a sad one, we trod among the tangled weeds, and almost hoped that our feet would sink into the hollow of a witch's grave. Such vestiges were to be found within the memory of man, but have vanished now, and with them, I believe, all traces of the precise spot of the executions. On the long and broad ridge of the eminence, there is no very decided elevation of any one point, nor other prominent marks, except the decayed stumps of two trees, standing near each other, and here and there the rocky substance of the hill, peeping just above the wood-wax.

There are few such prospects of town and village, woodland and cultivated field, steeples and country seats, as we beheld from this unhappy spot. No blight had fallen on old Essex ; all was prosperity and riches, healthfully distributed. Before us lay our native town, extending from the foot of the hill to the harbor, level as a chess board, embraced by two arms of the sea, and filling the whole peninsula with a close assemblage of wooden roofs, overtopped by many a spire, and intermixed with frequent heaps of verdure, where

trees threw up their shade from unseen trunks. Beyond was the bay and its islands, almost the only
objects, in a country unmarked by strong natural features, on which time and human toil had produced no
change. Retaining these portions of the scene, and
also the peaceful glory and tender gloom of the declining sun, we threw, in imagination, a veil of deep
forest over the land, and pictured a few scattered villages, and this old town itself a village, as when the
prince of hell bore sway there. The idea thus gained
of its former aspect, its quaint edifices standing far
apart, with peaked roofs and projecting stories, and
its single meeting-house pointing up a tall spire in
the midst; the vision, in short, of the town in 1692,
served to introduce a wondrous tale of those old
times.

I had brought the manuscript in my pocket. It
was one of a series written years ago, when my pen,
now sluggish and perhaps feeble, because I have not
much to hope or fear, was driven by stronger external
motives, and a more passionate impulse within, than I
am fated to feel again. Three or four of these tales
had appeared in the "Token," after a long time and
various adventures, but had encumbered me with no
troublesome notoriety, even in my birthplace. One
great heap had met a brighter destiny: they had fed
the flames; thoughts meant to delight the world and
endure for ages had perished in a moment, and stirred
not a single heart but mine. The story now to be introduced, and another, chanced to be in kinder custody
at the time, and thus, by no conspicuous merits of
their own, escaped destruction.

The ladies, in consideration that I had never before
intruded my performances on them, by any but the

legitimate medium, through the press, consented to hear me read. I made them sit down on a moss-grown rock, close by the spot where we chose to believe that the death tree had stood. After a little hesitation on my part, caused by a dread of renewing my acquaintance with fantasies that had lost their charm in the ceaseless flux of mind, I began the tale, which opened darkly with the discovery of a murder.

------------

A hundred years, and nearly half that time, have elapsed since the body of a murdered man was found, at about the distance of three miles, on the old road to Boston. He lay in a solitary spot, on the bank of a small lake, which the severe frost of December had covered with a sheet of ice. Beneath this, it seemed to have been the intention of the murderer to conceal his victim in a chill and watery grave, the ice being deeply hacked, perhaps with the weapon that had slain him, though its solidity was too stubborn for the patience of a man with blood upon his hand. The corpse therefore reclined on the earth, but was separated from the road by a thick growth of dwarf pines. There had been a slight fall of snow during the night, and as if nature were shocked at the deed, and strove to hide it with her frozen tears, a little drifted heap had partly buried the body, and lay deepest over the pale dead face. An early traveller, whose dog had led him to the spot, ventured to uncover the features, but was affrighted by their expression. A look of evil and scornful triumph had hardened on them, and made death so life-like and so terrible, that the beholder at once took flight, as swiftly as if the stiffened corpse would rise up and follow.

I read on, and identified the body as that of a young man, a stranger in the country, but resident during several preceding months in the town which lay at our feet. The story described, at some length, the excitement caused by the murder, the unavailing quest after the perpetrator, the funeral ceremonies, and other commonplace matters, in the course of which, I brought forward the personages who were to move among the succeeding events. They were but three. A young man and his sister; the former characterized by a diseased imagination and morbid feelings; the latter, beautiful and virtuous, and instilling something of her own excellence into the wild heart of her brother, but not enough to cure the deep taint of his nature. The third person was a wizard; a small, gray, withered man, with fiendish ingenuity in devising evil, and superhuman power to execute it, but senseless as an idiot and feebler than a child to all better purposes. The central scene of the story was an interview between this wretch and Leonard Doane, in the wizard's hut, situated beneath a range of rocks at some distance from the town. They sat beside a mouldering fire, while a tempest of wintry rain was beating on the roof. The young man spoke of the closeness of the tie which united him and Alice, the consecrated fervor of their affection from childhood upwards, their sense of lonely sufficiency to each other, because they only of their race had escaped death, in a night attack by the Indians. He related his discovery or suspicion of a secret sympathy between his sister and Walter Brome, and told how a distempered jealousy had maddened him. In the following passage, I threw a glimmering light on the mystery of the tale.

" Searching," continued Leonard, "into the breast of Walter Brome, I at length found a cause why Alice must inevitably love him. For he was my very counterpart! I compared his mind by each individual portion, and as a whole, with mine. There was a resemblance from which I shrunk with sickness, and loathing, and horror, as if my own features had come and stared upon me in a solitary place, or had met me in struggling through a crowd. Nay! the very same thoughts would often express themselves in the same words from our lips, proving a hateful sympathy in our secret souls. His education, indeed, in the cities of the old world, and mine in this rude wilderness, had wrought a superficial difference. The evil of his character, also, had been strengthened and rendered prominent by a reckless and ungoverned life, while mine had been softened and purified by the gentle and holy nature of Alice. But my soul had been conscious of the germ of all the fierce and deep passions, and of all the many varieties of wickedness, which accident had brought to their full maturity in him. Nor will I deny that, in the accursed one, I could see the withered blossom of every virtue, which, by a happier culture, had been made to bring forth fruit in me. Now, here was a man whom Alice might love with all the strength of sisterly affection, added to that impure passion which alone engrosses all the heart. The stranger would have more than the love which had been gathered to me from the many graves of our household — and I be desolate! "

Leonard Doane went on to describe the insane hatred that had kindled his heart into a volume of hellish flame. It appeared, indeed, that his jealousy had grounds, so far as that Walter Brome had actually sought the love of Alice, who also had betrayed an undefinable, but powerful interest in the unknown youth. The latter, in spite of his passion for Alice, seemed to return the loathful antipathy of her brother; the similarity of their dispositions made them like joint possessors of an individual nature, which could not become wholly the property of one, unless by the extinction of the other. At last, with the same devil in each bosom, they chanced to meet, they two on a lonely road. While Leonard spoke, the wizard had sat listening to what he already knew, yet with tokens of pleasurable interest, manifested by flashes of expression across his vacant features, by grisly smiles and by a word here and there, mysteriously filling up some void in the narrative. But when the young man told how Walter Brome had taunted him with indubitable proofs of the shame of Alice, and, before the triumphant sneer could vanish from his face, had died by her brother's hand, the wizard laughed aloud. Leonard started, but just then a gust of wind came down the chimney, forming itself into a close resemblance of the slow, unvaried laughter, by which he had been interrupted. "I was deceived," thought he; and thus pursued his fearful story.

---

"I trod out his accursed soul, and knew that he was dead; for my spirit bounded as if a chain had fallen from it and left me free. But the burst of exulting certainty soon fled, and was succeeded by a torpor over my brain and a dimness before my eyes, with the sensation of one who struggles through a dream. So

I bent down over the body of Walter Brome, gazing into his face, and striving to make my soul glad with the thought, that he, in very truth, lay dead before me. I know not what space of time I had thus stood, nor how the vision came. But it seemed to me that the irrevocable years since childhood had rolled back, and a scene, that had long been confused and broken in my memory, arrayed itself with all its first distinctness. Methought I stood a weeping infant by my father's hearth; by the cold and blood-stained hearth where he lay dead. I heard the childish wail of Alice, and my own cry arose with hers, as we beheld the features of our parent, fierce with the strife and distorted with the pain, in which his spirit had passed away. As I gazed, a cold wind whistled by, and waved my father's hair. Immediately I stood again in the lonesome road, no more a sinless child, but a man of blood, whose tears were falling fast over the face of his dead enemy. But the delusion was not wholly gone; that face still wore a likeness of my father; and because my soul shrank from the fixed glare of the eyes, I bore the body to the lake, and would have buried it there. But before his icy sepulchre was hewn, I heard the voices of two travellers and fled."

_____

Such was the dreadful confession of Leonard Doane. And now tortured by the idea of his sister's guilt, yet sometimes yielding to a conviction of her purity; stung with remorse for the death of Walter Brome, and shuddering with a deeper sense of some unutterable crime, perpetrated, as he imagined, in madness or a dream; moved also by dark impulses, as if a fiend were whispering him to meditate violence against the life of Alice; he had sought this interview with the wizard, who, on certain conditions, had no power to withhold his aid in unravelling the mystery. The tale drew near its close.

---

The moon was bright on high; the blue firmament appeared to glow with an inherent brightness; the greater stars were burning in their spheres; the northern lights threw their mysterious glare far over the horizon; the few small clouds aloft were burdened with radiance; but the sky, with all its variety of light, was scarcely so brilliant as the earth. The rain of the preceding night had frozen as it fell, and, by that simple magic, had wrought wonders. The trees were hung with diamonds and many-colored gems; the houses were overlaid with silver, and the streets paved with slippery brightness; a frigid glory was flung over all familiar things, from the cottage chimney to the steeple of the meeting-house, that gleamed upward to the sky. This living world, where we sit by our firesides, or go forth to meet beings like ourselves, seemed rather the creation of wizard power, with so much of resemblance to known objects that a man might shudder at the ghostly shape of his old beloved dwelling, and the shadow of a ghostly tree before his door. One looked to behold inhabitants suited to such a town, glittering in icy garments, with motionless features, cold, sparkling eyes, and just sensation enough in their frozen hearts to shiver at each other's presence.

---

By this fantastic piece of description, and more in the same style, I intended to throw a ghostly glimmer

round the reader, so that his imagination might view
the town through a medium that should take off its
every-day aspect, and make it a proper theatre for so
wild a scene as the final one. Amid this unearthly
show, the wretched brother and sister were represented
as setting forth, at midnight, through the gleaming
streets, and directing their steps to a graveyard, where
all the dead had been laid, from the first corpse in that
ancient town, to the murdered man who was buried
three days before. As they went, they seemed to see
the wizard gliding by their sides, or walking dimly on
the path before them. But here I paused, and gazed
into the faces of my two fair auditors, to judge
whether, even on the hill where so many had been
brought to death by wilder tales than this, I might
venture to proceed. Their bright eyes were fixed on
me ; their lips apart. I took courage, and led the
fated pair to a new made grave, where for a few moments, in the bright and silent midnight, they stood
alone. But suddenly there was a multitude of people
among the graves.

Each family tomb had given up its inhabitants, who,
one by one, through distant years, had been borne to
its dark chamber, but now came forth and stood in a
pale group together. There was the gray ancestor, the
aged mother, and all their descendants, some withered
and full of years, like themselves, and others in their
prime ; there, too, were the children who went prattling
to the tomb, and there the maiden who yielded her
early beauty to death's embrace, before passion had
polluted it. Husbands and wives arose, who had lain
many years side by side, and young mothers who had

forgotten to kiss their first babes, though pillowed so long on their bosoms. Many had been buried in the habiliments of life, and still wore their ancient garb; some were old defenders of the infant colony, and gleamed forth in their steel-caps and bright breast-plates, as if starting up at an Indian war-cry; other venerable shapes had been pastors of the church, fa-mous among the New England clergy, and now leaned with hands clasped over their gravestones, ready to call the congregation to prayer. There stood the early settlers, those old illustrious ones, the heroes of tradition and fireside legends, the men of history whose features had been so long beneath the sod that few alive could have remembered them. There, too, were faces of former towns-people, dimly recollected from childhood, and others, whom Leonard and Alice had wept in later years, but who now were most terrible of all, by their ghastly smile of recognition. All, in short, were there; the dead of other generations, whose moss-grown names could scarce be read upon their tombstones, and their successors, whose graves were not yet green; all whom black funerals had followed slowly thither now reappeared where the mourners left them. Yet none but souls accursed were there, and fiends counterfeiting the likeness of departed saints.

The countenances of those venerable men, whose very features had been hallowed by lives of piety, were contorted now by intolerable pain or hellish passion, and now by an unearthly and derisive merriment. Had the pastors prayed, all saintlike as they seemed, it had been blasphemy. The chaste matrons, too, and the maidens with untasted lips, who had slept in their virgin graves apart from all other dust, now wore a look from which the two trembling mortals shrank, as if the unimaginable sin of twenty worlds were collected there. The faces of fond lovers, even of such as had pined into the tomb, because there their treasure was, were bent on one another with glances of hatred and smiles of bitter scorn, passions that are to devils what love is to the blest. At times, the features of those who had passed from a holy life to heaven would vary to and fro, between their assumed aspect and the fiendish lineaments whence they had been transformed. The whole miserable multitude, both sinful souls and false spectres of good men, groaned horribly and gnashed their teeth, as they looked upward to the calm loveliness of the midnight sky, and beheld those homes of bliss where they must never dwell. Such was the apparition, though too shadowy for language to portray; for here would be the moonbeams on the ice, glittering through a warrior's breastplate, and there the letters of a tombstone, on the form that stood before it; and whenever a breeze went by, it swept the old men's hoary heads, the women's fearful beauty, and all the unreal throng, into one indistinguishable cloud together.

---

I dare not give the remainder of the scene, except in a very brief epitome. This company of devils and condemned souls had come on a holiday, to revel in the discovery of a complicated crime; as foul a one as ever was imagined in their dreadful abode. In the course of the tale, the reader had been permitted to discover that all the incidents were results of the machinations of the wizard, who had cunningly devised that Walter Brome should tempt his unknown sister to guilt and shame, and himself perish by the hand of his twin-brother. I described the glee of the fiends at this hideous conception, and their eagerness to know if it were consummated. The story concluded with the Appeal of Alice to the spectre of Walter Brome ; his reply, absolving her from every stain ; and the trembling awe with which ghost and devil fled, as from the sinless presence of an angel.

The sun had gone down. While I held my page of wonders in the fading light, and read how Alice and her brother were left alone among the graves, my voice mingled with the sigh of a summer wind, which passed over the hill - top, with the broad and hollow sound as of the flight of unseen spirits. Not a word was spoken till I added that the wizard's grave was close beside us, and that the wood-wax had sprouted originally from his unhallowed bones. The ladies started ; perhaps their cheeks might have grown pale had not the crimson west been blushing on them ; but after a moment they began to laugh, while the breeze took a livelier motion, as if responsive to their mirth. I kept an awful solemnity of visage, being, indeed, a little piqued that a narrative which had good authority in our ancient superstitions, and would have brought even a church deacon to Gallows Hill, in old witch times, should now be considered too grotesque and extravagant for timid maids to tremble at. Though it was past supper time, I detained them a while longer on the hill, and made a trial whether truth were more powerful than fiction.

We looked again towards the town, no longer arrayed in that icy splendor of earth, tree, and edifice, beneath the glow of a wintry midnight, which shining afar through the gloom of a century had made it appear

the very home of visions in visionary streets. An in-
distinctness had begun to creep over the mass of buildings and blend them with the intermingled tree-tops,
except where the roof of a statelier mansion, and the
steeples and brick towers of churches, caught the
brightness of some cloud that yet floated in the sunshine. Twilight over the landscape was congenial to
the obscurity of time. With such eloquence as my
share of feeling and fancy could supply, I called back
hoar antiquity, and bade my companions imagine an
ancient multitude of people, congregated on the hill-
side, spreading far below, clustering on the steep old
roofs, and climbing the adjacent heights, wherever a
glimpse of this spot might be obtained. I strove to
realize and faintly communicate the deep, unutterable
loathing and horror, the indignation, the affrighted
wonder, that wrinkled on every brow, and filled the
universal heart. See! the whole crowd turns pale and
shrinks within itself, as the virtuous emerge from yonder street. Keeping pace with that devoted company,
I described them one by one; here tottered a woman
in her dotage, knowing neither the crime imputed her,
nor its punishment; there another, distracted by the
universal madness, till feverish dreams were remembered as realities, and she almost believed her guilt.
One, a proud man once, was so broken down by the
intolerable hatred heaped upon him, that he seemed
to hasten his steps, eager to hide himself in the grave
hastily dug at the foot of the gallows. As they went
slowly on, a mother looked behind, and beheld her
peaceful dwelling; she cast her eyes elsewhere, and
groaned inwardly yet with bitterest anguish, for there
was her little son among the accusers. I watched the
face of an ordained pastor, who walked onward to the

same death; his lips moved in prayer; no narrow petition for himself alone, but embracing all his fellow-sufferers and the frenzied multitude; he looked to Heaven and trod lightly up the hill.

Behind their victims came the afflicted, a guilty and miserable band; villains who had thus avenged themselves on their enemies, and viler wretches, whose cowardice had destroyed their friends; lunatics, whose ravings had chimed in with the madness of the land; and children, who had played a game that the imps of darkness might have envied them, since it disgraced an age, and dipped a people's hands in blood. In the rear of the procession rode a figure on horseback, so darkly conspicuous, so sternly triumphant, that my hearers mistook him for the visible presence of the fiend himself; but it was only his good friend, Cotton Mather, proud of his well-won dignity, as the representative of all the hateful features of his time; the one blood - thirsty man, in whom were concentrated those vices of spirit and errors of opinion that sufficed to madden the whole surrounding multitude. And thus I marshalled them onward, the innocent who were to die, and the guilty who were to grow old in long remorse — tracing their every step, by rock, and shrub, and broken track, till their shadowy visages had circled round the hill - top, where we stood. I plunged into my imagination for a blacker horror, and a deeper woe, and pictured the scaffold ——

But here my companions seized an arm on each side; their nerves were trembling; and, sweeter victory still, I had reached the seldom trodden places of their hearts, and found the well-spring of their tears. And now the past had done all it could. We slowly descended, watching the lights as they twinkled gradually through the town, and listening to the distant mirth of boys at play, and to the voice of a young girl warbling somewhere in the dusk, a pleasant sound to wanderers from old witch times. Yet, ere we left the hill, we could not but regret that there is nothing on its barren summit, no relic of old, nor lettered stone of later days, to assist the imagination in appealing to the heart. We build the memorial column on the height which our fathers made sacred with their blood, poured out in a holy cause. And here, in dark, funereal stone, should rise another monument, sadly commemorative of the errors of an earlier race, and not to be cast down, while the human heart has one infirmity that may result in crime.

ally through the town, and listening to the distant
shout of boys at play, and to the voice of a young girl,
warbling somewhere in the dusk, a pleasant sound to
wanderers from old witch times.  Yet, ere we left the
hill, we could not but regret that there is nothing on
its barren summit, no relic of old, nor lettered stone
of later days, to assist the imagination in appealing
to the heart.  We build the memorial column on the
height which our fathers made sacred with their blood,
poured out in a holy cause.  And here, in dark, tragic story, should rise another monument, sadly
commemorative of the errors of an earlier race; and
not to be cast down, while the human heart has one
infirmity that may result in crime.

# CHIEFLY ABOUT WAR MATTERS

# CHIEFLY ABOUT WAR MATTERS.

# CHIEFLY ABOUT WAR MATTERS.

## BY A PEACEABLE MAN.

———◇———

[This article appeared in the "Atlantic Monthly" for July, 1862, and is now first reprinted among Hawthorne's collected writings. The editor of the magazine objected to sundry paragraphs in the manuscript, and these were cancelled with the consent of the author, who himself supplied all the foot-notes that accompanied the article when it was published. It has seemed best to retain them in the present reproduction. One of the suppressed passages, in which President Lincoln is described, has since been printed, and is therefore restored to its proper place in the following pages. — G. P. L.]

THERE is no remoteness of life and thought, no hermetically sealed seclusion, except, possibly, that of the grave, into which the disturbing influences of this war do not penetrate. Of course, the general heart-quake of the country long ago knocked at my cottage-door, and compelled me, reluctantly, to suspend the contemplation of certain fantasies, to which, according to my harmless custom, I was endeavoring to give a sufficiently life-like aspect to admit of their figuring in a romance. As I make no pretensions to state-craft or soldiership, and could promote the common weal neither by valor nor counsel, it seemed, at first, a pity that I should be debarred from such unsubstantial business as I had contrived for myself, since nothing more genuine was to be substituted for it. But I magnanimously considered that there is a kind of treason in insulating one's self from the universal fear and sorrow, and thinking one's idle thoughts in the dread time of civil war; and could a man be so cold and hard-hearted, he would better deserve to be sent to Fort Warren than many who have found their way thither on the score of violent, but misdirected sympathies. I remembered the touching rebuke administered by King Charles to that rural squire the echo of whose hunting-horn came to the poor monarch's ear on the morning before a battle, where the sovereignty and constitution of England were to be set at a stake. So I gave myself up to reading newspapers and listening to the click of the telegraph, like other people; until, after a great many months of such pastime, it grew so abominably irksome that I determined to look a little more closely at matters with my own eyes.

Accordingly we set out — a friend and myself — towards Washington, while it was still the long, dreary January of our Northern year, though March in name; nor were we unwilling to clip a little margin off the five months' winter, during which there is nothing genial in New England save the fireside. It was a clear, frosty morning, when we started. The sun shone brightly on snow-covered hills in the neighborhood of Boston, and burnished the surface of frozen ponds; and the wintry weather kept along with us while we trundled through Worcester and Springfield, and all those old, familiar towns, and through the village-cities of Connecticut. In New York the streets were afloat with liquid mud and slosh. Over New Jersey there was still a thin covering of snow, with the face of Nature visible through the rents in her white shroud, though with little or no symptom of reviving life. But when we reached Philadelphia, the air was mild and balmy; there was but a patch or two of dingy winter here and there, and the bare, brown fields about the city were ready to be green. We had met the Spring half-way, in her slow progress from the South; and if we kept onward at the same pace, and could get through the Rebel lines, we should soon come to fresh grass, fruit-blossoms, green peas, strawberries, and all such delights of early summer.

On our way, we heard many rumors of the war, but saw few signs of it. The people were staid and decorous, according to their ordinary fashion; and business seemed about as brisk as usual, — though, I suppose, it was considerably diverted from its customary channels into warlike ones. In the cities, especially in New York, there was a rather prominent display of military goods at the shop windows, — such as swords with gilded scabbards and trappings, epaulets, carabines, revolvers, and sometimes a great iron cannon at the edge of the pavement, as if Mars had dropped one of his pocket-pistols there, while hurrying to the field. As railway-companions, we had now and then a volunteer in his French-gray great-coat, returning from furlough, or a new-made officer travelling to join his regiment, in his new-made uniform, which was perhaps all of the military character that he had about him, — but proud of his eagle-buttons, and likely enough to do them honor before the gilt should be wholly dimmed. The country, in short, so far as bustle and movement went, was more quiet than in ordinary times, because so large a proportion of its restless elements had been drawn towards the seat of the conflict. But the air was full of a vague disturbance. To me, at least, it seemed so, emerging from such a solitude as has been hinted at, and the more impressible by rumors and indefinable presentiments, since I had not lived, like other men, in an atmosphere of continual talk about the war. A battle was momentarily expected on the Potomac; for, though our army was still on the hither side of the river, all of us were looking towards the mysterious and terrible Manassas, with the idea that somewhere in its neighborhood lay a ghastly battle-field, yet to be fought, but foredoomed of old to be bloodier than the one where we had reaped such shame. Of all haunted places, methinks such a des-tined field should be thickest thronged with ugly phan-toms, ominous of mischief through ages beforehand.

Beyond Philadelphia there was a much greater abundance of military people. Between Baltimore and Washington a guard seemed to hold every station along the railroad; and frequently, on the hill-sides, we saw a collection of weather-beaten tents, the peaks of which, blackened with smoke, indicated that they had been made comfortable by stove-heat throughout the winter. At several commanding positions we saw fortifications, with the muzzles of cannon protruding from the ramparts, the slopes of which were made of the yellow earth of that region, and still unsodded; whereas, till these troublous times, there have been no forts but what were grass-grown with the lapse of at least a lifetime of peace. Our stopping-places were thronged with soldiers, some of whom came through the cars asking for newspapers that contained accounts of the battle between the Merrimack and Monitor, which had been fought the day before. A railway-train met us, conveying a regiment out of Washington to some unknown point; and reaching the capital, we filed out of the station between lines of soldiers, with shouldered muskets, putting us in mind of similar spectacles at the gates of European cities. It was not without sorrow that we saw the free circulation of the nation's life-blood (at the very heart, moreover) clogged with such strictures as these, which have caused chronic diseases in almost all countries save our own. Will the time ever come again, in America, when we may live half a score of years without once seeing the likeness of a soldier, except it be in the festal march of a company on its summer tour? Not in this generation, I fear, nor in the next, nor till the Millennium; and even that blessed epoch, as the prophecies seem to intimate, will advance to the sound of the trumpet.

One terrible idea occurs in reference to this matter. Even supposing the war should end to-morrow, and the army melt into the mass of the population within the year, what an incalculable preponderance will there be of military titles and pretensions for at least half a century to come! Every country-neighborhood will have its general or two, its three or four colonels, half a dozen majors, and captains without end, — besides non-commissioned officers and privates, more than the recruiting offices ever knew of, — all with their campaign-stories, which will become the staple of fireside-talk forevermore. Military merit, or rather, since that is not so readily estimated, military notoriety, will be the measure of all claims to civil distinction. One bullet-headed general will succeed another in the Presidential chair; and veterans will hold the offices at home and abroad, and sit in Congress and the state legislatures, and fill all the avenues of public life. And yet I do not speak of this deprecatingly, since, very likely, it may substitute something more real and genuine, instead of the many shams on which men

have heretofore founded their claims to public regard;
but it behooves civilians to consider their wretched
prospects in the future, and assume the military button
before it is too late.

We were not in time to see Washington as a camp.
On the very day of our arrival sixty thousand men
had crossed the Potomac on their march towards Manassas; and almost with their first step into the Virginia mud, the phantasmagory of a countless host and
impregnable ramparts, before which they had so long
remained quiescent, dissolved quite away. It was as
if General McClellan had thrust his sword into a gigantic enemy, and, beholding him suddenly collapse, had
discovered to himself and the world that he had merely
punctured an enormously swollen bladder. There are
instances of a similar character in old romances, where
great armies are long kept at bay by the arts of nec-
romancers, who build airy towers and battlements,
and muster warriors of terrible aspect, and thus feign
a defence of seeming impregnability, until some bolder
champion of the besiegers dashes forward to try an
encounter with the foremost foeman, and finds him
melt away in the death-grapple. With such heroic
adventures let the march upon Manassas be hereafter
reckoned. The whole business, though connected with
the destinies of a nation, takes inevitably a tinge of
the ludicrous. The vast preparation of men and warlike material, — the majestic patience and docility
with which the people waited through those weary and
dreary months, — the martial skill, courage, and caution, with which our movement was ultimately made,
— and, at last, the tremendous shock with which we
were brought suddenly up against nothing at all! The
Southerners show little sense of humor nowadays, but

I think they must have meant to provoke a laugh at our expense, when they planted those Quaker guns. At all events, no other Rebel artillery has played upon us with such overwhelming effect.

The troops being gone, we had the better leisure and opportunity to look into other matters. It is natural enough to suppose that the centre and heart of Washington is the Capitol; and certainly, in its outward aspect, the world has not many statelier or more beautiful edifices, nor any, I should suppose, more skilfully adapted to legislative purposes, and to all accompanying needs. But, etc., etc.[1]

.   .   .   .   .   .   .   .   .

We found one man, however, at the Capitol, who was satisfactorily adequate to the business which brought him thither. In quest of him, we went through halls, galleries, and corridors, and ascended a noble staircase, balustraded with a dark and beautifully variegated marble from Tennessee, the richness of which is quite a sufficient cause for objecting to the secession of that State. At last we came to a barrier of pine boards, built right across the stairs. Knocking at a rough, temporary door, we thrust a card beneath; and in a minute or two it was opened by a person in his shirt-sleeves, a middle-aged figure, neither tall nor short, of Teutonic build and aspect, with an ample beard of a ruddy tinge and chestnut hair. He looked at us, in the first place, with keen and somewhat guarded eyes, as if it were not his practice to vouchsafe

[1] We omit several paragraphs here, in which the author speaks of some prominent Members of Congress with a freedom that seems to have been not unkindly meant, but might be liable to misconstruction. As he admits that he never listened to an important debate, we can hardly recognize his qualifications to estimate these gentlemen, in their legislative and oratorical capacities.

any great warmth of greeting, except upon sure ground of observation.  Soon, however, his look grew kindly and genial (not that it had ever been in the least degree repulsive, but only reserved), and Leutze allowed us to gaze at the cartoon of his great fresco, and talked about it unaffectedly, as only a man of true genius can speak of his own works.  Meanwhile the noble design spoke for itself upon the wall.  A sketch in color, which we saw afterwards, helped us to form some distant and flickering notion of what the picture will be, a few months hence, when these bare outlines, already so rich in thought and suggestiveness, shall glow with a fire of their own, — a fire which, I truly believe, will consume every other pictorial decoration of the Capitol, or, at least, will compel us to banish those stiff and respectable productions to some less conspicuous gallery.  The work will be emphatically original and American, embracing characteristics that neither art nor literature have yet dealt with, and producing new forms of artistic beauty from the natural features of the Rocky-Mountain region, which Leutze seems to have studied broadly and minutely.  The garb of the hunters and wanderers of those deserts, too, under his free and natural management, is shown as the most picturesque of costumes.  But it would be doing this admirable painter no kind office to overlay his picture with any more of my colorless and uncertain words; so I shall merely add that it looked full of energy, hope, progress, irrepressible movement onward, all represented in a momentary pause of triumph; and it was most cheering to feel its good augury at this dismal time, when our country might seem to have arrived at such a deadly stand-still.

It was an absolute comfort, indeed, to find Leutze

so quietly busy at this great national work, which is destined to glow for centuries on the walls of the Capitol, if that edifice shall stand, or must share its fate, if treason shall succeed in subverting it with the Union which it represents. It was delightful to see him so calmly elaborating his design, while other men doubted and feared, or hoped treacherously, and whispered to one another that the nation would exist only a little longer, or that, if a remnant still held together, its centre and seat of government would be far northward and westward of Washington. But the artist keeps right on, firm of heart and hand, drawing his outlines with an unwavering pencil, beautifying and idealizing our rude, material life, and thus manifesting that we have an indefeasible claim to a more enduring national existence. In honest truth, what with the hope-inspiring influence of the design, and what with Leutze's undisturbed evolvement of it, I was exceedingly encouraged, and allowed these cheerful auguries to weigh against a sinister omen that was pointed out to me in another part of the Capitol. The freestone walls of the central edifice are pervaded with great cracks, and threaten to come thundering down, under the immense weight of the iron dome, — an appropriate catastrophe enough, if it should occur on the day when we drop the Southern stars out of our flag.

Everybody seems to be at Washington, and yet there is a singular dearth of imperatively noticeable people there. I question whether there are half a dozen individuals, in all kinds of eminence, at whom a stranger, wearied with the contact of a hundred moderate celebrities, would turn round to snatch a second glance. Secretary Seward, to be sure, — a pale, large-nosed, elderly man, of moderate stature, with a decided originality of gait and aspect, and a cigar in his mouth, — etc., etc.[1]

. . . . . . . . . .

Of course, there was one other personage, in the class of statesmen, whom I should have been truly mortified to leave Washington without seeing; since (temporarily, at least, and by force of circumstances) he was the man of men. But a private grief had built up a barrier about him, impeding the customary free intercourse of Americans with their chief magistrate; so that I might have come away without a glimpse of his very remarkable physiognomy, save for a semi-official opportunity of which I was glad to take advantage. The fact is, we were invited to annex ourselves, as supernumeraries, to a deputation that was about to wait upon the President, from a Massachusetts whip-factory, with a present of a splendid whip.

Our immediate party consisted only of four or five (including Major Ben Perley Poore, with his notebook and pencil), but we were joined by several other persons, who seemed to have been lounging about the precincts of the White House, under the spacious porch, or within the hall, and who swarmed in with us to take the chances of a presentation. Nine o'clock had been appointed as the time for receiving the deputation, and we were punctual to the moment; but not so the President, who sent us word that he was eating his breakfast, and would come as soon as he could. His appetite, we were glad to think, must have been a

---

[1] We are again compelled to interfere with our friend's license of personal description and criticism. Even Cabinet Ministers (to whom the next few pages of the article were devoted) had their private immunities, which ought to be conscientiously observed, — unless, indeed, the writer chanced to have some very piquant motives for violating them.

pretty fair one ; for we waited about half an hour in one of the antechambers, and then were ushered into a reception-room, in one corner of which sat the Secretaries of War and of the Treasury, expecting, like ourselves, the termination of the Presidential breakfast. During this interval there were several new additions to our group, one or two of whom were in a working-garb, so that we formed a very miscellaneous collection of people, mostly unknown to each other, and without any common sponsor, but all with an equal right to look our head-servant in the face.

By and by there was a little stir on the staircase and in the passage-way, and in lounged a tall, loose-jointed figure, of an exaggerated Yankee port and demeanor, whom (as being about the homeliest man I ever saw, yet by no means repulsive or disagreeable) it was impossible not to recognize as Uncle Abe.

Unquestionably, Western man though he be, and Kentuckian by birth, President Lincoln is the essential representative of all Yankees, and the veritable specimen, physically, of what the world seems determined to regard as our characteristic qualities. It is the strangest and yet the fittest thing in the jumble of human vicissitudes, that he, out of so many millions, unlooked for, unselected by any intelligible process that could be based upon his genuine qualities, unknown to those who chose him, and unsuspected of what endowments may adapt him for his tremendous responsibility, should have found the way open for him to fling his lank personality into the chair of state, — where, I presume, it was his first impulse to throw his legs on the council - table, and tell the Cabinet Ministers a story. There is no describing his lengthy awkwardness, nor the uncouthness of his movement; and yet it seemed as if I had been in the habit of seeing him daily, and had shaken hands with him a thousand times in some village street; so true was he to the aspect of the pattern American, though with a certain extravagance which, possibly, I exaggerated still further by the delighted eagerness with which I took it in. If put to guess his calling and livelihood, I should have taken him for a country schoolmaster as soon as anything else. He was dressed in a rusty black frockcoat and pantaloons, unbrushed, and worn so faithfully that the suit had adapted itself to the curves and angularities of his figure, and had grown to be an outer skin of the man. He had shabby slippers on his feet. His hair was black, still unmixed with gray, stiff, somewhat bushy, and had apparently been acquainted with neither brush nor comb that morning, after the disarrangement of the pillow; and as to a night-cap, Uncle Abe probably knows nothing of such effeminacies. His complexion is dark and sallow, betokening, I fear, an insalubrious atmosphere around the White House; he has thick black eyebrows and an impending brow; his nose is large, and the lines about his mouth are very strongly defined.

The whole physiognomy is as coarse a one as you would meet anywhere in the length and breadth of the States ; but, withal, it is redeemed, illuminated, softened, and brightened by a kindly though serious look out of his eyes, and an expression of homely sagacity, that seems weighted with rich results of village experience. A great deal of native sense ; no bookish cultivation, no refinement ; honest at heart, and thoroughly so, and yet, in some sort, sly, — at least, endowed with a sort of tact and wisdom that are akin to craft, and would impel him, I think, to take an antagonist in flank, rather than to make a bull-run at him right in front. But, on the whole, I like this sallow, queer, sagacious visage, with the homely human sympathies that warmed it; and, for my small share in the matter, would as lief have Uncle Abe for a ruler as any man whom it would have been practicable to put in his place.

Immediately on his entrance the President accosted our member of Congress, who had us in charge, and, with a comical twist of his face, made some jocular remark about the length of his breakfast. He then greeted us all round, not waiting for an introduction, but shaking and squeezing everybody's hand with the utmost cordiality, whether the individual's name was announced to him or not. His manner towards us was wholly without pretence, but yet had a kind of natural dignity, quite sufficient to keep the forwardest of us from clapping him on the shoulder and asking him for a story. A mutual acquaintance being established, our leader took the whip out of its case, and began to read the address of presentation. The whip was an exceedingly long one, its handle wrought in ivory (by some artist in the Massachusetts State Prison, I believe), and ornamented with a medallion of the President, and other equally beautiful devices; and along its whole length there was a succession of golden bands and ferrules. The address was shorter than the whip, but equally well made, consisting chiefly of an explanatory description of these artistic designs, and closing with a hint that the gift was a suggestive and emblematic one, and that the President would recognize the use to which such an instrument should be put.

This suggestion gave Uncle Abe rather a delicate

task in his reply, because, slight as the matter seemed, it apparently called for some declaration, or intimation, or faint foreshadowing of policy in reference to the conduct of the war, and the final treatment of the Rebels. But the President's Yankee aptness and not-to-be-caughtness stood him in good stead, and he jerked or wiggled himself out of the dilemma with an uncouth dexterity that was entirely in character; although, without his gesticulation of eye and mouth, — and especially the flourish of the whip, with which he imagined himself touching up a pair of fat horses, — I doubt whether his words would be worth recording, even if I could remember them. The gist of the reply was, that he accepted the whip as an emblem of peace, not punishment; and, this great affair over, we retired out of the presence in high good-humor, only regretting that we could not have seen the President sit down and fold up his legs (which is said to be a most extraordinary spectacle), or have heard him tell one of those delectable stories for which he is so celebrated. A good many of them are afloat upon the common talk of Washington, and are certainly the aptest, pithiest, and funniest little things imaginable; though, to be sure, they smack of the frontier freedom, and would not always bear repetition in a drawing-room, or on the immaculate page of the Atlantic.[1]

[1] The above passage relating to President Lincoln was one of those omitted from the article as originally published, and the following note was appended to explain the omission, which had been indicated by a line of points : —

We are compelled to omit two or three pages, in which the author describes the interview, and gives his idea of the personal appearance and deportment of the President. The sketch appears to have been written in a benign spirit, and perhaps conveys a not inaccurate impression of its august subject; but it lacks *reverence*, and it pains us to see a gentleman of ripe age, and who has spent years under the

Good Heavens! what liberties have I been taking with one of the potentates of the earth, and the man on whose conduct more important consequences depend than on that of any other historical personage of the century! But with whom is an American citizen entitled to take a liberty, if not with his own chief magistrate? However, lest the above allusions to President Lincoln's little peculiarities (already well known to the country and to the world) should be misinterpreted, I deem it proper to say a word or two in regard to him, of unfeigned respect and measurable confidence. He is evidently a man of keen faculties, and, what is still more to the purpose, of powerful character. As to his integrity, the people have that intuition of it which is never deceived. Before he actually entered upon his great office, and for a considerable time afterwards, there is no reason to suppose that he adequately estimated the gigantic task about to be imposed on him, or, at least, had any distinct idea how it was to be managed; and I presume there may have been more than one veteran politician who proposed to himself to take the power out of President Lincoln's hands into his own, leaving our honest friend only the public responsibility for the good or ill success of the career. The extremely imperfect development of his statesmanly qualities, at that period, may have justified such designs. But the President is teachable by events, and has now spent a year in a very arduous course of education; he has a flexible mind, capable of much expansion, and convertible towards far loftier studies and activities than those of his early life; and if he came to Washington a back-

corrective influence of foreign institutions, falling into the characteristic and most ominous fault of Young America.

woods humorist, he has already transformed himself
into as good a statesman (to speak moderately) as his
prime-minister.

Among other excursions to camps and places of interest in the neighborhood of Washington, we went,
one day, to Alexandria.  It is a little port on the Potomac, with one or two shabby wharves and docks, resembling those of a fishing-village in New England,
and the respectable old brick town rising gently behind.  In peaceful times it no doubt bore an aspect
of decorous quietude and dulness; but it was now
thronged with the Northern soldiery, whose stir and
bustle contrasted strikingly with the many closed
warehouses, the absence of citizens from their customary haunts, and the lack of any symptom of healthy
activity, while army-wagons trundled heavily over the
pavements, and sentinels paced the sidewalks, and
mounted dragoons dashed to and fro on military errands.  I tried to imagine how very disagreeable the
presence of a Southern army would be in a sober
town of Massachusetts; and the thought considerably
lessened my wonder at the cold and shy regards that
are cast upon our troops, the gloom, the sullen demeanor, the declared or scarcely hidden sympathy
with rebellion, which are so frequent here.  It is a
strange thing in human life, that the greatest errors
both of men and women often spring from their sweetest and most generous qualities; and so, undoubtedly,
thousands of warm-hearted, sympathetic, and impulsive persons have joined the Rebels, not from any real
zeal for the cause, but because, between two conflicting loyalties, they chose that which necessarily lay
nearest the heart.  There never existed any other
government against which treason was so easy, and

could defend itself by such plausible arguments, as against that of the United States. The anomaly of two allegiances (of which that of the State comes nearest home to a man's feelings, and includes the altar and the hearth, while the General Government claims his devotion only to an airy mode of law, and has no symbol but a flag) is exceedingly mischievous in this point of view; for it has converted crowds of honest people into traitors, who seem to themselves not merely innocent, but patriotic, and who die for a bad cause with as quiet a conscience as if it were the best. In the vast extent of our country, — too vast by far to be taken into one small human heart, — we inevitably limit to our own State, or, at farthest, to our own section, that sentiment of physical love for the soil which renders an Englishman, for example, so intensely sensitive to the dignity and well-being of his little island, that one hostile foot, treading anywhere upon it, would make a bruise on each individual breast. If a man loves his own State, therefore, and is content to be ruined with her, let us shoot him, if we can, but allow him an honorable burial in the soil he fights for.[1]

In Alexandria, we visited the tavern in which Colonel Ellsworth was killed, and saw the spot where he fell, and the stairs below, whence Jackson fired the fatal shot, and where he himself was slain a moment afterwards; so that the assassin and his victim must have met on the threshold of the spirit-world, and perhaps came to a better understanding before they had taken many steps on the other side. Ellsworth was

---

[1] We do not thoroughly comprehend the author's drift in the foregoing paragraph, but are inclined to think its tone reprehensible, and its tendency impolitic in the present stage of our national difficulties.

too generous to bear an immortal grudge for a deed like that, done in hot blood, and by no skulking enemy. The memorial-hunters have completely cut away the original wood-work around the spot, with their pocket-knives; and the staircase, balustrade, and floor, as well as the adjacent doors and door-frames, have recently been renewed; the walls, moreover, are covered with new paper-hangings, the former having been torn off in tatters; and thus it becomes something like a metaphysical question whether the place of the murder actually exists.

Driving out of Alexandria, we stopped on the edge of the city to inspect an old slave-pen, which is one of the lions of the place, but a very poor one; and a little farther on, we came to a brick church where Washington used sometimes to attend service, — a pre-Revolutionary edifice, with ivy growing over its walls, though not very luxuriantly. Reaching the open country, we saw forts and camps on all sides; some of the tents being placed immediately on the ground, while others were raised over a basement of logs, laid lengthwise, like those of a log-hut, or driven vertically into the soil in a circle, — thus forming a solid wall, the chinks closed up with Virginia mud, and above it the pyramidal shelter of the tent. Here were in progress all the occupations, and all the idleness, of the soldier in the tented field; some were cooking the company-rations in pots hung over fires in the open air; some played at ball, or developed their muscular power by gymnastic exercise; some read newspapers; some smoked cigars or pipes; and many were cleaning their arms and accoutrements, — the more carefully, perhaps, because their division was to be reviewed by the Commander-in-Chief that afternoon; others sat on the

ground, while their comrades cut their hair, — it being a soldierly fashion (and for excellent reasons) to
crop it within an inch of the skull; others, finally, lay
asleep in breast-high tents, with their legs protruding
into the open air.

We paid a visit to Fort Ellsworth, and from its
ramparts (which have been heaped up out of the
muddy soil within the last few months, and will require still a year or two to make them verdant) we
had a beautiful view of the Potomac, a truly majestic
river, and the surrounding country. The fortifications,
so numerous in all this region, and now so unsightly
with their bare, precipitous sides, will remain as historic monuments, grass-grown and picturesque memorials of an epoch of terror and suffering: they will
serve to make our country dearer and more interesting
to us, and afford fit soil for poetry to root itself in:
for this is a plant which thrives best in spots where
blood has been spilt long ago, and grows in abundant
clusters in old ditches, such as the moat around Fort
Ellsworth will be a century hence. It may seem to
be paying dear for what many will reckon but a worthless weed; but the more historical associations we can
link with our localities, the richer will be the daily life
that feeds upon the past, and the more valuable the
things that have been long established: so that our
children will be less prodigal than their fathers in sac-
rificing good institutions to passionate impulses and
impracticable theories. This herb of grace, let us
hope, may be found in the old footprints of the war.

Even in an æsthetic point of view, however, the
war has done a great deal of enduring mischief, by
causing the devastation of great tracts of woodland
scenery, in which this part of Virginia would appear

to have been very rich. Around all the encampments, and everywhere along the road, we saw the bare sites of what had evidently been tracts of hard-wood forest, indicated by the unsightly stumps of well-grown trees, not smoothly felled by regular axe-men, but hacked, haggled, and unevenly amputated, as by a sword, or other miserable tool, in an unskilful hand. Fifty years will not repair this desolation. An army destroys everything before and around it, even to the very grass; for the sites of the encampments are converted into barren esplanades, like those of the squares in French cities, where not a blade of grass is allowed to grow. As to the other symptoms of devastation and obstruction, such as deserted houses, unfenced fields, and a general aspect of nakedness and ruin, I know not how much may be due to a normal lack of neatness in the rural life of Virginia, which puts a squalid face even upon a prosperous state of things; but undoubtedly the war must have spoilt what was good, and made the bad a great deal worse. The carcasses of horses were scattered along the wayside.

One very pregnant token of a social system thoroughly disturbed was presented by a party of contrabands, escaping out of the mysterious depths of Secessia; and its strangeness consisted in the leisurely delay with which they trudged forward, as dreading no pursuer, and encountering nobody to turn them back. They were unlike the specimens of their race whom we are accustomed to see at the North, and, in my judgment, were far more agreeable. So rudely were they attired, — as if their garb had grown upon them spontaneously, — so picturesquely natural in manners, and wearing such a crust of primeval simplicity (which is quite polished away from the northern black man), that they seemed a kind of creature by themselves, not altogether human, but perhaps quite as good, and akin to the fauns and rustic deities of olden times. I wonder whether I shall excite anybody's wrath by saying this. It is no great matter. At all events, I felt most kindly towards these poor fugitives, but knew not precisely what to wish in their behalf, nor in the least how to help them. For the sake of the manhood which is latent in them, I would not have turned them back; but I should have felt almost as reluctant, on their own account, to hasten them forward to the stranger's land; and I think my prevalent idea was, that, whoever may be benefited by the results of this war, it will not be the present generation of negroes, the childhood of whose race is now gone forever, and who must henceforth fight a hard battle with the world, on very unequal terms. On behalf of my own race, I am glad and can only hope that an inscrutable Providence means good to both parties.

There is an historical circumstance, known to few, that connects the children of the Puritans with these Africans of Virginia in a very singular way. They are our brethren, as being lineal descendants from the Mayflower, the fated womb of which, in her first voyage, sent forth a brood of Pilgrims on Plymouth Rock, and, in a subsequent one, spawned slaves upon the Southern soil, — a monstrous birth, but with which we have an instinctive sense of kindred, and so are stirred by an irresistible impulse to attempt their rescue, even at the cost of blood and ruin. The character of our sacred ship, I fear, may suffer a little by this revelation; but we must let her white progeny offset her dark one, — and two such portents never sprang from an identical source before.

While we drove onward, a young officer on horse-back looked earnestly into the carriage, and recognized some faces that he had seen before ; so he rode along by our side, and we pestered him with queries and observations, to which he responded more civilly than they deserved. He was on General McClellan's staff, and a gallant cavalier, high-booted, with a revolver in his belt, and mounted on a noble horse, which trotted hard and high without disturbing the rider in his accustomed seat. His face had a healthy hue of exposure and an expression of careless hardihood ; and, as I looked at him, it seemed to me that the war had brought good fortune to the youth of this epoch, if to none beside ; since they now make it their daily business to ride a horse and handle a sword, instead of lounging listlessly through the duties, occupations, pleasures — all tedious alike — to which the artificial state of society limits a peaceful generation. The atmosphere of the camp and the smoke of the battle-field are morally invigorating ; the hardy virtues flourish in them, the nonsense dies like a wilted weed. The enervating effects of centuries of civilization vanish at once, and leave these young men to enjoy a life of hardship, and the exhilarating sense of danger, — to kill men blamelessly, or to be killed gloriously, — and to be happy in following out their native instincts of destruction, precisely in the spirit of Homer's heroes, only with some considerable change of mode. One touch of Nature makes not only the whole world, but all time, akin. Set men face to face, with weapons in their hands, and they are as ready to slaughter one another now, after playing at peace and good-will for so many years, as in the rudest ages, that never heard of peace-societies, and thought no wine so deli-

cious as what they quaffed from an enemy's skull.
Indeed, if the report of a Congressional committee
may be trusted, that old-fashioned kind of goblet has
again come into use, at the expense of our Northern
head-pieces, — a costly drinking-cup to him that fur-
nishes it! Heaven forgive me for seeming to jest
upon such a subject! — only, it is so odd, when we
measure our advances from barbarism, and find ourselves just here! [1]

We now approached General McClellan's headquarters, which, at that time, were established at
Fairfield Seminary. The edifice was situated on a
gentle elevation, amid very agreeable scenery, and, at
a distance, looked like a gentleman's seat. Preparations were going forward for reviewing a division of
ten or twelve thousand men, the various regiments
composing which had begun to array themselves on an
extensive plain, where, methought, there was a more
convenient place for a battle than is usually found
in this broken and difficult country. Two thousand
cavalry made a portion of the troops to be reviewed.
By and by we saw a pretty numerous troop of mounted
officers, who were congregated on a distant part of the
plain, and whom we finally ascertained to be the Commander-in-Chief's staff, with McClellan himself at
their head. Our party managed to establish itself in
a position conveniently close to the General, to whom,
moreover, we had the honor of an introduction; and
he bowed, on his horseback, with a good deal of dignity and martial courtesy, but no airs nor fuss nor

[1] We hardly expected this outbreak in favor of war from the
Peaceable Man; but the justice of our cause makes us all soldiers at
heart, however quiet in our outward life. We have heard of twenty
Quakers in a single company of a Pennsylvania regiment.

pretension beyond what his character and rank inevitably gave him.

Now, at that juncture, and, in fact, up to the present moment, there was, and is, a most fierce and bitter outcry, and detraction loud and low, against General McClellan, accusing him of sloth, imbecility, cowardice, treasonable purposes, and, in short, utterly denying his ability as a soldier, and questioning his integrity as a man. Nor was this to be wondered at; for when before, in all history, do we find a general in command of half a million of men, and in presence of an enemy inferior in numbers and no better disciplined than his own troops, leaving it still debatable, after the better part of a year, whether he is a soldier or no? The question would seem to answer itself in the very asking. Nevertheless, being most profoundly ignorant of the art of war, like the majority of the General's critics, and, on the other hand, having some considerable impressibility by men's characters, I was glad of the opportunity to look him in the face, and to feel whatever influence might reach me from his sphere. So I stared at him, as the phrase goes, with all the eyes I had; and the reader shall have the benefit of what I saw, — to which he is the more welcome, because, in writing this article, I feel disposed to be singularly frank, and can scarcely restrain myself from telling truths the utterance of which I should get slender thanks for.

The General was dressed in a simple, dark-blue uniform, without epaulets, booted to the knee, and with a cloth cap upon his head; and, at first sight, you might have taken him for a corporal of dragoons, of particularly neat and soldier-like aspect, and in the prime of his age and strength. He is only of middling stature,

but his build is very compact and sturdy, with broad
shoulders and a look of great physical vigor, which, in
fact, he is said to possess, — he and Beauregard having
been rivals in that particular, and both distinguished
above other men. His complexion is dark and sanguine, with dark hair. He has a strong, bold, soldierly face, full of decision ; a Roman nose, by no
means a thin prominence, but very thick and firm ;
and if he follows it (which I should think likely), it
may be pretty confidently trusted to guide him aright.
His profile would make a more effective likeness than
the full face, which, however, is much better in the
real man than in any photograph that I have seen.
His forehead is not remarkably large, but comes forward at the eyebrows ; it is not the brow nor countenance of a prominently intellectual man (not a natural student, I mean, or abstract thinker), but of one
whose office it is to handle things practically and to
bring about tangible results. His face looked capable of being very stern, but wore, in its repose, when
I saw it, an aspect pleasant and dignified ; it is not,
in its character, an American face, nor an English
one. The man on whom he fixes his eye is conscious
of him. In his natural disposition, he seems calm
and self - possessed, sustaining his great responsibilities cheerfully, without shrinking, or weariness, or
spasmodic effort, or damage to his health, but all
with quiet, deep - drawn breaths ; just as his broad
shoulders would bear up a heavy burden without ach-
ing beneath it.

After we had had sufficient time to peruse the man
(so far as it could be done with one pair of very atten-
tive eyes), the General rode off, followed by his caval-
cade, and was lost to sight among the troops. They

received him with loud shouts, by the eager uproar of which — now near, now in the centre, now on the outskirts of the division, and now sweeping back towards us in a great volume of sound — we could trace his progress through the ranks. If he is a coward, or a traitor, or a humbug, or anything less than a brave, true, and able man, that mass of intelligent soldiers, whose lives and honor he had in charge, were utterly deceived, and so was this present writer; for they believed in him, and so did I; and had I stood in the ranks, I should have shouted with the lustiest of them. Of course I may be mistaken; my opinion on such a point is worth nothing, although my impression may be worth a little more; neither do I consider the General's antecedents as bearing very decided testimony to his practical soldiership. A thorough knowledge of the science of war seems to be conceded to him; he is allowed to be a good military critic; but all this is possible without his possessing any positive qualities of a great general, just as a literary critic may show the profoundest acquaintance with the principles of epic poetry without being able to produce a single stanza of an epic poem. Nevertheless, I shall not give up my faith in General McClellan's soldiership until he is defeated, nor in his courage and integrity even then.

Another of our excursions was to Harper's Ferry, — the Directors of the Baltimore and Ohio Railroad having kindly invited us to accompany them on the first trip over the newly laid track, after its breaking up by the Rebels. It began to rain, in the early morning, pretty soon after we left Washington, and continued to pour a cataract throughout the day; so that the aspect of the country was dreary, where it would otherwise have been delightful, as we entered among the hill-scenery that is formed by the subsiding swells of the Al-leghanies. The latter part of our journey lay along the shore of the Potomac, in its upper course, where the margin of that noble river is bordered by gray, over-hanging crags, beneath which — and sometimes right through them — the railroad takes its way. In one place the Rebels had attempted to arrest a train by pre-cipitating an immense mass of rock down upon the track, by the side of which it still lay, deeply imbed-ded in the ground, and looking as if it might have lain there since the Deluge. The scenery grew even more picturesque as we proceeded, the bluffs becoming very bold in their descent upon the river, which, at Har-per's Ferry, presents as striking a vista among the hills as a painter could desire to see. But a beautiful landscape is a luxury, and luxuries are thrown away amid discomfort ; and when we alighted into the tena-cious mud and almost fathomless puddle, on the hither side of the Ferry (the ultimate point to which the cars proceeded, since the railroad bridge had been destroyed by the Rebels), I cannot remember that any very rap-turous emotions were awakened by the scenery.

We paddled and floundered over the ruins of the track, and, scrambling down an embankment, crossed the Potomac by a pontoon-bridge, a thousand feet in length, over the narrow line of which — level with the river, and rising and subsiding with it — General Banks had recently led his whole army, with its pon-derous artillery and heavily laden wagons. Yet our own tread made it vibrate. The broken bridge of the railroad was a little below us, and at the base of one of its massive piers, in the rocky bed of the river, lay a locomotive, which the Rebels had precipitated there.

As we passed over, we looked towards the Virginia shore, and beheld the little town of Harper's Ferry, gathered about the base of a round hill and climbing up its steep acclivity; so that it somewhat resembled the Etruscan cities which I have seen among the Apennines, rushing, as it were, down an apparently breakneck height. About midway of the ascent stood a shabby brick church, towards which a difficult path went scrambling up the precipice, indicating, one would say, a very fervent aspiration on the part of the worshippers, unless there was some easier mode of access in another direction. Immediately on the shore of the Potomac, and extending back towards the town, lay the dismal ruins of the United States arsenal and armory, consisting of piles of broken bricks and a waste of shapeless demolition, amid which we saw gunbarrels in heaps of hundreds together. They were the relics of the conflagration, bent with the heat of the fire and rusted with the wintry rain to which they had since been exposed. The brightest sunshine could not have made the scene cheerful, nor have taken away the gloom from the dilapidated town; for, besides the natural shabbiness, and decayed, unthrifty look of a Virginian village, it has an inexpressible forlornness resulting from the devastations of war and its occupation by both armies alternately. Yet there would be a less striking contrast between Southern and New-England villages, if the former were as much in the habit of using white paint as we are. It is prodigiously efficacious in putting a bright face upon a bad matter.

There was one small shop, which appeared to have nothing for sale. A single man and one or two boys were all the inhabitants in view, except the Yankee sentinels and soldiers, belonging to Massachusetts regiments, who were scattered about pretty numerously. A guard-house stood on the slope of the hill; and in the level street at its base were the offices of the Provost-Marshal and other military authorities, to whom we forthwith reported ourselves. The Provost-Marshal kindly sent a corporal to guide us to the little building which John Brown seized upon as his fortress, and which, after it was stormed by the United States marines, became his temporary prison. It is an old engine-house, rusty and shabby, like every other work of man's hands in this God-forsaken town, and stands fronting upon the river, only a short distance from the bank, nearly at the point where the pontoon-bridge touches the Virginia shore. In its front wall, on each side of the door, are two or three ragged loop-holes, which John Brown perforated for his defence, knocking out merely a brick or two, so as to give himself and his garrison a sight over their rifles. Through these orifices the sturdy old man dealt a good deal of deadly mischief among his assailants, until they broke down the door by thrusting against it with a ladder, and tumbled headlong in upon him. I shall not pretend to be an admirer of old John Brown, any farther than sympathy with Whittier's excellent ballad about him may go; nor did I expect ever to shrink so unutterably from any apophthegm of a sage, whose happy lips have uttered a hundred golden sentences, as from that saying (perhaps falsely attributed to so honored a source), that the death of this blood-stained fanatic has "made the Gallows as venerable as the Cross!" Nobody was ever more justly hanged. He won his martyrdom fairly, and took it firmly. He himself, I am persuaded (such was his natural integrity), would have acknowledged that Virginia had a right to take the life which he had staked and lost; although it would have been better for her, in the hour that is fast coming, if she could generously have forgotten the criminality of his attempt in its enormous folly. On the other hand, any common-sensible man, looking at the matter unsentimentally, must have felt a certain intellectual satisfaction in seeing him hanged, if it were only in requital of his preposterous miscalculation of possibilities.[1]

But, coolly as I seem to say these things, my Yankee heart stirred triumphantly when I saw the use to which John Brown's fortress and prison-house has now been put. What right have I to complain of any other man's foolish impulses, when I cannot possibly control my own? The engine-house is now a place of confinement for Rebel prisoners.

A Massachusetts soldier stood on guard, but readily permitted our whole party to enter. It was a wretched place. A room of perhaps twenty-five feet square occupied the whole interior of the building, having an iron stove in its centre, whence a rusty funnel ascended towards a hole in the roof, which served the purposes of ventilation, as well as for the exit of smoke. We found ourselves right in the midst of the Rebels, some of whom lay on heaps of straw, asleep, or, at all events, giving no sign of consciousness; others sat in the corners of the room, huddled close together, and staring with a lazy kind of interest at the visitors; two were astride of some planks, playing with the dirtiest pack of cards that I ever happened to see. There was only one figure in the least military among all these

[1] Can it be a son of old Massachusetts who utters this abominable sentiment? For shame.

twenty prisoners of war, — a man with a dark, intelligent, moustached face, wearing a shabby cotton uniform, which he had contrived to arrange with a degree of soldierly smartness, though it had evidently borne the brunt of a very filthy campaign. He stood erect, and talked freely with those who addressed him, telling them his place of residence, the number of his regiment, the circumstances of his capture, and such other particulars as their Northern inquisitiveness prompted them to ask. I liked the manliness of his deportment; he was neither ashamed, nor afraid, nor in the slightest degree sullen, peppery, or contumacious, but bore himself as if whatever animosity he had felt towards his enemies was left upon the battle-field, and would not be resumed till he had again a weapon in his hand.

Neither could I detect a trace of hostile feeling in the countenance, words, or manner of any prisoner there. Almost to a man, they were simple, bumpkin-like fellows, dressed in homespun clothes, with faces singularly vacant of meaning, but sufficiently good-humored : a breed of men, in short, such as I did not suppose to exist in this country, although I have seen their like in some other parts of the world. They were peasants, and of a very low order: a class of people with whom our Northern rural population has not a single trait in common. They were exceedingly respectful, — more so than a rustic New-Englander ever dreams of being towards anybody, except perhaps his minister; and had they worn any hats, they would probably have been self-constrained to take them off, under the unusual circumstance of being permitted to hold conversation with well-dressed persons. It is my belief that not a single bumpkin of them all (the mous-

tached soldier always excepted) had the remotest comprehension of what they had been fighting for, or how
they had deserved to be shut up in that dreary hole ;
nor, possibly, did they care to inquire into this latter
mystery, but took it as a godsend to be suffered to
lie here in a heap of unwashed human bodies, well
warmed and well foddered to-day, and without the
necessity of bothering themselves about the possible
hunger and cold of to-morrow. Their dark prison-life
may have seemed to them the sunshine of all their
lifetime.

There was one poor wretch, a wild-beast of a man,
at whom I gazed with greater interest than at his fellows ; although I know not that each one of them, in
their semi-barbarous moral state, might not have been
capable of the same savage impulse that had made
this particular individual a horror to all beholders.
At the close of some battle or skirmish, a wounded
Union soldier had crept on hands and knees to his
feet, and besought his assistance, — not dreaming that
any creature in human shape, in the Christian land
where they had so recently been brethren, could refuse it. But this man (this fiend, if you prefer to call
him so, though I would not advise it) flung a bitter
curse at the poor Northerner, and absolutely trampled
the soul out of his body, as he lay writhing beneath
his feet. The fellow's face was horribly ugly ; but I
am not quite sure that I should have noticed it, if I
had not known his story. He spoke not a word, and
met nobody's eye, but kept staring upward into the
smoky vacancy towards the ceiling, where, it might
be, he beheld a continual portraiture of his victim's
horror-stricken agonies. I rather fancy, however, that
his moral sense was yet too torpid to trouble him with

such remorseful visions, and that, for his own part, he might have had very agreeable reminiscences of the soldier's death, if other eyes had not been bent reproachfully upon him and warned him that something was amiss. It was this reproach in other men's eyes that made him look aside. He was a wild-beast, as I began with saying, — an unsophisticated wild-beast, — while the rest of us are partially tamed, though still the scent of blood excites some of the savage instincts of our nature. What this wretch needed, in order to make him capable of the degree of mercy and benevolence that exists in us, was simply such a measure of moral and intellectual development as we have received; and, in my mind, the present war is so well justified by no other consideration as by the probability that it will free this class of Southern whites from a thraldom in which they scarcely begin to be responsible beings. So far as the education of the heart is concerned, the negroes have apparently the advantage of them; and as to other schooling, it is practically unattainable by black or white.

Looking round at these poor prisoners, therefore, it struck me as an immense absurdity that they should fancy us their enemies; since, whether we intend it so or no, they have a far greater stake on our success than we can possibly have. For ourselves, the balance of advantages between defeat and triumph may admit of question. For them, all truly valuable things are dependent on our complete success; for thence would come the regeneration of a people, — the removal of a foul scurf that has overgrown their life, and keeps them in a state of disease and decrepitude, one of the chief symptoms of which is, that, the more they suffer and are debased, the more they imagine themselves strong and beautiful. No human effort, on a grand scale, has ever yet resulted according to the purpose of its projectors. The advantages are always incidental. Man's accidents are God's purposes. We miss the good we sought, and do the good we little cared for.[1]

Our Government evidently knows when and where to lay its finger upon its most available citizens; for, quite unexpectedly, we were joined with some other gentlemen, scarcely less competent than ourselves, in a commission to proceed to Fortress Monroe and examine into things in general. Of course, official propriety compels us to be extremely guarded in our description of the interesting objects which this expedition opened to our view. There can be no harm, however, in stating that we were received by the commander of the fortress with a kind of acid good-nature, or mild cynicism, that indicated him to be a humorist, characterized by certain rather pungent peculiarities, yet of no unamiable cast. He is a small, thin old gentleman, set off by a large pair of brilliant epaulets, — the only pair, so far as my observation went, that adorn the shoulders of any officer in the Union army. Either for our inspection, or because the matter had already been arranged, he drew out a regiment of Zouaves that formed the principal part of his garrison, and appeared at their head, sitting on horseback with rigid perpendicularity, and affording us a vivid idea of the disciplinarian of Baron Steuben's school.

There can be no question of the General's military qualities; he must have been especially useful in con-

[1] The author seems to imagine that he has compressed a great deal of meaning into these little, hard, dry pellets of aphoristic wisdom. We disagree with him. The counsels of wise and good men are often coincident with the purposes of Providence; and the present war promises to illustrate our remark.

verting raw recruits into trained and efficient soldiers.
But valor and martial skill are of so evanescent a
character (hardly less fleeting than a woman's beauty),
that Government has perhaps taken the safer course in
assigning to this gallant officer, though distinguished
in former wars, no more active duty than the guardianship of an apparently impregnable fortress. The ideas
of military men solidify and fossilize so fast, while
military science makes such rapid advances, that even
here there might be a difficulty. An active, diversified, and therefore a youthful, ingenuity is required
by the quick exigencies of this singular war. Fortress Monroe, for example, in spite of the massive solidity of its ramparts, its broad and deep moat, and
all the contrivances of defence that were known at the
not very remote epoch of its construction, is now pronounced absolutely incapable of resisting the novel
modes of assault which may be brought to bear upon
it. It can only be the flexible talent of a young man
that will evolve a new efficiency out of its obsolete
strength.

It is a pity that old men grow unfit for war, not
only by their incapacity for new ideas, but by the
peaceful and unadventurous tendencies that gradually
possess themselves of the once turbulent disposition,
which used to snuff the battle-smoke as its congenial
atmosphere. It is a pity; because it would be such
an economy of human existence, if time-stricken people (whose value I have the better right to estimate,
as reckoning myself one of them) could snatch from
their juniors the exclusive privilege of carrying on the
war. In case of death upon the battle-field, how unequal would be the comparative sacrifice ! On one
part, a few unenjoyable years, the little remnant of a

life grown torpid; on the other, the many fervent summers of manhood in its spring and prime, with all that they include of possible benefit to mankind. Then, too, a bullet offers such a brief and easy way, such a pretty little orifice, through which the weary spirit might seize the opportunity to be exhaled! If I had the ordering of these matters, fifty should be the tenderest age at which a recruit might be accepted for training; at fifty-five or sixty, I would consider him eligible for most kinds of military duty and exposure, excluding that of a forlorn hope, which no soldier should be permitted to volunteer upon, short of the ripe age of seventy. As a general rule, these venerable combatants should have the preference for all dangerous and honorable service in the order of their seniority, with a distinction in favor of those whose infirmities might render their lives less worth the keeping. Methinks there would be no more Bull Runs; a warrior with gout in his toe, or rheumatism in his joints, or with one foot in the grave, would make a sorry fugitive!

On this admirable system, the productive part of the population would be undisturbed even by the bloodiest war; and, best of all, those thousands upon thousands of our Northern girls, whose proper mates will perish in camp-hospitals or on Southern battle-fields, would avoid their doom of forlorn old-maidenhood. But, no doubt, the plan will be pooh-poohed down by the War Department; though it could scarcely be more disastrous than the one on which we began the war, when a young army was struck with paralysis through the age of its commander.

The waters around Fortress Monroe were thronged with a gallant array of ships of war and transports,

wearing the Union flag, — "Old Glory," as I hear it
called in these days. A little withdrawn from our national fleet lay two French frigates, and, in another
direction, an English sloop, under that banner which
always makes itself visible, like a red portent in the
air, wherever there is strife. In pursuance of our
official duty (which had no ascertainable limits), we
went on board the flag-ship, and were shown over
every part of her, and down into her depths, inspect-
ing her gallant crew, her powerful armament, her
mighty engines, and her furnaces, where the fires are
always kept burning, as well at midnight as at noon,
so that it would require only five minutes to put the
vessel under full steam. This vigilance has been felt
necessary ever since the Merrimack made that terrible dash from Norfolk. Splendid as she is, however,
and provided with all but the very latest improvements
in naval armament, the Minnesota belongs to a class
of vessels that will be built no more, nor ever fight
another battle, — being as much a thing of the past
as any of the ships of Queen Elizabeth's time, which
grappled with the galleons of the Spanish Armada.

On her quarter-deck, an elderly flag-officer was pac-
ing to and fro, with a self-conscious dignity to which
a touch of the gout or rheumatism perhaps contributed a little additional stiffness. He seemed to be a
gallant gentleman, but of the old, slow, and pompous
school of naval worthies, who have grown up amid
rules, forms, and etiquette which were adopted full-
blown from the British navy into ours, and are somewhat too cumbrous for the quick spirit of to-day. This
order of nautical heroes will probably go down, along
with the ships in which they fought valorously and
strutted most intolerably. How can an admiral con-

descend to go to sea in an iron pot? What space and elbow-room can be found for quarter-deck dignity in the cramped lookout of the Monitor, or even in the twenty-feet diameter of her cheese-box? All the pomp and splendor of naval warfare are gone by. Henceforth there must come up a race of enginemen and smoke-blackened cannoneers, who will hammer away at their enemies under the direction of a single pair of eyes; and even heroism — so deadly a gripe is Science laying on our noble possibilities — will become a quality of very minor importance, when its possessor cannot break through the iron crust of his own armament and give the world a glimpse of it.

At no great distance from the Minnesota lay the strangest-looking craft I ever saw. It was a platform of iron, so nearly on a level with the water that the swash of the waves broke over it, under the impulse of a very moderate breeze; and on this platform was raised a circular structure, likewise of iron, and rather broad and capacious, but of no great height. It could not be called a vessel at all; it was a machine, — and I have seen one of somewhat similar appearance employed in cleaning out the docks; or, for lack of a better similitude, it looked like a gigantic rat-trap. It was ugly, questionable, suspicious, evidently mischievous, — nay, I will allow myself to call it devilish; for this was the new war-fiend, destined, along with others of the same breed, to annihilate whole navies and batter down old supremacies. The wooden walls of Old England cease to exist, and a whole history of naval renown reaches its period, now that the Monitor comes smoking into view; while the billows dash over what seems her deck, and storms bury even her turret in green water, as she burrows and snorts

along, oftener under the surface than above. The singularity of the object has betrayed me into a more ambitious vein of description than I often indulge ; and,
after all, I might as well have contented myself with
simply saying that she looked very queer.

Going on board, we were surprised at the extent and
convenience of her interior accommodations. There is
a spacious ward-room, nine or ten feet in height, besides a private cabin for the commander, and sleeping accommodations on an ample scale ; the whole well
lighted and ventilated, though beneath the surface of
the water. Forward, or aft (for it is impossible to
tell stem from stern), the crew are relatively quite as
well provided for as the officers. It was like finding
a palace, with all its conveniences, under the sea. The
inaccessibility, the apparent impregnability, of this
submerged iron fortress are most satisfactory; the
officers and crew get down through a little hole in the
deck, hermetically seal themselves, and go below ; and
until they see fit to reappear, there would seem to be
no power given to man whereby they can be brought
to light. A storm of cannon-shot damages them no
more than a handful of dried peas. We saw the shot-
marks made by the great artillery of the Merrimack
on the outer casing of the iron tower ; they were about
the breadth and depth of shallow saucers, almost imperceptible dents, with no corresponding bulge on the
interior surface. In fact, the thing looked altogether
too safe ; though it may not prove quite an agreeable
predicament to be thus boxed up in impenetrable iron,
with the possibility, one would imagine, of being sent
to the bottom of the sea, and, even there, not drowned,
but stifled. Nothing, however, can exceed the confidence of the officers in this new craft. It was pleasant

to see their benign exultation in her powers of mischief, and the delight with which they exhibited the circumvolutory movement of the tower, the quick thrusting forth of the immense guns to deliver their ponderous missiles, and then the immediate recoil, and the security behind the closed port-holes. Yet even this will not long be the last and most terrible improvement in the science of war. Already we hear of vessels the armament of which is to act entirely beneath the surface of the water; so that, with no other external symptoms than a great bubbling and foaming, and gush of smoke, and belch of smothered thunder out of the yeasty waves, there shall be a deadly fight going on below, — and, by and by, a sucking whirlpool, as one of the ships goes down.

The Monitor was certainly an object of great interest; but on our way to Newport News, whither we next went, we saw a spectacle that affected us with far profounder emotion. It was the sight of the few sticks that are left of the frigate Congress, stranded near the shore, — and still more, the masts of the Cumberland rising midway out of the water, with a tattered rag of a pennant fluttering from one of them. The invisible hull of the latter ship seems to be careened over, so that the three masts stand slantwise; the rigging looks quite unimpaired, except that a few ropes dangle loosely from the yards. The flag (which never was struck, thank Heaven!) is entirely hidden under the waters of the bay, but is still doubtless waving in its old place, although it floats to and fro with the swell and reflux of the tide, instead of rustling on the breeze. A remnant of the dead crew still man the sunken ship, and sometimes a drowned body floats up to the surface.

That was a noble fight. When was ever a better word spoken than that of Commodore Smith, the father of the commander of the Congress, when he heard that his son's ship was surrendered? "Then Joe's dead!" said he; and so it proved. Nor can any warrior be more certain of enduring renown than the gallant Morris, who fought so well the final battle of the old system of naval warfare, and won glory for his country and himself out of inevitable disaster and defeat. That last gun from the Cumberland, when her deck was half submerged, sounded the requiem of many sinking ships. Then went down all the navies of Europe, and our own, Old Ironsides and all, and Trafalgar and a thousand other fights became only a memory, never to be acted over again; and thus our brave countrymen come last in the long procession of heroic sailors that includes Blake and Nelson, and so many mariners of England, and other mariners as brave as they, whose renown is our native inheritance. There will be other battles, but no more such tests of seamanship and manhood as the battles of the past; and, moreover, the Millennium is certainly approaching, because human strife is to be transferred from the heart and personality of man into cunning contrivances of machinery, which by and by will fight out our wars with only the clank and smash of iron, strewing the field with broken engines, but damaging nobody's little finger except by accident. Such is obviously the tendency of modern improvement. But, in the meanwhile, so long as manhood retains any part of its pristine value, no country can afford to let gallantry like that of Morris and his crew, any more than that of the brave Worden, pass unhonored and unrewarded. If the Government do nothing, let the people take the matter into their own hands, and cities give him swords, gold boxes, festivals of triumph, and, if he needs it, heaps of gold. Let poets brood upon the theme, and make themselves sensible how much of the past and future is contained within its compass, till its spirit shall flash forth in the lightning of a song!

From these various excursions, and a good many others (including one to Manassas), we gained a pretty lively idea of what was going on ; but, after all, if compelled to pass a rainy day in the hall and parlors of Willard's Hotel, it proved about as profitably spent as if we had floundered through miles of Virginia mud, in quest of interesting matter. This hotel, in fact, may be much more justly called the centre of Washington and the Union than either the Capitol, the White House, or the State Department. Everybody may be seen there. It is the meeting-place of the true representatives of the country, — not such as are chosen blindly and amiss by electors who take a folded ballot from the hand of a local politician, and thrust it into the ballot-box unread, but men who gravitate or are attracted hither by real business, or a native impulse to breathe the intensest atmosphere of the nation's life, or a genuine anxiety to see how this life-and-death struggle is going to deal with us. Nor these only, but all manner of loafers. Never, in any other spot, was there such a miscellany of people. You exchange nods with governors of sovereign States ; you elbow illustrious men, and tread on the toes of generals ; you hear statesmen and orators speaking in their familiar tones. You are mixed up with office-seekers, wire-pullers, inventors, artists, poets, prosers (including editors, army-correspondents, *attachés* of foreign journals, and long-winded talkers), clerks, diplomatists, mail-contractors, railway-directors, until your own identity is lost among them. Occasionally you talk with a man whom you have never before heard of, and are struck by the brightness of a thought, and fancy that there is more wisdom hidden among the obscure than is anywhere revealed among the famous. You adopt the universal habit of the place, and call for a mint-julep, a whiskey-skin, a gin-cocktail, a brandy-smash, or a glass of pure Old Rye ; for the conviviality of Washington sets in at an early hour, and, so far as I had an opportunity of observing, never terminates at any hour, and all these drinks are continually in request by almost all these people. A constant atmosphere of cigar-smoke, too, envelops the motley crowd, and forms a sympathetic medium, in which men meet more closely and talk more frankly than in any other kind of air. If legislators would smoke in session, they might speak truer words, and fewer of them, and bring about more valuable results.

It is curious to observe what antiquated figures and costumes sometimes make their appearance at Willard's. You meet elderly men with frilled shirt-fronts, for example, the fashion of which adornment passed away from among the people of this world half a century ago. It is as if one of Stuart's portraits were walking abroad. I see no way of accounting for this, except that the trouble of the times, the impiety of traitors, and the peril of our sacred Union and Constitution have disturbed, in their honored graves, some of the venerable fathers of the country, and summoned them forth to protest against the meditated and half-accomplished sacrilege. If it be so, their wonted fires are not altogether extinguished in their ashes, — in their throats, I might rather say, — for I beheld one of these excellent old men quaffing such a horn of Bourbon whiskey as a toper of the present century would be loath to venture upon. But, really, one would be glad to know where these strange figures come from. It shows, at any rate, how many remote, decaying villages and country-neighborhoods of the North, and forest-nooks of the West, and old mansion-houses in cities, are shaken by the tremor of our native soil, so that men long hidden in retirement put on the garments of their youth and hurry out to inquire what is the matter. The old men whom we see here have generally more marked faces than the young ones, and naturally enough; since it must be an extraordinary vigor and renewability of life that can overcome the rusty sloth of age, and keep the senior flexible enough to take an interest in new things; whereas hundreds of commonplace young men come hither to stare with eyes of vacant wonder, and with vague hopes of finding out what they are fit for. And this war (we may say so much in its favor) has been the means of discovering that important secret to not a few.

We saw at Willard's many who had thus found out for themselves, that, when Nature gives a young man no other utilizable faculty, she must be understood as intending him for a soldier. The bulk of the army had moved out of Washington before we reached the city; yet it seemed to me that at least two thirds of the guests and idlers at the hotel wore one or another token of the military profession. Many of them, no doubt, were self-commissioned officers, and had put on the buttons and the shoulder-straps, and booted themselves to the knees, merely because captain, in these days, is so good a travelling-name. The majority, however, had been duly appointed by the President, but might be none the better warriors for that. It was pleasant, occasionally, to distinguish a grizzly veteran among this crowd of carpet-knights, — the trained soldier of a lifetime, long ago from West Point, who had spent his prime upon the frontier, and very likely could show an Indian bullet-mark on his breast, — if such decorations, won in an obscure warfare, were worth the showing now.

The question often occurred to me, — and, to say the truth, it added an indefinable piquancy to the scene, — what proportion of all these people, whether soldiers or civilians, were true at heart to the Union, and what part were tainted, more or less, with treasonable sympathies and wishes, even if such had never blossomed into purpose. Traitors there were among them, — no doubt of that, — civil servants of the public, very reputable persons, who yet deserved to dangle from a cord; or men who buttoned military coats over their breasts, hiding perilous secrets there, which might bring the gallant officer to stand pale-faced before a file of musketeers, with his open grave behind him. But, without insisting upon such picturesque criminality and punishment as this, an observer, who kept both his eyes and heart open, would find it by no means difficult to discern that many residents and visitors of Washington so far sided with the South as to desire nothing more nor better than to see everything reëstablished a little worse than its former basis. If the cabinet of Richmond were transferred to the Federal city, and the North awfully snubbed, at least, and driven back within its old political limits, they would deem it a happy day. It is no wonder, and, if we look at the matter generously, no unpardonable crime.

Very excellent people hereabouts remember the many dynasties in which the Southern character has been predominant, and contrast the genial courtesy, the warm and graceful freedom of that region, with what they call (though I utterly disagree with them) the frigidity of our Northern manners, and the Western plainness of the President. They have a conscientious, though mistaken belief, that the South was driven out of the Union by intolerable wrong on our part, and that we are responsible for having compelled true patriots to love only half their country instead of the whole, and brave soldiers to draw their swords against the Constitution which they would once have died for, — to draw them, too, with a bitterness of animosity which is the only symptom of brotherhood (since brothers hate each other best) that any longer exists. They whisper these things with tears in their eyes, and shake their heads, and stoop their poor old shoulders, at the tidings of another and another Northern victory, which, in their opinion, puts farther off the remote, the already impossible, chance of a reunion.

I am sorry for them, though it is by no means a sorrow without hope. Since the matter has gone so far, there seems to be no way but to go on winning victories, and establishing peace and a truer union in another generation, at the expense, probably, of greater trouble, in the present one, than any other people ever voluntarily suffered. We woo the South " as the Lion wooes his bride;" it is a rough courtship, but perhaps love and a quiet household may come of it at last. Or, if we stop short of that blessed consummation, heaven was heaven still, as Milton sings, after Lucifer and a third part of the angels had seceded from its golden palaces, — and perhaps all the more heavenly, because so many gloomy brows, and soured, vindictive hearts, had gone to plot ineffectual schemes of mischief elsewhere.[1]

[1] We regret the innuendo in the concluding sentence. The war can never be allowed to terminate, except in the complete triumph of Northern principles. We hold the event in our own hands, and may choose whether to terminate it by the methods already so successfully used, or by other means equally within our control, and calculated to be still more speedily efficacious. In truth, the work is already done. We should be sorry to cast a doubt on the Peaceable Man's loyalty, but he will allow us to say that we consider him premature in his kindly feelings towards traitors and sympathizers with treason. As the author himself says of John Brown (and, so applied, we thought it an atrociously cold-blooded *dictum*), " any common-sensible man would feel an intellectual satisfaction in seeing them hanged, were it only for their preposterous miscalculation of possibilities." There are some degrees of absurdity that put Reason herself into a rage, and affect us like an intolerable crime, — which this Rebellion is, into the bargain.

# LIFE OF FRANKLIN PIERCE.

# LIFE OF FRANKLIN PIERCE.

## PREFACE.

THE author of this memoir — being so little of a politician that he scarcely feels entitled to call himself a member of any party — would not voluntarily have undertaken the work here offered to the public. Neither can he flatter himself that he has been remarkably successful in the performance of his task, viewing it in the light of a political biography, and as a representation of the principles and acts of a public man, intended to operate upon the minds of multitudes during a presidential canvass. This species of writing is too remote from his customary occupations — and, he may add, from his tastes — to be very satisfactorily done, without more time and practice than he would be willing to expend for such a purpose. If this little biography have any value, it is probably of another kind — as the narrative of one who knew the individual of whom he treats, at a period of life when character could be read with undoubting accuracy, and who, consequently, in judging of the motives of his subsequent conduct, has an advantage over much more competent observers, whose knowledge of the man may have commenced at a later date. Nor can it be considered improper (at least the author will never feel it so, although some foolish delicacy be sacrificed in the undertaking), that when a friend, dear to him almost from boyish days, stands up before his country, misrepresented by indiscriminate abuse, on the one hand, and by aimless praise, on the other, he should be sketched by one who has had opportunities of knowing him well, and who is certainly inclined to tell the truth.

It is perhaps right to say, that while this biography is so far sanctioned by General Pierce, as it comprises a generally correct narrative of the principal events of his life, the author does not understand him as thereby necessarily indorsing all the sentiments put forth by himself, in the progress of the work. These are the author's own speculations upon the facts before him, and may, or may not, be in accordance with the ideas of the individual whose life he writes. That individual's opinions, however, — so far as it is necessary to know them, — may be read, in his straightforward and consistent deeds, with more certainty than those of almost any other man now before the public.

The author, while collecting his materials, has received liberal aid from all manner of people — Whigs and Democrats, congressmen, astute lawyers, grim old generals of militia, and gallant young officers of the Mexican war — most of whom, however, he must needs say, have rather abounded in eulogy of General Pierce than in such anecdotical matter as is calculated for a biography. Among the gentlemen to whom he is substantially indebted, he would mention Hon. C. G. Atherton, Hon. S. H. Ayer, Hon. Joseph Hall, Chief Justice Gilchrist, Isaac O. Barnes, Esq., Col. T. J. Whipple, and Mr. C. J. Smith. He has likewise derived much assistance from an able and accurate sketch, that originally appeared in the "Boston Post," and was drawn up, as he believes, by the junior editor of that journal.

CONCORD, MASS., *August* 27, 1852.

# CHAPTER I.

### HIS PARENTAGE AND EARLY LIFE.

FRANKLIN PIERCE was born at Hillsborough, in the State of New Hampshire, on the 23d of November, 1804. His native county, at the period of his birth, covered a much more extensive territory than at present, and might reckon among its children many memorable men, and some illustrious ones. General Stark, the hero of Bennington, Daniel Webster, Levi Woodbury, Jeremiah Smith, the eminent jurist, and governor of the state, General James Miller, General McNeil, Senator Atherton, were natives of old Hillsborough County.

General Benjamin Pierce, the father of Franklin, was one of the earliest settlers in the town of Hillsborough, and contributed as much as any other man to the growth and prosperity of the county. He was born in 1757, at Chelmsford, now Lowell, in Massachusetts. Losing his parents early, he grew up under the care of an uncle, amid such circumstances of simple fare, hard labor, and scanty education as usually fell to the lot of a New England yeoman's family some eighty or a hundred years ago. On the 19th of April, 1775, being then less than eighteen years of age, the stripling was at the plough, when tidings reached him of the bloodshed at Lexington and Concord. He immediately loosened the ox chain, left the plough in the furrow, took his uncle's gun and equipments, and set forth towards the scene of action. From that day, for more than seven years, he never saw his native place. He enlisted in the army, was present at the battle of Bunker Hill, and after serving through the whole Revolutionary War, and fighting his way upward from the lowest grade, returned, at last, a thorough soldier, and commander of a company. He was retained in the army as long as that body of veterans had a united existence ; and, being finally disbanded, at West Point, in 1784, was left with no other reward, for nine years of toil and danger, than the nominal amount of his pay in the Continental currency — then so depreciated as to be almost worthless.

In 1785, being employed as agent to explore a tract of wild land, he purchased a lot of fifty acres in what is now the town of Hillsborough. In the spring of the succeeding year, he built himself a log hut, and began the clearing and cultivation of his tract. Another year beheld him married to his first wife, Elizabeth Andrews, who died within a twelvemonth after their union, leaving a daughter, the present widow of General John McNeil. In 1789, he married Anna Kendrick, with whom he lived about half a century, and who bore him eight children, of whom Franklin was the sixth.

Although the revolutionary soldier had thus betaken himself to the wilderness for a subsistence, his professional merits were not forgotten by those who had witnessed his military career. As early as 1786, he was appointed brigade major of the militia of Hillsborough County, then first organized and formed into a brigade. And it was a still stronger testimonial to his character as a soldier, that, nearly fifteen years afterwards, during the presidency of John Adams, he was offered a high command in the northern division of the army which was proposed to be levied in antici- pation of a war with the French republic. Inflexibly democratic in his political faith, however, Major Pierce refused to be implicated in a policy which he could not approve. " No, gentlemen," said he to the delegates who urged his acceptance of the commission, " poor as I am, and acceptable as would be the position under other circumstances, I would sooner go to yonder mountains, dig me a cave, and live on roast potatoes, than be instrumental in promoting the objects for which that army is to be raised ! " This same fidelity to his principles marked every public, as well as pri- vate, action of his life.

In his own neighborhood, among those who knew him best, he early gained an influence that was never lost nor diminished, but continued to spread wider during the whole of his long life. In 1789, he was elected to the state legislature and retained that posi- tion for thirteen successive years, until chosen a mem- ber of the council. During the same period, he was active in his military duties, as a field officer, and fi- nally general, of the militia of the county; and Miller, McNeil, and others learned of him, in this capacity, the soldier - like discipline which was afterwards dis- played on the battle fields of the northern frontier.

The history, character, and circumstances of Gen- eral Benjamin Pierce, though here but briefly touched upon, are essential parts of the biography of his son, both as indicating some of the native traits which the latter has inherited, and as showing the influences amid which he grew up. At Franklin Pierce's birth, and for many years subsequent, his father was the

most active and public-spirited man within his sphere;
a most decided Democrat, and supporter of Jefferson
and Madison; a practical farmer, moreover, not rich,
but independent, exercising a liberal hospitality, and
noted for the kindness and generosity of his character; a man of the people, but whose natural qualities
inevitably made him a leader among them.  From infancy upward, the boy had before his eyes, as the
model on which he might instinctively form himself,
one of the best specimens of sterling New England
character, developed in a life of simple habits, yet of
elevated action.  Patriotism, such as it had been in
revolutionary days, was taught him by his father, as
early as his mother taught him religion.  He became
early imbued, too, with the military spirit which the
old soldier had retained from his long service, and
which was kept active by the constant alarms and warlike preparations of the first twelve years of the present century.  If any man is bound, by birth and youthful training, to show himself a brave, faithful, and
able citizen of his native country, it is the son of such
a father.

At the commencement of the war of 1812, Franklin
Pierce was a few months under eight years of age.
The old general, his father, sent two of his sons into
the army; and as his eldest daughter was soon afterwards married to Major McNeil, there were few families that had so large a personal stake in the war as
that of General Benjamin Pierce.  He himself, both
in his public capacity as a member of the council, and
by his great local influence in his own county, lent a
strenuous support to the national administration.  It
is attributable to his sagacity and energy, that New
Hampshire — then under a federal governor — was

saved the disgrace of participation in the questionable, if not treasonable projects of the Hartford Convention. He identified himself with the cause of the country, and was doubtless as thoroughly alive with patriotic zeal, at this eventful period, as in the old days of Bunker Hill, and Saratoga, and Yorktown. The general not only took a prominent part at all public meetings, but was ever ready for the informal discussion of political affairs at all places of casual resort, where — in accordance with the custom of the time and country — the minds of men were made to operate effectually upon each other. Franklin Pierce was a frequent auditor of these controversies. The intentness with which he watched the old general, and listened to his arguments, is still remembered ; and, at this day, in his most earnest moods, there are gesticulations and movements that bring up the image of his father to those who recollect the latter on those occasions of the display of homely, native eloquence. No mode of education could be conceived, better adapted to imbue a youth with the principles and sentiment of democratic institutions ; it brought him into the most familiar contact with the popular mind, and made his own mind a part of it.

Franklin's father had felt, through life, the disadvantages of a defective education ; although, in his peculiar sphere of action, it might be doubted whether he did not gain more than he lost, by being thrown on his own resources, and compelled to study men and their actual affairs, rather than books. But he determined to afford his son all the opportunities of improvement which he himself had lacked. Franklin, accordingly, was early sent to the academy at Hancock, and afterwards to that of Francestown, where he was received into the family of General Pierce's old and steadfast friend, Peter Woodbury, father of the late eminent judge. It is scarcely more than a year ago, at the semi-centennial celebration of the academy, that Franklin Pierce, the mature and distinguished man, paid a beautiful tribute to the character of Madam Woodbury, in affectionate remembrance of the motherly kindness experienced at her hands by the school-boy.

The old people of his neighborhood give a very delightful picture of Franklin at this early age. They describe him as a beautiful boy, with blue eyes, light curling hair, and a sweet expression of face. The traits presented of him indicate moral symmetry, kindliness, and a delicate texture of sentiment, rather than marked prominences of character. His instructors testify to his propriety of conduct, his fellow-pupils to his sweetness of disposition and cordial sympathy. One of the latter, being older than most of his companions, and less advanced in his studies, found it difficult to keep up with his class ; and he remembers how perseveringly, while the other boys were at play, Franklin spent the noon recess, for many weeks together, in aiding him in his lessons. These attributes, proper to a generous and affectionate nature, have remained with him through life. Lending their color to his deportment, and softening his manners, they are, perhaps, even now, the characteristics by which most of those who casually meet him would be inclined to identify the man. But there are other qualities, not then developed, but which have subsequently attained a firm and manly growth, and are recognized as his leading traits among those who really know him. Franklin Pierce's development, indeed, has always been the reverse of premature; the boy did not show the germ of all that was in the man, nor, perhaps, did the young man adequately foreshow the mature one.

In 1820, at the age of sixteen, he became a student of Bowdoin College, at Brunswick, Maine. It was in the autumn of the next year that the author of this memoir entered the class below him; but our college reminiscences, however interesting to the parties concerned, are not exactly the material for a biography. He was then a youth, with the boy and man in him, vivacious, mirthful, slender, of a fair complexion, with light hair that had a curl in it: his bright and cheerful aspect made a kind of sunshine, both as regarded its radiance and its warmth; insomuch that no shyness of disposition, in his associates, could well resist its influence. We soon became acquainted, and were more especially drawn together as members of the same college society. There were two of these institutions, dividing the college between them, and typifying, respectively, and with singular accuracy of feature, the respectable conservative, and the progressive or democratic parties. Pierce's native tendencies inevitably drew him to the latter.

His chum was Zenas Caldwell, several years older than himself, a member of the Methodist persuasion, a pure-minded, studious, devoutly religious character; endowed thus early in life with the authority of a grave and sagacious turn of mind. The friendship between Pierce and him appeared to be mutually strong, and was of itself a pledge of correct deportment in the former. His chief friend, I think, was a classmate named Little, a young man of most estimable qualities and high intellectual promise; one of those fortunate characters whom an early death so canonizes in the remembrance of their companions, that the perfect fulfilment of a long life would scarcely give them a higher place. Jonathan Cilley, of my own class, — whose untimely fate is still mournfully remembered, — a person of very marked ability and great social influence, was another of Pierce's friends. All these have long been dead. There are others, still alive, who would meet Franklin Pierce, at this day, with as warm a pressure of the hand, and the same confidence in his kindly feelings, as when they parted from him nearly thirty years ago.

Pierce's class was small, but composed of individuals seriously intent on the duties and studies of their college life. They were not boys, but, for the most part, well advanced towards maturity ; and, having wrought out their own means of education, were little inclined to neglect the opportunities that had been won at so much cost. They knew the value of time, and had a sense of the responsibilities of their position. Their first scholar — the present Professor Stowe — has long since established his rank among the first scholars of the country. It could have been no easy task to hold successful rivalry with students so much in earnest as these were. During the earlier part of his college course, it may be doubted whether Pierce was distinguished for scholarship. But, for the last two years, he appeared to grow more intent on the business in hand, and, without losing any of his vivacious qualities as a companion, was evidently resolved to gain an honorable elevation in his class. His habits of attention, and obedience to college discipline, were of the strictest character ; he rose progressively in scholarship, and took a highly creditable degree.[1]

[1] See note at close of this Life.

The first civil office, I imagine, which Franklin Pierce ever held, was that of chairman of the standing committee of the Athenæan Society, of which, as above hinted, we were both members; and, having myself held a place on the committee, I can bear testimony to his having discharged not only his own share of the duties, but that of his colleagues. I remember, likewise, that the only military service of my life was as a private soldier in a college company, of which Pierce was one of the officers. He entered into this latter business, or pastime, with an earnestness with which I could not pretend to compete, and at which, perhaps, he would now be inclined to smile. His slender and youthful figure rises before my mind's eye, at this moment, with the air and step of a veteran of the school of Steuben; as well became the son of a revolutionary hero, who had probably drilled under the old baron's orders. Indeed, at this time, and for some years afterwards, Pierce's ambition seemed to be of a military cast. Until reflection had tempered his first predilections, and other varieties of success had rewarded his efforts, he would have preferred, I believe, the honors of the battle field to any laurels more peacefully won. And it was remarkable how, with all the invariable gentleness of his demeanor, he perfectly gave, nevertheless, the impression of a high and fearless spirit. His friends were as sure of his courage, while yet untried, as now, when it has been displayed so brilliantly in famous battles.

At this early period of his life, he was distinguished by the same fascination of manner that has since proved so magical in winning him an unbounded personal popularity. It is wronging him, however, to call this peculiarity a mere effect of manner; its source lies deep in the kindliness of his nature, and in the liberal, generous, catholic sympathy, that embraces all who are worthy of it. Few men possess any thing like it; so irresistible as it is, so sure to draw forth an undoubting confidence, and so true to the promise which it gives. This frankness, this democracy of good feeling, has not been chilled by the society of politicians, nor polished down into mere courtesy by his intercourse with the most refined men of the day. It belongs to him at this moment, and will never leave him. A little while ago, after his return from Mexico, he darted across the street to exchange a hearty gripe of the hand with a rough countryman upon his cart — a man who used to " live with his father," as the general explained the matter to his companions. Other men assume this manner, more or less skilfully; but with Frank Pierce it is an innate characteristic; nor will it ever lose its charm unless his heart should grow narrower and colder — a misfortune not to be anticipated, even in the dangerous atmosphere of elevated rank, whither he seems destined to ascend.

There is little else that it is worth while to relate as regards his college course, unless it be that, during one of his winter vacations, Pierce taught a country school. So many of the statesmen of New England have performed their first public service in the character of pedagogue, that it seems almost a necessary step on the ladder of advancement.

## CHAPTER II.

HIS SERVICES IN THE STATE AND NATIONAL LEGISLATURES.

AFTER leaving college, in the year 1824, Franklin Pierce returned to Hillsborough. His father, now in a green old age, continued to take a prominent part in the affairs of the day, but likewise made his declining years rich and picturesque with recollections of the heroic times through which he had lived. On the 26th of December, 1825, it being his sixty-seventh birthday, General Benjamin Pierce prepared a festival for his comrades in arms, the survivors of the Revolution, eighteen of whom, all inhabitants of Hillsborough, assembled at his house. The ages of these veterans ranged from fifty-nine up to the patriarchal venerableness of nearly ninety. They spent the day in festivity, in calling up reminiscences of the great men whom they had known, and the great deeds which they had helped to do, and in reviving the old sentiments of the era of 'seventy-six. At nightfall, after a manly and pathetic farewell from their host, they separated — "prepared," as the old general expressed it, " at the first tap of the shrouded drum, to move and join their beloved Washington, and the rest of their comrades, who fought and bled at their sides." A scene like this must have been profitable for a young man to witness, as being likely to give him a stronger sense than most of us can attain of the value of that Union which these old heroes had risked so much to consolidate — of that common country which they had sacrificed everything to create; and patriotism must have been communicated from their hearts to his, with somewhat of the warmth and freshness of a new-born sentiment. No youth was ever more fortunate than Franklin Pierce, through the whole of his early life, in this most desirable species of moral education.

Having chosen the law as a profession, Franklin became a student in the office of Judge Woodbury, of Portsmouth. Allusion has already been made to the friendship between General Benjamin Pierce and Peter Woodbury, the father of the judge. The early progress of Levi Woodbury towards eminence had been facilitated by the powerful influence of his father's friend. It was a worthy and honorable kind of patronage, and bestowed only as the great abilities of the recipient vindicated his claim to it. Few young men have met with such early success in life, or have deserved it so eminently, as did Judge Woodbury. At the age of twenty-seven, he was appointed to the bench of the Supreme Court of the state, on the earnest recommendation of old General Pierce. The opponents of the measure ridiculed him as the " baby judge; " but his conduct in that high office showed the prescient judgment of the friend who had known him from a child, and had seen in his young manhood already the wisdom of ripened age. It was some years afterwards when Franklin Pierce entered the office of Judge Woodbury as a student. In the interval, the judge had been elected governor, and, after a term of office that thoroughly tested the integrity of his democratic principles, had lost his second election, and returned to the profession of the law.

The last two years of Pierce's preparatory studies were spent at the law school of Northampton, in Massachusetts, and in the office of Judge Parker at Amherst. In 1827, being admitted to the bar, he began

the practice of his profession at Hillsborough. It is
an interesting fact, considered in reference to his subsequent splendid career as an advocate, that he did not,
at the outset, give promise of distinguished success.
His first case was a failure, and perhaps a somewhat
marked one. But it is remembered that this defeat,
however mortifying at the moment, did but serve to
make him aware of the latent resources of his mind,
the full command of which he was far from having
yet attained. To a friend, an older practitioner, who
addressed him with some expression of condolence and
encouragement, Pierce replied, — and it was a kind of
self-assertion which no triumph would have drawn out,
— "I do not need that. I will try nine hundred and
ninety-nine cases, if clients will continue to trust me,
and, if I fail just as I have to-day, will try the thou-
sandth. I shall live to argue cases in this court house
in a manner that will mortify neither myself nor my
friends." It is in such moments of defeat that character and ability are most fairly tested ; they would irre-
mediably crush a youth devoid of real energy, and, being neither more nor less than his just desert, would
be accepted as such. But a failure of this kind serves
an opposite purpose to a mind in which the strongest
and richest qualities lie deep, and, from their very size
and mass, cannot at once be rendered available. It pro-
vokes an innate self-confidence, while, at the same time,
it sternly indicates the sedulous cultivation, the earnest
effort, the toil, the agony, which are the conditions of
ultimate success. It is, indeed, one of the best modes
of discipline that experience can administer, and may
reasonably be counted a fortunate event in the life of
a young man vigorous enough to overcome the momentary depression.

Pierce's distinction at the bar, however, did not immediately follow; nor did he acquire what we may designate as positive eminence until some years after this period. The enticements of political life — so especially fascinating to a young lawyer, but so irregular in its tendencies, and so inimical to steady professional labor — had begun to operate upon him. His father's prominent position in the politics of the state made it almost impossible that the son should stand aloof. In 1827, the same year when Franklin began the practice of the law, General Benjamin Pierce had been elected governor of New Hampshire. He was defeated in the election of 1828, but was again successful in that of the subsequent year. During these years, the contest for the presidency had been fought with a fervor that drew almost everybody into it, on one side or the other, and had terminated in the triumph of Andrew Jackson. Franklin Pierce, in advance of his father's decision, though not in opposition to it, had declared himself for the illustrious man whose military renown was destined to be thrown into the shade by a civil administration, the most splendid and powerful that ever adorned the annals of our country. I love to record of the subject of this memoir that his first political faith was pledged to that great leader of the democracy.

I remember meeting Pierce about this period, and catching from him some faint reflection of the zeal with which he was now stepping into the political arena. My sympathies and opinions, it is true, — so far as I had any in public affairs, — had, from the first, been enlisted on the same side with his own. But I was now made strongly sensible of an increased development of my friend's mind, by means of which he possessed a vastly greater power than heretofore over the minds with which he came in contact. This progressive growth has continued to be one of his remarkable characteristics. Of most men you early know the mental gauge and measurement, and do not subsequently have much occasion to change it. Not so with Pierce: his tendency was not merely high, but towards a point which rose higher and higher, as the aspirant tended upward. Since we parted, studious days had educated him ; life, too, and his own exertions in it, and his native habit of close and accurate observation, had likewise begun to educate him.

The town of Hillsborough, in 1829, gave Franklin Pierce his first public honor, by electing him its representative in the legislature of the state. His whole service in that body comprised four years, in the two latter of which he was elected Speaker by a vote of one hundred and fifty-five against fifty-eight for other candidates. This overpowering majority evinced the confidence which his character inspired, and which, during his whole career, it has invariably commanded, in advance of what might be termed positive proof, although the result has never failed to justify it. I still recollect his description of the feelings with which he entered on his arduous duties — the feverish night that preceded his taking the chair — the doubt, the struggle with himself — all ending in perfect calmness, full self-possession, and free power of action when the crisis actually came.

He had all the natural gifts that adapted him for the post ; courtesy, firmness, quickness and accuracy of judgment, and a clearness of mental perception that brought its own regularity into the scene of confused and entangled debate ; and to these qualities he added whatever was to be attained by laborious study of parliamentary rules. His merit as a presiding officer was universally acknowledged. It is rare that a man combines so much impulse with so great a power of regulating the impulses of himself and others as Franklin Pierce. The faculty, here exercised and improved, of controlling an assembly while agitated by tumultuous controversy, was afterwards called into play upon a higher field ; for, during his congressional service, Pierce was often summoned to preside in committee of the whole, when a turbulent debate was expected to demand peculiar energy in the chair.

He was elected a member of Congress in 1833, being young for the station, as he has always been for every public station that he has filled. A different kind of man — a man conscious that accident alone had elevated him, and therefore nervously anxious to prove himself equal to his fortunes — would thus have been impelled to spasmodic efforts. He would have thrust himself forward in debate, taking the word out of the mouths of renowned orators, and thereby winning notoriety, as at least the glittering counterfeit of true celebrity. Had Pierce, with his genuine ability, practised this course ; had he possessed even an ordinary love of display, and had he acted upon it with his inherent tact and skill, taking advantage of fair occasions to prove the power and substance that were in him, it would greatly have facilitated the task of his biographer.

To aim at personal distinction, however, as an object independent of the public service, would have been contrary to all the foregone and subsequent manifestations of his life. He was never wanting to the occasion ; but he waited for the occasion to bring him inevitably forward. When he spoke, it was not only because he was fully master of the subject, but because the exigency demanded him, and because no other and older man could perform the same duty as well as himself. Of the copious eloquence — and some of it, no doubt, of a high order — which Buncombe has called forth, not a paragraph, nor a period, is attributable to Franklin Pierce. He had no need of these devices to fortify his constituents in their high opinion of him; nor did he fail to perceive that such was not the method to acquire real weight in the body of which he was a member. In truth, he has no fluency of words, except when an earnest meaning and purpose supply their own expression. Every one of his speeches in Congress, and, we may say, in every other hall of oratory, or on any stump that he may have mounted, was drawn forth by the perception that it was needed, was directed to a full exposition of the subject, and (rarest of all) was limited by what he really had to say. Even the graces of the orator were never elaborated, never assumed for their own sake, but were legitimately derived from the force of his conceptions, and from the impulsive warmth which accompanies the glow of thought. Owing to these peculiarities, — for such, unfortunately, they may be termed, in reference to what are usually the characteristics of a legislative career, — his position before the country was less conspicuous than that of many men who could claim nothing like Pierce's actual influence in the national councils. His speeches, in their muscular texture and close grasp of their subject, resembled the brief but pregnant arguments and expositions of the sages of the Continental Congress, rather than the immeasurable harangues which are now the order of the day.

His congressional life, though it made comparatively so little show, was full of labor, directed to substantial objects. He was a member of the judiciary and other important committees; and the drudgery of the committee room, where so much of the real public business of the country is transacted, fell in large measure to his lot. Thus, even as a legislator, he may be said to have been a man of deeds, not words; and when he spoke upon any subject with which his duty, as chairman or member of a committee, had brought him in relation, his words had the weight of deeds, from the meaning, the directness, and the truth, that he conveyed into them. His merits made themselves known and felt in the sphere where they were exercised; and he was early appreciated by one who seldom erred in his estimate of men, whether in their moral or intellectual aspect. His intercourse with President Jackson was frequent and free, and marked by friendly regard on the part of the latter. In the stormiest periods of his administration, Pierce came frankly to his aid. The confidence then established was never lost; and when Jackson was on his death-bed, being visited by a gentleman from the North (himself formerly a democratic member of Congress), the old hero spoke with energy of Franklin Pierce's ability and patriotism, and remarked, as with prophetic foresight of his young friend's destiny, that "the interests of the country would be safe in such hands."

One of President Jackson's measures, which had Pierce's approval and support, was his veto of the Maysville Road Bill. This bill was part of a system of vast public works, principally railroads and canals, which it was proposed to undertake at the expense of

the national treasury — a policy not then of recent
origin, but which had been fostered by John Quincy
Adams, and had attained a gigantic growth at the
close of his presidency. The estimate of works undertaken or projected, at the commencement of Jackson's
administration, amounted to considerably more than
a hundred millions of dollars. The expenditure of
this enormous sum, and doubtless other incalculable
amounts, in progressive increase, was to be for purposes often of unascertained utility, and was to pass
through the agents and officers of the federal government — a means of political corruption not safely
to be trusted even in the purest hands. The peril to
the individuality of the states, from a system tending
so directly to consolidate the powers of government
towards a common centre, was obvious. The result
might have been, with the lapse of time and the increased activity of the disease, to place the capital of
our federative Union in a position resembling that of
imperial Rome, where each once independent state
was a subject province, and all the highways of the
world were said to meet in her forum. It was against
this system, so dangerous to liberty and to public and
private integrity, that Jackson declared war, by the
famous Maysville veto.

It would be an absurd interpretation of Pierce's
course, in regard to this and similar measures, to suppose him hostile either to internal or coastwise improvements, so far as they may legitimately be the
business of the general government. He was aware of
the immense importance of our internal commerce, and
was ever ready to vote such appropriations as might be
necessary for promoting it, when asked for in an honest spirit, and at points where they were really needed.

He doubted, indeed, the constitutional power of Congress to undertake, by building roads through the wilderness or opening unfrequented rivers, to create commerce where it did not yet exist; but he never denied or questioned the right and duty to remove obstructions in the way of inland trade, and to afford it every facility, when the nature and necessity of things had brought it into genuine existence. And he agreed with the best and wisest statesmen in believing that this distinction involved the true principle on which legislation, for the purpose here discussed, should proceed.

While a member of the House of Representatives, he delivered a forcible speech against the bill authorizing appropriations for the Military Academy at West Point. He was decidedly opposed to that institution as then and at present organized. We allude to the subject in illustration of the generous frankness with which, years afterwards, when the battle smoke of Mexico had baptized him also a soldier, he acknowledged himself in the wrong, and bore testimony to the brilliant services which the graduates of the Academy, trained to soldiership from boyhood, had rendered to their country. And if he has made no other such acknowledgment of past error, committed in his legislative capacity, it is but fair to believe that it is because his reason and conscience accuse him of no other wrong.

It was while in the lower house of Congress that Franklin Pierce took that stand on the slavery question from which he has never since swerved a hair's breadth. He fully recognized, by his votes and by his voice, the rights pledged to the South by the Constitution. This, at the period when he so declared himself, was comparatively an easy thing to do. But when it became more difficult, when the first imperceptible movement of agitation had grown to be almost a convulsion, his course was still the same. Nor did he ever shun the obloquy that sometimes threatened to pursue the northern man who dared to love that great and sacred reality — his whole, united, native country — better than the mistiness of a philanthropic theory.

He continued in the House of Representatives four years. If, at this period of his life, he rendered unobtrusive, though not unimportant, services to the public, it must also have been a time of vast intellectual advantage to himself. Amidst great national affairs, he was acquiring the best of all educations for future eminence and leadership. In the midst of statesmen, he grew to be a statesman. Studious, as all his speeches prove him to be, of history, he beheld it demonstrating itself before his eyes. As regards this sort of training, much of its good or ill effect depends on the natural force and depth of the man. Many, no doubt, by early mixture with politics, become the mere politicians of the moment, — a class of men sufficiently abundant among us, — acquiring only a knack and cunning, which guide them tolerably well through immediate difficulties, without instructing them in the great rules of higher policy. But when the actual observation of public measures goes hand in hand with study, when the mind is capable of comparing the present with its analogies in the past, and of grasping the principle that belongs to both, this is to have history for a living tutor. If the student be fit for such instruction, he will be seen to act afterwards with the elevation of a high ideal, and with the expediency, the sagacity, the instinct of what is fit and practicable, which make the advantage of the man of actual affairs over the mere theorist.

And it was another advantage of his being brought early into the sphere of national interests, and continuing there for a series of years, that it enabled him to overcome any narrow and sectional prejudices. Without loving New England less, he loved the broad area of the country more. He thus retained that equal sentiment of patriotism for the whole land with which his father had imbued him, and which is perhaps apt to be impaired in the hearts of those who come late to the national legislature, after long training in the narrower fields of the separate states. His sense of the value of the Union, which had been taught him at the fireside, from earliest infancy, by the stories of patriotic valor that he there heard, was now strengthened by friendly association with its representatives from every quarter. It is this youthful sentiment of Americanism, so happily developed by after circumstances, that we see operating through all his public life, and making him as tender of what he considers due to the South as of the rights of his own land of hills.

Franklin Pierce had scarcely reached the legal age for such elevation, when, in 1837, he was elected to the Senate of the United States. He took his seat at the commencement of the presidency of Mr. Van Buren. Never before nor since has the Senate been more venerable for the array of veteran and celebrated statesmen than at that time. Calhoun, Webster, and Clay had lost nothing of their intellectual might. Benton, Silas Wright, Woodbury, Buchanan, and Walker were members; and many even of the less eminent names were such as have gained historic place — men of powerful eloquence, and worthy to be leaders of the

respective parties which they espoused. To this dignified body (composed of individuals some of whom were
older in political experience than he in his mortal life)
Pierce came as the youngest member of the Senate.
With his usual tact and exquisite sense of propriety,
he saw that it was not the time for him to step forward
prominently on this highest theatre in the land. He
beheld these great combatants doing battle before the
eyes of the nation, and engrossing its whole regards.
There was hardly an avenue to reputation save what
was occupied by one or another of those gigantic figures.

Modes of public service remained, however, requiring high ability, but with which few men of competent
endowments would have been content to occupy themselves. Pierce had already demonstrated the possibility of obtaining an enviable position among his associates, without the windy notoriety which a member of
Congress may readily manufacture for himself by the
lavish expenditure of breath that had been better
spared. In the more elevated field of the Senate, he
pursued the same course as while a representative, and
with more than equal results.

Among other committees, he was a member of that
upon revolutionary pensions. Of this subject he made
himself thoroughly master, and was recognized by the
Senate as an unquestionable authority. In 1840, in
reference to several bills for the relief of claimants
under the pension law, he delivered a speech which
finely illustrates as well the sympathies as the justice
of the man, showing how vividly he could feel, and,
at the same time, how powerless were his feelings to
turn him aside from the strict line of public integrity.
The merits and sacrifices of the people of the Revolu-

tion have never been stated with more earnest gratitude than in the following passage : —

" I am not insensible, Mr. President, of the advantages with which claims of this character always come before Congress. They are supposed to be based on services for which no man entertains a higher estimate than myself — services beyond all praise, and above all price. But, while warm and glowing with the glorious recollections which a recurrence to that period of our history can never fail to awaken ; while we cherish with emotions of pride, reverence, and affection the memory of those brave men who are no longer with us ; while we provide, with a liberal hand, for such as survive, and for the widows of the deceased ; while we would accord to the heirs, whether in the second or third generation, every dollar to which they can establish a just claim, — I trust we shall not, in the strong current of our sympathies, forget what becomes us as the descendants of such men. They would teach us to legislate upon our judgment, upon our sober sense of right, and not upon our impulses or our sympathies. No, sir ; we may act in this way, if we choose, when dispensing our own means, but we are not at liberty to do it when dispensing the means of our constituents.

" If we were to legislate upon our sympathies — yet more I will admit — if we were to yield to that sense of just and grateful remuneration which presses itself upon every man's heart, there would be scarcely a limit for our bounty. The whole exchequer could not answer the demand. To the patriotism, the courage, and the sacrifices of the people of that day, we owe, under Providence, all that we now most highly prize, and what we shall transmit to our children as the richest legacy they can inherit. The War of the Revolution, it has been justly remarked, was not a war of armies merely — it was the war of nearly a whole people, and such a people as the world had never before seen, in a death struggle for liberty.

"The losses, sacrifices, and sufferings of that period were common to all classes and conditions of life. Those who remained at home suffered hardly less than those who entered upon the active strife. The aged father and mother underwent not less than the son, who would have been the comfort and stay of their declining years, now called to perform a yet higher duty — to follow the standard of his bleeding country. The young mother, with her helpless children, excites not less deeply our sympathies, contending with want, and dragging out years of weary and toilsome days and anxious nights, than the husband in the field, following the fortunes of our arms without the common habiliments to protect his person, or the requisite sustenance to support his strength. Sir, I never think of that patient, enduring, self-sacrificing army, which crossed the Delaware in December, 1777, marching barefooted upon frozen ground to encounter the foe, and leaving bloody footprints for miles behind them — I never think of their sufferings during that terrible winter without involuntarily inquiring, Where then were their families? Who lit up the cheerful fire upon their hearths at home? Who spoke the word of comfort and encouragement? Nay, sir, who furnished protection from the rigors of winter, and brought them the necessary means of subsistence?

"The true and simple answer to these questions would disclose an amount of suffering and anguish, mental and physical, such as might not have been found in the ranks of the armies — not even in the severest trial of that fortitude which never faltered, and that power of endurance which seemed to know no limit. All this no man feels more deeply than I do. But they were common sacrifices in a common cause, ultimately crowned with the reward of liberty. They have an everlasting claim upon our gratitude, and are destined, as I trust, by their heroic example, to exert an abiding influence upon our latest posterity."

With this heartfelt recognition of the debt of gratitude due to those excellent men, the senator enters into an analysis of the claims presented, and proves them to be void of justice. The whole speech is a good exponent of his character; full of the truest sympathy, but, above all things, just, and not to be misled, on the public behalf, by those impulses that would be most apt to sway the private man. The mere pecuniary amount saved to the nation by his scrutiny into affairs of this kind, though great, was, after all, but a minor consideration. The danger lay in establishing a corrupt system, and placing a wrong precedent upon the statute book. Instances might be adduced, on the other hand, which show him not less scrupulous of the just rights of the claimants than careful of the public interests.

Another subject upon which he came forward was the military establishment and the natural defences of the country. In looking through the columns of the "Congressional Globe," we find abundant evidences of Senator Pierce's laborious and unostentatious discharge of his duties — reports of committees, brief remarks, and, here and there, a longer speech, always full of matter, and evincing a thoroughly-digested knowledge of the subject. Not having been written out by himself, however, these speeches are no fair specimens of his oratory, except as regards the train of argument and substantial thought; and adhering very closely to the business in hand, they seldom present passages that could be quoted, without tearing them forcibly, as it were, out of the context, and thus mangling the fragments which we might offer to the reader. As we have already remarked, he seems, as a debater, to revive the old type of the Revolutionary Congress, or to bring back the noble days of the Long Parliament of England, before eloquence had become what it is now, a knack, and a thing valued for itself. Like those strenuous orators, he speaks with the earnestness of honest conviction, and out of the fervor of his heart, and because the occasion and his deep sense of it constrain him.

By the defeat of Mr. Van Buren, in the presidential election of 1840, the administration of government was transferred, for the first time in twelve years, to the Whigs. An extra session of Congress was summoned to assemble in June, 1841, by President Harrison, who, however, died before it came together. At this extra session, it was the purpose of the whig party, under the leadership of Henry Clay, to overthrow all the great measures which the successive democratic administrations had established. The subtreasury was to be demolished; a national bank was to be incorporated; a high tariff of duties was to be imposed, for purposes of protection and abundant revenue. The whig administration possessed a majority, both in the Senate and the House. It was a dark period for the Democracy, so long unaccustomed to defeat, and now beholding all that they had won for the cause of national progress, after the arduous struggle of so many years, apparently about to be swept away.

The sterling influence which Franklin Pierce now exercised is well described in the following remarks of the Hon. A. O. P. Nicholson : —

"The power of an organized minority was never more clearly exhibited than in this contest. The democratic senators acted in strict concert, meeting night after night for consultation, arranging their plan of battle, selecting their champions for the coming day, assigning to each man his proper duty, and looking carefully to the popular judgment for a final victory. In these consultations, no man's voice was heard with more profound respect than that of Franklin Pierce. His counsels were characterized by so thorough a knowledge of human nature, by so much solid common sense, by such devotion to democratic principles, that, although among the youngest of the senators, it was deemed important that all their conclusions should be submitted to his sanction.

"Although known to be ardent in his temperament, he was also known to act with prudence and caution. His impetuosity in debate was only the result of the deep convictions which controlled his mind. He enjoyed the unbounded confidence of Calhoun, Buchanan, Wright, Woodbury, Walker, King, Benton, and indeed of the entire democratic portion of the Senate. When he rose in the Senate or in the committee room, he was heard with the profoundest attention ; and again and again was he greeted by these veteran Democrats as one of our ablest champions. His speeches, during this session, will compare with those of any other senator. If it be asked why he did not receive higher distinction, I answer, that such men as Calhoun, Wright, Buchanan, and Woodbury were the acknowledged leaders of the Democracy. The eyes of the nation were on them. The hopes of their party were reposed in them. The brightness of these luminaries was too great to allow the brilliancy of so young a man to attract especial attention. But ask any one of these veterans how Franklin Pierce ranked in the Senate, and he will tell you, that, to stand in the front rank for talents, eloquence, and statesmanship, he only lacked a few more years."

In the course of this session he made a very powerful speech in favor of Mr. Buchanan's resolution, calling on the President to furnish the names of persons removed from office since the 4th of March, 1841. The Whigs, in 1840, as in the subsequent canvass of 1848, had professed a purpose to abolish the system of official removals on account of political opinion, but, immediately on coming into power, had commenced a proscription infinitely beyond the example of the democratic party. This course, with an army of office seekers besieging the departments, was unquestionably difficult to avoid, and perhaps, on the whole, not desirable to be avoided. But it was rendered astounding by the sturdy effrontry with which the gentlemen in power denied that their present practice had falsified any of their past professions. A few of the closing paragraphs of Senator Pierce's highly effective speech, being more easily separable than the rest, may here be cited.

" One word more, and I leave this subject, — a painful one to me, from the beginning to the end. The senator from North Carolina, in the course of his remarks the other day, asked, ' Do gentlemen expect that their friends are to be retained in office against the will of the nation ? Are they so unreasonable as to expect what the circumstances and the *necessity* of the case forbid ? ' What our expectations were is not the question now; but what were your pledges and promises before the people. On a previous occasion, the distinguished senator from Kentucky made a similar remark : *'An ungracious task, but the nation demands it!'* Sir, this demand of the nation, — this plea of STATE NECESSITY, — let me tell gentlemen, is as old as the history of wrong and oppression. It has been the standing plea, the never-failing resort of despotism.

" The great Julius found it a convenient plea when he restored the *dignity* of the Roman Senate, but destroyed its *independence.* It gave countenance to and justified all the atrocities of the Inquisition in Spain. It forced out the stifled groans that issued from the Black Hole of Calcutta. It was written in tears upon the Bridge of Sighs in Venice, and pointed to those dark recesses upon whose gloomy thresholds there was never seen a returning footprint.

" It was the plea of the austere and ambitious Strafford, in the days of Charles I. It filled the Bastile of France, and lent its sanction to the terrible atrocities perpetrated there. It was this plea that snatched the mild, eloquent, and patriotic Camille Desmoulins from his young and beautiful wife, and hurried him to the guillotine with thousands of others equally unoffending and innocent. It was upon this plea that the greatest of generals, if not men, — you cannot mistake me, — I mean him, the presence of whose very ashes within the last few months sufficed to stir the hearts of a continent, — it was upon this plea that he abjured the noble wife who had thrown light and gladness around his humbler days, and, by her own lofty energies and high intellect, had encouraged his aspirations. It was upon this plea that he committed that worst and most fatal act of his eventful life. Upon this, too, he drew around his person the imperial purple. It has in all times, and in every age, been the foe of liberty and the indispensable stay of usurpation.

"Where were the chains of despotism ever thrown around the freedom of speech and of the press but on this plea of STATE NECESSITY? Let the spirit of Charles X. and of his ministers answer.

"It is cold, selfish, heartless, and has always been regardless of age, sex, condition, services, or any of the incidents of life that appeal to patriotism or humanity. Wherever its authority has been acknowledged, it has assailed men who stood by their country when she needed strong arms and bold hearts, and has assailed them when, maimed and disabled in her service, they could no longer brandish a weapon in her defence. It has afflicted the feeble and dependent wife for the imaginary faults of the husband. It has stricken down Innocence in its beauty, Youth in its freshness, Manhood in its vigor, and Age in its feebleness and decrepitude. Whatever other plea or apology may be set up for the sweeping, ruthless exercise of this civil guillotine at the present day, in the name of LIBERTY let us be spared this fearful one of STATE NECESSITY, in this early age of the Republic, upon the floor of the American Senate, in the face of a people yet free!"

In June, 1842, he signified his purpose of retiring from the Senate.

It was now more than sixteen years since the author of this sketch had been accustomed to meet Frank Pierce (that familiar name, which the nation is adopt-

ing as one of its household words) in habits of daily
intercourse. Our modes of life had since been as different as could well be imagined; our culture and labor were entirely unlike; there was hardly a single
object or aspiration in common between us. Still we
had occasionally met, and always on the old ground of
friendly confidence. There were sympathies that had
not been suffered to die out. Had we lived more constantly together, it is not impossible that the relation
might have been changed by the various accidents and
attritions of life; but having no mutual events, and
few mutual interests, the tie of early friendship remained the same as when we parted. The modifica-
tions which I saw in his character were those of growth
and development; new qualities came out, or displayed
themselves more prominently, but always in harmony
with those heretofore known. Always I was sensible
of progress in him; a characteristic — as, I believe,
has been said in the foregoing pages — more perceptible
in Franklin Pierce than in any other person with whom
I have been acquainted. He widened, deepened, rose
to a higher point, and thus ever made himself equal to
the ever-heightening occasion. This peculiarity of intellectual growth, continued beyond the ordinary period, has its analogy in his physical constitution — it
being a fact that he continued to grow in stature between his twenty-first and twenty-fifth years.

He had not met with that misfortune, which, it is
to be feared, befalls many men who throw their ardor
into politics. The pursuit had taken nothing from
the frankness of his nature; now, as ever, he used direct means to gain honorable ends; and his subtlety
— for, after all, his heart and purpose were not such
as he that runs may read — had the depth of wisdom,

and never any quality of cunning. In great part, this undeteriorated manhood was due to his original nobil-ity of nature. Yet it may not be unjust to attribute it, in some degree, to the singular good fortune of his life. He had never, in all his career, found it neces-sary to stoop. Office had sought him ; he had not begged it, nor manœuvred for it, nor crept towards it — arts which too frequently bring a man, morally bowed and degraded, to a position which should be one of dignity, but in which he will vainly essay to stand upright.

In our earlier meetings, after Pierce had begun to come forward in public life, I could discern that his ambition was aroused. He felt a young man's enjoy-ment of success, so early and so distinguished. But as years went on, such motives seemed to be less in-fluential with him. He was cured of ambition, as, one after another, its objects came to him unsought. His domestic position, likewise, had contributed to direct his tastes and wishes towards the pursuits of private life. In 1834 he had married Jane Means, a daugh-ter of the Rev. Dr. Appleton, a former president of Bowdoin College. Three sons, the first of whom died in early infancy, were born to him ; and, having hith-erto been kept poor by his public service, he no doubt became sensible of the expediency of making some provision for the future. Such, it may be presumed, were the considerations that induced his resignation of the senatorship, greatly to the regret of all parties. The senators gathered around him, as he was about to quit the chamber; political opponents took leave of him as of a personal friend ; and no departing mem-ber has ever retired from that dignified body amid warmer wishes for his happiness than those that at-tended Franklin Pierce.

His father had died three years before, in 1839, at the mansion which he built, after the original log-cabin grew too narrow for his rising family and fortunes. The mansion was spacious, as the liberal hospitality of the occupant required, and stood on a little eminence, surrounded by verdure and abundance, and a happy population, where, half a century before, the revolutionary soldier had come alone into the wilderness, and levelled the primeval forest trees. After being spared to behold the distinction of his son, he departed this life at the age of eighty-one years, in perfect peace, and, until within a few hours of his death, in the full possession of his intellectual powers. His last act was one of charity to a poor neighbor — a fitting close to a life that had abounded in such deeds. Governor Pierce was a man of admirable qualities — brave, active, public-spirited, endowed with natural authority, courteous yet simple in his manners; and in his son we may perceive these same attributes, modified and softened by a finer texture of character, illuminated by higher intellectual culture, and polished by a larger intercourse with the world, but as substantial and sterling as in the good old patriot.

Franklin Pierce had removed from Hillsborough in 1838, and taken up his residence at Concord, the capital of New Hampshire. On this occasion, the citizens of his native town invited him to a public dinner, in token of their affection and respect. In accordance with his usual taste, he gratefully accepted the kindly sentiment, but declined the public demonstration of it.

## CHAPTER III.

HIS SUCCESS AT THE BAR.

FRANKLIN PIERCE'S earliest effort at the bar, as we have already observed, was an unsuccessful one ; but instead of discouraging him, the failure had only served to awaken the consciousness of latent power, and the resolution to bring it out. Since those days, he had indeed gained reputation as a lawyer. So much, however, was the tenor of his legal life broken up by the months of public service subtracted from each year, and such was the inevitable tendency of his thoughts towards political subjects, that he could but very partially avail himself of the opportunities of professional advancement. But on retiring from the Senate, he appears to have started immediately into full practice. Though the people of New Hampshire already knew him well, yet his brilliant achievements as an advocate brought him more into their view, and into closer relations with them, than he had ever before been. He now met his countrymen, as represented in the jury box, face to face, and made them feel what manner of man he was. Their sentiment towards him soon grew to be nothing short of enthusiasm ; love, pride, the sense of brotherhood, affectionate sympathy, and perfect trust, all mingled in it. It was the influence of a great heart pervading the general heart, and throbbing with it in the same pulsation.

It has never been the writer's good fortune to listen to one of Franklin Pierce's public speeches, whether at the bar or elsewhere ; nor, by diligent inquiry, has he been able to gain a very definite idea of the mode in which he produces his effects. To me, therefore, his forensic displays are in the same category with those of Patrick Henry, or any other orator whose tongue, beyond the memory of man, has mouldered into dust. His power results, no doubt, in great measure, from the earnestness with which he imbues himself with the conception of his client's cause; insomuch that he makes it entirely his own, and, never undertaking a case which he believes to be unjust, contends with his whole heart and conscience, as well as intellectual force, for victory. His labor in the preparation of his cases is said to be unremitting; and he throws himself with such energy into a trial of importance as wholly to exhaust his strength.

Few lawyers, probably, have been interested in a wider variety of business than he; its scope comprehends the great causes where immense pecuniary interests are concerned — from which, however, he is always ready to turn aside, to defend the humble rights of the poor man, or give his protection to one unjustly accused. As one of my correspondents observes, "When an applicant has interested him by a recital of oppression, fraud, or wrong, General Pierce never investigates the man's estate before engaging in his business; neither does he calculate whose path he may cross. I have been privy to several instances of the noblest independence on his part, in pursuing, to the disrepute of those who stood well in the community, the weal of an obscure client with a good cause."

In the practice of the law, as Pierce pursued it, in one or another of the court houses of New Hampshire, the rumor of each successive struggle and success resounded over the rugged hills, and perished without a record. Those mighty efforts, into which he put all his strength, before a county court, and addressing a jury of yeomen, have necessarily been, as regards the evanescent memory of any particular trial, like the eloquence that is sometimes poured out in a dream. In other spheres of action, with no greater expenditure of mental energy, words have been spoken that endure from age to age — deeds done that harden into history. But this, perhaps the most earnest portion of Franklin Pierce's life, has left few materials from which it can be written. There is before me only one report of a case in which he was engaged — the defence of the Wentworths, at a preliminary examination, on a charge of murder. His speech occupied four hours in the delivery, and handles a confused medley of facts with masterly skill, bringing them to bear one upon another, and making the entire mass, as it were, transparent, so that the truth may be seen through it. The whole hangs together too closely to permit the quotation of passages.

The writer has been favored with communications from two individuals, who have enjoyed the best of opportunities to become acquainted with General Pierce's character as a lawyer. The following is the graceful and generous tribute of a gentleman, who, of late, more frequently than any other, has been opposed to him at the bar : —

" General Pierce cannot be said to have commenced his career at the bar, in earnest, until after his resignation of the office of senator, in 1842. And it is a convincing proof of his eminent powers that he at once placed himself in the very first rank at a bar so distinguished for ability as that of New Hampshire. It is confessed by all, who have the means of knowledge and judgment on this subject, that in no state of the Union are causes tried with more industry of preparation, skill, perseverance, energy, or vehement effort to succeed.

"During much of this time, my practice in our courts was suspended; and it is only within three or four years that I have had opportunities of intimately knowing his powers as an advocate, by being associated with him at the bar; and, most of all, of appreciating and feeling that power, by being opposed to him in the trial of causes before juries. Far more than any other man, whom it has been my fortune to meet, he makes himself *felt* by one who tries a case against him. From the first, he impresses on his opponent a consciousness of the necessity of a deadly struggle, not only in order to win the victory, but to avoid defeat.

"His vigilance and perseverance, omitting nothing in the preparation and introduction of testimony, even to the minutest details, which can be useful to his clients; his watchful attention, seizing on every weak point in the opposite case; his quickness and readiness; his sound and excellent judgment; his keen insight into character and motives, his almost intuitive knowledge of men; his ingenious and powerful cross-examinations; his adroitness in turning aside troublesome testimony, and availing himself of every favorable point; his quick sense of the ridiculous; his pathetic appeals to the feelings; his sustained eloquence, and remarkably energetic declamation, — all mark him for a ' leader.'

"From the beginning to the end of the trial of a case, nothing with him is neglected, which can by possibility honorably conduce to success. His manner is

always respectful and deferential to the court, captivating to the jury, and calculated to conciliate the
good will even of those who would be otherwise indifferent spectators. In short, he plays the part of a
successful actor ; successful, because he always identi-
fies himself with his part, and in him it is not acting.

" Perhaps, as would be expected by those who know
his generosity of heart, and his scorn of everything
like oppression or extortion, he is most powerful in his
indignant denunciations of fraud or injustice, and his
addresses to the feelings in behalf of the poor and
lowly, and the sufferers under wrong. I remember to
have heard of his extraordinary power on one occasion,
when a person, who had offered to procure arrears of
a pension for revolutionary services, had appropriated
to himself a most unreasonable share of the money.
General Pierce spoke of the frequency of these instances, and, before the numerous audience, offered
his aid, freely and gratuitously, to redress the wrongs
of any widow or representative of a revolutionary officer or soldier who had been made the subject of such
extortion.

". The reply of the poor man, in the anecdote related
by Lord Campbell of Harry Erskine, would be appli-
cable, as exhibiting a feeling kindred to that with
which General Pierce is regarded : 'There's no a puir
man in a' Scotland need to want a friend or fear an
enemy, sae lang as Harry Erskine lives!' "

We next give his aspect as seen from the bench, in
the following carefully prepared and discriminating
article, from the chief justice of New Hampshire : —

" In attempting to estimate the character and qualifications of Mr. Pierce as a lawyer and an advocate,
we undertake a delicate, but, at the same time, an

agreeable task. The profession of the law, practised by men of liberal and enlightened minds, and unstained by the sordidness which more or less affects all human pursuits, invariably confers honor upon and is honored by its followers. An integrity above suspicion, an eloquence alike vigorous and persuasive, and an intuitive sagacity have earned for Mr. Pierce the reputation that always follows them.

" The last case of paramount importance in which he was engaged as counsel was that of Morrison *v.* Philbrick, tried in the month of February, 1852, at the Court of Common Pleas for the county of Belknap. There was on both sides an array of eminent professional talent, Messrs. Pierce, Bell, and Bellows appearing for the defendant, and Messrs. Atherton and Whipple for the plaintiff. The case was one of almost unequalled interest to the public generally, and to the inhabitants of the country lying around the lower part of Lake Winnipiseogee. A company, commonly called the Lake Company, had become the owners of many of the outlets of the streams supplying the lake, and by means of their works at such places, and at Union Bridge, a few miles below, were enabled to keep back the waters of the lake, and to use them as occasion should require, to supply the mills at Lowell. The plaintiff alleged that the dam at Union Bridge had caused the water to rise higher than was done by the dam that existed in the year 1828, and that he was essentially injured thereby. The case had been on trial nearly seven weeks. Evidence equivalent to the testimony of one hundred and eighty witnesses had been laid before the jury. Upon this immense mass of facts, involving a great number of issues, Mr. Pierce was to meet his most formidable opponent in the state, Mr. Atherton. In that gentleman are united many of the rarest qualifications of an advocate. Of inimitable self-possession; with a coolness and clearness of intellect which no sudden emergencies can disturb; with that confidence in his resources which nothing but native strength, aided by the most thorough training, can bestow; with a felicity and fertility of illustration, the result alike of an exquisite natural taste and a cultivation of those studies which refine while they strengthen the mind for forensic contests, — Mr. Atherton's argument was listened to with an earnestness and interest which showed the conviction of his audience that no ordinary man was addressing them.

"No one who witnessed that memorable trial will soon forget the argument of Mr. Pierce on that occasion. He was the counsel for the defendant, and was therefore to precede Mr. Atherton. He was to analyze and unfold to the jury this vast body of evidence under the watchful eyes of an opponent at once enterprising and cautious, and before whom it was necessary to be both bold and skilful. He was to place himself in the position of the jury, to see the evidence as they would be likely to regard it, to understand the character of their minds, and what views would be the most likely to impress them. He was not only to be familiar with his own case, but to anticipate that of his opponent, and answer as he best might the argument of the counsel. And most admirably did he discharge the duties he had assumed on behalf of his client. Eminently graceful and attractive in his manner at all times, his demeanor was then precisely what it should have been, showing a manly confidence in himself and his case, and a courteous deference to the tribunal he was addressing. His erect and manly figure, his easy and unembarrassed air, bespoke the favorable attention of his audience. His earnest devotion to his cause, his deep emotion, evidently suppressed, but for that very reason all the more interesting, diffused themselves like electricity through his hearers. And when, as often happened, in the course of his argument, his clear and musical accents fell upon the ear in eloquent and pointed sentences, gratifying the taste while they satisfied the reason, no man could avoid turning to his neighbor, and expressing by his looks that pleasure which the very depth of his interest forbade him to express in words. And when the long trial was over, every one remembered with satisfaction that these two distinguished gentlemen had met each other during a most exciting and exhausting trial of seven weeks, and that no unkind words, or captious passages, had occurred between them to diminish their mutual respect, or that in which they were held by their fellow-citizens.

"In the above remarks, we have indicated a few of Mr. Pierce's characteristics as an advocate ; but he possesses other endowments, to which we have not alluded. In the first place, as he is a perfectly fearless man, so he is a perfectly fearless advocate ; and true courage is as necessary to the civilian as to the soldier, and smiles and frowns Mr. Pierce disregards alike in the undaunted discharge of his duty. He never fears to uphold his client, however unpopular his cause may seem to be for the moment. It is this courage which kindles his eloquence, inspires his conduct, and gives direction and firmness to his skill. This it is which impels him onward, at all risks, to lay bare every 'mystery of iniquity' which he believes is threatening his case. He does not ask himself whether his opponent be not a man of wealth and influence, of whom it might be for his interest to speak with care and circumspection ; but he devotes himself with a ready zeal to his cause, careless of aught but how he may best discharge his duty. His argumentative powers are of the highest order. He never takes before the court a position which he believes untenable. He has a quick and sure perception of his points, and the power of enforcing them by apt and pertinent illustrations. He sees the relative importance and weight of different views, and can assign to each its proper place, and brings forward the main body of his reasoning in prominent relief, without distracting the attention by unimportant particulars. And above all, he has the good sense, so rarely shown by many, to stop when he has said all that is necessary for the elucidation of his subject. With a proper confidence in his own perceptions, he states his views so pertinently and in such precise and logical terms, that they cannot but be felt and appreciated. He never mystifies; he never attempts to pervert words from their proper and legitimate meaning, to answer a temporary purpose.

" His demeanor at the bar may be pronounced faultless. His courtesy in the court house, like his courtesy elsewhere, is that which springs from self-respect and from a kindly heart, disposing its owner to say and do kindly things. But he would be a courageous man who, presuming upon the affability of Mr. Pierce's manner, would venture a second time to attack him; for he would long remember the rebuke that followed his first attack. There is a ready repartee and a quick and cutting sarcasm in his manner when he chooses to

display it, which it requires a man of considerable
nerve to withstand. He is peculiarly happy in the
examination of witnesses — that art in which so few
excel. He never browbeats, he never attempts to ter-
rify. He is never rude or discourteous. But the
equivocating witness soon discovers that his falsehood
is hunted out of its recesses with an unsparing determination. If he is dogged and surly, he is met by a
spirit as resolute as his own. If he is smooth and
plausible, the veil is lifted from him by a firm but
graceful hand. If he is pompous and vain, no ridicule was ever more perfect than that to which he lis-
tens with astonished and mortified ears.

"The eloquence of Mr. Pierce is of a character not
to be easily forgotten. He understands men, their
passions and their feelings. He knows the way to
their hearts, and can make them vibrate to his touch.
His language always attracts the hearer. A graceful
and manly carriage, bespeaking him at once the gentleman and the true man ; a manner warmed by the
ardent glow of an earnest belief ; an enunciation ringing, distinct, and impressive beyond that of most men ;
a command of brilliant and expressive language ; and
an accurate taste, together with a sagacious and instinctive insight into the points of his case, are the
secrets of his success. It is thus that audiences are
moved and truth ascertained; and he will ever be the
most successful advocate who can approach the nearest
to this lofty and difficult position.

"Mr. Pierce's views as a constitutional lawyer are
such as have been advocated by the ablest minds of
America. They are those which, taking their rise in
the heroic age of the country, were transmitted to him
by a noble father, worthy of the times in which he lived,

worthy of that Revolution which he assisted in bringing about. He believes that the Constitution was made, not to be subverted, but to be sacredly preserved; that a republic is perfectly consistent with the conservation of law, of rational submission to right authority, and of true self-government. Equally removed from that malignant hostility to order which characterizes the demagogues who are eager to rise upon the ruins even of freedom, and from that barren and bigoted narrowness which would oppose all rational freedom of opinion, he is, in its loftiest and most ennobling sense, a friend of that Union, without which the honored name of American citizen would become a by-word among the nations. And if, as we fervently pray and confidently expect he will, Mr. Pierce shall display before the great tribunals of the nation the courage, the consistency, the sagacity, and the sense of honor, which have already secured for him so many thousands of devoted friends, and which have signalized both his private and professional life, his administration will long be held in grateful remembrance as one of which the sense of right and the sagacity to perceive it, a clear insight into the true destinies of the country and a determination to uphold them at whatever sacrifice, were the predominant characteristics."

It may appear singular that Franklin Pierce has not taken up his residence in some metropolis, where his great forensic abilities would so readily find a more conspicuous theatre, and a far richer remuneration than heretofore. He himself, it is understood, has sometimes contemplated a removal, and, two or three years since, had almost determined on settling in Baltimore. But his native state, where he is known so well, and regarded with so much familiar affection, which he has served so faithfully, and which rewards him so generously with its confidence, New Hampshire, with its granite hills, must always be his home. He will dwell there, except when public duty for a season shall summon him away; he will die there, and give his dust to its soil.

It was at his option, in 1846, to accept the highest legal position in the country, setting aside the bench, and the one which undoubtedly would most have gratified his professional aspirations. President Polk, with whom he had been associated on the most friendly terms in Congress, now offered him the post of attorney general of the United States. "In tendering to you this position in my cabinet," writes the President, "I have been governed by the high estimate which I place upon your character and eminent qualifications to fill it." The letter, in which this proposal is declined, shows so much of the writer's real self that we quote a portion of it.

"Although the early years of my manhood were devoted to public life, it was never really suited to my taste. I longed, as I am sure you must often have done, for the quiet and independence that belong only to the private citizen; and now, at forty, I feel that desire stronger than ever.

"Coming so unexpectedly as this offer does, it would be difficult, if not impossible, to arrange the business of an extensive practice, between this and the first of November, in a manner at all satisfactory to myself, or to those who have committed their interests to my care, and who rely on my services. Besides, you know that Mrs. Pierce's health, while at Washington, was very delicate. It is, I fear, even more so now; and the responsibilities which the proposed change would

necessarily impose upon her ought, probably, in themselves, to constitute an insurmountable objection to
leaving our quiet home for a public station at Washington.

"When I resigned my seat in the Senate in 1842, I
did it with the fixed purpose never again to be voluntarily separated from my family for any considerable
length of time, except at the call of my country in
time of war ; and yet this consequence, for the reason
before stated, and on account of climate, would be very
likely to result from my acceptance.

"These are some of the considerations which have
influenced my decision. You will, I am sure, appreciate my motives. You will not believe that I have
weighed my personal convenience and ease against the
public interest, especially as the office is one which, if
not sought, would be readily accepted by gentlemen
who could bring to your aid attainments and qualifications vastly superior to mine."

Previous to the offer of the attorney-generalship, the
appointment of United States Senator had been tendered to Pierce by Governor Steele, and declined. It
is unquestionable that, at this period, he hoped and expected to spend a life of professional toil in a private
station, undistinguished except by the exercise of his
great talents in peaceful pursuits. But such was not
his destiny. The contingency to which he referred in
the above letter, as the sole exception to his purpose of
never being separated from his family, was now about
to occur. Nor did he fail to comport himself as not
only that intimation, but the whole tenor of his character, gave reason to anticipate.

During the years embraced in this chapter, — between 1842 and 1847, — he had constantly taken an

efficient interest in the politics of the state, but had uniformly declined the honors which New Hampshire was at all times ready to confer upon him. A democratic convention nominated him for governor, but could not obtain his acquiescence. One of the occasions on which he most strenuously exerted himself was in holding the democratic party loyal to its principles, in opposition to the course of John P. Hale. This gentleman, then a representative in Congress, had broken with his party on no less important a point than the annexation of Texas. He has never since acted with the Democracy, and has long been a leader of the free soil party.

In 1844 died Frank Robert, son of Franklin Pierce, aged four years, a little boy of rare beauty and promise, and whose death was the greatest affliction that his father has experienced. His only surviving child is a son, now eleven years old.

## CHAPTER IV.

### THE MEXICAN WAR.

When Franklin Pierce declined the honorable offer of the attorney-generalship of the United States, he intimated that there might be one contingency in which he would feel it his duty to give up the cherished purpose of spending the remainder of his life in a private station. That exceptional case was brought about, in 1847, by the Mexican War. He showed his readiness to redeem the pledge by enrolling himself as the earliest volunteer of a company raised in Concord, and went through the regular drill, with his fellow-soldiers, as a private in the ranks. On the passage of the bill for the increase of the army, he received the appointment of colonel of the Ninth Regiment, which was the quota of New England towards the ten that were to be raised. And shortly afterwards, — in March, 1847, — he was commissioned as brigadier-general in the army; his brigade consisting of regiments from the extreme north, the extreme west, and the extreme south of the Union.

There is nothing in any other country similar to what we see in our own, when the blast of the trumpet at once converts men of peaceful pursuits into warriors. Every war in which America has been engaged has done this; the valor that wins our battles is not the trained hardihood of veterans, but a native and spontaneous fire; and there is surely a chivalrous beauty in the devotion of the citizen soldier to his country's cause, which the man who makes arms his profession, and is but doing his regular business on the field of battle, cannot pretend to rival. Taking the Mexican War as a specimen, this peculiar composition of an American army, as well in respect to its officers as its private soldiers, seems to create a spirit of romantic adventure which more than supplies the place of disciplined courage.

The author saw General Pierce in Boston, on the eve of his departure for Vera Cruz. He had been intensely occupied, since his appointment, in effecting the arrangements necessary on leaving his affairs, as well as by the preparations, military and personal, demanded by the expedition. The transports were waiting at Newport to receive the troops. He was now in the midst of bustle, with some of the officers of his command about him, mingled with the friends whom he was to leave behind. The severest point of the crisis was over, for he had already bidden his family farewell. His spirits appeared to have risen with the occasion. He was evidently in his element; nor, to say the truth, dangerous as was the path before him, could it be regretted that his life was now to have the opportunity of that species of success which — in his youth, at least — he had considered the best worth struggling for. He looked so fit to be a soldier, that it was impossible to doubt — not merely his good conduct, which was as certain before the event as afterwards, but — his good fortune in the field, and his fortunate return.

He sailed from Newport on the 27th of May, in the bark Kepler, having on board three companies of the Ninth Regiment of Infantry, together with Colonel Ransom, its commander, and the officers belonging to the detachment. The passage was long and tedious, with protracted calms, and so smooth a sea that a sail boat might have performed the voyage in safety. The Kepler arrived at Vera Cruz in precisely a month after her departure from the United States, without speaking a single vessel from the south during her passage, and, of course, receiving no intelligence as to the position and state of the army which these reënforcements were to join.

From a journal kept by General Pierce, and intended only for the perusal of his family and friends, we present some extracts. They are mere hasty jottings-down in camp, and at the intervals of weary marches, but will doubtless bring the reader closer to the man than any narrative which we could substitute.[1]

---

[1] In this reprint it has been thought expedient to omit the passages from General Pierce's journal.

. . . . . . . . . . . .

General Pierce's journal here terminates. In its clear and simple narrative, the reader cannot fail to see — although it was written with no purpose of displaying them — the native qualities of a born soldier, together with the sagacity of an experienced one. He had proved himself, moreover, physically apt for war, by his easy endurance of the fatigues of the march; every step of which (as was the case with few other officers) was performed either on horseback or on foot. Nature, indeed, has endowed him with a rare elasticity both of mind and body; he springs up from pressure like a well-tempered sword. After the severest toil, a single night's rest does as much for him, in the way of refreshment, as a week could do for most other men.

His conduct on this adventurous march received the high encomiums of military men, and was honored with the commendation of the great soldier who is now his rival in the presidential contest. He reached the main army at Puebla on the 7th of August, with twenty-four hundred men, in fine order, and without the loss of a single wagon.

## CHAPTER V.

### HIS SERVICES IN THE VALLEY OF MEXICO.

GENERAL SCOTT, who was at Puebla with the main army, awaiting this reënforcement, began his march towards the city of Mexico on the day after General Pierce's arrival. The battle of Contreras was fought on the 19th of August.

The enemy's force consisted of about seven thousand men, posted in a strongly-intrenched camp, under General Valencia, one of the bravest and ablest of the Mexican commanders. The object of the commanding general appears to have been to cut off the communications of these detached troops with Santa Anna's main army, and thus to have them entirely at his mercy. For this purpose a portion of the American forces were ordered to move against Valencia's left flank, and, by occupying strong positions in the villages and on the roads towards the city, to prevent reënforcements from reaching him. In the mean time, to draw the enemy's attention from this movement, a vigorous onset was made upon his front; and as the operations upon his flank were not immediately and fully carried out according to the plan, this front demonstration assumed the character of a fierce and desperate attack, upon which the fortunes of the day much depended. General Pierce's brigade formed a part of the force engaged in this latter movement, in which four thousand newly-recruited men, unable to bring their artillery to bear, contended against seven thousand disciplined soldiers, protected by intrenchments, and showering round shot and shells against the assailing troops.

The ground in front was of the rudest and roughest character. The troops made their way with difficulty over a broken tract called the Pedregal, bristling with sharp points of rocks, and which is represented as having been the crater of a now exhausted and extinct volcano. The enemy had thrown out skirmishers, who were posted in great force among the crevices and inequalities of this broken ground, and vigorously resisted the American advance; while the artillery of

the intrenched camp played upon our troops, and shattered the very rocks over which they were to pass.

General Pierce's immediate command had never before been under such a fire of artillery. The enemy's
range was a little too high, or the havoc in our ranks
must have been dreadful. In the midst of this fire,
General Pierce, being the only officer mounted in the
brigade, leaped his horse upon an abrupt eminence,
and addressed the colonels and captains of the regiments, as they passed, in a few stirring words — re-
minding them of the honor of their country, of the
victory their steady valor would contribute to achieve.
Pressing forward to the head of the column, he had
nearly reached the practicable ground that lay beyond,
when his horse slipped among the rocks, thrust his
foot into a crevice, and fell, breaking his own leg, and
crushing his rider heavily beneath him.

Pierce's mounted orderly soon came to his assistance. The general was stunned, and almost insensible.
When partially recovered, he found himself suffering
from severe bruises, and especially from a sprain of the
left knee, which was undermost when the horse came
down. The orderly assisted him to reach the shelter
of a projecting rock ; and as they made their way
thither, a shell fell close beside them and exploded,
covering them with earth. " That was a lucky miss,"
said Pierce calmly. Leaving him in such shelter as
the rock afforded, the orderly went in search of aid,
and was fortunate to meet with Dr. Ritchie, of Virginia, who was attached to Pierce's brigade, and was
following in close proximity to the advancing column.
The doctor administered to him as well as the circumstances would admit. Immediately on recovering his
full consciousness, General Pierce had become anxious

to rejoin his troops; and now, in opposition to Dr. Ritchie's advice and remonstrances, he determined to proceed to the front.

With pain and difficulty, and leaning on his order- ly's arm, he reached the battery commanded by Cap- tain McGruder, where he found the horse of Lieuten- ant Johnson, who had just before received a mortal wound. In compliance with his wishes, he was as- sisted into the saddle; and, in answer to a remark that he would be unable to keep his seat, "Then," said the general, " you must tie me on." Whether his pre- caution was actually taken is a point on which author- ities differ; but at all events, with injuries so severe as would have sent almost any other man to the hos- pital, he rode forward into the battle.

The contest was kept up until nightfall, without forcing Valencia's intrenchment. General Pierce re- mained in the saddle until eleven o'clock at night. Finding himself, at nine o'clock, the senior officer in the field, he, in that capacity, withdrew the troops from their advanced position, and concentrated them at the point where they were to pass the night. At eleven, beneath a torrent of rain, destitute of a tent or other protection, and without food or refreshment, he lay down on an ammunition wagon, but was prevented by the pain of his injuries, especially that of his wounded knee, from finding any repose. At one o'clock came orders from General Scott to put the brigade into a new position, in front of the enemy's works, pre- paratory to taking part in the contemplated operations of the next morning. During the night, the troops appointed for that service, under Riley, Shields, Smith, and Cadwallader, had occupied the villages and roads between Valencia's position and the city; so that, with daylight, the commanding general's scheme of the battle was ready to be carried out, as it had originally existed in his mind.

At daylight, accordingly, Valencia's intrenched camp was assaulted. General Pierce was soon in the saddle at the head of his brigade, which retained its position in front, thus serving to attract the enemy's attention, and divert him from the true point of attack. The camp was stormed in the rear by the American troops, led on by Riley, Cadwallader, and Dimmick ; and in the short space of seventeen minutes it had fallen into the hands of the assailants, together with a multitude of prisoners. The remnant of the routed enemy fled towards Churubusco. As Pierce led his brigade in pursuit, crossing the battle-field, and passing through the works that had just been stormed, he found the road and adjacent fields everywhere strewn with the dead and dying. The pursuit was continued until one o'clock, when the foremost of the Americans arrived in front of the strong Mexican positions at Churubusco and San Antonio, where Santa Anna's army had been compelled to make a stand, and where the great conflict of the day commenced.

General Santa Anna entertained the design of withdrawing his forces towards the city. In order to intercept this movement, Pierce's brigade, with other troops, was ordered to pursue a route by which the enemy could be attacked in the rear. Colonel Noah E. Smith (a patriotic American, long resident in Mexico, whose local and topographical knowledge proved eminently serviceable) had offered to point out the road, and was sent to summon General Pierce to the presence of the commander-in-chief. When he met Pierce, near Coyacan, at the head of his brigade, the heavy fire of the batteries had commenced. "He was exceedingly thin," writes Colonel Smith, "worn down by the fatigue and pain of the day and night before, and then evidently suffering severely. Still there was a glow in his eye, as the cannon boomed, that showed within him a spirit ready for the conflict." He rode up to General Scott, who was at this time sitting on horseback beneath a tree, near the church of Coyacan, issuing orders to different individuals of his staff. Our account of this interview is chiefly taken from the narrative of Colonel Smith, corroborated by other testimony.

The commander-in-chief had already heard of the accident that befell Pierce the day before; and as the latter approached, General Scott could not but notice the marks of pain and physical exhaustion against which only the sturdiest constancy of will could have enabled him to bear up. "Pierce, my dear fellow," said he, — and that epithet of familiar kindness and friendship, upon the battle-field, was the highest of military commendation from such a man, — "you are badly injured; you are not fit to be in your saddle." "Yes, general, I am," replied Pierce, "in a case like this." "You cannot touch your foot to the stirrup," said Scott. "One of them I can," answered Pierce. The general looked again at Pierce's almost disabled figure, and seemed on the point of taking his irrevocable resolution. "You are rash, General Pierce," said he; "we shall lose you, and we cannot spare you. It is my duty to order you back to St. Augustine." "For God's sake, general," exclaimed Pierce, "don't say that! This is the last great battle, and I must lead my brigade!" The commander-in-chief made no further remonstrance, but gave the order for Pierce to advance with his brigade.

The way lay through thick standing corn, and over marshy ground intersected with ditches, which were filled, or partially so, with water. Over some of the narrower of these Pierce leaped his horse. When the brigade had advanced about a mile, however, it found itself impeded by a ditch ten or twelve feet wide, and six or eight feet deep. It being impossible to leap it, General Pierce was lifted from his saddle, and in some incomprehensible way, hurt as he was, contrived to wade or scramble across this obstacle, leaving his horse on the hither side. The troops were now under fire. In the excitement of the battle he forgot his injury, and hurried forward, leading the brigade, a distance of two or three hundred yards. But the exhaustion of his frame, and particularly the anguish of his knee, — made more intolerable by such free use of it, — was greater than any strength of nerve, or any degree of mental energy, could struggle against. He fell, faint and almost insensible, within full range of the enemy's fire. It was proposed to bear him off the field; but, as some of his soldiers approached to lift him, he became aware of their purpose, and was partially revived by his determination to resist it. "No," said he, with all the strength he had left, "don't carry me off! Let me lie here!" And there he lay, under the tremendous fire of Churubusco, until the enemy, in total rout, was driven from the field.

Immediately after the victory, when the city of Mexico lay at the mercy of the American commander, and might have been entered that very night, Santa Anna sent a flag of truce, proposing an armistice, with a view to negotiations for peace. It cannot be considered in any other light than as a very high and signal compliment to his gallantry in the field that General Pierce was appointed, by the commander-in-chief, one of the commissioners on our part, together with General Quitman and General Persifer F. Smith, to arrange the terms of this armistice. Pierce was unable to walk, or to mount his horse without assistance, when intelligence of his appointment reached him. He had not taken off his spurs, nor slept an hour, for two nights ; but he immediately obeyed the summons, was assisted into the saddle, and rode to Tacubaya, where, at the house of the British consul-general, the American and Mexican commissioners were assembled. The conference began late in the afternoon, and continued till four o'clock the next morning, when the articles were signed. Pierce then proceeded to the quarters of General Worth, in the village of Tacubaya, where he obtained an hour or two of repose.

The expectation of General Scott, that further bloodshed might be avoided by means of the armistice, proved deceptive. Military operations, after a temporary interruption, were actively renewed ; and on the 8th of September was fought the bloody battle of Molino del Rey, one of the fiercest and most destructive of the war.

In this conflict general Worth, with three thousand troops, attacked and routed fourteen thousand Mexicans, driving them under the protection of the Castle of Chepultepec. Perceiving the obstinacy with which the field was contested, the commander-in-chief dispatched an order to General Pierce to advance to the support of General Worth's division. He moved forward with rapidity ; and although the battle was won just as he reached the field, he interposed his brigade between Worth and the retreating enemy, and thus drew upon himself the fire of Chepultepec. A shell came streaming from the castle, and, bursting within a few feet of him, startled his horse, which was near plunging over an adjacent precipice. Continuing a long time under fire, Pierce's brigade was engaged in removing the wounded and the captured ammunition. While thus occupied, he led a portion of his command to repel the attacks of the enemy's skirmishers.

There remained but one other battle, — that of Chepultepec, — which was fought on the 13th of September. On the preceding day (although the injuries and the over-exertion resulting from previous marches and battles had greatly enfeebled him), General Pierce had acted with his brigade. In obedience to orders, it had occupied the field of Molino del Rey. Contrary to expectation, it was found that the enemy's force had been withdrawn from this position. Pierce remained in the field until noon, when, it being certain that the anticipated attack would not take place before the following day, he returned to the quarters of General Worth, which were near at hand. There he became extremely ill, and was unable to leave his bed for the thirty-six hours next ensuing. In the mean time, the Castle of Chepultepec was stormed by the troops under Generals Pillow and Quitman. Pierce's brigade behaved itself gallantly, and suffered severely ; and that accomplished officer, Colonel Ransom, leading the Ninth Regiment to the attack, was shot through the head, and fell, with many other brave men, in that last battle of the war.

The American troops, under Quitman and Worth, had established themselves within the limits of the city, having possession of the gates of Belen and of San Cosma, but, up till nightfall, had met with a vigorous resistance from the Mexicans, led on by Santa Anna in person. They had still, apparently, a desperate task before them. It was anticipated that, with the next morning's light, our troops would be ordered to storm the citadel, and the city of Mexico itself. When this was told to Pierce, upon his sick-bed, he rose, and attempted to dress himself; but Captain Hardcastle, who had brought the intelligence from Worth, prevailed upon him to remain in bed, and not to exhaust his scanty strength until the imminence of the occasion should require his presence. Pierce acquiesced for the time, but again arose, in the course of the night, and made his way to the trenches, where he reported himself to General Quitman, with whose division was a part of his brigade. Quitman's share in the anticipated assault, it was supposed, owing to the position which his troops occupied, would be more perilous than that of Worth.

But the last great battle had been fought. In the morning, it was discovered that the citadel had been abandoned, and that Santa Anna had withdrawn his army from the city.

There never was a more gallant body of officers than those who came from civil life into the army on occasion of the Mexican War. All of them, from the rank of general downward, appear to have been animated by the spirit of young knights, in times of chivalry, when fighting for their spurs. Hitherto known only as peaceful citizens, they felt it incumbent on them, by daring and desperate valor, to prove their fitness to be intrusted with the guardianship of their country's honor. The old and trained soldier, already distinguished on former fields, was free to be discreet as well as brave; but these untried warriors were in a different position, and therefore rushed on perils with a recklessness that found its penalty on every battle-field — not one of which was won without a grievous sacrifice of the best blood of America. In this band of gallant men, it is not too much to say, General Pierce was as distinguished for what we must term his temerity in personal exposure, as for the higher traits of leadership, wherever there was an opportunity for their display.

He had manifested, moreover, other and better qual-ities than these, and such as it affords his biographer far greater pleasure to record. His tenderness of heart, his sympathy, his brotherly or paternal care for his men, had been displayed in a hundred instances, and had gained him the enthusiastic affection of all who served under his command. During the passage from America, under the tropics, he would go down into the stifling air of the hold, with a lemon, a cup of tea, and, better and more efficacious than all, a kind word for the sick. While encamped before Vera Cruz, he gave up his own tent to a sick comrade, and went him-self to lodge in the pestilential city. On the march, and even on the battle-field, he found occasion to ex-ercise those feelings of humanity which show most beautifully there. And, in the hospitals of Mexico, he went among the diseased and wounded soldiers, cheering them with his voice and the magic of his kindness, inquiring into their wants, and relieving them to the utmost of his pecuniary means. There was not a man of his brigade but loved him, and would have followed him to death, or have sacrificed his own life in his general's defence.

The officers of the old army, whose profession was war, and who well knew what a soldier was and ought to be, fully recognized his merit. An instance of their honorable testimony in his behalf may fitly be recorded here. It was after General Pierce had returned to the United States. At a dinner in the halls of Montezuma, at which forty or fifty of the brave men above alluded to were present, a young officer of the New England Regiment was called on for a toast. He made an address, in which he spoke with irrepressible enthusiasm of General Pierce, and begged to propose his health. One of the officers of the old line rose, and observed that none of the recently appointed generals commanded more unanimous and universal respect; that General Pierce had appreciated the scientific knowledge of the regular military men, and had acquired their respect by the independence, firmness, and promptitude with which he exercised his own judgment, and acted on the intelligence derived from them. In concluding this tribute of high, but well-considered praise, the speaker very cordially acquiesced in the health of General Pierce, and proposed that it should be drunk standing, with three times three.

General Pierce remained in Mexico until December, when, as the warfare was over, and peace on the point of being concluded, he set out on his return. In nine months, crowded full of incident, he had seen far more of actual service than many professional soldiers during their whole lives. As soon as the treaty of peace was signed, he gave up his commission, and returned to the practice of the law, again proposing to spend the remainder of his days in the bosom of his family. All the dreams of his youth were now fulfilled; the military ardor, that had struck an hereditary root in his breast, had enjoyed its scope, and was satisfied; and he flattered himself that no circumstances could hereafter occur to draw him from the retirement of domestic peace. New Hampshire received him with even more enthusiastic affection than ever. At his departure, he had received a splendid sword at the hands of many of his friends, in token of their confidence; he had shown himself well worthy to wear and able to use a soldier's weapon; and his native state now gave him another, the testimonial of approved valor and warlike conduct.

## CHAPTER VI.

### THE COMPROMISE AND OTHER MATTERS.

THE intervening years, since General Pierce's return from Mexico, and until the present time, have been spent in the laborious exercise of the legal profession, — an employment scarcely varied or interrupted, except by those episodes of political activity which a man of public influence finds it impossible to avoid, and in which, if his opinions are matter of conscience with him, he feels it his duty to interest himself.

In the presidential canvass of 1848 he used his best efforts (and with success, so far as New Hampshire was concerned) in behalf of the candidate of his party. A truer and better speech has never been uttered on a similar occasion than one which he made (during a hurried half hour, snatched from the court room) in October of the above year, before the democratic state convention, then in session at Concord. It is an invariable characteristic of General Pierce's popular addresses, that they evince a genuine respect for the people; he makes his appeal to their intelligence, their patriotism, and their integrity, and, never doubtful of their upright purpose, proves his faith in the great mind and heart of the country both by what he says and by what he refrains from saying. He never yet was guilty of an effort to cajole his fellow-citizens, to operate upon their credulity, or to trick them even into what was right; and therefore all the victories which he has ever won in popular assemblies have been triumphs doubly honored, being as creditable to his audiences as to himself.

When the series of measures known under the collective term of The Compromise were passed by Congress in 1850, and put to so searching a test here at the North the reverence of the people for the Constitution and their attachment to the Union, General Pierce was true to the principles which he had long ago avowed. At an early period of his congressional service he had made known, with the perfect frankness of his character, those opinions upon the slavery question which he has never since seen occasion to change in the slightest degree. There is an unbroken consistency in his action with regard to this matter. It is entirely of a piece, from his first entrance upon public life until the moment when he came forward, while many were faltering, to throw the great weight of his character and influence into the scale in favor of those measures through which it was intended to redeem the pledges of the Constitution, and to preserve and renew the old love and harmony among the sisterhood of States. His approval embraced the whole series of these acts, as well those which bore hard upon northern views and sentiments as those in which the South deemed itself to have made more than reciprocal concessions.

No friend nor enemy that knew Franklin Pierce would have expected him to act otherwise. With his view of the whole subject, whether looking at it through the medium of his conscience, his feelings, or his intellect, it was impossible for him not to take his stand as the unshaken advocate of Union, and of the mutual steps of compromise which that great object unquestionably demanded. The fiercest, the least scrupulous, and the most consistent of those who battle against slavery recognize the same fact that he does. They see that merely human wisdom and human efforts cannot subvert it, except by tearing to pieces the Constitution, breaking the pledges which it sanctions, and severing into distracted fragments that common country which Providence brought into one nation, through a continued miracle of almost two hundred years, from the first settlement of the American wilderness until the Revolution. In the days when, a young member of Congress, he first raised his voice against agitation, Pierce saw these perils and their consequences. He considered, too, that the evil would be certain, while the good was, at best, a contingency, and (to the clear, practical foresight with which he looked into the future) scarcely so much as that, attended as the movement was and must be during its progress, with the aggravated injury of those whose condition it aimed to ameliorate, and terminating, in its possible triumph, — if such possibility there were, — with the ruin of two races which now dwelt together in greater peace and affection, it is not too much to say, than had ever elsewhere existed between the taskmaster and the serf.

Of course, there is another view of all these matters. The theorist may take that view in his closet; the philanthropist by profession may strive to act upon it uncompromisingly, amid the tumult and warfare of his life. But the statesman of practical sagacity — who loves his country as it is, and evolves good from things as they exist, and who demands to feel his firm grasp upon a better reality before he quits the one already gained — will be likely here, with all the greatest statesmen of America, to stand in the attitude of a conservative. Such, at all events, will be the attitude of Franklin Pierce. We have sketched some of the influences amid which he grew up, inheriting his father's love of country, mindful of the old patriot's valor in so many conflicts of the Revolution, and having close before his eyes the example of brothers and relatives, more than one of whom have bled for America, both at the extremest north and farthest south; himself, too, in early manhood, serving the Union in its legislative halls, and, at a maturer age, leading his fellow-citizens, his brethren, from the widest-sundered states, to redden the same battle-fields with their kindred blood, to unite their breath into one shout of victory, and perhaps to sleep, side by side, with the same sod over them. Such a man, with such hereditary recollections, and such a personal experience, must not narrow himself to adopt the cause of one section of his native country against another. He will stand up, as he has always stood, among the patriots of the whole land. And if the work of antislavery agitation, which it is undeniable leaves most men who earnestly engage in it with only half a country in their affections, — if this work must be done, let others do it.

Those northern men, therefore, who deem the great cause of human welfare as represented and involved in this present hostility against southern institutions, and who conceive that the world stands still except so

far as that goes forward, — these, it may be allowed,
can scarcely give their sympathy or their confidence
to the subject of this memoir. But there is still another view, and probably as wise a one. It looks
upon slavery as one of those evils which divine Providence does not leave to be remedied by human contrivances, but which, in its own good time, by some
means impossible to be anticipated, but of the simplest
and easiest operation, when all its uses shall have been
fulfilled, it causes to vanish like a dream. There is
no instance, in all history, of the human will and intellect having perfected any great moral reform by
methods which it adapted to that end; but the progress of the world, at every step, leaves some evil or
wrong on the path behind it, which the wisest of mankind, of their own set purpose, could never have found
the way to rectify. Whatever contributes to the great
cause of good, contributes to all its subdivisions and
varieties; and, on this score, the lover of his race, the
enthusiast, the philanthropist of whatever theory, might
lend his aid to put a man, like the one before us, into
the leadership of the world's affairs.

How firm and conscientious was General Pierce's
support of The Compromise may be estimated from
his conduct in reference to the Reverend John Atwood.
In the foregoing pages it has come oftener in our way
to illustrate the bland and prepossessing features of
General Pierce's character, than those sterner ones
which must necessarily form the bones, so to speak,
the massive skeleton, of any man who retains an upright attitude amidst the sinister influences of public
life. The transaction now alluded to affords a favorable opportunity for indicating some of these latter
traits.

In October, 1850, a democratic convention, held at Concord, nominated Mr. Atwood as the party's regular candidate for governor. The Compromise, then recent, was inevitably a prominent element in the discussions of the convention ; and a series of resolutions were adopted, bearing reference to this great subject, fully and unreservedly indorsing the measures comprehended under it, and declaring the principles on which the Democracy of the state was about to engage in the gubernatorial contest. Mr. Atwood accepted the nomination, acceding to the platform thus tendered him, taking exceptions to none of the individual resolutions, and, of course, pledging himself to the whole by the very act of assuming the candidacy, which was predicated upon them.

The reverend candidate, we should conceive, is a well-meaning, and probably an amiable man. In ordinary circumstances, he would, doubtless, have gone through the canvass triumphantly, and have administered the high office to which he aspired with no discredit to the party that had placed him at its head. But the disturbed state of the public mind on the Compromise question rendered the season a very critical one ; and Mr. Atwood, unfortunately, had that fatal weakness of character, which, however respectably it may pass in quiet times, is always bound to make itself pitiably manifest under the pressure of a crisis. A letter was addressed to him by a committee, representing the party opposed to The Compromise, and with whom, it may be supposed, were included those who held the more thorough-going degrees of antislavery sentiment. The purpose of the letter was to draw out an expression of Mr. Atwood's opinion on the abolition movement generally, and with an especial reference to the Fugitive Slave Law, and whether, as chief magistrate of the state, he would favor any attempt for its repeal. In an answer of considerable length the candidate expressed sentiments that brought him unquestionably within the free soil pale, and favored his correspondents, moreover, with a pretty decided judgment as to the unconstitutional, unjust, and oppressive character of the Fugitive Slave Act.

During a space of about two months, this very important document was kept from the public eye. Rumors of its existence, however, became gradually noised abroad, and necessarily attracted the attention of Mr. Atwood's democratic friends. Inquiries being made, he acknowledged the existence of the letter, but averred that it had never been delivered, that it was merely a rough draught, and that he had hitherto kept it within his own control, with a view to more careful consideration. In accordance with the advice of friends, he expressed a determination, and apparently in good faith, to suppress the letter, and thus to sever all connection with the antislavery party. This, however, was now beyond his power. A copy of the letter had been taken; it was published, with high commendations, in the antislavery newspapers; and Mr. Atwood was exhibited in the awkward predicament of directly avowing sentiments on the one hand which he had implicitly disavowed on the other, of accepting a nomination based on principles diametrically opposite.

The candidate appears to have apprehended this disclosure, and he hurried to Concord, and sought counsel of General Pierce, with whom he was on terms of personal kindness, and between whom and himself, heretofore, there had never been a shade of political

difference. An interview with the general and one or
two other gentlemen ensued. Mr. Atwood was cau-
tioned against saying or writing a word that might be
repugnant to his feelings or his principles; but, voluntarily, and at his own suggestion, he now wrote for
publication a second letter, in which he retracted every
objectionable feature of his former one, and took decided ground in favor of The Compromise, including
all its individual measures. Had he adhered to this
latter position, he might have come out of the affair,
if not with the credit of consistency, yet, at least, as a
successful candidate in the impending election. But
his evil fate, or, rather, the natural infirmity of his
character, was not so to be thrown off. The very next
day, unhappily, he fell into the hands of some of his
antislavery friends, to whom he avowed a constant adherence to the principles of his first letter, describing
the second as having been drawn from him by impor-
tunity, in an excited state of his mind, and without a
full realization of its purport.

It would be needlessly cruel to Mr. Atwood to trace
with minuteness the further details of this affair. It
is impossible to withold from him a certain sympathy,
or to avoid feeling that a very worthy man, as the world
goes, had entangled himself in an inextricable knot of
duplicity and tergiversation, by an ill-advised effort to
be two opposite things at once. For the sake of true
manhood, we gladly turn to consider the course adopted
by General Pierce.

The election for governor was now at a distance of
only a few weeks; and it could not be otherwise than
a most hazardous movement for the democratic party,
at so late a period, to discard a candidate with whom
the people had become familiar. It involved nothing

less than the imminent peril of that political suprem-
acy which the party had so long enjoyed. With Mr.
Atwood as candidate, success might still be considered
certain. To a short-sighted and a weak man, it would
have appeared the obvious policy to patch up the difficulty, and, at all events, to conquer, under whatever
leadership, and with whatever allies. But it was one
of those junctures which test the difference between
the man of principle and the mere politician — the
man of moral courage and him who yields to temporary expediency. General Pierce could not consent
that his party should gain a nominal triumph, at the
expense of what he looked upon as its real integrity
and life. With this view of the matter, he had no
hesitation in his course; nor could the motives which
otherwise would have been strongest with him — pity
for the situation of an unfortunate individual, a personal friend, a Democrat, as Mr. Atwood describes
himself, of nearly fifty years' standing — incline him
to mercy, where it would have been fatal to his sense
of right. He took decided ground against Mr. Atwood. The convention met again, and nominated
another candidate. Mr. Atwood went into the field as
the candidate of the antislavery party, drew off a sufficient body of Democrats to defeat the election by the
people, but was himself defeated in the legislature.

Thus, after exhibiting to the eyes of mankind (or
such portion of mankind as chanced to be looking in
that direction) the absurd spectacle of a gentleman
of extremely moderate stride attempting a feat that
would have baffled a Colossus, — to support himself,
namely, on both margins of the impassable chasm
that has always divided the antislavery faction from
the New Hampshire Democracy, — this ill-fated man

attempted first to throw himself upon one side of
the gulf, then on the other, and finally tumbled headlong into the bottomless depth between.  His case
presents a painful but very curious and instructive
instance of the troubles that beset weakness, in those
emergencies which demand steadfast moral strength
and energy — of which latter type of manly character
there can be no truer example than Franklin Pierce.

In the autumn of 1850, in pursuance of a vote of
the people, a convention assembled at Concord for the
revision of the Constitution of New Hampshire.  General Pierce was elected its president by an almost
unanimous vote — a very high mark of the affectionate confidence which the state, for so long a time and
in such a variety of modes, had manifested in him.
It was so much the higher, as the convention included
New Hampshire's most eminent citizens, among whom
was Judge Woodbury.

General Pierce's conduct, as presiding officer, was
satisfactory to all parties ; and one of his political opponents (Professor Sanborn, of Dartmouth College)
has ably sketched him, both in that aspect and as a
debater.

" In drawing the portraits of the distinguished
members of the constitutional convention," writes the
professor, " to pass Frank Pierce unnoticed would be
as absurd as to enact one of Shakspeare's dramas without its principal hero.  I give my impressions of the
man as I saw him in the convention ; for I would not
undertake to vouch for the truth or falsehood of those
veracious organs of public sentiment, at the capital,
which have loaded him in turn with indiscriminate
praise and abuse.  As a presiding officer, it would
be difficult to find his equal.  In proposing questions

to the house, he never hesitates or blunders. In deciding points of order, he is both prompt and impartial. His treatment of every member of the convention was characterized by uniform courtesy and kindness. The deportment of the presiding officer of a deliberative body usually gives tone to the debates. If he is harsh, morose, or abrupt in his manner, the speakers are apt to catch his spirit by the force of involuntary sympathy. The same is true, to some extent, of the principal debaters in such a body. When a man of strong prejudices and harsh temper rises to address a public assembly, his indwelling antipathies speak from every feature of his face and from every motion of his person. The audience at once brace themselves against his assaults, and condemn his opinions before they are heard. The well-known character of an orator persuades or dissuades quite as forcibly as the language he utters. Some men never rise to address a deliberative assembly without conciliating good will in advance. The smile that plays upon the speaker's face awakens emotions of complacency in those who hear, even before he speaks. So does that weight of character, which is the matured fruit of long public services and acknowledged worth, soothe, in advance, the irritated and angry crowd.

"Mr. Pierce possesses unquestioned ability as a public speaker. Few men, in our country, better understand the means of swaying a popular assembly, or employ them with greater success. His forte lies in moving the passions of those whom he addresses. He knows how to call into vigorous action both the sympathies and antipathies of those who listen to him. I do not mean to imply by these remarks that his oratory is deficient in argument or sound reasoning. On the contrary, he seizes with great power upon the strong points of his subject, and presents them clearly, forcibly, and eloquently. As a prompt and ready debater, always prepared for assault or defence, he has few equals. In these encounters, he appears to great advantage, from his happy faculty of turning little incidents, unexpectedly occurring, to his own account. A word carelessly dropped, or an unguarded allusion to individuals or parties by an opponent, is frequently converted into a powerful weapon of assault, by this skilful advocate. He has been so much in office that he may be said to have been educated in public life. He is most thoroughly versed in all the tactics of debate. He is not only remarkably fluent in his elocution, but remarkably correct. He seldom miscalls or repeats a word. His style is not overloaded with ornament, and yet he draws liberally upon the treasury of rhetoric. His figures are often beautiful and striking, never incongruous. He is always listened to with respectful attention, if he does not always command conviction. From his whole course in the convention, a disinterested spectator could not fail to form a very favorable opinion, not only of his talent and eloquence, but of his generosity and magnanimity."

Among other antiquated relics of the past, and mouldy types of prejudices that ought now to be forgotten, and of which it was the object of the present convention to purge the Constitution of New Hampshire, there is a provision that certain state offices should be held only by Protestants. Since General Pierce's nomination for the presidency, the existence of this religious test has been brought as a charge against him, as if, in spite of his continued efforts to remove it, he were personally responsible for its remaining on the statute book.

General Pierce has naturally a strong endowment of religious feeling. At no period of his life, as is well known to his friends, have the sacred relations of the human soul been a matter of indifference with him; and, of more recent years, whatever circumstances of good or evil fortune may have befallen him, they have alike served to deepen this powerful sentiment. Whether in sorrow or success, he has learned, in his own behalf, the great lesson, that religious faith is the most valuable and most sacred of human possessions; but, with this sense, there has come no narrowness or illiberality, but a wide-embracing sympathy for the modes of Christian worship, and a reverence for individual belief, as a matter between the Deity and man's soul, and with which no other has a right to interfere. With the feeling here described, and with his acute intellectual perception of the abortive character of all intolerant measures, as defeating their own ends, it strikes one as nothing less than ludicrous that he should be charged with desiring to retain this obsolete enactment, standing, as it does, as a merely gratuitous and otherwise inoperative stigma upon the fair reputation of his native state. Even supposing no higher motives to have influenced him, it would have sufficed to secure his best efforts for the repeal of the religious test that so many of the Catholics have always been found in the advance-guard of freedom, marching onward with the progressive party; and that, whether in peace or war, they have performed for their adopted country the hard toil and the gallant services which she has a right to expect from her most faithful citizens.

The truth is that, ever since his entrance upon public life, on all occasions, — and often making the occasion where he found none, — General Pierce has done his utmost to obliterate this obnoxious feature from the Constitution. He has repeatedly advocated the calling of a convention mainly for this purpose. In that of 1850, he both spoke and voted in favor of the abolition of the test, and, with the aid of Judge Woodbury and other democratic members, attained his purpose, so far as the convention possessed any power or responsibility in the matter. That the measure was ultimately defeated is due to other causes, either temporary or of long continuance ; and to some of them it is attributable that the enlightened public sentiment of New Hampshire was not, long since, made to operate upon this enactment, so anomalous in the fundamental law of a free state.

In order to the validity of the amendments passed by the convention, it was necessary that the people should subsequently act upon them, and pass a vote of two thirds in favor of their adoption. The amendments proposed by the convention of 1850 were numerous. The Constitution had been modified in many and very important particulars, in respect to which the popular mind had not previously been made familiar, and on which it had not anticipated the necessity of passing judgment. In March, 1851, when the vote of the people was taken upon these measures, the Atwood controversy was at its height, and threw all matters of less immediate interest into the background. During the interval since the adjournment of the convention, the whig newspapers had been indefatigable in their attempts to put its proceedings in an odious light before the people. There had been no period, for many years, in which sinister influences rendered it so difficult to draw out an efficient expression of the will of the

Democracy as on this occasion. It was the result of all these obstacles that the doings of the constitutional convention were rejected in the mass.

In the ensuing April, the convention reassembled, in order to receive the unfavorable verdict of the people upon its proposed amendments. At the suggestion of General Pierce, the amendment abolishing the religious test was again brought forward, and, in spite of the opposition of the leading whig members, was a second time submitted to the people. Nor did his struggle in behalf of this enlightened movement terminate here. At the democratic caucus, in Concord, preliminary to the town meeting, he urged upon his political friends the repeal of the test, as a party measure; and again, at the town meeting itself, while the balloting was going forward, he advocated it on the higher ground of religious freedom, and of reverence for what is inviolable in the human soul. Had the amendment passed, the credit would have belonged to no man more than to General Pierce; and that it failed, and that the free Constitution of New Hampshire is still disgraced by a provision which even monarchical England has cast off, is a responsibility which must rest elsewhere than on his head.

In September, 1851, died that eminent statesman and jurist, Levi Woodbury, then occupying the elevated post of judge of the Supreme Court of the United States. The connection between him and General Pierce, beginning in the early youth of the latter, had been sustained through all the subsequent years. They sat together, with but one intervening chair between, in the national Senate; they were always advocates of the same great measures, and held, through life, a harmony of opinion and action, which was never more cônspicu-

ous than in the few months that preceded Judge
Woodbury's death. At a meeting of the bar, after his
decease, General Pierce uttered some remarks, full of
sensibility, in which he referred to the circumstances
that had made this friendship an inheritance on his
part. Had Judge Woodbury survived, it is not im-
probable that his more advanced age, his great public
services, and equally distinguished zeal in behalf of
the Union might have placed him in the position now
occupied by the subject of this memoir. Fortunate
the state which, after losing such a son, can still point
to another, not less worthy to take upon him the charge
of the nation's welfare.

We have now finished our record of Franklin Pierce's
life, and have only to describe the posture of affairs
which, without his own purpose and against his wish,
has placed him before the people of the United States
as a candidate for the presidency.

## CHAPTER VII.

### HIS NOMINATION FOR THE PRESIDENCY.

On the 12th of June, 1852, the democratic national
convention assembled at Baltimore, in order to select
a candidate for the presidency of the United States.
Many names, eminently distinguished in peace and
war, had been brought before the public, during several
months previous ; and among them, though by no
means occupying a very prominent place, was the
name of Franklin Pierce. In January of this year,
the Democracy of New Hampshire had signified its
preference of General Pierce as a presidential candi-

date in the approaching canvass — a demonstration which drew from him the following response, addressed to his friend, Mr. Atherton : —

"I am far from being insensible to the generous confidence so often manifested towards me by the people of this state; and although the object indicated in the resolution, having particular reference to myself, be not one of desire on my part, the expression is not on that account less gratifying.

"Doubtless the spontaneous and just appreciation of an intelligent people is the best earthly reward for earnest and cheerful sevices rendered to one's state and country; and while it is a matter of unfeigned regret that my life has been so barren of usefulness, I shall ever hold this and similar tributes among my most cherished recollections.

"To these, my sincere and grateful acknowledgments, I desire to add that the same motives which induced me, several years ago, to retire from public life, and which since that time controlled my judgment in this respect, now impel me to say that the use of my name in any event, before the democratic national convention at Baltimore, to which you are a delegate, would be utterly repugnant to my taste and wishes."

The sentiments expressed in the above letter were genuine, and from his heart. He had looked long and closely at the effects of high public station on the character and happiness, and on what is the innermost and dearest part of a man's possessions — his independence; and he had satisfied himself that office, however elevated, should be avoided for one's own sake, or accepted only as a good citizen would make any other sacrifice, at the call and at the need of his country.

As the time for the assembling of the national con-

vention drew near, there were other sufficient indications of his sincerity in declining a stake in the great
game. A circular letter was addressed, by Major Scott,
of Virginia, to the distinguished Democrats whose
claims had heretofore been publicly discussed, request-
ing a statement of their opinions on several points, and
inquiring what would be the course of each of these
gentlemen, in certain contingencies, in case of his attaining the presidency. These queries, it may be presumed, were of such a nature that General Pierce
might have answered them, had he seen fit to do so,
to the satisfaction of Major Scott himself, or to that of
the southern democratic party, whom it seemed his
purpose to represent. With not more than one exception, the other statesmen and soldiers, to whom the
circular had been sent, made a response. General
Pierce preserved an unbroken silence. It was equivalent to the withdrawal of all claims which he might
be supposed to possess, in reference to the contemplated office; and he thereby repeated, to the delegates of the national party, the same avowal of dis-
taste for public life which he had already made known
to the Democracy of his native state. He had thus
done everything in his power, actively or passively,—
everything that he could have done, without showing
such an estimate of his position before the country as
was inconsistent with the modesty of his character, —
to avoid the perilous and burdensome honor of the
candidacy.

The convention met, at the date above mentioned,
and continued its sessions during four days. Thirty-
five ballotings were held, with a continually decreasing
prospect that the friends of any one of the gentlemen
hitherto prominent before the people would succeed in

obtaining the two thirds vote that was requisite for a nomination. Thus far, not a vote had been thrown for General Pierce; but, at the thirty-sixth ballot, the delegation of old Virginia brought forward his name. In the course of several more trials, his strength increased, very gradually at first, but afterwards with a growing impetus, until, at the forty-ninth ballot, the votes were for Franklin Pierce two hundred and eighty-two, and eleven for all other candidates. Thus Franklin Pierce became the nominee of the convention; and as quickly as the lightning flash could blazen it abroad his name was on every tongue, from end to end of this vast country. Within an hour he grew to be illustrious.

It would be a pretension, which we do not mean to put forward, to assert that, whether considering the length and amount of his public services, or his prominence before the country, General Pierce stood on equal ground with several of the distinguished men whose claims, to use the customary phrase, had been rejected in favor of his own. But no man, be his public services or sacrifices what they might, ever did or ever could possess, in the slightest degree, what we may term a legitimate claim to be elevated to the rulership of a free people. The nation would degrade itself, and violate every principle upon which its institutions are founded, by offering its majestic obedience to one of its citizens as a reward for whatever splendor of achievement. The conqueror may assert a claim, such as it is, to the sovereignty of the people whom he subjugates; but, with us Americans, when a statesman comes to the chief direction of affairs, it is at the summons of the nation, addressed to the servant whom it deems best fitted to spend his wisdom, his strength, and his life in its behalf. On this principle, which is obviously the correct one, a candidate's previous services are entitled to consideration only as they indicate the qualities which may enable him to render higher services in the position which his countrymen choose that he shall occupy. What he has done is of no importance, except as proving what he can do. And it is on this score, because they see in his public course the irrefragable evidences of patriotism, integrity, and courage, and because they recognize in him the noble gift of natural authority, and have a prescience of the stately endowment of administrative genius, that his fellow-citizens are about to summon Franklin Pierce to the presidency. To those who know him well, the event comes, not like accident, but as a consummation which might have been anticipated, from its innate fitness, and as the final step of a career which, all along, has tended thitherward.

It is not as a reward that he will take upon him the mighty burden of this office, of which the toil and awful responsibility whiten the statesman's head, and in which, as in more than one instance we have seen, the warrior encounters a deadlier risk than in the battlefield. When General Pierce received the news of his nomination, it affected him with no thrill of joy, but a sadness, which, for many days, was perceptible in his deportment. It awoke in his heart the sense of religious dependence — a sentiment that has been growing continually stronger, through all the trials and experiences of his life; and there was nothing feigned in that passage of his beautiful letter, accepting the nomination, in which he expresses his reliance upon heavenly support.

The committee, appointed by the Baltimore conven-

tion, conveyed to him the intelligence of his nomination in the following terms : —

"A national convention of the democratic republican party, which met in Baltimore on the first Tuesday in June, unanimously nominated you as a candidate for the high trust of the President of the United
States. We have been delegated to acquaint you with
the nomination, and earnestly to request that you will
accept it. Persuaded as we are that this office should
never be pursued by an unchastened ambition, it cannot be refused by a dutiful patriotism.

"The circumstances under which you will be presented for the canvass of your countrymen seem to us
propitious to the interests which the constitution in-
trusts to our Federal Union, and must be auspicious
to your own name. You come before the people without the impulse of personal wishes, and free from
selfish expectations. You are identified with none of
the distractions which have recently disturbed our
country, whilst you are known to be faithful to the
constitution — to all its guaranties and compromises.
You will be free to exercise your tried abilities, within
the path of duty, in protecting that repose we happily
enjoy, and in giving efficacy and control to those car-
dinal principles that have already illustrated the party
which has now selected you as its leader — principles
that regard the security and prosperity of the whole
country, and the paramount power of its laws, as in-
dissolubly associated with the perpetuity of our civil
and religious liberties.

"The convention did not pretermit the duty of reit-
erating those principles, and you will find them prominently set forth in the resolutions it adopted. To
these we respectfully invite your attention.

"It is firmly believed that to your talents and patriotism the security of our holy Union, with its ex-
panded and expanding interests, may be wisely trusted,
and that, amid all the perils which may assail the constitution, you will have the heart to love and the arm
to defend it."

We quote likewise General Pierce's reply : —

"I have the honor to acknowledge your personal
kindness in presenting me, this day, your letter, officially informing me of my nomination, by the democratic national convention, as a candidate for the presidency of the United States. The surprise with which
I received the intelligence of my nomination was not
unmingled with painful solicitude ; and yet it is proper
for me to say that the manner in which it was conferred was peculiarly gratifying.

"The delegation from New Hampshire, with all the
glow of state pride, and with all the warmth of personal regard, would not have submitted my name to
the convention, nor would they have cast a vote for
me, under circumstances other than those which occurred.

"I shall always cherish with pride and gratitude
the recollection of the fact that the voice which first
pronounced, and pronounced alone, came from the
Mother of States — a pride and gratitude rising above
any consequences that can betide me personally. May
I not regard it as a fact pointing to the overthrow of
sectional jealousies, and looking to the permanent life
and vigor of the Union, cemented by the blood of
those who have passed to their reward ? — a Union
wonderful in its formation, boundless in its hopes,
amazing in its destiny.

"I accept the nomination, relying upon an abiding

devotion to the interests, honor, and glory of the whole country, but, above and beyond all, upon a Power superior to all human might — a Power which, from the first gun of the Revolution, in every crisis through which we have passed, in every hour of acknowledged peril, when the dark clouds had shut down over us, has interposed as if to baffle human wisdom, outmarch human forecast, and bring out of darkness the rainbow of promise. Weak myself, faith and hope repose there in security.

" I accept the nomination upon the platform adopted by the convention, not because this is expected of me as a candidate, but because the principles it embraces command the approbation of my judgment; and with them, I believe I can safely say, there has been no word or act of my life in conflict."

The news of his nomination went abroad over the Union, and, far and wide, there came a response, in which was distinguishable a truer appreciation of some of General Pierce's leading traits than could have been anticipated, considering the unobtrusive tenor of his legislative life, and the lapse of time since he had entirely withdrawn himself from the nation's eye. It was the marvellous and mystic influence of character, in regard to which the judgment of the people is so seldom found erroneous, and which conveys the perception of itself through some medium higher and deeper than the intellect. Everywhere the country knows that a man of steadfast will, true heart, and generous qualities has been brought forward, to receive the suffrages of his fellow-citizens.

He comes before the people of the United States at a remarkable era in the history of this country and of the world. The two great parties of the nation appear — at least to an observer somewhat removed from both — to have nearly merged into one another; for they preserve the attitude of political antagonism rather through the effect of their old organizations than because any great and radical principles are at present in dispute between them. The measures advocated by the one party, and resisted by the other, through a long series of years, have now ceased to be the pivots on which the election turns. The prominent statesmen, so long identified with those measures, will henceforth relinquish their controlling influence over public affairs. Both parties, it may likewise be said, are united in one common purpose, — that of preserving our sacred Union, as the immovable basis from which the destinies, not of America alone, but of mankind at large, may be carried upward and consummated. And thus men stand together, in unwonted quiet and harmony, awaiting the new movement in advance which all these tokens indicate.

It remains for the citizens of this great country to decide, within the next few weeks, whether they will retard the steps of human progress by placing at its head an illustrious soldier, indeed, a patriot, and one indelibly stamped into the history of the past, but who has already done his work, and has not in him the spirit of the present or of the coming time ; or whether they will put their trust in a new man, whom a life of energy and various activity has tested, but not worn out, and advance with him into the auspicious epoch upon which we are about to enter.

# NOTE.

WE have done far less than justice to Franklin Pierce's college standing, in our statement on page 355. Some circumstances connected with this matter are too characteristic not to be reported.

During the first two years, Pierce was extremely inattentive to his college duties, bestowing only such modicum of time upon them as was requisite to supply the merest superficial acquaintance with the course of study for the recitation room. The consequence was that when the relative standing of the members of the class was first authoritatively ascertained, in the junior year, he found himself occupying precisely the lowest position in point of scholarship. In the first mortification of wounded pride, he resolved never to attend another recitation, and accordingly absented himself from college exercises of all kinds for several days, expecting and desiring that some form of punishment, such as suspension or expulsion, would be the result. The faculty of the college, however, with a wise lenity, took no notice of this behavior ; and at last, having had time to grow cool, and moved by the grief of his friend Little and another classmate, Pierce determined to resume the routine of college duties. "But," said he to his friends, "if I do so, you shall see a change ! "

Accordingly, from that time forward, he devoted himself to study. His mind, having run wild for so long a period, could be reclaimed only by the severest efforts of an iron resolution ; and for three months afterwards, he rose at four in the morning, toiled all day over his books, and retired only at midnight, allowing himself but four hours for sleep. With habit and exercise, he acquired command over his intellectual powers, and was no longer under the necessity of application so intense. But from the moment when he made his resolve until the close of his college life, he never incurred a censure, never was absent (and then unavoidably) but from two college exercises, never went into the recitation room without a thorough acquaintance with the subject to be recited, and finally graduated as the third scholar of his class. Nothing save the low standard of his previous scholarship prevented his taking a yet higher rank.

The moral of this little story lies in the stern and continued exercise of self-controlling will, which redeemed him from indolence, completely changed the aspect of his character, and made this the turning point of his life.

# APPENDIX.

# BIOGRAPHICAL SKETCH

OF

# NATHANIEL HAWTHORNE.

## I.

THE lives of great men are written gradually. It often takes as long to construct a true biography as it took the person who is the subject of it to complete his career; and when the work is done, it is found to consist of many volumes, produced by a variety of authors. We receive views from different observers, and by putting them together are able to form our own estimate. What the man really was not even himself could know; much less can we. Hence all that we accomplish, in any case, is to approximate to the reality. While we flatter ourselves that we have imprinted on our minds an exact image of the individual, we actually secure nothing but a typical likeness. This likeness, however, is amplified and strengthened by successive efforts to paint a correct portrait. If the faces of people belonging to several generations of a family be photographed upon one plate, they combine to form a single distinct countenance, which shows a general resemblance to them all: in somewhat the same way, every sketch of a distinguished man helps to fix the lines of that typical semblance of him which is all that the world can hope to preserve.

This principle applies to the case of Hawthorne, notwithstanding that the details of his career are comparatively few, and must be marshalled in much the same way each time that it is attempted to review them. The veritable history of his life would be the history of his mental development, recording, like Wordsworth's " Prelude," the growth of a poet's mind ; and on glancing back over it he too might have said, in Wordsworth's phrases : —

> " Wisdom and spirit of the universe !
> . . . . . . . . . .
>
> By day or star-light thus from my first dawn
> Of childhood didst thou intertwine for me
> The passions that build up the human soul;
> Not with the mean and vulgar works of man,
> But with high objects, with enduring things —
> With life and nature, purifying thus
> The elements of feeling and of thought,
> And sanctifying by such discipline
> Both pain and fear, until we recognize
> A grandeur in the beatings of the heart."

But a record of that kind, except where an autobiography exists, can be had only by indirect means. We must resort to tracing the outward facts of the life, and must try to infer the interior relations.

Nathaniel Hawthorne was born on the Fourth of July, 1804, at Salem, Massachusetts, in a house numbered twenty-one, Union Street. The house is still standing, although somewhat reduced in size and still more reduced in circumstances. The character of the neighborhood has declined very much since the period when Hawthorne involuntarily became a resident there. As the building stands to-day it makes the impression simply of an exceedingly plain, exceedingly old-fashioned, solid, comfortable abode, which in its prime must have been regarded as proof of a sufficient but modest prosperity on the part of the occupant. It is clapboarded, is two stories high, and has a gambrel roof, immediately beneath which is a large garret that doubtless served the boy-child well as a place for play and a stimulant for the sense of mystery. A single massive chimney, rising from the centre, emphasizes by its style the antiquity of the building, and has the air of holding it together. The cobble-stoned street in front is narrow, and although it runs from the house towards the water-side, where once an extensive commerce was carried on, and debouches not far from the Custom House where Hawthorne in middle life found plenty of occupation as Surveyor, it is now silent and deserted.

He was the second of three children born to Nathaniel Hathorne, sea-captain, and Elizabeth Clarke Manning. The eldest was Elizabeth Manning Hathorne, who came into the world March 7, 1802 ; the last was Maria Louisa, born January 9, 1808, and lost in the steamer Henry Clay, which was burned on the Hudson River, July 27, 1852. Elizabeth survived all the members of the family, dying on the 1st of January, 1883, when almost eighty-one years old, at Montserrat, a hamlet in the township of Beverly, near Salem. In early manhood, certainly at about the time when he began to publish, the young Nathaniel changed the spelling of his surname to Hawthorne; an alteration also adopted by his sisters. This is believed to have been merely a return to a mode of spelling practised by the English progenitors of the line, although none of the American ancestors had sanctioned it.

" The fact that he was born in Salem," writes Dr. George B. Loring, who knew him as a fellow-towns-

man, " may not amount to much to other people, but
it amounted to a great deal to him. The sturdy and
defiant spirit of his progenitor, who first landed on
these shores, found a congenial abode among the people
of Naumkeag, after having vainly endeavored to accommodate itself to the more imposing ecclesiasticism
of Winthrop and his colony at Trimountain, and of
Endicott at his new home. He was a stern Separatist
. . . but he was also a warrior, a politician, a legal
adviser, a merchant, an orator with persuasive speech.
. . . He had great powers of mind and body, and
forms a conspicuous figure in that imposing and heroic group which stands around the cradle of New
England. The generations of the family that followed
took active and prominent part in the manly adventures which marked our entire colonial period. . . .
It was among the family traditions gathered from the
Indian wars, the tragic and awful spectre of the witchcraft delusion, the wild life of the privateer, that he
[Nathaniel] first saw the light."

The progenitor here referred to is William Hathorne, who came to America with John Winthrop in
1630. He had grants of land in Dorchester, but was
considered so desirable a citizen that the town of Salem offered him other lands if he would settle there;
which he did. It has not been ascertained from what
place William Hathorne originally came. His elder
brother Robert is known to have written to him in
1653 from the village of Bray, in Berkshire, England; but Nathaniel Hawthorne says in the "American Note-Books " that William was a younger brother
of a family having for its seat a place called Wigcastle,
in Wiltshire. He became, however, a person of note
and of great usefulness in the community with which

he cast his lot, in the new England. Hathorne Street in Salem perpetuates his name to-day, as Lathrop Street does that of Captain Thomas Lathrop, who commanded one of the companies of Essex militia, when John Hathorne was quartermaster of the forces ; Thomas Lathrop, who marched his men to Deerfield in 1675, to protect frontier inhabitants from the Indians, and perished with his whole troop, in the massacre at Bloody Brook. The year after that, William Hathorne also took the field against the Indians, in Maine, and conducted a highly successful campaign there, under great hardships. He had been the captain of the first military organization in Salem, and rose to be major. He served for a number of years as deputy in the Great and General Court ; was a tax-collector, a magistrate, and a bold advocate of colonial self-government. Although opposed to religious persecution, as a magistrate he inflicted cruelties on the Quakers, causing a woman on one occasion to be whipped through Salem, Boston, and Dedham. " The figure of that first ancestor," Hawthorne wrote in " The Custom House," " invested by family tradition with a dim and dusky grandeur, was present to my boyish imagination as far back as I can remember ; " so that it is by no means idle to reckon the history of his own family as among the important elements influencing the bent of his genius. John, the son of William, was likewise a public character ; he, too, became a representative, a member of the Governor's council, a magistrate and a military officer, and saw active service as a soldier in the expedition which he headed against St. John, in 1696. But he is chiefly remembered as the judge who presided over the witch-craft trials and displayed great harshness and bigotry

## HATHORNE FAMILY OF SALEM, MASSACHUSETTS.

Hathorne =

Robert Hathorne writes to his brother, William, from Bray (Berks), 1 April, 1653.

William, came in the Arbella, with John Winthrop 1630; first of Dorchester; afterwards of Salem; deputy, speaker of the House, Assistant, Major commanding in Indian Wars; ob. 1681 in 74th year of his age. Will proved 28 June, 1681. = Anne

Elizabeth (?) = Capt. Richard Davenport killed by lightning 15 July, 1665.

John Hathorne = Sarah of Salem and Lynn, died in Lynn 12 Dec. 1676. Will sworn to 25-1-1677.

Nathaniel named in his father's will.

Phebe b. in Lynn 22 March, 1665.

Ebenezer b. in Lynn — March, 1656.

Mary b. in Lynn — July, 1653; d. 31 Dec. 1676.

William b. in Lynn 1651; d. 14 Sept. 1676.

Elizabeth b. 22 July, 1649: m. 20-9-1672 to Israel Porter.

Anna born 12 Dec. 1643; m. 27 Jan. 1664-5 to Joseph Porter.

William = Sarah b. 1 Apr. 1645; d. 14 July, 1676. Captain.

Ruth dau. of Lieut. George Gardner; married 22-1-1674-5.

Priscilla bapt. at Salem 22 July, 1649; m. 15 Jan. 1669 to Jonathan Shore.

John bapt. at Salem 18 Oct. 1646.

Sarah bapt. at Salem 2 June, 1644.

Nathaniel b. 11 Aug. 1639.

John b. 4 Aug. 1641 = Ruth dau. representative; Assistant; Judge in Witchcraft cases; Judge Sup. Court 1702-15; Colonel; died 10 May, 1717; will proved 27 June, 1717.

Eleazer b. 1 Aug. 1637; m. 28-6-1663, Abigail, dau. of Capt. George Curwen, of Salem.

Sarah born 11 March, 1644-5; m. 13 April, 1665, to Joseph Coker of Newbury, and died 8 Feb'y, 1688.

(dau.) = Helwise

Gervice Helwise in "Urop," according to his gr. father's will.

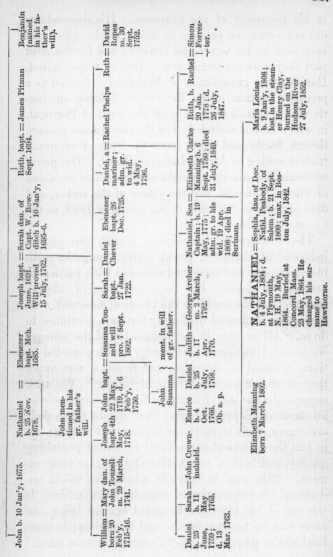

John b. 10 Jan'y, 1675.

Nathaniel b. 25 Nov. 1678.

John mentioned in his gr. father's will.

Ebenezer bapt. Mch. 1685.

Joseph bapt. June, 1681. = Sarah dau. of Capt. W. Bowditch b. 10 Jan'y, 1695-6. Will proved 15 July, 1762.

Ruth, bapt. = James Pitman Sept. 1694.

Benjamin (named in his father's will).

William = Mary dau. of born 20 John Touzell Feb'y, m. 29 March, 1715-16. 1741.

Joseph bapt. 4th May, 1718.

John bapt. 22 May, 1719, d. 6 Feb'y, 1750.

Susanna Touzell will pro. 7 Sept. 1802. = Daniel Chever

Sarah bapt. 27 Jan. 1722.

Ebenezer bapt. 26 Dec. 1725.

Daniel, a = Rachel Phelps mariner; adm. gr. to wid. 4 May, 1796.

Ruth = David Ropes m. 30 Sept. 1752.

John Susanna } ment. in will of gr. father.

Daniel b. 23 June, 1759; d. 13 Mar. 1763.

Sarah = John Crown- b. 11 inshield. May 1763.

Eunice b. 4 Oct. 1766. Ob. s. p.

Daniel b. 25 July, 1768.

Judith = George Archer b. 17 m. 2 March, Apr. 1792. 1770.

Nathaniel, Sea = Elizabeth Clarke Captain; b. 19 Manning b. 6 May, 1775; Sept. 1780; died adm. gr. to his 31 July, 1849. wid. 19 Apr., 1808; died in Surinam.

Ruth, b. Rachel = Simon 20 Jan. Forres- 1778; d. ter. 26 July, 1847.

Elizabeth Manning born 7 March, 1802.

NATHANIEL = Sophia, dau. of Doc. b. 4 July, 1804; d. Nathl. Peabody, of at Plymouth, Salem; b. 21 Sept. N. H. 19 May, 1809; mar. in Bos- 1864. Buried at ton July, 1842. Concord, Mass. 23 May, 1864. He changed his surname to Hawthorne.

Maria Louisa b. 9 Jan'y, 1808; lost in the steamer Henry Clay, burned on the Hudson River 27 July, 1852.

in his treatment of the prisoners. His descendants did not retain the position in public affairs which had been held by his father and himself; and for the most part they were sea-faring men. One of them, indeed, Daniel — the grandfather of Nathaniel — figured as a privateer captain in the Revolution, fighting one battle with a British troop-ship off the coast of Portugal, in which he was wounded; but the rest led the obscure though hardy and semi-romantic lives of maritime traders sailing to Africa, India, or Brazil. The privateersman had among his eight children three boys, one of whom, Nathaniel, was the father of the author, and died of fever in Surinam, in the spring of 1808, at the age of thirty-three.

The founders of the American branch were men of independent character, proud, active, energetic, capable of extreme sternness and endowed with passionate natures, no doubt. But they were men of affairs; they touched the world on the practical side, and, even during the decline of the family fortunes, continued to do so. All at once, in the personality of the younger Nathaniel Hawthorne, this energy which persisted in them reversed its direction, and found a new outlet through the channel of literary expression. We must suppose that he included among his own characteristics all those of his predecessors; their innate force, their endurance, their capacity for impassioned feeling; but in him these elements were fused by a finer prevailing quality, and held in firm balance by his rare temperament. This must be borne in mind, if we would understand the conjunction of opposite traits in him. It was one of his principles to guard against being run away with by his imagination, and to cultivate in practical affairs what he called " a morose common sense."

There has been attributed to him by some of those who knew him a certain good - humored gruffness, which might be explained as a heritage from the self-assertive vitality of his ancestors. While at Liverpool he wrote to one of his intimates in this country, and in doing so made reference to another acquaintance as a "wretch," to be away from whom made exile endurable. The letter passed into the hands of the acquaintance thus stigmatized long after Hawthorne was in his grave ; but he declared himself to be in no wise disturbed by it, because he knew that the remark was not meant seriously, being only one of the occasional explosions of a " sea - dog " forcefulness, which had come into the writer's blood from his skipper forefathers. Hawthorne had, in fact, parted on friendly terms from the gentleman of whom he thus wrote. On the other hand we have the traits of sensitiveness, great delicacy, reserve and reverie, drawn from both his father and his mother. Captain Hathorne had been a man of fine presence, handsome, kindly, and rather silent ; a reader, likewise ; and his son's resemblance to him was so marked that a strange sailor stopped Hawthorne on the steps of the Salem Custom House, many years afterward, to ask him if he were not a son or nephew of the Captain, whom he had known.

His mother belonged to an excellent family, the Mannings, of English stock, settled in Salem and Ipswich ever since 1680, and still well represented in the former place. She, too, was a very reserved person ; had a stately, aristocratic manner ; is remembered as possessing a peculiar and striking beauty. Her education was of that simple, austere, but judicious and perfected kind that — without taking any

very wide range — gave to New England women in
the earlier part of this century a sedate freedom and
a cultivated judgment, which all the assumed improvements in pedagogy and the general relations of
men and women since then have hardly surpassed.
She was a pious woman, a sincere and devoted wife, a
mother whose teachings could not fail to impress upon
her children a bias towards the best things in life.
Nathaniel's sister Elizabeth, although a recluse to the
end of her days, and wholly unknown to the public,
gave in her own case evidence indisputable of the fine
influences which had moulded her own childhood and
that of her brother. She showed a quiet, unspoiled,
and ardent love of Nature, and was to the last not
only an assiduous reader of books but also a very
discriminating one. The range of her reading was
very wide, but she never made any more display of it
than Hawthorne did of his. An intuitive judgment
of character was hers, which was really startling at
times : merely from the perusal of a book or the inspection of a portrait, she would arrive at accurate
estimates of character which revealed a power of facile
and comprehensive insight; and her letters, even in
old age, flowed spontaneously into utterance of the
same finished kind that distinguished Nathaniel Hawthorne's epistolary style. How fresh and various, too,
was her interest in the affairs of the world! For
many years she had not gone farther from her secluded abode in a farm - house at Montserrat, than
to Beverly or Salem ; yet I remember that, only six
months before her death, she wrote a letter to her
niece, a large part of which was devoted to the campaign of the English in Egypt, then progressing : with
a lively and clear comprehension she discussed the

difficulties of the situation, and expressed the utmost concern for the success of the English army, at the same time that she laughed at herself for displaying, as an old woman, so much anxiety about the matter. Now, a mother who could bring up her daughter in such a way as to make all this possible and natural, must be given much credit for her share in developing an illustrious son. Let us not forget that it was to his mother that Goethe owed in good measure the foundation of his greatness. Mrs. Hathorne had large, very luminous gray eyes, which were reproduced in her son's; so that, on both sides, his parentage entitled him to the impressive personal appearance which distinguished him. In mature life he became somewhat estranged from her, but their mutual love was presumably suspended only for a time, and he was with her at her death, in 1849. She lived long enough to see him famous as the author of "Twice-Told Tales"; but "The Scarlet Letter" had not been written when she died.

She, as well as her husband, was one of a family of eight brothers and sisters; these were the children of Richard Manning. Two of the brothers, Richard and Robert, were living in Salem when she was left a widow; Robert being eminent in New England at that time as a horticulturist. She was without resources, other than her husband's earnings, and Robert undertook to provide for her. Accordingly, she removed with her young family to the Manning homestead on Herbert Street, the next street east of Union Street, where Nathaniel was born. This homestead stood upon a piece of land running through to Union Street, and adjoining the garden attached to Hawthorne's birthplace. At that time Dr. Nathaniel Peabody, a physician, occupied a house in a brick block on the opposite side of Union Street; and there in 1809, September 21st, was born his daughter, Sophia A. Peabody, who afterwards became Hawthorne's wife. Her birthplace, therefore, was but a few rods distant from that of her future husband. Sophia Peabody's eldest sister, Mary, who married Horace Mann, noted as an educator and an abolitionist, remembers the child Nathaniel, who was then about five years old. He used to make his appearance in the garden of the Herbert Street mansion, running and dancing about there at play, a vivacious, golden-haired boy. The next oldest sister, who was the first of this family to make the acquaintance of the young author some thirty years later on, was Miss Elizabeth P. Peabody, who has taken an important part in developing the Kindergarten in America. There were plenty of books in the Manning house, and Nathaniel very soon got at them. Among the authors whom he earliest came to know were Shakespeare, Milton, Pope, Thomson, and Rousseau. The " Castle of Indolence " was one of his favorite volumes. Subsequently, he read the whole of the " Newgate Calendar," and became intensely absorbed in Bunyan's " Pilgrim's Progress," which undoubtedly left very deep impressions upon him, traceable in the various allusions to it scattered through his works. He also made himself familiar with Spenser's " Faërie Queen," Froissart's " Chronicles," and Clarendon's " History of the Rebellion."

" Being a healthy boy, with strong out-of-door instincts planted in him by inheritance from his seafaring sire, it might have been that he would not have been brought so early to an intimacy with books, but for an accident similar to that which played a part in the boyhoods of Scott and Dickens. When he was nine years old, he was struck on the foot by a ball, and made seriously lame. The earliest fragment of his writing now extant is a letter to his uncle Robert Manning, at that time 'in Raymond, Maine, written from Salem, December 9, 1813. It announces that the foot is no better, and that a new doctor is to be sent for. 'Maybe,' the boy writes, 'he will do me some good, for Dr. B—— has not, and I don't know as Dr. K—— will.' He adds that it is now four weeks since he has been to school, 'and I don't know but it will be four weeks longer.' . . . But the trouble was destined to last much longer than even the young seer had projected his gaze. There was some threat of deformity, and it was not until he was nearly twelve that he became quite well. Meantime, his kind school-master, Dr. Worcester, . . . came to hear him his lessons at home. The good pedagogue does not figure after this in Hawthorne's history; but a copy of Worcester's Dictionary still exists and is in present use, which bears in a tremulous writing on the fly-leaf the legend : 'Nathaniel Hawthorne Esq., with the respects of J. E. Worcester.' For a long time, in the worst of his lameness, the gentle boy was forced to lie prostrate, and choosing the floor for his couch, he would read there all day long. He was extremely fond of cats — a taste which he kept through life; and during this illness, forced to odd resorts for amusement, he knitted a pair of socks for the cat who reigned in the household at the time. When tired of reading, he constructed houses of books for the same feline pet, building walls for her to leap, and perhaps erecting triumphal arches for her to pass under." [1]

[1] *A Study of Hawthorne,* III., 67-69.

The lexicographer, Dr. Worcester, was then living at Salem in charge of a school, which he kept for a few years; and it was with him that Hawthorne was carrying on his primary studies. He also went to dancing-school, was fond of fishing as well as of taking long walks, and doubtless engaged in the sundry occupations and sports, neither more nor less extraordinary than these, common to lads of his age. He already displayed a tendency towards dry humor. As he brought home from school frequent reports of having had a bout at fisticuffs with another pupil named John Knights, his sister Elizabeth asked him: "Why do you fight with John Knights so often?" "I can't help it," he answered: "John Knights is a boy of very quarrelsome disposition."

But all this time an interior growth, of which we can have no direct account, was proceeding in his mind. The loss of the father whom he had had so little chance to see and know and be fondled by, no doubt produced a profound effect upon him. While still a very young child he would rouse himself from long broodings, to exclaim with an impressive shaking of the head: "There, mother! I is going away to sea some time; and I 'll never come back again!" The thought of that absent one, whose barque had glided out of Salem harbor bound upon a terrestrial voyage, but had carried him softly away to the unseen world, must have been incessantly with the boy; and it would naturally melt into what he heard of the strange, shadowy history of his ancestors, and mix itself with the ever-present hush of settled grief in his mother's dwelling, and blend with his unconscious observations of the old town in which he lived. Salem then was much younger in time, but much older to the eye, than it is now. In "Alice Doane's Appeal" he has sketched a rapid bird's-eye view of it as it appeared to him when he was a young man. Describing his approach with his sisters to Witch Hill, he says : "We . . . began to ascend a hill which at a distance, by its dark slope and the even line of its summit, resembled a green rampart along the road; . . . but, strange to tell, though the whole slope and summit were of a peculiarly deep green, scarce a blade of grass was visible from the base upward. This deceitful verdure was occasioned by a plentiful crop of 'wood-wax,' which wears the same dark and gloomy green throughout the summer, except at one short period, when it puts forth a profusion of yellow blossoms. At that season, to a distant spectator the hill appears absolutely overlaid with gold, or covered with a glory of sunshine even under a clouded sky." This wood-wax, it may be said, is a weed which grows nowhere but in Essex County, and, having been native in England, was undoubtedly brought over by the Pilgrims. He goes on : "There are few such prospects of town and village, woodland and cultivated field, steeples and country-seats, as we beheld from this unhappy spot. . . . Before us lay our native town, extending from the foot of the hill to the harbor, level as a chess-board, embraced by two arms of the sea, and filling the whole peninsula with a close assemblage of wooden roofs, overtopped by many a spire and intermixed with frequent heaps of verdure. . . . Retaining these portions of the scene, and also the peaceful glory and tender gloom of the declining sun, we threw in imagination a deep veil of forest over the land, and pictured a few scattered villages here and there and this old town itself a village, as when the prince of Hell bore sway there. The idea thus

gained of its former aspect, its quaint edifices standing far apart with peaked roofs and projecting stories,
and its single meeting-house pointing up a tall spire
in the midst; the vision, in short, of the town in 1692,
served to introduce a wondrous tale." There were
in fact several old houses of the kind here described
still extant during Hawthorne's boyhood, and he went
every Sunday to service in the First Church, in whose
congregation his forefathers had held a pew for a hundred and seventy years. It is easy to see how some of
the materials for "The House of the Seven Gables"
and "The Scarlet Letter" were already depositing
themselves in the form of indelible recollections and
suggestions taken from his surroundings.

Oppressed by her great sorrow, his mother had shut
herself away, after her husband's death, from all society except that of her immediate relatives. This was
perhaps not a very extraordinary circumstance, nor
one that need be construed as denoting a morbid disposition; but it was one which must have distinctly
affected the tone of her son's meditations. In 1818,
when he was fourteen years old, she retired to a still
deeper seclusion, in Maine; but the occasion of this
was simply that her brother Robert, having purchased
the seven-mile-square township of Raymond, in that
State, had built a house there, intending to found a
new home. The year that Hawthorne passed in that
spot, amid the breezy life of the forest, fishing and
shooting, watching the traits and customs of lumber-
men and country-folk, and drinking in the tonic of a
companionship with untamed nature, was to him a
happy and profitable one. "We are all very well,"
he wrote thence to his Uncle Robert, in May, 1819:
"The fences are all finished, and the garden is laid

out and planted. . . . I have shot a partridge and a
henhawk, and caught eighteen large trout out of our
brook. I am sorry you intend to send me to school
again." He had been to the place before, probably
for short visits, when his Uncle Richard was staying
there, and his memories of it were always agreeable
ones. To Mr. James T. Fields, he said in 1863 : " I
lived in Maine like a bird of the air, so perfect was
the freedom I enjoyed. But it was there I first got
my cursed habits of solitude." " During the moonlight nights of winter he would skate until midnight
all alone upon Sebago Lake, with the deep shadows of
the icy hills on either hand. When he found himself
far away from his home and weary with the exercise of
skating, he would sometimes take refuge in a log-cabin,
where half a tree would be burning on the broad
hearth. He would sit in the ample chimney, and look
at the stars through the great aperture through which
the flames went roaring up. ' Ah,' he said, ' how well
I recall the summer days, also, when with my gun I
roamed through the woods of Maine !' " [1]

Hawthorne at this time had an intention of following
the example of his father and grandfather, and going
to sea ; but this was frustrated by the course of events.
His mother, it is probable, would strongly have objected to it. In a boyish journal kept while he was at
Raymond he mentions a gentleman having come with
a boat to take one or two persons out on " the Great
Pond," and adds : " He was kind enough to say that
I might go (with my mother's consent), which she
gave after much coaxing. Since the loss of my father
she dreads to have any one belonging to her go upon
the water." And again : " A young man named

[1] *Yesterdays With Authors,* p. 113.

Henry Jackson, Jr., was drowned two days ago, up in Crooked River. . . . I read one of the Psalms to my mother this morning, and it plainly declares twenty-six times that 'God's mercy endureth forever.' . . . Mother is sad; says she shall not consent any more to my swimming in the mill-pond with the boys, fearing that in sport my mouth might get kicked open, and then sorrow for a dead son be added to that for a dead father, which she says would break her heart. I love to swim, but I shall not disobey my mother." This same journal, which seems to have laid the basis of his life-long habit of keeping note-books, was begun at the suggestion of Mr. Richard Manning, who gave him a blank-book, with advice that he should use it for recording his thoughts, " as the best means of his securing for mature years command of thought and language." In it were made a number of entries which testify plainly to his keenness of observation both of people and scenery, to his sense of humor and his shrewdness. Here are a few : —

" Swapped pocket-knives with Robinson Cook yesterday. Jacob Dingley says that he cheated me, but I think not, for I cut a fishing-pole this morning and did it well; besides, he is a Quaker, and they never cheat."

" This morning the bucket got off the chain, and dropped back into the well. I wanted to go down on the stones and get it. Mother would not consent, for fear the well might cave in, but hired Samuel Shaw to go down. In the goodness of her heart, she thought the son of old Mrs. Shaw not quite so good as the son of the Widow Hathorne."

Of a trout that he saw caught by some men : —
" This trout had a droll-looking hooked nose, and they

tried to make me believe that, if the line had been in my hands, I should have been obliged to let go, or have been pulled out of the boat. They are men, and have a right to say so. I am a boy, and have a right to think differently."

" We could see the White Hills to the northwest, though Mr. Little said they were eighty miles away ; and grand old Rattlesnake to the northeast, in its immense jacket of green oak, looked more inviting than I had ever seen it; while Frye's Island, with its close growth of great trees growing to the very edge of the water, looked like a monstrous green raft, floating to the southeastward. Whichever way the eye turned, something charming appeared."

The mental clearness, the sharpness of vision, and the competence of the language in this early note-book are remarkable, considering the youth and inexperience of the writer ; and there is one sketch of " a solemn-faced old horse " at the grist-mill, which exhibits a delightful boyish humor with a dash of pathos in it, and at the same time is the first instance on record of a mild approach by Hawthorne to the writing of fiction : —

" He had brought for his owner some bags of corn to be ground, who, after carrying them into the mill, walked up to Uncle Richard's store, leaving his half-starved animal in the cold wind with nothing to eat, while the corn was being turned into meal. I felt sorry, and, nobody being near, thought it best to have a talk with the old nag, and said, ' Good morning, Mr. Horse, how are you to-day ? ' ' Good morning, youngster,' said he, just as plain as a horse can speak; and then said, ' I am almost dead, and I wish I was quite. I am hungry, have had no breakfast, and must

stand here tied by the head while they are grinding
the corn, and until master drinks two or three glasses
of rum at the store, then drag the meal and him up
the Ben Ham Hill home, and am now so weak that I
can hardly stand.  Oh dear, I am in a bad way;' and
the old creature cried.  I almost cried myself.  Just
then the miller went down-stairs to the meal-trough;
I heard his feet on the steps, and not thinking much
what I was doing, ran into the mill, and, taking the
four-quart toll-dish nearly full of corn out of the hopper, carried it out, and poured it into the trough before the horse, and placed the dish back before the
miller came up from below.  When I got out, the
horse was laughing, but he had to eat slowly, because
the bits were in his mouth.  I told him that I was
sorry, but did not know how to take them out, and
should not dare to if I did. . . . At last the horse
winked and stuck out his lip ever so far, and then
said, ' The last kernel is gone ; ' then he laughed a little, then shook one ear, then the other; then he shut
his eyes.  I jumped up and said : ' How do you feel,
old fellow ; any better ?'  He opened his eyes, and
looking at me kindly answered, 'Very much,' and then
blew his nose exceedingly loud, but he did not wipe it.
Perhaps he had no wiper.  I then asked him if his
master whipped him much.  He answered, ' Not much
lately.  He used to till my hide got hardened, but
now he has a white-oak goad-stick with an iron brad
in its end, with which he jabs my hind-quarters and
hurts me awfully.' . . . The goad with the iron brad
was in the wagon, and snatching it out I struck the
end against a stone, and the stabber flew into the mill-
pond.  ' There,' says I, ' old colt,' as I threw the goad
back into the wagon, ' he won't harpoon you again with

*that* iron.' The poor old brute understood well enough what I said, for I looked him in the eye and spoke horse language."

Mother and uncles could hardly have missed observing in him many tokens of a gifted intelligence and an uncommon individuality. The perception of these, added to Mrs. Hawthorne's dread of the sea, may have led to the decision which was taken to send him to college. In 1819 he went back to Salem, to continue his schooling ; and one year later, March 7, 1820, wrote to his mother, who was still at Raymond : " I have left school, and have begun to fit for College, under Benjamin L. Oliver, Lawyer. So you are in great danger of having one learned man in your family. . . . Shall you want me to be a Minister, Doctor, or Lawyer ? A minister I will not be." Miss E. P. Peabody remembers another letter of his, in which he touched the same problem, thus : " I do not want to be a doctor and live by men's diseases, nor a minister to live by their sins, nor a lawyer and live by their quarrels. So I don't see that there is anything left but for me to be an author. How would you like some day to see a whole shelf full of books written by your son, with ' Hathorne's Works ' printed on the backs ? " There appears to have been but little difficulty for him in settling the problem of his future occupation. During part of August and September he amused himself by writing three numbers of a miniature weekly paper called " The Spectator ; " and in October we find that he had been composing poetry and sending it to his sister Elizabeth, who was also exercising herself in verse. At this time he was employed as a clerk, for a part of each day, in the office of another uncle, William Manning, proprietor of a great

line of stages which then had extensive connections
throughout New England; but he did not find the
task congenial. "No man," he informed his sister,
"can be a poet and a book-keeper at the same time;"
from which one infers his distinct belief that literature
was his natural vocation. The idea of remaining dependent for four years more on the bounty of his Uncle Robert, who had so generously taken the place of
a father in giving him a support and education, oppressed him, and he even contemplated not going to
college; but go he finally did, taking up his residence
at Bowdoin with the class of 1821.

The village of Brunswick, where Bowdoin College is
situated, some thirty miles from Raymond, stands on
high ground beside the Androscoggin River, which is
there crossed by a bridge running zig-zag from bank
to bank, resting on various rocky ledges and producing
a picturesque effect. The village itself is ranged on
two sides of a broad street, which meets the river at
right angles, and has a mall in the centre that, in Hawthorne's time, was little more than a swamp. This
street, then known as "sixteen-rod road," from its
width, continues in a straight line to Casco Bay, only
a few miles off; so that the new student was still near
the sea and had a good course for his walks. If Har-
vard fifty and even twenty-five years ago had the look
of a rural college, Bowdoin was by comparison an
academy in a wilderness. "If this institution," says
Hawthorne in "Fanshawe," where he describes it under the name of Harley College, "did not offer all the
advantages of elder and prouder seminaries, its deficiencies were compensated to its students by the in-
culcation of regular habits, and of a deep and awful
sense of religion, which seldom deserted them in their

course through life. The mild and gentle rule . . .
was more destructive to vice than a sterner sway ; and
though youth is never without its follies, they have seldom been more harmless than they were here." The
local resources for amusement or dissipation must have
been very limited, and the demands of the curriculum
not very severe. Details of Hawthorne's four years'
stay at college are not forthcoming, otherwise than in
small quantity. His comrades who survived him never
have been able to give any very vivid picture of the
life there, or to recall any anecdotes of Hawthorne :
the whole episode has slipped away, like a dream from
which fragmentary glimpses alone remain. By one of
those unaccountable associations with trifles, which out-
last more important memories, Professor Calvin Stowe
(to whom the authoress of "Uncle Tom's Cabin" was
afterwards married) remembers seeing Hawthorne,
then a member of the class below him, crossing the
college-yard one stormy day, attired in a brass-but-
toned blue coat, with an umbrella over his head. The
wind caught the umbrella and turned it inside out ;
and what stamped the incident on Professor Stowe's
mind was the silent but terrible and consuming wrath
with which Hawthorne regarded the implement in its
utterly subverted and useless state, as he tried to rear-
range it. Incidents of no greater moment and the
general effect of his presence seem to have created
the belief among his fellows that, beneath the bashful
quietude of his exterior, was stored a capability of ex-
erting tremendous force in some form or other. He
was seventeen when he entered college, — tall, broad-
chested, with clear, lustrous gray eyes,[1] a fresh com-

[1] Both his friends, George William Curtis and George S. Hillard,
in writing about him, have made the mistake of assigning to him

plexion, and long hair: his classmates were so impressed with his masculine beauty, and perhaps with a sense of occult power in him, that they nicknamed him Oberon. Although unusually calm-tempered, however, he was quick to resent disrespectful treatment (as he had been with John Knights), and his vigorous, athletic frame made him a formidable adversary. In the same class with him were Henry W. Longfellow; George Barrell Cheever, since famous as a divine, and destined to make a great stir in Salem by a satire in verse called "Deacon Giles's Distillery," which cost him a thirty days' imprisonment, together with the loss of his pastorate ; also John S. C. Abbott, the writer of popular histories; and Horatio Bridge, afterwards Lieutenant in the United States Navy, and now Commander. Bridge and Franklin Pierce, who studied in the class above him, were his most intimate friends. He boarded in a house which had a stairway on the outside, ascending to the second story; he took part, I suppose, in the " rope-pulls " and " hold-ins " between Freshmen and Sophomores, if those customs were practised .then ; he was fined for card-playing and for neglect of theme ; entered the Athenæan Society, which had a library of eight hundred volumes ; tried to read Hume's " History of England," but found it "abominably dull," and postponed the attempt; was fond of whittling, and destroyed some of his furniture in gratifying that taste. Such are the insignificant particulars to which we are confined in attempting to form an idea of the externals of his college-life. Pierce was chairman of the Athenæan Society, and also organized a military company, which Hawthorne joined.

black or dark eyes ; an error perhaps due to the depth of shadowed cavity in which they were seen under the high and massive forehead.

In the Preface to " The Snow-Image" we are given a glimpse of the simple amusements which occupied his leisure : " While we were lads together at a country college, gathering blueberries in study hours under those tall academic pines ; or watching the great logs as they tumbled along the current of the Androscoggin ; or shooting pigeons and gray squirrels in the woods ; or bat-fowling in the summer-twilight ; or catching trouts in that shadowy little stream which, I suppose, is still wandering riverward through the forest." He became proficient in Latin. Longfellow was wont to recall how he would rise at recitation, standing slightly sidewise — attitude indicative of his ingrained shyness — and read from the Roman classics translations which had a peculiar elegance and charm. In writing English, too, he won a reputation, and Professor Newman was often so struck with the beauty of his work in this kind that he would read them in the evening to his own family. Professor Packard says : " His themes were written in the sustained, finished style that gives to his mature productions an inimitable charm. The recollection is very distinct of Hawthorne's reluctant step and averted look, when he presented himself at the professor's study and submitted a composition which no man in his class could equal."

Hawthorne always looked back with satisfaction to those simple and placid days. In 1852 he revisited the scene where they were passed, in order to be present at the semi-centennial anniversary of the founding of the college. A letter, from Concord (October 13, 1852), to Lieutenant Bridge, now for the first time published, contains the following reference to that event : —

"I meant to have told you about my visit to Bruns-wick. . . . Only eight of our classmates were present, and they were a set of dismal old fellows, whose heads looked as if they had been out in a pretty copious shower of snow. The whole intermediate quarter of a century vanished, and it seemed to me as if they had undergone the miserable transformation in the course of a single night — especially as I myself felt just about as young as when I graduated. They flattered me with the assurance that time had touched me ten-derly; but alas! they were each a mirror in which I beheld the reflection of my own age. I did not arrive till after the public exercises were nearly over — and very luckily, too, for my praises had been sounded by orator and poet, and of course my blushes would have been quite oppressive."

Hawthorne's rank in his class entitled him to a "part" at Commencement, but the fact that he had not cultivated declamation debarred him from that honor; and so he passed quietly away from the life of Bowdoin and settled down to his career. "I have thought much upon the subject," he wrote to his sister, just before graduation, "and have come to the con-clusion that I shall never make a distinguished figure in the world, and all I hope or wish is to plod along with the multitude." But declamation was not essen-tial to his success, which was to be achieved in anything but a declamatory fashion.

## II.

In one sense it was all very simple, this childhood and youth and early training of Hawthorne. We can see that the conditions were not complicated and were quite homely. But the influence of good literature had been at work upon the excellent mental substance derived from a father who was fond of reading and a mother who had the plain elementary virtues on which so much depends, and great purity of soul. The composure and finish of style which he already had at command on going to college were ripened amid the homely conditions aforesaid : there must have been an atmosphere of culture in his home, unpretentious though the mode of life there was. His sister, as I have mentioned, showed much the same tone, the same commanding ease, in her writing. There existed a dignity, a reserve, an instinctive refinement in this old-fashioned household, which moved its members to appropriate the best means of expression as by natural right. They appear to have treated the most ordinary affairs of life with a quiet stateliness, as if human existence were really a thing to be considered with respect, and with a frank interest that might occasionally even admit of enthusiasm or strong feeling with regard to an experience, although thousands of beings might have passed through it before. Our new horizons, physically enlarged by rapid travel, our omnifarious culture, our passion for obtaining a glaze of cosmopolitanism to cover the common clay from which we are all moulded, do not often yield us anything essentially better than the narrow limits of the little world in which Hawthorne grew up. He was now to go back to Salem, which he once spoke of as being apparently for him " the inevitable centre of the universe ; " and the conditions there were not radically altered from what they had been before. We can form an outline of him as he was then, or at most a water-color sketch presenting the fresh hues of youth,

the strong manly frame of the young graduate, his fine
deep-lighted eyes, and sensitively retiring ways. But
we have now to imagine the change that took place
in him from the recent college Senior to the maturing
man; change that gradually transforms him from the
visionary outline of that earlier period to a solid reality of flesh and blood, a virile and efficient person
who still, while developing, did not lose the delicate
sensibility of his young prime.

His family having reëstablished themselves in Salem,
at the old Herbert Street house, he settled himself with
them, and stayed there until December, 1828, meanwhile publishing "Fanshawe" anonymously. They
then moved to a smaller house on Dearborn Street,
North Salem; but after four years they again took up
their abode in the Herbert Street homestead. Hawthorne wrote industriously; first the "Seven Tales of
my Native Land," which he burned, and subsequently
the sketches and stories which, after appearing in current periodicals, were collected as "Twice-Told Tales."
In 1830 he took a carriage trip through parts of Connecticut. "I meet with many marvellous adventures,"
was a part of his news on this occasion, but they were
in reality adventures of a very tame description. He
visited New York and New Hampshire and Nan-
tucket, thus extending slightly his knowledge of men
and places. A great deal of discursive reading was
also accomplished. In 1836 he went to Boston to edit
for Mr. S. G. Goodrich "The American Magazine of
Useful and Entertaining Knowledge." It did not
turn out to be either useful or entertaining for the
editor, who was to be paid but $500 a year for his
drudgery, and in fact received only a small part of
that sum. Through Goodrich, he became a copious

contributor to " The Token," in the pages of which his tales first came to be generally known ; but he gave up the magazine after a four months' misery of editorship, and sought refuge once more in his native town.

Salem was an isolated place, was not even joined to the outer world by its present link of railroad with Boston, and afforded no very generous diet for a young, vigorous, hungry intellect like that of Hawthorne. Surroundings, however, cannot make a mind, though they may color its processes. He proceeded to extract what he could from the material at hand. " His mode of life at this period was fitted to nurture his imagination, but must have put the endurance of his nerves to the severest test. The statement that for several years ' he never saw the sun ' is entirely an error. In summer he was up shortly after sunrise, and would go down to bathe in the sea; but it is true that he seldom chose to walk in the town except at night, and it is said that he was extremely fond of going to fires if they occurred after dark. The morning was chiefly given to study, the afternoon to writing, and in the evening he would take long walks, exploring the coast from Gloucester to Marblehead and Lynn — a range of many miles. . . . Sometimes he took the day for his rambles, wandering perhaps over Endicott's ancient Orchard Farm and among the antique houses and grassy cellars of old Salem Village, the witchcraft ground ; or losing himself among the pines of Montserrat and in the silence of the Great Pastures, or strolling along the beaches to talk with old sailors and fishermen." " He had little communication with even the members of his family. Frequently his meals were brought and left at his locked door, and it was not often that the four inmates of the old Herbert Street mansion met in family circle. He never read his stories aloud to his mother and sisters, as might be imagined from the picture which Mr. Fields draws of the young author reciting his new productions to his listening family; though, when they met, he sometimes read older literature to them. It was the custom in this household for the members to remain very much by themselves: the three ladies were perhaps nearly as rigorous recluses as himself ; and, speaking of the isolation which reigned among them, Hawthorne once said, ' We do not even *live* at our house ! ' But still the presence of this near and gentle element is not to be underrated, as forming a very great compensation in the cold and difficult morning of his life." Of self-reliant mind, accustomed to solitude and fond of reading, it was not strange that they should have fallen into these habits, which, however peculiarly they may strike others, did not necessarily spring from a morbid disposition, and never prevented the Hawthornes from according a kindly reception to their friends.

Nathaniel Hawthorne's own associates were not numerous. There was a good society in the town, for Salem was not, strictly speaking, provincial, but — aided in a degree by the separateness of its situation — retained very much its old independence as a commercial capital. There were people of wealth and cultivation, of good lineage in our simple domestic kind, who made considerable display in their entertainments and were addicted to impressive absences in Paris and London. Among these Hawthorne did not show himself at all. His preference was for individuals who had no pretensions whatever in the social way. Among his friends was one William B. Pike, a carpenter's son, who, after acquiring an ordinary public-school education without passing through the higher grades, adopted his father's trade, became a Methodist class-leader, secondly a disciple of Swedenborg, and at length a successful politician, being appointed Collector of the port of Salem by President Pierce. He is described as having " a strongly marked, benignant face, indicative of intelligence and individuality. He was gray at twenty, and always looked older than his years. . . . He had a keen sense of the ludicrous, a vivid recollection of localities and incidents, a quick apprehension of peculiarities and traits, and was a most graphic and entertaining narrator." [1] As Mr. James has said : " Hawthorne had a democratic strain in his composition, a relish for the common stuff of human nature. He liked to fraternize with plain people, to take them on their own terms." It was the most natural thing in the world for him to fancy such a man as Pike is represented to have been. His Society in college was the one which displayed a democratic tendency; and, in addition to making friends with persons of this stamp, men of some education and much innate " go," he had a taste for loitering in taverns where he could observe character in the rough, without being called upon to take an active share in talk. "Men," we are told, "who did not meddle with him he loved, men who made no demands on him, who offered him the repose of genial companionship. His life-long friends were of this description, and his loyalty to them was chivalrous and fearless, and so generous that when they differed from him on matters of opinion he rose at once above the difference and ad-

[1] *Hawthorne and his Friends: Harper's Magazine,* vol. 63 (July, 1881).

hered to them for what they really were." Inevitably, such a basis for the selection of companions, coupled with his extreme reserve, subjected him to criticism; but when, in 1835, his former classmate, the Rev. George B. Cheever, was thrown into jail on account of the satirical temperance pamphlet which has already been referred to in this sketch, Hawthorne emerged from his strict privacy, and daily visited the imprisoned clergyman. He showed no especial love for his native place, and in return it never made of him a popular idol. At this initial epoch of his career as an author there probably did not exist that active ill-will which his chapter on the Custom House afterwards engendered; he was in fact too little known to be an object of malice or envy, and his humble friendships could not be made the ground of unfavorable insinuations. The town, however, was not congenial to him, and the profound retirement in which he dwelt, the slow toil with scanty meed of praise or gold, and the long waiting for recognition, doubtless weighed upon and preyed upon him.

To stop at that would be to make a superficial summary. His seclusion was also of the highest utility to him, nay, almost indispensable to his development; for his mind, which seemed to be only creeping, was making long strides of growth in an original direction, unhindered by arbitrary necessities or by factitious influences.

Nevertheless, the process had gone on long enough; and it was well that circumstances now occurred to bring it to a close, to establish new relations, and draw him somewhat farther into the general circle of human movement. Dr. Peabody, who has been spoken of on a preceding page as living on the opposite side of Union Street from Hawthorne's birthplace, had, during the vicissitudes of the young author's education and journeys to and fro, changed his residence and gone to Boston. No acquaintance had as yet sprung up between the two families which had been domiciled so near together, but in 1832 the Peabodys returned to Salem; and Miss Elizabeth, who followed in 1836, having been greatly struck by the story of " The Gentle Boy," and excited as to the authorship, set on foot an investigation which resulted in her meeting Hawthorne. It is an evidence of the approachableness, after all, of his secluded family, that Miss Louisa Hawthorne should have received her readily and with graciousness. Miss Peabody, having formerly seen one of Miss Hawthorne's letters, had supposed that she must be the writer of the stories, under shelter of a masculine name. She now learned her mistake. Months passed without any response being made to her advance. But when the first volume of " Twice-Told Tales " was issued, Hawthorne sent it to her with his compliments. Up to this time she had not obtained even a glimpse of him anywhere; and, in acknowledging his gift, she proposed that he should call at her father's house; but although matters had proceeded thus far, and Dr. Peabody lived within three minutes' walk of Herbert Street, Hawthorne still did not come. It was more than a year afterward that she addressed an inquiry to him about a new magazine, and in closing asked him to bring his sisters to call in the evening of the same day. This time he made his appearance, was induced to accept an invitation to another house, and thus was led into beginning a social intercourse which, though not extensive, was unequalled in his previous experience.

About a week after the first call, he came again. Miss Sophia Peabody, who was an invalid, had been unable to appear before, but this time she entered the room ; and it was thus that Hawthorne met the lady whom he was to make his wife some two or three years later. She was now about twenty-nine, and younger by five years than Hawthorne. In childhood her health had received a serious shock from the heroic treatment then upheld by physicians, which favored a free use of mercury, so that it became necessary from that time on to nurse her with the utmost care. Many years of invalidism had she suffered, being compelled to stay in a darkened room through long spaces of time, and although a sojourn in Cuba had greatly benefited her, it was believed she could never be quite restored to a normal state of well-being. Despite such serious obstacles, she had gently persisted in reading and study ; she drew and painted, and no fear of flippant remark deterred her from attempting even to learn Hebrew. At the same time she was a woman of the most exquisitely natural cultivation conceivable. A temperament inclined like hers, from the beginning, to a sweet equanimity, may have been assisted towards its proper culmination by the habit of patience likely enough to result from the continued endurance of pain ; but a serenity so benign and so purely feminine and trustful as that which she not displayed, but spontaneously exhaled, must have rested on a primary and plenary inspiration of goodness. All that she knew or saw sank into her mind and took a place in the interior harmony of it, without ruffling the surface ; and all that she thought or uttered seemed to gain a fragrance and a flower-like quality from having sprung thence. Neither were strength of character and practical good sense absent from the company of her calm wisdom and refinement. In brief, no fitter mate for Hawthorne could have existed.

Soon after their acquaintance began, she showed him, one evening, a large outline drawing which she had made, to illustrate "The Gentle Boy," and asked him: "Does that look like Ilbrahim?"

Hawthorne, without other demonstration, replied quietly: "Ilbrahim will never look otherwise to me."

The drawing was shown to Washington Allston, who accorded it his praise; and a Miss Burleigh, who was among the earliest admirers of Hawthorne's genius, having offered to pay the cost of an engraving from it, the design was reproduced and printed with a new special edition of the story, accompanied by a Preface, and a Dedication to Miss Sophia Peabody. The three sisters and two brothers who composed the family of Dr. Peabody were strongly imbued with intellectual tastes: nothing of importance in literature, art, or the philosophy of education escaped them, when once it was brought to their notice by the facilities of the time. Miss Sophia was not only well read and a very graceful amateur in the practice of drawing and painting, but evinced furthermore a somewhat remarkable skill in sculpture. About the year 1831, she modelled a bust of Laura Bridgman, the blind girl, who was then a child of twelve years. This portrait not only was said to be a very good likeness, but — although it is marred by a representation of the peculiar band used to protect the eyes of the patient — has considerable artistic value, and attains very nearly to a classic purity of form and treatment. Miss Peabody also executed a medallion portrait, in relief, of Charles Emerson, the brilliant brother of Ralph Waldo Emer-

son, whose great promise was frustrated by his premature death. This medallion was done from memory.
The artist had once seen Mr. Emerson while he was
lecturing, and was so strongly impressed by his eloquent profile that, on going home, she made a memory-
sketch of it in pencil, which supplied a germ for the
portrait in clay which she attempted after his death.

The appearance of the "Twice-Told Tales" in book-
form had, like that of the " Gentle Boy " design, been
due to the kindness of a friend. In this case it was
Lieutenant Bridge who became responsible for the expense; and the volume met with, if not much pecuniary success, a gratifying literary renown. The author
sent a copy to Longfellow, who acknowledged it cordially; and then Hawthorne wrote him as follows: —

" By some witchcraft or other — for I really cannot
assign any reasonable cause — I have been carried
apart from the main current of life, and find it impossible to get back again. Since we last met, which
you remember was in Sawtell's room, where you read
a farewell poem to the relics of the class — ever since
that time I have secluded myself from society; and
yet I never meant any such thing nor dreamed what
sort of life I was going to lead. . . . For the last
ten years I have not lived, but only dreamed of living. . . .

" As to my literary efforts, I do not think much of
them, neither is it worth while to be ashamed of them.
They would have been better, I trust, if written under
more favorable circumstances."

But Longfellow broke out, as it were, into an exulting cry over them, which echoed from the pages of the
next " North American Review." [1] His notice was

hardly a criticism ; it was a eulogy, bristling with the adornment of frequent references to European litera-ture ; but it is worth while to recall a few of its sen-tences.

"When a star rises in the heavens," said Longfel-low, "people gaze after it for a season with the naked eye, and with such telescopes as they may find. In the stream of thought, which flows so peacefully deep and clear through this book, we see the bright reflec-tion of a spiritual star, after which men will be prone to gaze 'with the naked eye and with the spy-glasses of criticism.' . . . To this little work we would say, 'Live ever, sweet, sweet book.' It comes from the hand of a man of genius. Everything about it has the freshness of morning and of May. . . . The book, though in prose, is nevertheless written by a poet. He looks upon all things in a spirit of love and with lively sympathies. A calm, thoughtful face seems to· be looking at you from every page; with now and then a pleasant smile, and now a shade of sadness steal-ing over its features. Sometimes, though not often, it glares wildly at you, with a strange and painful ex-pression, as, in the German romance, the bronze knocker of the Archivarius Lindhorst makes up faces at the student Anselm. . . . One of the prominent characteristics of these tales is that they are national in their character. The author has wisely chosen his themes among the traditions of New England. . . . This is the right material for story. It seems as nat-ural to make tales out of old tumble-down traditions as canes and snuff-boxes out of old steeples, or trees planted by great men."

This hearty utterance of Longfellow's not only was of advantage to the young author publicly, but also doubtless threw a bright ray of encouragement into the morning-dusk which was then the pervading atmosphere of his little study, which he termed his " owl's nest." " I have to-day," he wrote back, " received and read with huge delight, your review of ' Hawthorne's Twice-Told Tales.' I frankly own that I was not without hopes that you would do this kind office for the book ; though I could not have anticipated how very kindly it would be done. Whether or no the public will agree to the praise which you bestow on me, there are at least five persons who think you the most sagacious critic on earth, viz., my mother and two sisters, my old maiden aunt, and finally the strongest believer of the whole five, my own self. If I doubt the sincerity and earnestness of any of my critics, it shall be of those who censure me. Hard would be the lot of a poor scribbler, if he may not have this privilege."

His pleasant intimacy with the Peabodys went on ; the dawn of his new epoch broadened, and he began to see in Miss Sophia Peabody the figure upon which his hopes, his plans for the future converged. Her father's house stood on the edge of the Charter Street Burying-Ground, oldest of the Salem cemeteries. "A three-story wooden house " — thus he has described it — " perhaps a century old, low-studded, with a square front, standing right upon the street, and a small enclosed porch, containing the main entrance, affording a glimpse up and down the street through an oval window on each side : its characteristic was decent respectability, not sinking below the level of the genteel." In his " Note-Books " (July 4, 1837) he speaks of the old graveyard. "A slate gravestone round the borders, to the memory of ' Col. John Hathorne Esq.,' who died in 1717. This was the witch-judge. The stone is sunk deep into the earth, and leans forward, and the grass grows very long around it. . . . Other Hathornes lie buried in a range with him on either side. . . . It gives strange ideas, to think how convenient to Dr. P——'s family this burial-ground is,— the monuments standing almost within arm's reach of the side-windows of the parlor — and there being a little gate from the back-yard through which we step forth upon those old graves aforesaid. And the tomb of the P—— family is right in front, and close to the gate." Among the other Hathornes interred there are Captain Daniel, the privateersman, and a Mr. John Hathorne, "grandson of the Hon. John Hathorne," who died in 1758. The specification of his grandfather's name, with the prefix, shows that the relentless condemner of witches was still held in honor at Salem, in the middle of the eighteenth century. Dr. Peabody's house and this adjoining burial-ground form the scene of the unfinished "Dolliver Romance," and also supply the setting for the first part of "Dr. Grimshawe's Secret." In the latter we find it pictured with a Rembrandtesque depth of tone : —

" It stood in a shabby by-street and cornered on a graveyard. . . . Here were old brick tombs with curious sculpture on them, and quaint gravestones, some of which bore puffy little cherubs, and one or two others the effigies of eminent Puritans, wrought out to a button, a fold of the ruff, and a wrinkle of the skull-cap. . . . Here used to be some specimens of English garden flowers, which could not be accounted for — unless, perhaps, they had sprung from some English maiden's heart, where the intense love of those homely things and regret of them in the foreign

land, had conspired together to keep their vivifying
principle. . . . Thus rippled and surged with its hundreds of little billows the old graveyard about the
house which cornered upon it; it made the street
gloomy so that people did not altogether like to pass
along the high wooden fence that shut it in; and the
old house itself, covering ground which else had been
thickly sown with bodies, partook of its dreariness, because it hardly seemed possible that the dead people
should not get up out of their graves and steal in to
warm themselves at this convenient fireside."

This was the place in which Hawthorne conducted
his courtship; but we ought not to lose sight of the
fact that, in the account above quoted, he was writing
imaginatively, indulging his fancy, and dwelling on
particular points for the sake of heightening the effect.
It is not probable that he associated gloomy fantasies
with his own experience as it progressed in these surroundings. Here as elsewhere it is important to bear
in mind the distinction which Dr. Loring has made:
" Throughout life," he declares, " Hawthorne led a
twofold existence — a real and a supernatural. As a
man, he was the realest of men. From childhood to
old age, he had great physical powers. His massive
head sat upon a strong and muscular neck, and his
chest was broad and capacious. His strength was
great; his hand and foot were large and well made.
. . . In walking, he had a firm step and a great stride
without effort. In early manhood he had abounding
health, a good digestion, a hearty enjoyment of food.
His excellent physical condition gave him a placid and
even temper, a cheerful spirit. He was a silent man
and often a moody one, but never irritable or morose;
his organization was too grand for that. He was a

most delightful companion. In conversation he was never controversial, never authoritative, and never absorbing. In a multitude his silence was oppressive; but with a single companion his talk flowed on sensibly, quietly, and full of wisdom and shrewdness. He discussed books with wonderful acuteness, sometimes with startling power, and with an unexpected verdict, as if Shakespeare were discussing Ben Jonson. He analyzed men, their characters and motives and capacity, with great penetration, impartially if a stranger or an enemy, with the tenderest and most touching justice if a friend. He was fond of the companionship of all who were in sympathy with this real and human side of his life." But there was another side of his being, for which we may adopt the name that Dr. Loring has given it, the "supernatural." It was this which gave him his high distinction. " When he entered upon his work as a writer, he left" behind him his other and accustomed personality by which he was known in general intercourse. " In this work he allowed no interference, he asked for no aid. He was shy of those whose intellectual power and literary fame might seem to give them a right to enter his sanctuary. In an assembly of illustrious authors and thinkers, he floated, reserved and silent, around the margin in the twilight of the room, and at last vanished into the outer darkness ; and when he was gone, Mr. Emerson said of him : ' Hawthorne rides well his horse of the night.' The working of his mind was so sacred and mysterious to him that he was impatient of any attempt at familiarity or even intimacy with the divine power within him. His love of personal solitude was a ruling passion, his intellectual solitude was an overpowering necessity. . . . Hawthorne said himself that his work grew in his brain as it went on, and was beyond his control or direction, for nature was his guide. . . . I have often thought that he understood his own greatness so imperfectly, that he dared not expose the mystery to others, and that the sacredness of his genius was to him like the sacredness of his love."

And did not Hawthorne write to his betrothed wife ? — " Lights and shadows are continually flitting across my inward sky, and I know not whence they come nor whither they go ; nor do I inquire too closely into them. It is dangerous to look too minutely into such phenomena." What we may collect and set down of mere fact about his surroundings and his acts relates itself, therefore, mainly to his outwardly real existence, to the mere shell or mask of him, which was all that anybody could behold with the eyes ; and as for the interior and ideal existence, it is not likely that we shall securely penetrate very far, where his own impartial and introverted gaze stopped short. It is but a rough method to infer with brusque self-confidence that we may judge from a few words here and there the whole of his thought and feeling. A fair enough notion may be formed as to the status of his postcollegiate life in Salem, from the data we have, but we can do no more than guess at its formative influence upon his genius. And I should be sorry to give an impression that because his courtship went on in the old house by the graveyard, of which he has written so soberly, there was any shadow of melancholy upon that initiatory period of a new happiness. His reflections concerning the spot had to do with his imaginative, or if one choose, his " supernatural," existence ; what actually passed there had to do with the

real and the personal, and with the life of the affections. We may be sure that the meeting of two such
perfected spirits, so in harmony one with another, was
attended with no qualified degree of joy. If it was
calm and reticent, without rush of excitement or exuberant utterance, this was because movement at its
acme becomes akin to rest. Let us leave his love in
that sanctity which, in his own mind, it shared with
his genius.

Picturesquely considered, however, — and the picturesque never goes very deep, — it is certainly interesting to observe that Hawthorne and his wife, both
of Salem families, should have been born on opposite
sides of the same street, within the sound of a voice;
should have gone in separate directions, remaining un-
aware of each other's existence; and then should finally
have met, when well beyond their first youth, in an old
house on the borders of the ancient burial-ground in
which the ancestors of both reposed, within hail of the
spot where both had first seen the light.

When they became engaged, there was opposition
to the match on the part of Hawthorne's family, who
regarded the seemingly confirmed invalidism of Miss
Peabody as an insuperable objection; but this could
not be allowed to stand in the way of a union so evidently pointed out by providential circumstance and
inherent adaptability in those who were to be the parties to it. The engagement was a long one; but in
the interval before her marriage Miss Peabody's health
materially improved.

## III.

The new turn of affairs of course made Hawthorne impatient to find some employment more immediately productive than that with the pen. He was profoundly dissatisfied, also, with his elimination from the active life of the world. "I am tired of being an ornament!" he said with great emphasis, to a friend. "I want a little piece of land of my own, big enough to stand upon, big enough to be buried in. I want to have something to do with this material world." And, striking his hand vigorously upon a table that stood by: "If I could only make tables," he declared, "I should feel myself more of a man."

President Van Buren had entered on the second year of his term, and Mr. Bancroft, the historian, was Collector of the port of Boston. One evening the latter was speaking, in a circle of whig friends, of the splendid things which the democratic administration was doing for literary men.

"But there's Hawthorne," suggested Miss Elizabeth Peabody, who was present. "You've done nothing for him."

"He won't take anything," was the answer: "he has been offered places."

In fact, Hawthorne's friends in political life, Pierce and Jonathan Cilley, had urged him to enter politics; and at one time he had been offered a post in the West Indies, but refused it because he would not live in a slaveholding community.

"I happen to know," said Miss Peabody, "that he would be very glad of employment."

The result was that a small position in the Boston

Custom House was soon awarded to the young author. On going down from Salem to inquire about it, he received another and better appointment as weigher and gauger. His friend Pike was installed there at the same time. To Longfellow, Hawthorne wrote in good spirits: —

"I have no reason to doubt my capacity to fulfil the duties ; for I don't know what they are. They tell me that a considerable portion of my time will be unoccupied, the which I mean to employ in sketches of my new experience, under some such titles as follows : ' Scenes In Dock,' ' Voyages at Anchor,' ' Nibblings of a Wharf Rat,' ' Trials of a Tide-Waiter,' ' Romance of the Revenue Service,' together with an ethical work in two volumes on the subject of Duties ; the first volume to treat of moral duties and the second of duties imposed by the revenue laws, which I begin to consider the most important."

His hopes regarding unoccupied time were not fulfilled ; he was unable to write with freedom during his term of service in Boston, and the best result of it for us is contained in those letters, extracts from which Mrs. Hawthorne published in the first volume of the "American Note-Books." The benefit to him lay in the moderate salary of $1,200, from which the cheapness of living at that time and his habitual economy enabled him to lay up something ; and in the contact with others which his work involved. He might have saved time for writing if he had chosen ; but the wages of the wharf laborers depended on the number of hours they worked, and Hawthorne — true to his instinct of democratic sympathy and of justice — made it a point to reach the wharf at the earliest hour, no matter what the weather might be, solely for the con-

venience of the men. " It pleased me," he says in one
of his letters, " to think that I also had a part to act
in the material and tangible business of life, and that
a portion of all this industry could not have gone on
without my presence."

But when he had had two years of this sort of toil
the Whigs elected a President, and Hawthorne was
dropped from the civil service. The project of an
ideal community just then presented itself, and from
Boston he went to Brook Farm, close by in Roxbury.
The era of Transcendentalism had arrived, and Dr.
George Ripley, an enthusiastic student of philosophy
and a man of wide information, sought to give the new
tendencies a practical turn in the establishment of a
modified socialistic community. The Industrial Association which he proposed to plant at West Roxbury
was wisely planned with reference to the conditions of ·
American life; it had no affinity with the erratic views
of Enfantin or St. Simon, nor did it in the least partake of the errors of Robert Owen regarding the relation of the sexes; although it agreed with Fourier and
Owen both, if I understand the aim rightly, in respect
of labor. Dr. Ripley's simple object was to distrib-
ute labor in such a way as to give all men time for
culture, and to free their minds from the debasing influence of a merely selfish competition. "A few men
of like views and feelings," one of his sympathizers has
said, " grouped themselves around him, not as their
master, but as their friend and brother, and the community at Brook Farm was instituted." Charles A.
Dana and Minot Pratt were leading spirits in the enterprise; the young Brownson, George William Curtis,
and Horace Sumner (a younger brother of Charles)
were also engaged in it, at various times. The place

was a kind of granary of true grit. Hawthorne has characterized the community in that remark which he applied to Blithedale : " They were mostly individuals who had gone through such an experience as to disgust them with ordinary pursuits, but who were not yet so old, nor had suffered so deeply, as to lose their faith in the better time to come." Miss E. P. Peabody had at that time left Salem and begun a publishing business in Boston, being one of the first women of our time to embark in an occupation thought to appertain exclusively to men ; and at her rooms some of the preliminary meetings of the new association were held. Thus it happened that the scheme was speedily brought to Hawthorne's notice. When his accession to the ranks was announced, Dr. Ripley, as he said to the present writer, felt as if a miracle had occurred, " or as if the heavens would presently be opened and we should see Jacob's Ladder before us. But we never came any nearer to having *that*, than our old ladder in the barn, from floor to hayloft." Besides his belief in the theory of an improved condition of society, and his desire to forward its accomplishment, Hawthorne had two objects in joining the community : one of which was to secure a suitable and economical home after marriage ; the other, to hit upon a mode of life which should equalize the sum of his exertions between body and brain. Many persons went thither in just the same frame of mind.

From a distance, the life that was led there has a very pretty and idyllic look. There was teaching, and there was intellectual talk ; there was hard domestic and farming work in pleasant companionship, and a general effort to be disinterested. The various buildings in which the associators found shelter were baptized with cheerful and sentimental names ; The Hive, The Pilgrim House, The Nest, The Eyrie, and The Cottage. The young women sang as they washed the dishes, and the more prepossessing and eligible of the yeomen sometimes volunteered to help them with their unpoetic and saponaceous task. The costume of the men included a blouse of checked or plaided stuff, belted at the waist, and a rough straw hat ; and the women also wore hats, in defiance of the fashion then ruling, and chose calico for their gowns. In the evenings, poems and essays composed by the members, or else a play of Shakespeare, would be read aloud in the principal gathering held at one of the houses. A great deal of individual liberty was allowed, and Hawthorne probably availed himself of this to keep as much as possible out of sight. One might fancy, on a casual glance, that Brook Farm was the scene of a prolonged picnic. But it was not so at all. Hawthorne had hoped that by devoting six hours a day to mechanical employments, he could earn the time he needed for writing ; but, as it proved, the manual labor more nearly consumed sixteen hours, according to Dr. Ripley, who declared of Hawthorne that " he worked like a dragon ! "

Sundry of Hawthorne's common sense observations and conclusions upon the advisability of his remaining at the farm are to be found in his " Note-Books," and have often been quoted and criticised. They show that, as might be expected in a person of candor and good judgment, he was considering the whole phenomenon upon the practical side. There is an instructive passage also in " The Blithedale Romance," which undoubtedly refers to his own experience : —

" Though fond of society, I was so constituted as to

need these occasional retirements, even in a life like that of Blithedale, which was itself characterized by a remoteness from the world. Unless renewed by a yet further withdrawal towards the inner circle of self-communion, I lost the better part of my individuality. My thoughts became of little worth, and my sensibilities grew as arid as a tuft of moss . . . crumbling in the sunshine, after long expectance of a shower."

The whole thing was an experiment for everybody concerned, and Hawthorne found it best to withdraw from a further prosecution thereof, as persons were constantly doing who had come to see if the life would suit them. He had contributed a thousand dollars (the chief part of his savings in the Custom House) to the funds of the establishment; and, some time after he quitted the place, an effort was made among the most influential gentlemen of Brook Farm to restore this sum to him, although they were not, I believe, bound to do so. Whether or not they ever carried out this purpose has not been learned. The community flourished for four years and was financially sound, but in 1844 it entered into bonds of brotherhood with a Fourieristic organization in New York, began to build a Phalanstery, attempted to enlarge its range of industry, and came to grief. No one of its chief adherents has ever written its history; but perhaps Mr. Frothingham is right in saying that "Aspirations have no history." [1] At all events Hawthorne, in " The Blithedale Romance," which explicitly disclaims any close adherence to facts or any criticism on the experiment, has furnished the best chronicle it has had, so far as the spirit of the scheme is concerned.

Having tried the utmost isolation for ten years in

[1] *Transcendentalism in New England.*

Salem, and finding it unsatisfactory ; and having made a venture in an opposite extreme at Brook Farm, which was scarcely more to his liking, Hawthorne had unconsciously passed through the best of preparation for that family life of comparative freedom, and of solitude alternating with a gentle and perfect companionship, on which he was about to enter. In July, 1842, Rev. James Freeman Clarke, of Boston, received the following note, dated from 54 Pinckney Street, which was the residence of Hawthorne's friend, George S. Hillard : —

My dear Sir, — Though personally a stranger to you, I am about to request of you the greatest favor which I can receive from any man. I am to be married to Miss Sophia Peabody ; and it is our mutual desire that you should perform the ceremony. Unless it should be decidedly a rainy day, a carriage will call for you at half past eleven o'clock in the forenoon.

Very respectfully yours,

Nathaniel Hawthorne.

The wedding took place quietly, and Hawthorne carried his bride to the Manse at Concord, the old parsonage of that town. It belonged to the descendants of Dr. Ezra Ripley, who had been pastor there at the close of the last century ; they were relatives of the George Ripley with whom Hawthorne had so recently been associated at Brook Farm. Hawthorne had succeeded in hiring the place for a time, and was happy in beginning his married life in a house so well in keeping with his tastes. The best account of this, his first sojourn in Concord, is to be found in the " American Note-Books," and in the Introduction to the "Mosses from an Old Manse." Here his first child was born, a daughter, to whom the name of Una[1] was given, from "The Faërie Queen"; and here he saw something of Emerson and of Margaret Fuller. Among his visitors, who were never many, was George Stillman Hillard, a Democrat, a lawyer, an editor, an orator in high favor with the Bostonians, and the author of several works both of travel and of an educational kind. Mr. George P. Bradford, with whom Hawthorne had talked and toiled at Brook Farm, was a cousin of the Ripleys, and also came hither as a friend. Another Brook Farmer appeared at the Manse, in the person of one Frank Farley, a man of some originality, who had written a little book on natural scenery and had been a frontiersman, but was subject to a mild, loquacious form of insanity. (Mention of him as "Mr. F—— " is made in the "American Note-Books," under date of June 6 and June 10, 1844.) A writer in one of the magazines has recorded the impression which Hawthorne left on the minds of others who saw him during this period, but did not know him. Among the villagers "a report was current that this man Hawthorne was somewhat uncanny — in point of fact, not altogether sane. My friend, the son of a Concord farmer and at that time a raw college youth, had heard these bucolic whisperings as to the sanity of the recluse dweller at the ancient parsonage; but he knew nothing of the man, had read none of his productions, and of course took no interest in what was said or surmised about him. And one day, casting his eye toward the Manse as he was passing, he saw Hawthorne up the pathway, standing with folded arms in motionless attitude, and with eyes fixed upon

[1] She died, unmarried, in September, 1877.

the ground. ' Poor fellow,' was his unspoken comment: ' he does look as if he might be daft.' And when, on his return a full hour afterward, Hawthorne was still standing in the same place and attitude, the lad's very natural conclusion was, ' The man *is* daft, sure enough ! ' " Mr. Thomas Wentworth Higginson has presented quite a different view, in his " Short Studies of American Authors." He says : —

" The self-contained purpose of Hawthorne, the large resources, the waiting power, — these seem to the imagination to imply an ample basis of physical life ; and certainly his stately and noble port is inseparable, in my memory, from these characteristics. Vivid as this impression is, I yet saw him but twice, and never spoke to him. I first met him on a summer morning, in Concord, as he was walking along the road near the Old Manse, with his wife by his side and a noble looking baby-boy in a little wagon which the father was pushing. I remember him as tall, firm, and strong in bearing. . . . When I passed, Hawthorne lifted upon me his great gray eyes with a look too keen to seem indifferent, too shy to be sympathetic — and that was all." [1]

Hawthorne's plan of life was settled ; he was happily married, and the problems of his youth were solved : his character and his genius were formed. From this point on, therefore, his works and his " Note-Books " impart the essentials of his career. The main business of the biographer is, after this, to put together that which will help to make real the picture of the author grappling with those transient emergencies that consti-

[1] The allusion to a baby-boy is confusing, because Mr. Julian Hawthorne was not born at Concord, and when the family returned thither to occupy The Wayside, he was about six years old.

tute the tangible part of his history. A few extracts from letters written to Horatio Bridge, heretofore unpublished, come under this head.

*Concord, March* 25, 1843.— " I did not come to see you, because I was very short of cash — having been disappointed in money that I had expected from three or four sources. My difficulties of this kind sometimes make me sigh for the regular monthly payments of the Custom House. The system of slack payments in this country is most abominable. . . . I find no difference in anybody in this respect, for all do wrong alike. —— is just as certain to disappoint me in money matters as any little pitiful scoundrel among the booksellers. For my part, I am compelled to disappoint those who put faith in my engagements; and so it goes round."

The following piece of advice with regard to notes for the " Journal of an African Cruiser," by Mr. Bridge, which Hawthorne was to edit, is worth observing and has never before been given to the public : —

" I would advise you not to stick too accurately to the bare facts, either in your descriptions or your narratives; else your hand will be cramped, and the result will be a want of freedom that will deprive you of a higher truth than that which you strive to attain. Allow your fancy pretty free license, and omit no heightening touches merely because they did not chance to happen before your eyes. If they did not happen, they at least ought — which is all that concerns you. This is the secret of all entertaining travellers. . . . Begin to write always before the impression of novelty has worn off from your mind ; else you will soon begin to think that the peculiarities which at first interested you are not worth recording; yet these slight peculiarities are the very things that make the most vivid impression upon the reader." In this same letter (May 3, 1843) he reverts to the financial difficulty, and speaks of a desire to obtain office again, but adds: " It is rather singular that I should need an office; for nobody's scribblings seem to be more acceptable to the public than mine; and yet I still find it a tough match to gain a respectable living by my pen."

By November of 1844 he had put things seriously in train for procuring another government position; Polk having been elected to the Presidency. There was a rumor that Tyler had actually fixed upon Hawthorne for the postmastership of Salem, but had been induced to withdraw the name; and this was the office upon which he fixed his hope; but a hostile party made itself felt in Salem, which raised all possible obstacles, and apparently Hawthorne's former chief, Mr. Bancroft, — it may have been for some reason connected with political management, — opposed his nomination. Early in October, 1845, Hawthorne made his farewell to the Old Manse, never to return to the shelter of its venerable and high-shouldered roof. Once more he went to Salem, and halted in Herbert Street. The postmastership had proved unattainable, but there was a prospect of his becoming Naval Officer or Surveyor. The latter position was given him at length; but not until the spring of 1846. On first arriving at Salem, he wrote to Bridge: " Here I am, again established — in the old chamber where I wasted so many years of my life. I find it rather favorable to my literary duties; for I have already begun to sketch out the story for Wiley & Put-

nam," an allusion to something intended to fill out a
volume of the " Mosses," already negotiated for. After his installation as Surveyor he wrote, speaking
of his " moderate prosperity," and said further : " I
have written nothing for the press since my entrance
into office, but intend to begin soon. My ' Mosses '
seem to have met with good acceptance." Time went
on, however, and he remained, so far as literary production was concerned, inert. He had left the Manning homestead and hired a house in Chestnut Street,
which he kept for a year and a half. During this
period Mrs. Hawthorne went to Boston for a time,
and in Carver Street, Boston, was born their second
child and only son, Mr. Julian Hawthorne, who has
since made a reputation for himself as a novelist.
From Chestnut Street he went to another house, in
Mall Street ; and it was there that " The Scarlet Letter " was finished, in 1850, four years after he had announced to Bridge that he intended soon to begin
composition. The Custom House routine disturbed
his creative moods and caused a gradual postponement
of literary effort. Of the figure that he made while
fulfilling the functions assigned to him, slight traces
have been left. We are told, for example, that two
Shakers, leaders in their community, visited the Custom House one day, and were conducted through its
several departments. On the way out, they passed
Hawthorne, and no sooner had they left his room
than, the door being shut behind them, the elder
brother asked with great interest who that man was.
After referring to the strong face, " and those eyes,
the most wonderful he had ever beheld," he said :
" Mark my words, that man will in some way make a
deep impression upon the world." It is also remem-

bered that a rough and overbearing sea-captain attempted to interfere with Hawthorne's exercise of his duty as an inspector of the customs, in charge of the ship. His attempt "was met with such a terrific uprising of spiritual and physical wrath that the dismayed captain fled up the wharf" and took refuge with the Collector, "inquiring with a sailor's emotion and a sailor's tongue : ' What in God's name have you sent on board my ship for an inspector?'" Unexpectedly, in the winter of 1849, he was deprived of his surveyorship ; a great surprise to him, because he had understood certain of his fellow-citizens of Salem to have given a pledge that they would not seek his removal, and it appeared that they had, notwithstanding, gone to work to oust him.

On finding himself superseded, he walked away from the Custom House, returned home, and entering sat down in the nearest chair, without uttering a word. Mrs. Hawthorne asked him if he was well.

" Well enough," was the answer.

" What is the matter, then?" said she. " Are you ' decapitated?' "

He replied with gloom that he was, and that the occurrence was no joke.

"Oh," said his wife, gayly, " now you can write your Romance !" For he had told her several times that he had a romance "growling" in him.

" Write my Romance !" he exclaimed. " But what are we to do for bread and rice, next week?"

" I will take care of that," she answered. " And I will tell Ann to put a fire in your study, now."

Hawthorne was oppressed with anxiety as to means of support for his wife and children ; the necessity of writing for immediate returns always had a deterrent

and paralyzing effect on his genius; and he was
amazed that Mrs. Hawthorne should take his calamity with so much lightness. He questioned her again
regarding the wherewithal to meet their current needs,
knowing well that he himself had no fund in reserve.
His habit had been to hand her the instalments of
salary as they came to him from the office; and when
he was in need of money for himself he drew again
upon her for it. He therefore supposed that everything had been used up from week to week. But Mrs.
Hawthorne now disclosed the fact that she had about
a hundred and fifty dollars, a sum which for them was
a considerable one, their manner of living being extremely plain. Greatly astonished, he asked her where
she had obtained so much.

"You earned it," she replied, cheerily.

Mrs. Hawthorne was in fact overjoyed, on his account, that he had lost his place; feeling as she did
that he would now resume his proper employment.
The fire was built in the study, and Hawthorne, stim-
ulated by his wife's good spirits, set at once about writing "The Scarlet Letter."

Some six months of time were required for its
completion, and Mrs. Hawthorne, who was aware that
her savings would be consumed in a third of that
space, applied herself to increasing the small stock of
cash, so that her husband's mind might remain free
and buoyant for his writing. She began making little
cambric lamp-shades, which she decorated with delicate outline drawings and sent to Boston for sale.
They were readily purchased, and, by continuing their
manufacture, this devoted wife contrived to defray the
expenses of the household until the book was finished.

Mr. James T. Fields, the publisher, who was already

an acquaintance, and eventually became a friend, of Hawthorne's had been told of the work, and went down to Salem to suggest bringing it out. This was before the story had been fully elaborated into its present form. Hawthorne had written steadily all day, and every day, from the start, but, remembering in what small quantity his books sold, he had come to consider this new attempt a forlorn hope. Mr. Fields found him despondent, and thus narrates the close of the interview: —

" I looked at my watch and found that the train would soon be starting for Boston, and I knew there was not much time to lose in trying to discover what had been his literary work during these last few years in Salem. I remember that I pressed him to reveal to me what he had been writing. He shook his head, and gave me to understand that he had produced nothing. At that moment I caught sight of a bureau or set of drawers near where we were sitting; and immediately it occurred to me that, hidden away somewhere in that article of furniture, was a story or stories by the author of the ' Twice-Told Tales,' and I became so confident that I charged him vehemently with the fact. He seemed surprised, I thought, but shook his head again ; and I rose to take my leave, begging him not to come into the cold entry, saying I would come back and see him again in a few days. I was hurrying down the stairs when he called after me from the chamber, asking me to stop a moment. Then, quickly stepping into the entry with a roll of manuscript in his hands, he said : ' How in Heaven's name did you know this thing was here ? As you have found me out, take what I have written, and tell me, after you get home and have time to read it, if it is good for anything. It is either very good or very bad — I don't know which.' On my way up to Boston I read the germ of ' The Scarlet Letter ; ' before I slept that night I wrote him a note all aglow with admiration of the marvellous story he had put into my hands."

In a letter to Bridge (April 10, 1850), the author said : " ' The Scarlet Letter ' has sold well, the first edition having been exhausted in ten days, and the second (5,000 in all) promising to go off rapidly." Speaking of the excitement created among his townspeople by the introductory account of the Custom House, he continued : " As to the Salem people, I really thought I had been exceedingly good-natured in my treatment of them. They certainly do not deserve good usage at my hands, after permitting me . . . to be deliberately lied down, not merely once but at two separate attacks, on two false indictments, without hardly a voice being raised on my behalf; and then sending one of their false witnesses to Congress and choosing another as their Mayor. I feel an infinite contempt for them, and probably have expressed more of it than I intended ; for my preliminary chapter has caused the greatest uproar that ever happened here since witch-times. If I escape from town without being tarred and feathered, I shall consider it good luck. I wish they *would* tar and feather me — it would be such an entirely new distinction for a literary man ! And from such judges as my fellow-citizens, I should look upon it as a higher honor than a laurel-crown." In the same letter he states that he has taken a house in Lenox, and shall move to it on the 1st of May : " I thank Mrs. Bridge for her good wishes as respects my future removals from office ; but I should be sorry to anticipate such bad fortune as ever again being appointed to me."

Previous to this, he had written : " I long to get into the country, for my health latterly is not quite what it has been for many years past. I should not long stand such a life of bodily inactivity and mental exertion as I have led for the last few months. An hour or two of daily labor in a garden, and a daily ramble in country air or on the sea-shore, would keep me all right. Here I hardly go out once a week. . . . I detest this town so much, that I hate to go into the streets, or to have the people see me. Anywhere else I should at once be another man."

It was not a very comfortable home, that small red wooden house at Lenox, overlooking the beautiful valley of the Housatonic and surrounded by mountains; but both Hawthorne and his wife bravely made the best of it. Mrs. Hawthorne ornamented an entire set of plain furniture, painted a dull yellow, with copies from Flaxman's outlines, executed with great perfection ; and, poor as the place was, it soon became invested by its occupants with something of a poetic atmosphere. After a summer's rest, Hawthorne began "The House of the Seven Gables ; " writing to Bridge in October : —

" I am getting so deep into my own book, that I am afraid it will be impossible for me to attend properly to my editorial duties " (connected with a new edition of Lieutenant Bridge's " Journal of an African Cruiser "). . . . " Una and Julian grow apace, and so do our chickens, of which we have two broods. There is one difficulty about these chickens, as well as about the older fowls. We have become so intimately acquainted with every individual of them, that it really

Lenox, Jany 27. 1851

Dear Fields,

I intend to put the House of the Seven Gables into the express man's hands to-day; so that, if you do not soon receive it, you may conclude that it has miscarried — in which case, I shall not consent to the Universe existing a moment longer. I have no copy of it, except the wildest scrawl of a first draught; so that it could never be restored.

It has met with extraordinary success from that portion of the public to whose judgment it has been submitted; — viz, from my wife. I likewise prefer it to the Scarlet Letter; but an author's opinion of his book, just after completing it, is worth little or nothing; he being then in the hot or cold fit of a fever, and certain to rate it too high or too low.

I had something else to say, but have forgotten what.

Ronly Yours

Nath. Hawthorne.

seems like cannibalism to think of eating them. What is to be done?"

His task occupied him all winter. To Mr. Fields at length, on the 27th of January, 1851, he sent the following message: —

"I intend to put 'The House of the Seven Gables' into the expressman's hands to-day; so that, if you do not soon receive it, you may conclude that it has miscarried — in which case, I shall not consent to the universe existing a moment longer. I have no copy of it, except the wildest scribble of a first draught; so that it could never be restored.

"It has met with extraordinary success from that portion of the public to whose judgment it has been submitted: viz. from my wife. I likewise prefer it to 'The Scarlet Letter;' but an author's opinion of his book, just after completing it, is worth little or nothing; he being then in the hot or cold fit of a fever, and certain to rate it too high or too low. It has undoubtedly one disadvantage in being brought so close to the present time, whereby its romantic improbabilities become more glaring."

The fac simile of a part of the above letter which is reproduced here serves as a fairly good specimen of Hawthorne's handwriting. At the time when it was written, he was not very well, and the fatigue of his long labor upon the book rendered the chirography somewhat less clear in this case than it often was. The lettering in his manuscripts was somewhat larger, and was still more distinct than that in his correspondence.

After the new romance had come out and had met with a flattering reception, he inquired of Bridge (July 22, 1851) : "Why did you not write and tell me how you liked (or how you did not like) 'The House of

the Seven Gables?' Did you feel shy about expressing an unfavorable opinion? It would not have hurt
me in the least, though I am always glad to please
you; but I rather think I have reached the stage
when I do not care very essentially one way or the
other for anybody's opinion on any one production.
On this last romance, for instance, I have heard and
seen such diversity of judgment that I should be altogether bewildered if I attempted to strike a balance;
— so I take nobody's estimate but my own. I think
it is a work more characteristic of my mind, and more
natural and proper for me to write, than ' The Scarlet
Letter' — but for that very reason less likely to interest
the public. . . . As long as people will buy, I shall
keep at work, and I find that my facility of labor increases with the demand for it."

In the May of 1851 another daughter was added
to his family. Hawthorne, like his father, had one son
and two daughters. Of this youngest one he wrote to
Pike, two months after her birth: "She is a very
bright and healthy child. . . . I think I feel more interest in her than I did in the other children at the
same age, from the consideration that she is to be the
daughter of my age — the comfort (so it is to be
hoped) of my declining years." There are some other
interesting points in this communication. " What a
sad account you give of your solitude, in your letter!
I am not likely ever to have that feeling of loneliness
which you express; and I most heartily wish you
would take measures to remedy it in your own case,
by marrying. . . . Whenever you find it quite intolerable (and I can hardly help wishing that it may become so soon), do come to me. By the way, if I continue to prosper as hitherto in the literary line, I shall

soon be in a condition to buy a place; and if you should hear of one, say worth from $1,500 to $2,000, I wish you would keep your eye on it for me. I should wish it to be on the sea-coast, or at all events within easy access to the sea. Very little land would suit my purpose, but I want a good house, with space inside. . . . I find that I do not feel at home among these hills, and should not consider myself permanently settled here. I do not get acclimated to the peculiar state of the atmosphere; and, except in midwinter, I am continually catching cold, and am never so vigorous as I used to be on the sea-coast. . . . Why did you not express your opinion of 'The House of the Seven Gables?' . . . I should receive friendly censure with just as much equanimity as if it were praise; though certainly I had rather you would like the book than not. At any rate, it has sold finely, and seems to have pleased a good many people better than the other; and I must confess that I myself am among the number. . . . When I write another romance I shall take the Community for a subject, and shall give some of my experiences at Brook Farm."

On the first day of December, 1851, he left Lenox with his wife and children, betaking himself for the winter to West Newton, a suburban village a few miles west of Boston, on the Charles River; there to remain until he could effect the purchase of a house which could serve him as a settled home. The house that he finally selected was an old one in the town of Concord, about a mile easterly from the centre of the village on the road to Lexington, and was then the property of Mrs. Bronson Alcott. During the winter at West Newton he wrote "The Blithedale Romance," which was published early in 1852. In the brief term of two years and a half from the moment of his leaving the Custom House at Salem, he had thus produced four books, — "The Scarlet Letter," "The House of the Seven Gables," "A Wonder-Book for Boys and Girls," and "The Blithedale Romance," — three of them being the principal works of his lifetime, with which "The Marble Faun" alone stands in the same category. Early in the summer of 1852 he took up his residence in his new home, The Wayside, of which he thus discoursed to Mr. George William Curtis, on the 14th of July, 1852: —

MY DEAR HOWADJI, — I think (and am glad to think) that you will find it necessary to come hither in order to write your Concord Sketches; and as for my old house, you will understand it better after spending a day or two in it. Before Mr. Alcott took it in hand, it was a mean-looking affair, with two peaked gables; no suggestiveness about it and no venerableness, although from the style of its construction it seems to have survived beyond its first century. He added a porch in front, and a central peak, and a piazza at each end, and painted it a rusty olive hue, and invested the whole with a modest picturesqueness; all which improvements, together with its situation at the foot of a wooded hill, make it a place that one notices and remembers for a few moments after passing it. Mr. Alcott expended a good deal of taste and some money (to no great purpose) in forming the hillside behind the house into terraces, and building arbors and summer-houses of rough stems and branches and trees, on a system of his own. They must have been very pretty in their day, and are so still, although much decayed, and shattered more and more by every breeze that blows. The hill-side is covered chiefly with locust-trees, which come into luxuriant blossom in the month of June, and look and smell very sweetly, intermixed with a few young elms and some white-pines and infant oaks, — the whole forming rather a thicket than a wood. Nevertheless, there is some very good shade to be found there. I spend delectable hours there in the hottest part of the day, stretched out at my lazy length, with a book in my hand or an unwritten book in my thoughts. There is almost always a breeze stirring along the sides or brow of the hill.

From the hill-top there is a good view along the extensive level surfaces and gentle, hilly outlines, covered with wood, that characterize the scenery of Concord. We have not so much as a gleam of lake or river in the prospect; if there were, it would add greatly to the value of the place in my estimation.

The house stands within ten or fifteen feet of the old Boston road (along which the British marched and retreated), divided from it by a fence, and some trees and shrubbery of Mr. Alcott's setting out. Whereupon I have called it " The Wayside," which I think a better name and more morally suggestive than that which, as Mr. Alcott has since told me, he bestowed on it, — " The Hill-Side." In front of the house, on the opposite side of the road, I have eight acres of land, — the only valuable portion of the place in a farmer's eye, and which are capable of being made very fertile. On the hither side, my territory extends some little distance over the brow of the hill, and is absolutely good for nothing, in a productive point of view, though very good for many other purposes.

I know nothing of the history of the house, except Thoreau's telling me that it was inhabited a generation or two ago by a man who believed he should never die.[1] I believe, however, he is dead; at least, I hope so; else he may probably appear and dispute my title to his residence. . . .

I asked Ticknor to send a copy of " The Blithedale Romance" to you. Do not read it as if it had anything to do with Brook Farm (which essentially it has not), but merely for its own story and character.

Truly yours,    Nathaniel Hawthorne.

Quite possibly the name of The Wayside recommended itself to him by some association of thought like that which comes to light in the Preface to "The Snow-Image," where, speaking of the years immediately following his college course, he says: "I sat down by the wayside of life like a man under enchantment, and a shrubbery sprung up around me, and the bushes grew to be saplings, and the saplings became trees, until no exit appeared possible through the entangling depths of my obscurity." If so, the simile held good as to his home; for there, too, the shrubbery has sprung up and has grown to saplings and trees, until the house is embosomed in a wood, except for the opening along the road and a small amphitheatre of lawn overlooked by the evergreen-clad hill.

Hawthorne's old college friend, Franklin Pierce, after having been to Congress and having risen to the rank of general in the Mexican War, was nominated by the democratic party for the presidency of the United States, at the time when the romancer had established himself in this humble but charming old

---

[1] This is the first intimation of the story of *Septimius Felton,* so far as local setting is concerned. The scenery of that romance was obviously taken from The Wayside and its hill.

abode; and it became manifest that the candidate wanted Hawthorne to write a life of him, for use in the campaign. Hawthorne, on being pressed, consented to do so, and a letter which he addressed to Bridge, October 13, 1852, contains some extremely interesting confidences on the subject, which will be entirely new to readers. As they do Hawthorne credit, if considered fairly, and give a striking presentment of the impartiality with which he viewed all subjects, it seems to be proper to print them here.

He begins by speaking of "The Blithedale Romance," regarding which he says: "I doubt whether you will like it very well; but it has met with good success, and has brought me (besides its American circulation) a thousand dollars from England, whence likewise have come many favorable notices. Just at this time, I rather think your friend stands foremost there as an American fiction-monger. In a day or two I intend to begin a new romance, which, if possible, I intend to make more genial than the last.

" I did not send you the Life of Pierce, not considering it fairly one of my literary productions. . . . I was terribly reluctant to undertake this work, and tried to persuade Pierce, both by letter and *vivâ voce*, that I could not perform it as well as many others ; but he thought differently, and of course after a friendship of thirty years it was impossible to refuse my best efforts in his behalf, at the great pinch of his life. It was a bad book to write, for the gist of the matter lay in explaining how it happened, that with such extraordinary opportunities for eminent distinction, civil and military, as he has enjoyed, this crisis should have found him so obscure as he certainly was, in a national point of view. My heart absolutely sank at the dearth of available material. However, I have done the business, greatly to Frank's satisfaction; and, though I say it myself, it is judiciously done; and, without any sacrifice of truth, it puts him in as good a light as circumstances would admit. Other writers might have made larger claims for him, and have eulogized him more highly; but I doubt whether any other could have bestowed a better aspect of sincerity and reality on the narrative, and have secured all the credit possible for him without spoiling all by asserting too much. And though the story is true, yet it took a romancer to do it.

"Before undertaking it, I made an inward resolution that I would accept no office from him; but to say the truth, I doubt whether it would not be rather folly than heroism to adhere to this purpose, in case he should offer me anything particularly good. We shall see. A foreign mission I could not afford to take; — the consulship at Liverpool I might. . . . I have several invitations from English celebrities to come over there; and this office would make all straight. He certainly owes me something; for the biography has cost me hundreds of friends here at the North, who had a purer regard for me than Frank Pierce or any other politician ever gained, and who drop off from me like autumn leaves, in consequence of what I say on the slavery question. But they were my real sentiments, and I do not now regret that they are on record."

After discussing other topics, he observes further of Pierce: " I have come seriously to the conclusion that he has in him many of the chief elements of a great man; and that if he wins the election he may run a great career. His talents are administrative;

he has a subtle faculty of making affairs roll around according to his will, and of influencing their course without showing any trace of his action." Hawthorne did not feel very confident of his friend's election. " I love him," he adds, " and, oddly enough, there is a kind of pitying sentiment mixed with my affection for him just now."

Mr. Richard Henry Stoddard has set down his reminiscences of two visits paid to Hawthorne at the beginning and after the end of the campaign. In the summer of 1852, Mr. Stoddard was making a short stay in Boston, and dropped in at the Old Corner Bookstore to call upon Mr. Fields, who then had his headquarters there. He found Mr. Edwin P. Whipple, the lecturer and critic, sitting with the publisher.

" ' We are going to see Hawthorne,' Mr. Fields remarked, in an off-hand way, as if such a visit was the commonest thing in the world. ' Won't you come along ? ' He knew my admiration for Hawthorne, and that I desired to meet him, if I could do so without being considered an infliction. ' To be sure I will,' I replied. . . . When we were fairly seated in the train we met a friend of Hawthorne, whom Mr. Fields knew — a Colonel T. I. Whipple — who, like ourselves, was *en route* for Concord, . . . and as General Pierce was then the democratic candidate for the presidency, he was going to see Hawthorne, in order to furnish materials for that work.

" We reached The Wayside, where Hawthorne, who had no doubt been expecting visitors, met us at the door. I was introduced to him as being the only stranger of the party, and was greeted warmly, more so than I had dared to hope, remembering the stories

I had heard of his unconquerable shyness.  He threw open the door of the room on the left, and, telling us to make ourselves at home, disappeared with Colonel Whipple and his budget of biographical memoranda. We made ourselves at home, as he had desired, in what I suppose was the parlor — a cosy but plainly furnished room, with nothing to distinguish it from a thousand other " best rooms " in New England, except a fine engraving on the wall of one of Raphael's Madonnas.  We chatted a few moments, and then, as he did not return, we took a stroll over the grounds, under the direction of Mr. Fields.

" We had ascended the hill, and from its outlook were taking in the historic country about, when we were rejoined by Hawthorne in the old rustic summer-house.  As I was the stranger, he talked with me more than with the others, largely about myself and my verse-work, which he seemed to have followed with considerable attention ; and he mentioned an architectural poem of mine and compared it with his own modest mansion.

" ' If I could build like you,' he said, ' I, too, would have a castle in the air.'

" ' Give me The Wayside,' I replied, ' and you shall have all the air castles I can build.'

" As we rambled and talked, my heart went out towards this famous man, who did not look down upon me, as he might well have done, but took me up to himself as an equal and a friend.  Dinner was announced and eaten, a plain country dinner, with a bottle or two of *vin ordinaire,* and we started back to Boston."

Pierce having become President-Elect, Mr. Stoddard made another trip to Concord, in the winter of 1852–3, to ask Hawthorne's advice about getting a place in the Custom House. He was taken into the study (at that time in the southeast corner, on the ground-floor and facing the road), where there was a blazing wood-fire. The announcement of dinner cut short their conversation, but after dinner they again retired to the study, where, as Mr. Stoddard says, Hawthorne brought out some cigars, " which we smoked with a will and which I found stronger than I liked. Custom House matters were scarcely touched upon, and I was not sorry, for while they were my ostensible errand there, they were not half so interesting as the discursive talk of Hawthorne. He manifested a good deal of curiosity in regard to some old Brook Farmers whom I knew in a literary way, and I told him what they were doing, and gave him my impressions of the individuality of each. He listened, with an occasional twinkle of the eye, and I can see now that he was amused by my outspoken detestation of certain literary Philistines. . He was out-spoken, too, for he told me plainly that a volume of fairy stories I had just published was not simple enough for the young.

" What impressed me most at the time was not the drift of the conversation, but the graciousness of Hawthorne. He expressed the warmest interest in my affairs, and a willingness to serve me in every possible way. In a word, he was the soul of kindness, and when I forget him I shall have forgotten everything else."

When Mr. Stoddard got back to New York, he received this letter : —

Dear Stoddard :

I beg your pardon for not writing before ; but I have been very busy and not particularly well. I enclose a letter to Atherton. Roll up and pile up as much of a snow-ball as you can in the way of political interest; for there never was a fiercer time than this among the office-seekers. . . .

Atherton is a man of rather cold exterior ; but has a good heart — at least for a politician of a quarter of a century's standing. If it be certain that he cannot help you, he will probably tell you so. Perhaps it would be as well for you to apply for some place that has a literary fragrance about it — librarian to some department — the office that Lanman held. I don't know whether there is any other such office. Are you fond of brandy? Your strength of head (which you tell me you possess) may stand you in good stead in Washington ; for most of these public men are inveterate guzzlers, and love a man that can stand up to them in that particular. It would never do to let them see you corned, however. But I must leave you to find your way among them. If you have never associated with them heretofore, you will find them a new class, and very unlike poets.

I have finished the " Tanglewood Tales," and they will make a volume about the size of the " Wonder-Book," consisting of six myths — " The Minotaur," " The Golden Fleece," " The Story of Proserpine," etc., etc., etc., done up in excellent style, purified from all moral stain, re-created good as new, or better — and fully equal, in their way, to " Mother Goose." I never did anything so good as those old baby-stories.

In haste,                              Truly yours,
                              Nath. Hawthorne.

Nothing could more succinctly illustrate the readiness of Hawthorne's sympathies, and the companionable, cordial ease with which he treated a new friend who approached him in the right way, one who caught his fancy by a frank and simple independence, than this letter to Mr. Stoddard, whom he had spoken with only twice. At that very time his old disinclination to be intruded upon was as strong as ever; for Mr. Fields relates how, just before Hawthorne sailed for England, they walked together near the Old Manse and lay down in a secluded, grassy spot beside the Concord River, to watch the clouds and hear the birds sing. Suddenly, footsteps were heard approaching, and Hawthorne whispered in haste, with much solemnity: " Duck! or we shall be interrupted by somebody." So they were both obliged to prostrate themselves in the grass until the saunterer had passed out of sight.

The proposition to accept an office from Pierce was made to him as soon as the new President was inaugurated. Although Hawthorne had considered the possibility, as we have seen, and had decided what he could advantageously take if it were offered, he also had grave doubts with regard to taking any post whatever. When, therefore, the Liverpool consulate was tendered to him, he at first positively declined it. President Pierce, however, was much troubled by his refusal, and the intervention of Hawthorne's publisher, Mr. Ticknor, was sought. Mr. Ticknor urged him to reconsider, on the ground that it was a duty to his family; and Hawthorne, who also naturally felt a strong desire to see England, finally consented. His appointment was confirmed, March 26, 1853; but his predecessor was allowed, by resigning prospectively, to hold over for five months ; so that the departure for England was not effected until the midsummer of 1853.

## IV.

The twofold character of Hawthorne's mind is strongly manifested in the diverse nature of the interests which occupied him in Europe, and the tone with which he discussed them, alike in his journals, in his letters, in " Our Old Home," and " The Marble Faun." On the one side, we find the business-like official, attending methodically to the duties of his place, the careful father of a family looking out for his personal interests and the material welfare of his children in the future, the keen and cool-headed observer who is determined to contemplate all the novelties of strange scenes through no one's eyes but his own. On the other side, he presents himself to us as the man of reverie, whose observation of the actual constantly stimulates and brings into play a faculty that perceives more than the actual ; the delicate artist, whose sympathies are ready and true in the appreciation of whatever is picturesque or suggestive, or beautiful, whether in nature or in art.

Some of the letters which he wrote from Liverpool to his classmate, Horatio Bridge, throw light upon his own affairs and the deliberate way in which he considered them. For instance, under date of March 30, 1854, he wrote : —

" I like my office well enough, but my official duties and obligations are irksome to me beyond expression. Nevertheless, the emoluments will be a sufficient inducement to keep me here for four years, though they are not a quarter part what people suppose them. The value of the office varied between ten and fifteen thousand dollars during my predecessor's term, and it promises about the same now. Secretary Guthrie, however, has just cut off a large slice, by a circular. . . . Ask —— to show you a letter of mine, which I send by this steamer, for possible publication in the newspapers. It contains a statement of my doings in reference to the San Francisco [steamship] sufferers. The "Portsmouth Journal," it appears, published an attack on me, accusing me of refusing all assistance until compelled to act by Mr. Buchanan's orders; whereas I acted extra-officially on my own responsibility, throughout the whole affair. Buchanan refused to have anything to do with it. Alas! How we public men are calumniated. But I trust there will be no necessity for publishing my letter; for I desire only to glide noiselessly through my present phase of life.

"It sickens me to look back to America. I am sick to death of the continual fuss and tumult, and excitement and bad blood, which we keep up about political topics. If it were not for my children, I should probably never return, but, after quitting office, should go to Italy, to live and die there. If you and Mrs. Bridge would go, too, we might form a little colony amongst ourselves, and see our children grow up together. But it will never do to deprive them of their native land, which, I hope, will be a more comfortable and happy residence in their day than it has been in ours. In my opinion we are the most miserable people on earth." It appears, further, that the appointment of a consul for Manchester was contemplated, which, Hawthorne says, by withdrawing some of the

Liverpool perquisites, "would go far towards knocking this consulate in the head."

On April 17th, hearing that a bill had been introduced in Congress to put consuls upon salary, instead of granting them fees, he wrote : —

"I trust to Heaven no change whatever will be made in regard to the emoluments of the Liverpool consulate, unless indeed a salary is to be given in addition to the fees, in which case I should receive it very thankfully. This, however, is not to be expected. . . . A fixed salary (even if it should be larger than any salary now paid by government, with the exception of the President's own) will render the office not worth any man's holding. It is impossible (especially for a man with a family and keeping any kind of an establishment) not to spend a vast deal of money here. The office, unfortunately, is regarded as one of great dignity, and puts the holder on a level with the highest society, and compels him to associate on equal terms with men who spend more than my whole income on the mere entertainments and other trimmings and embroideries of their lives. Then I am bound to exercise some hospitality toward my own countrymen. I keep out of society as much as I decently can, and really practise as stern an economy as ever I did in my life; but nevertheless I have spent many thousands of dollars in the few months of my residence here, and cannot reasonably hope to spend less than $6,000 per annum, even after the expense of setting up an establishment is defrayed. All this is for the merely indispensable part of my living; and unless I make a hermit of myself and deprive my wife and children of all the pleasures and advantages of an English residence, I must inevitably exceed the sum named above.

. . . It would be the easiest thing in the world for me to run in debt, even taking my income at $15,-000 " (out of which all the clerks and certain other office expenses had to be paid), . . . " the largest sum that it ever reached in Crittenden's time. He had no family but a wife, and lived constantly at a boarding-house, and, nevertheless, went away (as he assured me) with an aggregate of only $25,000 derived from his savings.

" Now the American public can never be made to understand such a statement as the above; and they would grumble awfully if more than $6,000 per annum were allowed for a consul's salary." But Hawthorne concludes that it would not compensate him to retain the place with a salary even of $10,000; and that if the emoluments should be reduced from their then propor-tions, " the incumbent must be compelled to turn his official position to account by engaging in commerce — a course which ought not to be permitted, and which no Liverpool consul has ever adopted."

There are some references to President Pierce, in the Bridge correspondence, which possess exceptional interest; but I cite only one of them. The great honor of the immense publicity into which Pierce had come as the executive head of the nation, and the centre upon which many conflicting movements and machi-nations turned, created a danger of misunderstandings with some of his early and intimate friends. In dis-cussing one such case Hawthorne writes (May 1, 1854), with regard to maintaining a friendship for the Presi-dent : —

" You will say that it is easy for me to feel thus towards him, since he has done his very best on my behalf ; but the truth is (alas for poor human nature !)

I should probably have loved him better if I had never received any favor at his hands. But all this will come right again, after both he and I shall have returned into private life. It is some satisfaction, at any rate, that no one of his appointments was so favorably criticized as my own; and he should have my resignation by the very next mail, if it would really do him any good."

Mr. Pike, who still held a post in the Salem Custom House, had written to Hawthorne not long after his arrival in England, inquiring about the prospect of obtaining some employment in the consular service there; and Hawthorne replied, in a manner that leaves no doubt of his sagacity in perceiving the exact situation of affairs, with its bearings for both Pike and himself, nor of his determination neither to deceive himself nor to give his friend any but the real reasons why he discouraged the inquiry.

"LIVERPOOL, *September* 15, 1853.

DEAR PIKE, — I have been intending to write to you this some time, but wished to get some tolerably clear idea of the state of things here before communicating with you. I find that I have three persons in my office: the head-clerk, or vice-consul, at £200, the second clerk at £150, and the messenger, who does some writing, at £80. They are all honest and capable men, and do their duty to perfection. No American would take either of these places for twice the sums which they receive ; and no American, without some months' practice, would undertake the duty. Of the two I would rather displace the vice-consul than the second clerk, who does a great amount of labor, and has a remarkable variety of talent, — whereas the old gentleman, though perfect in his own track, is nothing

outside of it. I will not part with either of these men
unless compelled to do so ; and I don't think Secretary Marcy can compel me.

Now as to the Manchester branch, it brings me in
only about £200. There is a consular agent there,
all the business being transacted here in Liverpool.
The only reason for appointing an agent would be
that it might shut off all attempts to get a separate
consulate there. There is no danger, I presume, of
such an attempt for some time to come ; for Pierce
made a direct promise that the place should be kept
open for my benefit. Nevertheless efforts will be made
to fill it, and very possibly representations may be
made from the business men of Manchester that there
is necessity for a consul there. In a pecuniary point
of view, it would make very little difference to me
whether the place were filled by an independent consul or by a vice-consul of my own appointment, for the
latter would of course not be satisfied with less than
the whole £200. What I should like would be to
keep the place vacant and receive the proceeds as long
as possible, and at last, when I could do no better, to
give the office to you. No great generosity in that to
be sure. Thus I have put the matter fairly before
you. Do you tell me as frankly how your own affairs
stand, and whether you can live any longer in that
cursed old Custom House without hanging yourself.
Rather than that you should do so I would let you have
the place to-morrow, although it would pay you about
£100 less than your present office. I suppose as a
single man you might live within your income in Manchester ; but judging from my own experience as a
married man, it would be a very tight fit. With all
the economy I could use I have already got rid of $2,000

since landing in England. Hereafter I hope to spend less and save more.

In point of emolument, my office will turn out about what I expected. If I have ordinary luck I shall bag from $5,000 to $7,000 clear per annum: but to effect this I shall have to deny myself many things which I would gladly have. Colonel Crittenden told me that it cost him $4,000 to live with only his wife at a boarding-house, including a journey to London now and then. I am determined not to spend more than this, keeping house with my wife and children. I have hired a good house furnished at £160, on the other side of the River Mersey, at Rock Park, where there is good air and play-ground for the children; and I can come over to the city by steamboat every morning. I like the situation all the better because it will render it impossible for me to go to parties, or to give parties myself, and will keep me out of a good deal of nonsense.

Liverpool is the most detestable place as a residence that ever my lot was cast in, — smoky, noisy, dirty, pestilential; and the consulate is situated in the most detestable part of the city. The streets swarm with beggars by day and by night. You never saw the like; and I pray that you may never see it in America. It is worth while coming across the sea in order to feel one's heart warm towards his own country; and I feel it all the more because it is plain to be seen that a great many of the Englishmen whom I meet here dislike us, whatever they may pretend to the contrary.

My family and myself have suffered very much from the elements; there has not been what we should call a fair day since our arrival, nor a single day when a fire would not be agreeable. I long for one of our

sunny days, and one of our good hearty rains. It always threatens to rain, but seldom rains in good earnest. It never *does* rain, and it never *don't* rain; but
you are pretty sure to get a sprinkling if you go out
without an umbrella. Except by the fireside, I have
not once been as warm as I should like to be : but the
Englishmen call it a sultry day whenever the ther-
mometer rises above 60°. There has not been heat
enough in England this season to ripen an apple.

My wife and children often talk of you. Even the
baby has not forgotten you. Write often, and say as
much as you can about yourself, and as little as you
please about A——, N——, and B——, and all the
rest of those wretches of whom my soul was weary to
death before I made my escape.

Your friend ever,<br>NATH. HAWTHORNE.

Writing to Bridge again, November 28, 1854, he
continues, with regard to his consular prospects, by a
comparison between the pay received by English consuls and that allowed by the new bill to Americans.
Only $7,500 were to be paid the consul at Liverpool.
" Now I employ three clerks constantly," says Hawthorne " and sometimes more. The bill provides that
these clerks should be Americans; and the whole sum
allowed would not do much more than pay competent
Americans, whose salaries must be much higher than
would content Englishmen of equal qualifications.
No consul can keep the office at this rate, without engaging in business — which the bill forbids." He
adds that the notion that, by the proposed measure, a
fund would be gained from the larger consulates
towards paying the salaries of the smaller ones, was

mistaken, since " a large part of the income of this consulate arises from business which might just as well be transacted by a notary public as by a consul, and which a consul is therefore not officially bound to do. All such business as this the consul will cease to transact, the moment the avails of it go into the public treasury, instead of his own purse ; and thus there will be an immediate falling off of the office to a very considerable extent."

Later on, he says: " I should really be ashamed to tell you how much my income is taxed by the assistance which I find it absolutely necessary to render to American citizens, who come to me in difficulty or distress. Every day there is some new claimant, for whom the government makes no provision, and whom the consul must assist, if at all, out of his own pocket. It is impossible (or at any rate very disagreeable) to leave a countryman to starve in the streets, or to hand him over to the charities of an English work-house ; so I do my best for these poor devils. But I doubt whether they will meet with quite so good treatment after the passage of the consular bill. If the government chooses to starve the consul, a good many will starve with him."

The bill, nevertheless, was passed. Lieutenant Bridge, who was then stationed at Washington, had done all that he could to rouse an effectual opposition to its enactment; and his friend wrote to him from Liverpool (March 23, 1855) thus : —

" I thank you for your efforts against this bill ; but Providence is wiser than we are, and doubtless it will all turn out for the best. All through my life, I have had occasion to observe that what seemed to be misfortunes have proved, in the end, to be the best things that could possibly have happened to me; and so it will be with this — even though the mode in which it benefits me may never be made clear to my apprehension. It would seem to be a desirable thing enough that I should have had a sufficient income to live comfortably upon for the rest of my life, without the necessity of labor; but, on the other hand, I might have sunk prematurely into intellectual sluggishness — which now there will be no danger of my doing; though with a house and land of my own, and a good little sum at interest besides, I need not be under any very great anxiety about the future. When I contrast my present situation with what it was five years ago, I see a vast deal to be thankful for; and I still hope to thrive by my legitimate instrument — the pen. One consideration which goes very far towards reconciling me to quitting the office is my wife's health, with which the climate of England does not agree. . . . In short, we have wholly ceased to regret the action of Congress (which, nevertheless, was most unjust and absurd), and are looking at matters on the bright side. However, I shall be glad to get what advantage I can out of the office, and therefore I hope Pierce will give me as long a line as his conscience will let him."

Believing that the office of consul with a salary reduced to $7,500, which was only half the sum it had previously yielded in good years, would not be worth the sacrifice involved in giving himself up to its duties, he purposed resigning within a few months, taking a trip to Italy, and then going home. But, fortunately for his pecuniary welfare, the act of Congress had been so loosely framed (in harmony with the general ignorance on which it was based), that it was left to the President to reappoint old incumbents under the new system or not, as he pleased. Pierce accordingly let Hawthorne's commission run on without interruption, and the consul stayed through the rest of the administration's term.

While the matter was still in abeyance, however, the suggestion came from Bridge that he allow himself to be transferred to Lisbon as minister. The prospect was, in one way, seductive. Hawthorne was growing anxious about his wife's health, and felt that nothing could be more delightful than to take her to a warmer climate, which she needed, and thus avoid the temporary separation which might have to be undergone if he remained at Liverpool. The objections were, that he had no acquaintance with diplomacy, did not know Portuguese, and disliked forms and ceremonies. "You will observe," he wrote, " that the higher rank and position of a minister, as compared with a consul, have no weight with me. This is not the kind of honor of which I am ambitious." With a good deal of hesitation he came to the belief that it would be wise for him not to make the change. " But," he remarked, "it was a most kind and generous thing on the part of the President to entertain the idea." His friend, Mr. John O'Sullivan, who had been the founder and editor of the " Democratic Review," to which Hawthorne had contributed copiously during his residence at the Manse, was at this time accredited to the Court of Lisbon, and would doubtless have been provided for in some other way had Hawthorne been promoted to the place. The latter decided to stay at Liverpool, but to send Mrs. Hawthorne to Lisbon, where she would find not only milder air, but also friends in the minister and his wife. She sailed with her daughters in October, 1855, and returned in the following June.

Wearisome as the details of his office duty were to him, Hawthorne gave them more than a perfunctory attention. He became greatly aroused by the wrongs and cruelties endured by sailors on the high seas, and sent a long despatch on that subject to the Secretary of State, suggesting action for their relief. He even investigated such minutiæ as the candles used in the British navy, and sent samples of them to Bridge, thinking that it might be desirable to compare them with those in use on American war-ships. Opportunities, however, had occurred for several trips in various directions, to Wales, Furness Abbey, and the Lakes. London was visited just before Mrs. Hawthorne sailed; and during her absence he again went to the capital, and made a tour which included Glasgow, Edinburgh, York, Newcastle, and Salisbury. A few days before her expected return, he said in a letter to Bridge that unless she should prove to be perfectly free from the cough which had troubled her, "I shall make arrangements to give up the consulate in the latter part of autumn, and we will be off for Italy. I wish I were a little richer; but when I compare my situation with what it was before I wrote 'The Scarlet Letter,' I have reason to be satisfied with my run of luck. And, to say the truth, I had rather not be *too* prosperous: it may be a superstition, but it seems to me that the bitter is very apt to come with the sweet, and bright sunshine casts a dark shadow; so I content myself with a moderate portion of sugar, and about as much sunshine as that of an English summer's day. In this view of the matter, I am disposed to thank God for the gloom and chill of my early life, in the hope that my share of adversity came then, when I bore it alone; and that therefore it need not

come now, when the cloud would involve those whom
I love.

"I make my plans to return to America in about
two years from this time. For my own part, I should
be willing to stay abroad much longer, and perhaps
even to settle in Italy; but the children must not be
kept away so long as to lose their American characteristics; otherwise they will be exiles and outcasts
through life."

The presidential convention of the democratic party
was held early in the summer of 1856, and Buchanan,
the nminister at the Court of St. James, became the
candidate. Pierce had also been in the field, but was
defeated, and concerning this circumstance Hawthorne
wrote, characteristically : "I am sorry Frank has not
the nomination, if he wished it. Otherwise, I am glad
he is out of the scrape."

During the earlier part of his consulship, Hawthorne leased a pleasant dwelling at Rock Ferry, on
the opposite side of the Mersey from Liverpool, where
he was able to live without going much into society ;
and while Mrs. Hawthorne was in Portugal, he occupied simple quarters at a boarding-house. Afterwards
he settled at Southport for a number of months, in a
furnished house. He formed but one intimate friendship, that which attached him to Mr. Henry Bright, a
gentleman engaged in business, but gifted with a quick
and sympathetic mind and a taste for literature. In
London his chief friend was Mr. Francis Bennoch,
also a merchant, who consorted much with people of
creative genius, and delighted to gather them at his
table, where they were entertained with a cordial and
charming hospitality. Mr. Bright and Mr. Bennoch
have each published a book since then ; but although

Hawthorne met many persons eminent in literature, and enjoyed meeting them, it was not with any of their number that he formed the closest ties.

With relief he heard in April, 1857, that his resignation had been accepted. " Dear Bridge," he wrote, " I have received your letter, and the not unwelcome intelligence that there is another Liverpool consul now in existence. . . . I am going to Paris in a day or two, with my wife and children, and shall leave them there while I return here to await my successor." He then thanked Bridge for a newspaper paragraph which the latter had caused to be printed, explaining Hawthorne's position in resigning. " I was somewhat apprehensive that my resignation would have been misunderstood," he proceeded, " in consequence of a letter of General Cass to Lord Napier, in which he intimated that any consul found delinquent in certain matters should be compelled to retire. . . . But for your paragraph, I should have thought it necessary to enlighten the public on the true state of the case as regards the treatment of seamen on our merchant vessels, and I do not know but I may do it yet ; in which case I shall prove that General Cass made a most deplorable mistake in the above-mentioned letter to Lord Napier. I shall send the despatch to Ticknor, at any rate, for publication if necessary. I expect great pleasure during my stay on the Continent, and shall come home at last somewhat reluctantly. Your pledge on my behalf of a book shall be honored in good time, if God pleases."

The intention of taking his family at once to Paris was given up, and instead Hawthorne went with them to Manchester, the Lakes, and Scotland, and made a pilgrimage to Warwick and Coventry, besides visiting many other places. The new consul, however, postponed his coming until near the end of 1857. Not before January, 1858, did Hawthorne break away from the fascinations of England and cross to the Continent. When, after spending more than a year and a half in Italy, he again set foot in England, it was to establish himself at Redcar, a sea-side town in Yorkshire, where he finished " The Marble Faun " in October, 1859; and thence he betook himself to Leamington, which had greatly pleased him on a previous visit. Here his old friend, Mr. Hillard, called upon him ; and in an article printed in the "Atlantic Monthly," in 1870, he says : " The writer of this notice, who confesses to an insatiable passion for the possession of books, and an omnivorous appetite for their contents, was invited by him into his study, the invitation being accompanied with one of his peculiar and indescribable smiles, in which there lurked a consciousness of his (the writer's) weakness. The study was a small square room, with a table and chair, but absolutely not a single book. He liked writing better than reading." Mr. Hillard's implication, however, is a misleading one. " Hawthorne," says Mr. Fields, " was a hearty devourer of books, and in certain moods of mind it made very little difference what the volume before him happened to be. . . . He once told me that he found such delight in old advertisements in the newspaper files at the Boston Athenæum, that he had passed delicious hours among them. At other times he was very fastidious, and threw aside book after book, until he found the right one. De Quincey was a favorite with him, and the sermons of Laurence Sterne he once commended to me as the best sermons ever written." His correspondence was not " literary," to be sure ; but in his letters to Mr. Fields, who had to do so especially with books, occasional references to literature escape him, which did not ordinarily find their way into his letters to other people. From England, in 1854, he wrote to that gentleman : " I thank you for the books you sent me, and more especially for Mrs. Mowatt's 'Autobiography,' which seems to me an admirable book. Of all things I delight in autobiographies ; and I hardly ever read one that interested me so much." He did not read for erudition or for criticism, but he certainly read much, and books were companions to him. I have seen several catalogues of libraries which Hawthorne had marked carefully, proving that, although he made no annotations, he had studied the titles with a natural reader's loving fondness. His stay at Leamington was but a brief one, and for that reason he may well have been without books in his study at the moment; he never crowded them about himself, in the rooms where he worked, but his tower-study at The Wayside always contained a few volumes, and a few small pictures and ornaments — enough to relieve his eye or suggest a refreshment to his mind, without distracting him from composition or weakening the absorbed intensity of his thought.

The only approach to literary exertion made at Liverpool seems to have been the revision of the " Mosses from an Old Manse," for a reissue at the hands of Ticknor & Fields ; employment which led to some reflections upon his own earlier works.

"I am very glad that the 'Mosses' have come into the hands of our firm; and I return the copy sent me, after a careful revision. When I wrote those dreamy sketches, I little thought I should ever preface an edition for the press amid the bustling life of a Liverpool consulate. Upon my honor, I am not quite sure that I entirely comprehend my own meaning, in some of those blasted allegories; but I remember that I always had a meaning, or at least thought I had. I am a good deal changed since those times; and, to tell you the truth, my past self is not very much to my taste, as I see myself in this book. Yet certainly there is more in it than the public generally gave me credit for at the time it was written.

"But I don't think myself worthy of very much more credit than I got. It has been a very disagreeable task to read the book."

He was inveigled, however, into giving encouragement to that unfortunate woman, Miss Delia Bacon, who was engaged in the task of proving that Lord Bacon wrote Shakespeare's plays. He corresponded with her on the subject, and finally agreed, although not assenting to her theory, to write a preface for her book, which he did. She was dissatisfied because he did not accept her views entirely, grew very angry, and even broke off all relations with him, notwithstanding that he had paid the expenses of publication for her.

Arriving at Rome in February, 1858, Hawthorne lingered there until late in May, when he retired to Florence, and hired there the Villa Montauto, in the suburb of Bellosguardo. October found him again in Rome, where he spent the winter; leaving the Continent, finally, in June, 1859, for England and Redcar.

"I am afraid I have stayed away too long," he wrote from Bellosguardo, to Mr. Fields, in September, 1858, "and am forgotten by everybody. You have piled up the dusty remnants of my editions, I suppose, in that chamber over the shop, where you once took me to smoke a cigar, and have crossed my name out of your list of authors, without so much as asking whether I am dead or alive. But I like it well enough, nevertheless. It is pleasant to feel that at last I am away from America, — a satisfaction that I never enjoyed as long as I stayed in Liverpool, where it seemed to me that the quintessence of nasal and hand-shaking Yankeedom was continually filtered and sublimated through my consulate, on the way outward and homeward. I first got acquainted with my own countrymen there. At Rome, too, it was not much better. But here in Florence, and in the summer-time, and in this secluded villa, I have escaped from all my old tracks and am really remote.

"I like my present residence immensely. The house stands on a hill, overlooking Florence, and is big enough to quarter a regiment; insomuch that each member of the family, including servants, has a separate suite of apartments, and there are vast wildernesses of upper rooms, into which we have never yet sent exploring expeditions.

"At one end of the house there is a moss-grown tower haunted by the ghost of a monk, who was confined there in the thirteenth century, previous to being burned at the stake in the principal square of Florence. I hire this villa, tower and all, at twenty-eight dollars a month; but I mean to take it away bodily and clap it into a romance which I have in my head ready to be written out." Turning to the topic of home, he went on : " After so long an absence (more than five years already, which will be six before you see me at the Old Corner), it is not altogether delightful to think of returning. Everybody will be changed, and I, myself, no doubt, as much as anybody. . . . It won't do. I shall be forced to come back again and take refuge in a London lodging. London is like the grave in one respect, — any man can make himself at home there; and whenever a man finds himself homeless elsewhere, he had better either die or go to London.

"Speaking of the grave reminds me of old age and other disagreeable matters, and I would remark that one grows old in Italy twice or three times as fast as in other countries. I have three gray hairs now for one that I brought from England, and I shall look venerable indeed by the time I return next summer."

The "French and Italian Note-Books" are more prolific in literary hints than the English. At Rome and Florence the practical self, which was necessarily brought forward in the daily round at the consulate and left its impress on the letters to Lieutenant Bridge, retired into the background under the influence of scenes more purely picturesque and poetic than those of England; and the idealizing, imaginative faculty of Hawthorne, being freed from the restraint which had so long cramped it, gained in elasticity from day to day. Four years of confinement to business, broken only at intervals by short episodes of travel, had done no more than impede the current of fancy; had not dried it, nor choked the source. Mr. Fields assures us that, in England, Hawthorne told him he had no less than five romances in his mind, so well planned that he could write any one of them at short notice. But it is significant that, however favorable Italy might be for drawing out and giving free course to this current, he could do little there in the way of embodying his conceptions. He wrote out an extensive first draft of "The Marble Faun" while moving from place to place on the actual ground where the story is laid; but the work itself was written at Redcar, and in the communication last quoted from he had said: " I find this Italian atmosphere not favorable to the close toil of composition, although it is a very good air to dream in. I must breathe the fogs of old England, or the east-winds of Massachusetts, in order to put me into working-trim." Conditions other than physical were most probably responsible, in part, for this state of things. Strong as Hawthorne's nature was on the side of the real, the ideal force within him was so much more puissant, that when circumstances were all propitious — as they were in Italy — it obtained too commanding a sway over him. His dreams, in such case, would be apt to overcome him, to exist simply for their own sake instead of being subordinated to his will; and, in fine, to expend their witchery upon the air, instead of being imprisoned in the enduring form of a book. Being compounded in such singular wise of opposing qualities : the customary, prudential, common sensible ones, and the wise and visionary ones — the outward reticence, and (if we may say so) the inward eloquence — of which we now have a clearer view ; being so compounded, he positively needed something stern and adverse in his surroundings, it should seem, both as a satisfaction to the sturdier part of him, and as a healthful check which, by exciting reaction, would stimulate his imaginative mood. He must have precisely the right proportion between these counter influences, or else creation could not proceed. In the Salem Custom House and at the Liverpool consulate there had been too much of the hard commonplace : instead of serving as a convenient foil to the more expansive and lightsome tendencies of his genius, it had weighed them down. But in Italy there was too much freedom, not enough framework of the severe, the

roughly real and unpicturesque. Hawthorne's intellectual and poetic nature presents a spectacle somewhat like that of a granite rock upon which delicate
vines flourish at their best; but he was himself both
rock and vine. The delicate, aspiring tendrils and
the rich leafage of the plant, however, required a particular combination of soil and climate, in order to
grow well. When he was not hemmed in by the round
of official details, England afforded him that combination in bounteous measure.

On the publication of "The Marble Faun," the
author's friend, John Lothrop Motley, with whom he
had talked, of the contemplated romance, in Rome,
wrote to him from Walton-on-Thames (March 29,
1860) : —

"Everything that you have ever written, I believe,
I have read many times, and I am particularly vain
of having admired 'Sights from a Steeple,' when I
first read it in the Boston ' Token,' several hundred
years ago, when we were both younger than we are
now ; of having detected and cherished, at a later day,
an old Apple-Dealer, whom I believe you have un-
handsomely thrust out of your presence now that you
are grown so great. But the ' Romance of Monte
Beni ' has the additional charm for me, that it is the
first book of yours that I have read since I had the
privilege of making your personal acquaintance. My
memory goes back at once to those walks (alas, not
too frequent) we used to take along the Tiber, or in
the Campagna . . . and it is delightful to get hold of
the book now, and know that it is impossible for you
any longer, after waving your wand as you occasionally did then, indicating where the treasure was hidden, to sink it again beyond plummet's sound.

"I admire the book exceedingly . . . It is one which, for the first reading at least, I did n't like to hear aloud. . . . If I were composing an article for a review, of course I should feel obliged to show cause for my admiration; but I am only obeying an impulse. Permit me to say, however, that your style seems, if possible, more perfect than ever. . . . Believe me, I don't say to you half what I say behind your back; and I have said a dozen times that nobody can write English but you. With regard to the story, which has been somewhat criticized, I can only say that to me it is quite satisfactory. I like those shadowy, weird, fantastic, Hawthornesque shapes flitting through the golden gloom, which is the atmosphere of the book. I like the misty way in which the story is indicated rather than revealed; the outlines are quite definite enough from the beginning to the end, to those who have imagination enough to follow you in your airy flights. . . . The way in which the two victims dance through the Carnival on the last day is very striking. It is like a Greek tragedy in its effect, without being in the least Greek."

In this last sentence Mr. Motley struck out an apt distinction; for it is perhaps the foremost characteristic of Hawthorne as a writer that his fictions possessed a plastic repose, a perfection of form, which made them akin to classic models, at the same time that the spirit was throughout eminently that belonging to the mystic, capricious, irregular fantasy of the North.

Hawthorne thus made answer from Bath (April 1, 1860) : —

MY DEAR MOTLEY, — You are certainly that Gentle Reader for whom all my books were exclusively written. Nobody else (my wife excepted, who speaks so near me that I cannot tell her voice from my own) has ever said exactly what I love to hear. It is most satisfactory to be hit upon the raw, to be shot straight through the heart. It is not the quantity of your praise that I care so much about (though I gather it all up carefully, lavish as you are of it), but the kind, for you take the book precisely as I meant it; and if your note had come a few days sooner, I believe I would have printed it in a postscript which I have added to the second edition, because it explains better than I found possible to do the way in which my romance ought to be taken. . . . Now don't suppose that I fancy the book to be a tenth part as good as you say it is. You work out my imperfect efforts, and half make the book with your warm imagination, and see what I myself saw but could only hint at. Well, the romance is a success, even if it never finds another reader.

We spent the winter in Leamington, whither we had come from the sea-coast in October. I am sorry to say that it was another winter of sorrow and anxiety. . . . I have engaged our passages for June 16th. . . . Mrs. Hawthorne and the children will probably remain in Bath till the eve of our departure; but I intend to pay one more visit of a week or two to London, and shall certainly come and see you. I wonder at your lack of recognition of my social propensities. I take so much delight in my friends, that a little intercourse goes a great way, and illuminates my life before and after. . . .              Your friend,

NATHANIEL HAWTHORNE.

One may well linger here, for an instant, over the calm, confident, but deeply vibrating happiness from which those words sprang, concerning his wife, " who speaks so near me that I cannot tell her voice from my own ; " and one may profitably lay away, for instruction, the closing lines, — " I take so much delight in my friends, that a little intercourse goes a great way." The allusion to " another winter of sorrow and anxiety " carries us back to the previous winter, passed in Rome, during which Hawthorne's elder daughter underwent a prolonged attack of Roman fever. Illness again developed itself in his family while they were staying at Leamington.

In February of 1860 he wrote to Mr. Fields, who was then in Italy : —

" I thank you most heartily for your kind wishes in favor of the forthcoming work ['The Marble Faun'], and sincerely join my own prayers to yours in its behalf, without much confidence of a good result. My own opinion is, that I am not really a popular writer, and that what popularity I have gained is chiefly accidental, and owing to other causes than my own kind or degree of merit. Possibly I may (or may not) deserve something better than popularity ; but looking at all my productions, and especially this latter one, with a cold or critical eye, I can see that they do not make their appeal to the popular mind. It is odd enough, moreover, that my own individual taste is for quite another class of works than those which I myself am able to write. If I were to meet with such books as mine by another writer, I don't believe I should be able to get through them." At another time he had written of Anthony Trollope's novels : " They precisely suit my taste ; solid and substantial,

written on the strength of beef and through the inspiration of ale, and just as real as if some giant had
hewn a great lump out of the earth and put it under
a glass case, with all its inhabitants going about their
daily business and not suspecting that they were made
a show of."

Before leaving England for the last time, Hawthorne
went up alone to London, and spent a week or two
among his friends there, staying with Motley, and
meeting Lord Dufferin, the Honorable Mrs. Norton,
Leigh Hunt, Barry Cornwall, and many other agreeable and noted persons. "You would be stricken
dumb," he wrote to his wife, who remained at Bath,
" to see how quietly I accept a whole string of invitations, and, what is more, perform my engagements
without a murmur. . . . The stir of this London life,
somehow or other, has done me a wonderful deal of
good, and I feel better than for months past. This is
strange, for if I had my choice, I should leave undone
almost all the things I do." In the midst of these
social occupations he gave sittings to a young German-
American sculptor named Kuntze, who modelled a profile portrait of him in bas-relief. A farewell dinner
was given him at Barry Cornwall's ; and in June,
1860, he sailed for America, from which he had been
absent seven years.

There was not yet any serious sign of a failure in
his health ; but the illness in his family, lasting
through two winters, had worn severely upon him ; his
spirits had begun to droop. "I would gladly journal-
ize some of my proceedings, and describe things and
people ; but I find the same coldness and stiffness in
my pen as always since our return to England : " thus
he had written in his Note-Book, while making that

final London visit. In Italy, however, he had already shown symptoms of fatigue, saying to Mr. Fields: "I have had so many interruptions from things to see and things to suffer, that the story ['The Marble Faun'] has developed itself in a very imperfect way. . . . I could finish it in the time that I am to remain here, but my brain is tired of it just now." The voyage put fresh vigor into him, apparently. Mrs. Harriet Beecher Stowe and Professor Stowe were on board, with their daughters, and Mr. Fields, who was also a passenger, has said: "Hawthorne's love for the sea amounted to a passionate worship, and while I (the worst sailor probably on this planet) was longing, spite of the good company on board, to reach land as soon as possible, Hawthorne was constantly saying in his quiet, earnest way, 'I should like to sail on and on forever, and never touch the shore again.'" His inherited susceptibility to the fascination of the sea no doubt intensified his enjoyment, and he is reported to have talked in a strain of delightful humor while on shipboard.

For nearly a year after his return to The Wayside, there is an uneventful gap in his history, concerning which we have very few details. He set about improving his house, and added to it a wing at the back, which, having three stories, rose above the rest of the building, and thus supplied him with a study in the top room, which had the effect of a tower. Meanwhile the political quarrel between the North and the South was rapidly culminating; in a few months the Slave States began their secession, and the Civil War broke out. This affected Hawthorne so deeply that for some time he was unable to engage in imaginative work, and he now relinquished the custom he had maintained for so many years, of keeping a journal. But there are letters which define his state of mind, which make his position clear with regard to the question of the Union, and show the change in his feeling brought on by the course of events.

Several years before, while he was still consul, he thus confided to Bridge (January 9, 1857) his general opinion respecting the crisis which even then impended : —

" I regret that you think so doubtfully of the prospects of the Union ; for I should like well enough to hold on to the old thing. And yet I must confess that I sympathize to a large extent with the Northern feeling, and think it is about time for us to make a stand. If compelled to choose, I go for the North. At present, we have no country — at least, none in the sense in which an Englishman has a country. I never conceived, in reality, what a true and warm love of country is, till I witnessed it in the breasts of Englishmen. The States are too various and too extended to form really one country. New England is quite as large a lump of earth as my heart can really take in. . . . However, I have no kindred with nor leaning toward the Abolitionists."

When hostilities had begun, he wrote to the same friend, May 26, 1861 : —

" The war, strange to say, has had a beneficial effect upon my spirits, which were flagging woefully before it broke out. But it was delightful to share in the heroic sentiment of the time, and to feel that I had a country, a consciousness which seemed to make me young again. One thing as regards this matter I regret, and one thing I am glad of. The regrettable thing is that I am too old to shoulder a musket my-

self, and the joyful thing is that Julian is too young.
He drills constantly with a company of lads, and
means to enlist as soon as he reaches the minimum
age. But I trust we shall either be victorious or van-
quished by that time. Meantime, though I approve
the war as much as any man, I don't quite see what
we are fighting for or what definite result can be expected. If we pommel the South ever so hard, they
will love us none the better for it; and even if we
subjugate them, our next step should be to cut them
adrift, if we are fighting for the annihilation of slavery. To be sure, it may be a wise object, and offers
a tangible result and the only one which is consistent
with a future union between North and South. A
continuance of the war would soon make this plain
to us, and we should see the expediency of preparing
our black brethren for future citizenship, by allowing
them to fight for their own liberties and educating
them through heroic influences. Whatever happens
next, I must say that I rejoice that the old Union is
smashed. We never were one people, and never really
had a country since the Constitution was formed."

Thus, then, Hawthorne, who had been brought up
politically within the democratic party and thrice
held office under its *régime*, had reached the conclusion, four years in advance of the event, that it was
time for the North to "make a stand"; and now,
while muskets rattled their grim prelude to a long
and deadly conflict, he planted himself firmly on the
side of the government — was among the first, moreover, to resolve upon that policy of arming the negroes, which was so bitterly opposed and so slow of
adoption among even progressive reformers at the
North. In his solitude, out of the current of affairs,

trying to pursue his own peaceful, artistic calling, and little used to making utterances on public questions, it was not incumbent upon him nor proper to his character to blazon his beliefs where every one could see them. But, these private expressions being unknown, his silence was construed against him. One more reference to the war, occurring in a letter of October 12, 1861, to Lieutenant Bridge, should be recorded in this place : —

"I am glad you take such a hopeful view of our national prospects, so far as regards the war. . . . For my part, I don't hope (nor indeed wish) to see the Union restored as it was; amputation seems to me much the better plan, and all we ought to fight for is the liberty of selecting the point where our diseased members shall be lopped off. I would fight to the death for the Northern Slave-States, and let the rest go. . . . I have not found it possible to occupy my mind with its usual trash and nonsense during these anxious times ; but as the autumn advances, I find myself sitting down to my desk and blotting successive sheets of paper, as of yore. Very likely I may have something ready for the public long before the public is ready to receive it."

It will be seen that he was not hopeful as to the restoration of the entire Union, adhered to his first view indeed, that the scission of a part would be preferable. In declining a cordial invitation from Bridge to come to Washington, in February, 1862, he gave renewed emphasis to this opinion. "I am not very well," he said, "being mentally and physically languid ; but I suppose there is an even chance that the trip and change of scene might supply the energy which I lack." He announced that he had begun a new romance, and then turning to the questions of the day, remarked that he "should not much regret an ultimate separation," and that soon; adding that if a strong Union sentiment should not set in at the South, we ought to resolve ourselves into two nations at once. He was evidently growing despondent; a fact which may have been due in part to the physical and mental languor of which he told his friend. Misfortune had once more entered his household ; for one of his children was suffering from a peculiarly distressing malady, which imposed a heavy strain upon his nerves and troubled his heart. More than this, he mourned over the multitude of private griefs which he saw or apprehended on every side — griefs resulting from the slaughter that was going on at the seat of war — as acutely as if they had been his own losses. He could not shut out, by any wall of patriotic fire, the terrible shapes of fierce passion and the pathetic apparitions of those whose lives had been blasted by the tragedies of the field. His health, we have already noticed, had begun to falter while he was still abroad. Neither was he free from pecuniary anxieties. He had laid up a modest accumulation from his earnings in the consulate ; but the additions to his house, unambitious though they were, had cost a sum which was large in proportion to his resources ; the expense of living was increased by the war, and his pen was for the time being not productive. His income from his books was always scanty. He was too scrupulous to be willing to draw upon the principal which had been invested for the future support of his family; and there were times when he was harassed by the need of money. All these causes conspired to reduce his strength ; but the omnipresent misery of the war, and the destruction of the Union, which he believed to be inevitable, were perhaps the chief adverse factors in the case. " Hawthorne's life," Mr. Lowell has said to me, " was shortened by the war."

The romance mentioned as having been begun during this winter of 1861–62, was probably " Dr. Grimshawe's Secret," the first scheme of which appears as " The Ancestral Footstep ; " and it was afterwards merged in "Septimius Felton." Hawthorne, however, did not make satisfactory progress with this work; and throughout the summer of 1862 he seems to have given such energies as he could command to the preparation of the chapters of travel subsequently collected under the title, " Our Old Home." The latter volume appeared at a time of fervid, nay, violent public excitement, caused by the critical state of military matters, the unpopularity of the draft, the increasing boldness of the democratic party at the North in opposing the war and demanding its cessation. To Hawthorne it appeared no more than just that he should dedicate his book to the friend whose public act, in sending him abroad in the government service, had made it possible for him to gather the materials he had embodied in these reminiscences. But his publisher, Mr. Fields, knowing that ex-President Pierce was very generally held to be culpable for his deference towards Southern leaders who had done much to bring on the war, and that he was ranked among the men who were ready to vote against continuing the attempt to conquer the Confederacy, foresaw the clamor which would be raised against Hawthorne if, at such a moment, he linked his name publicly with that of Pierce. He remonstrated upon the proposed dedication. But Hawthorne was not to be turned aside from his purpose by any dread of an outcry which he considered unjust. " I find," he replied, " that it would be a piece of poltroonery in me to withdraw either the dedication or the dedicatory letter, . . . and if he [Pierce] is so exceedingly unpopular that his name is enough to sink the volume, there is so much the more need that an old friend should stand by him. I cannot, merely on account of pecuniary profit or literary reputation, go back from what I have deliberately felt and thought it right to do; and if I were to tear out the dedication, I should never look at the volume again without remorse and shame. . . . If the public of the North see fit to ostracize me for this, I can only say that I would gladly sacrifice a thousand or two of dollars rather than retain the good-will of such a herd of dolts and mean-spirited scoundrels." The language did not lack vigor and warmth; but Dr. Loring has stated that he spoke of the matter to the same effect, " not in the heat of passion, but with a calm and generous courage." The dedicatory letter was printed, of course, and drew down upon Hawthorne abundant condemnation; but he had maintained his integrity.

The shock of such an accident was by no means the right sort of tonic for a man of Hawthorne's sensitive disposition when he was already feeble and almost ill. In April, 1862, he had been to Washington, and the things that impressed him there were noted down in an " Atlantic Monthly " paper, entitled " Chiefly About War Matters." At Washington, also, Leutze painted a portrait of him for General Pierce. In July, he took a brief trip with his son to the Maine coast, and began a new journal. There were no other changes of scene for him ; the monotony of his life at The Wayside was seldom broken. That this period was for him one of unmitigated gloom cannot truthfully be predicated; he enjoyed his home, he had the society of his wife and children; he had many small and quiet pleasures. But there was likewise much to make him sorrowful, and the tide of vitality was steadily ebbing away. In May, 1863, James Russell Lowell invited him to Elmwood, and Hawthorne agreed to go, but he was finally prevented from doing so by a troublesome cold. The slow and mysterious disease, which was to prove fatal within a year, continued to make inroads upon his constitution. After the publication of "Our Old Home," in the autumn of 1863, there is no certain record of his condition or his proceedings, beyond this, that he went on declining, and that — having abandoned the two preceding phases of his new fiction — he attempted to write the resultant form of it, which was to have been brought out as " The Dolliver Romance."

Although the title had not yet been determined upon, he consented to begin a serial publication of the work in the " Atlantic Monthly " for January, 1864. But he wrote to Mr. Fields : " I don't see much probability of my having the first chapter of the Romance ready so soon as you want it. There are two or three chapters ready to be written, but I am not yet robust enough to begin, and I feel as if I should never carry it through. . . . I can think of no title for the unborn Romance. Always heretofore I have waited till it was quite complete, before attempting to name it, and I fear I shall have to do so now." On the 1st of December, he dispatched the manuscript of the first chapter, with the title of the whole. But he could not follow it up with more, and wrote, about the middle of January, 1864 : " I am not quite up to writing yet, but shall make an effort as soon as I see any hope of success." At the end of February: "I hardly know what to say to the public about this abortive Romance, though I know pretty well what the case will be. I shall never finish it. . . , I cannot finish it unless a great change comes over me ; and if I make too great an effort to do so, it will be my death." From this time on he accomplished no work which he was willing to send to the press, although he had among his papers the two fragmentary scenes from " The Dolliver Romance " that were posthumously printed.

The wife of ex-President Pierce died in December, 1863, and Hawthorne went to New Hampshire to attend the funeral. When he passed through Boston, on his return, he appeared to Mr. Fields ill and more nervous than usual. Dreary events seemed to thicken around his path. In the last days of March, 1864, Mr. Fields saw him again ; and by this time his appearance had greatly changed. "The light in his eye was as beautiful as ever, but his limbs were shrunken, and his usual stalwart vigor [was] utterly gone." A photograph taken not long before that date represents him with cheeks somewhat emaciated, and a worn, strangely anxious, half - appealing expression, which, while singularly delicate and noble, is extremely sad. Soon after this, in March, he set out for Washington with Mr. William Ticknor, Mr. Fields's senior partner in the publishing firm of Ticknor & Fields. The travelling companions spent two or three days in New York, and had got as far as Philadelphia, when Mr. Ticknor was taken suddenly ill, at the Continental Hotel, and died the next day. Stunned, wellnigh shattered by this sinister event, Hawthorne was almost incapacitated for action of any sort ; but there were kind and ready friends in Philadelphia who came

to his aid, and relieved him from the melancholy duty
which he would else have had to meet.   He returned
to Concord, in what forlorn state an extract from a
letter of Mrs. Hawthorne's may best convey : " He
came back unlooked for, that day ; and when I heard
a step on the piazza, I was lying on a couch and feeling quite indisposed.   But as soon as I saw him I
was frightened out of all knowledge of myself, — so
haggard, so white, so deeply scored with pain and fatigue was the face, so much more ill than ever I saw
him before."   Mrs. Hawthorne still hoped for some
favorable turn, if he could but obtain a complete
change of scene and escape from the austere New
England spring, into some warmer climate.   "He has
not smiled since he came home till to-day," she wrote,
" when I made him laugh, with Thackeray's humor,
in reading to him."   She was constant in her care ;
she would scarcely let him go up and down stairs
alone.   But not the most tender solicitude, nor any
encouragement of unquenchable hope, could now avail
to help him.

The only stratagem that could be devised to win
back health and strength was the plan proposed by
General Pierce, to take Hawthorne with him on an
easy journey by carriage into New Hampshire.   They
started in May, — the two old college-mates ; the ex-
President so lately widowed and still in the shadow
of his own bereavement, with the famous romancer
so mournfully broken, who was never more to be seen
in life by those to whom he was dearest.   From the
Pemigewasset House at Plymouth, New Hampshire,
where they had stopped for the night, General Pierce
sent the news on May 19, that Hawthorne was dead.
"He retired last night," wrote the General, "soon

after nine o'clock, and soon fell into a quiet slumber.
. . . At two o'clock I went to H——'s bedside; he
was apparently in a sound sleep; and I did not place
my hand upon him. At four o'clock I went into his
room again, and, as his position was unchanged, I
placed my hand upon him and found that life was
extinct. . . . He must have passed from natural slumber to that from which there is no waking, without the
slightest movement."

Hawthorne was buried in Sleepy Hollow Cemetery
at Concord, on the 24th of May, 1864. The grave was
made beneath the shadowing pines of a hill near one
of the borders of the beautiful, wooded burial-ground,
whence there is a peaceful view over the valley of the
Concord River. It was close to the slope where Thoreau now lies, and not far away is the grassy resting-place of Emerson. The spot was one for which Hawthorne had cherished an especial fondness. Emerson,
that day, stood beside the grave, and with him Longfellow and Lowell were present; Agassiz, Holmes,
James Freeman Clarke, Edwin Whipple, Pierce, and
Hillard, had all assembled to pay their last reverence.
A great multitude of people attended the funeral service at the old Unitarian First Church in the village,
and Mr. Clarke, who had performed the marriage ceremony for Hawthorne, conducted the rites above him
dead. It was a perfect day of spring; the roadside
banks were blue with violets, the orchards were in
bloom; and lilies of the valley, which were Hawthorne's
favorites among flowers, had blossomed early as if for
him, and were gathered in masses about him. Like a
requiem chant, the clear strains that Longfellow wrote
in memory of that hour still echo for us its tender solemnity:—

" How beautiful it was, that one bright day
　　In the long week of rain !
Though all its splendor could not chase away
　　The omnipresent pain.

" The lovely town was white with apple-blooms,
　　And the great elms o'erhead
Dark shadows wove on their aerial looms,
　　Shot through with golden thread.

" Across the meadows, by the gray old manse,
　　The historic river flowed ;
I was as one who wanders in a trance,
　　Unconscious of his road.

" The faces of familiar friends seemed strange ;
　　Their voices I could hear,
And yet the words they uttered seemed to change
　　Their meaning to the ear.

" For the one face I looked for was not there,
　　The one low voice was mute ;
Only an unseen presence filled the air,
　　And baffled my pursuit.

" Now I look back, and meadow, manse, and stream
　　Dimly my thought defines;
I only see — a dream within a dream —
　　The hill-top hearsed with pines.

" I only hear above his place of rest
　　Their tender undertone,
The infinite longings of a troubled breast,
　　The voice so like his own.

" There in seclusion and remote from men
　　The wizard hand lies cold,
Which at its topmost speed let fall the pen,
　　And left the tale half told.

"Ah, who shall lift that wand of magic power,
  And the lost clue regain?
The unfinished window in Aladdin's tower
  Unfinished must remain!"


## V.

This narrative of his career, in one sense so simple, so uneventful, has brought chiefly to the front, as we have followed it, a phase under which Hawthorne appears the most like other men; with motives easily understood, wishing to take his full share in human existence and its responsibilities; devoted in his domestic relations. Moderately ambitious of worldly welfare, but in poverty uncomplaining, he is so coolly practical in his view that he scarcely alludes to the products of his genius except as they may bear upon his material progress. Even this much of the character is uncommon, because of its sterling tone, the large, sustained manliness, and the success with which in the main it keeps itself firmly balanced; but it is a character not difficult to grasp, and one that appeals to every observer. It leaves out a great deal, however. The artist is absent from it. Neither is that essential mystery of organization included which held these elements together, united them with something of import far different, and converted the whole nature into a most extraordinary one, lifting it to a plane high above that on which it might, at first, seem to rest.

We know, from brief allusions in his "Note-Books," that Hawthorne was perfectly well aware of his high quality as an artist. He speaks of having won fame in his dismal room in Herbert Street; and at Arezzo, in 1858, the well "opposite Petrarch's birth-house"

which Boccaccio introduced into one of his stories, recalls to the American writer one of his own performances. "As I lingered round it I thought of my own
town-pump in old Salem, and wondered whether my
towns-people would ever point it out to strangers, and
whether the stranger would gaze at it with any degree
of such interest as I felt in Boccaccio's well. Oh,
certainly not; but I made that humble town-pump
the most celebrated structure in the good town. A
thousand and a thousand people had pumped there,
merely to water oxen or fill their tea-kettles; but
when once I grasped the handle, a rill gushed forth
that meandered as far as England, as far as India,
besides tasting pleasantly in every town and village
of our own country. I like to think of this, so long
after I did it, and so far from home, and am not
without hopes of some kindly local remembrance on
this score." [1] Such indications of the artistic consciousness are the merest ripples on the surface; the
deeper substance of it, with Hawthorne, always re-

---

[1] *French and Italian Note-Books*, May 30, 1858. A contributor to
*Appletons' Journal*, writing in 1875, describes a surviving specimen of
the old contrivances which then gave Salem its water-supply. "The
presumption is that a description of this particular one answers for
Hawthorne's pump, seeing that they were all alike. It is large
enough for a mausoleum and looks not unlike one, made of slabs of
dingy stone, like stained, gray gravestones set up on one end, in a
square at the foundation, but all inclining inward at the top, where
they are kept in position by a band of iron. A decaying segment of
log appears, in which the pump-handle works — in vain, now, however, since, being long out of use, it has no connection with the water
below; on the front side are two circular holes, like a pair of great
eyes, made for the insertion of the spouts; and, finally, a long-handled
iron dish, like a saucepan or warming-pan on a smaller scale, is attached
by an iron chain to the stone, by way of drinking-vessel. Altogether,
though it may not strike an old Salem resident in that way, it seems
to the stranger a very unique, antiquated, and remarkable structure."

mained out of sight. Letters, which are assumed to reveal so much of those who indite them, are, when we come to the fact, very insufficient exponents of character ; as, for instance, we may observe in the letters of Michael Angelo, whose mood and manner vary according to the person addressed. Correspondence, it is true, is appetizing to readers, and should be prized for the help it gives in defining an individual, but it does not always do full justice to the larger being included in the whole personality. Hawthorne's letters are more representative of those faculties by which he came into association with his fellows, than of those which tended to separate him from them by making him single and phenomenal, in his function as writer of romance. But in his actual presence there was a something which did most noticeably correspond to the hidden sources of his power, and visibly express them. There was the hale and vigorous port of a man well fitted by his physical constitution to meet the rudest emergency ; but there was also a temperament of which the reserve, the delicacy, the tremulous sensitiveness were equal to those of the most finely organized woman. " He was tall and strongly built," wrote his friend Hillard, " with broad shoulders, deep chest, a massive head. . . . He looked like a man who might have held the stroke oar in a University boat. . . . But, on the other hand, no man had more of the feminine element than he. He was feminine in his quick perceptions, his fine insight, his sensibility to beauty. . . . No man comprehended woman better than he. And his face was as mobile and rapid in its changes of expression as that of a young girl. . . . His eyes would darken visibly under the touch of a passing emotion, like the waters of a fountain ruffled by the breeze of summer.    So, too, he was the shyest of men." [1]

The same writer adds: "There was nothing morbid in his character or temperament. He was, indeed, much the reverse of morbid. No man of genius ever had less the infirmities of genius than he . . . Hawthorne was physically one of the healthiest of men. His pulse always kept even music. He cared nothing for wine or tobacco, or strong coffee or strong tea. He was a sound sleeper and an early riser. He was never moody or fitful or irritable. He was never unduly depressed or unreasonably elated. His spirits were not brilliant, but they were uniform, and, as Mrs. Hawthorne says, 'The airy splendor of his wit and humor was the light of his own home.'"

Dr. Loring has supplied another sketch of his appearance in general intercourse, which does a great deal to fill out our conception: —

"He knew no such thing as fear; was scrupulously honest; was unwavering in his fidelity; conscientious in the discharge of his duty. There may have been men of more latent power, but I have known no man more impressive, none in whom the great reposing strength seemed clad in such a robe of sweetness as he wore. I saw him on the day General Pierce was elected to the presidency. It was a bright and delicious day in late autumn. He was standing under the little shaded and embowered piazza of 'The Wayside,' at Concord, in the full vigor of his manhood, radiant with joy at the good fortune of his friend, and with that sad, shy smile playing over his face, which was so touching and charming. I have seen him fishing from the rocks of the Essex County shore at

[1] *Atlantic Monthly*, September, 1870, vol. 26, p. 257.

Swampscott, enjoying the bliss of absolute repose and the sweet uncertainty which attends the angler's line. I have sat with him in the dimly lighted room on autumnal evenings, cheerful and vocal with the cricket's chirp, and have heard his wise and sensible talk, uttered in that soft, melodious tone which gave such a peculiar charm to his utterances, — a tone so shy that an intruder would hush it into silence in an instant. I have strolled with him in the darkness of a summer night through the lanes of Concord, assured by his voice, which came up from the grass-grown roadside in a sort of mysterious murmur, that he was my companion still. And everywhere and at all times, he bore about him a strong and commanding presence and impression of unpretending power. I can hardly tell how Hawthorne succeeded in entertaining his companions and securing their entire confidence, unless it was that he displayed great good sense and acuteness and good temper in his intercourse with them, and never misled them by false promises or low appeals. This, in addition to his subtile genius, everywhere recognized and never wholly concealed to even the most commonplace associates, made him a most fascinating friend, as he was really and truly a man of rare quality among ordinary men." [1]

The earlier portraits of Hawthorne show the gentleness and the feminine traits in his disposition much more distinctly than those that are best known to the world. There is one, now owned by his cousin, Mr. Richard C. Manning, of Salem, which was painted in 1840 by Charles Osgood, an artist of Salem, and induced this comment from his sister Louisa: "The color is a little too high, to be sure, but perhaps it is

[1] *Papyrus Leaves*, pp. 261, 262.

a modest blush at the compliments which are paid to
your pen." Another, painted by a Mr. C. G. Thompson, at Boston, in 1850 (now owned by Mr. Julian
Hawthorne), resembles this, and presents, one would
say, the ideal Hawthorne of the "Twice-Told Tales"
and "The House of the Seven Gables." The face is
smooth shaven and the cheeks are somewhat slender,
making all the lines and features contribute to an effect of greater length and of more oval contour than
that given by the later representations. The color is
delicate; the large eyes look forth with peculiarly fascinating power from beneath a forehead of exceptional
height and harmonious prominence. The hair is long,
and recedes slightly on both sides of the forehead; a
single lock in the middle curving over and drooping
forward. There is less firmness about the lips than
was characteristic of them in his latter years; they
close softly, yet even in their pictured repose they
seem to be mobile and ready to quiver with response
to some emotion still undefined but liable to make itself felt at any instant. In its surrounding of long
hair, and of a collar rising above the jaws, with a large
black tie wound about the throat in the manner of a
stock but terminating in a large bow at the front, the
beardless countenance is stamped with a sort of prevalent aspect of the period when it was painted, which
gives it what we call the old-fashioned look. It is,
none the less, a striking one; one that arrests the
glance immediately, and holds it by a peculiar spell.
There is no suggestion of a smile or of cheeriness about
it; the eyes even look a little weary, as with too
much meditation in the brain behind them; there is
not a trace discernible of that sturdy, almost military,
resoluteness so marked in the familiar crayon portrait

by Rowse, executed after Hawthorne's return from
Italy and England. Here the face is pensive, timid,
fresh and impressionable as that of some studious un-
dergraduate unusually receptive of ideas, sentiments,
and observations : it is, indeed, quiet and thoughtful
to the verge of sadness. Longfellow kept always in
his study a black-and-white copy from this portrait,
and in speaking of it and of the subject's extreme shyness, said that to converse with Hawthorne was like
talking to a woman. The Thompson picture was reproduced in 1851, in a steel engraving of considerable
merit, and Hawthorne, thanking Mr. Fields for some
of the prints, wrote from Lenox : " The children recognized their venerable sire with great delight. My
wife complains somewhat of a want of cheerfulness in
the face ; and, to say the truth, it does appear to be
afflicted with a bedevilled melancholy ; but it will do
all the better for the author of ' The Scarlet Letter.'
In the expression there is a singular resemblance (which
I do not remember in Thompson's picture) to a miniature of my father."

In Rome, Miss Landor modelled a bust, the marble
copy of which is now in the Concord Public Library.
It is of life-size, and presents the head in a position
which raises the chin and inclines the plane of the face
slightly backward, so that the effigy might be taken
for that of an orator addressing a great audience.
This pose was selected by the sculptress because, after
due study, she was persuaded that when Hawthorne
became interested in conversation and kindled with the
desire to set forth his own view, he always raised his
head and spoke from a commanding attitude. She
chose to perpetuate a momentary action, instead of rendering his customary aspect of holding the chin some-

what down or on a firm level; and this may account
for the likeness not being satisfactory to the members of Hawthorne's own family. The bust, however,
renders impressively the magnificent proportions of
the neck and head and the whole physiognomy. The
mouth is not concealed, and, although it exhibits more
decision than that of the Thompson picture, it conveys
the same general impression of a quickly responsive
sensibility. Mr. Thompson made his painting when
Hawthorne was forty-six, and Miss Landor had
sittings from the author at the age of fifty-four; but
the difference in apparent maturity of power in the
face would indicate a much longer interval. This is
perhaps due to the difference in the means of representation, and to some defect of strength in Mr. Thompson's drawing; but perhaps also the decided change
in Hawthorne's general look, which began under the
greatly altered conditions attending his European life,
proceeded very rapidly. He allowed a thick mustache
to grow, during his last stay in England, and it was
then that Kuntze modelled his profile, which sets Hawthorne's features before us in a totally different way
from any of the other portraits. Unfortunately,
Kuntze's relief is reduced to a size below that of life,
and the features accordingly assume a cramped relation. The lofty forehead is given its due importance,
however, and concentration of impassioned energy is
conveyed by the outline of the face, from this point of
view. The chin, always forcible as well as delicate,
impresses one in this case with a sense of persistent
and enduring determination on the part of the original; and with this sense there is mingled an impression
of something that approaches sternness, caused, it may
be, by the hirsute upper lip. In considering these

several representations and the crayon by Rowse, together with the photographs taken after Hawthorne's
home-return, it is impossible not to observe that the
sturdier and more practical elements in the romancer
gained upon him, so far as personal appearance was
concerned, with advancing age and a wider experience of life in the large world. But such a series of
glimpses can do no more than to suggest disjointedly
the union in him of attributes positive and passive,
which always struck those who met him. A photograph which was secured before he left England de-
picts him in a mood and with an air that very happily convey this complete equipment of the man, this
wellnigh perfect combination of traits, which enabled
him by sympathy to run through the entire gamut of
human feeling. His friend, John Lothrop Motley,
induced him one day to enter a photographer's establishment, on the plea that he had business of his own
there. Hawthorne was given a book to read, while
waiting; and when the photographer was ready Motley
attracted his friend's attention. Hawthorne looked up
with a dawning smile, a bright, expectant glance, —
holding the book on his knee meanwhile, with a finger
in the place, — and instantly a perfect negative was
made. The resulting portraiture showed him absolutely as he was: a breathing form of human nobility;
a strong, masculine, self-contained nature, stored in a
stalwart frame — the face grown somewhat more ro-
tund than formerly, through material and professional
success, and lighted up with captivating but calm ge-
niality; while over the whole presence reigned an exquisite temperance of reserve, that held every faculty
in readiness to receive and record each finest fluctua-
tion of joy or sorrow, of earnest or of sport.

Such as he there appears, we shall do well to imagine him to ourselves.

The tendency at first, among those who judged him from his writings alone, was to set him down as a misanthrope. We need not go to the other extreme now. That he inclined to gravity, in his manner and in his habit of thought, seems to be beyond question; but he was not sombre. Neither was he hilarious. At home, though he was frequently silent, he never appeared to be so from depression, except in seasons of distress at the illness of members of the household; the prevailing effect of his presence, even when he was least communicative, being that of a cheerful calm with mellow humor underlying it. One of his children said to Mr. T. W. Higginson : " There was never such a playmate in all the world." On the other hand, I remember a letter from Hawthorne (no longer accessible for exact quotation), in which he frankly speaks of himself as taking constitutionally a somewhat despondent view of things. But if he did so, he never permitted the shadow to fall upon his friends. " I should fancy from your books," Hillard confessed in a letter to him, "that you were burdened with some secret sorrow, that you had some blue chamber in your soul, into which you hardly dared to enter yourself; but when I see you, you give me the impression of a man as healthy as Adam in Paradise." Mr. Hillard once told the present writer that he had sometimes walked twenty miles along the highway with Hawthorne, not a word being spoken during the entire tramp, and had nevertheless felt as if he were in constant communication with his friend. Mr. Curtis wrote many years ago : " His own sympathy was so broad and sure, that, although nothing had been said for hours, his companion knew that not a thing had escaped his eye, nor a single pulse of beauty in the day or scene or society failed to thrill his heart. In this way his silence was most social. Everything seemed to have been said."

His fondness for seclusion, his steady refusal to talk when he did not feel like talking, and his unobtrusive but immovable independence in opinion, together with his complete disregard of conventional requirements in social intercourse, prevented Hawthorne from ever becoming a popular man. But he was the object of a loving admiration and the sincerest friendship, on the part of certain few intimates. Those who knew him best, and had been longest in relations with him, insensibly — as one observer has well suggested — caught from his fine reticence a kindred reluctance to speak about him to others. A degree of reverence was blended with their friendship, which acquired for them a sacred privacy. Having sound health physically, as well as a healthy mind, he enjoyed out-door occupations — such as garden-work, rowing, fishing, and walking; but he never rode on horseback. He liked to make pedestrian trips through the country, stopping at haphazard in country taverns and farm-houses and listening to the conversation that went on there. In chance companionship of that sort, he could tolerate much freedom of speech, in consideration of the mother-wit that prompted it; but among men of his own class he never encouraged broad allusions. If anything that savored of the forbidden were introduced, he would not protest, but he at once turned the conversation towards some worthier subject. The practical vein in Hawthorne — his ingrained sympathy with the work-a-day world in which his father and his forefathers had busied themselves — adapted him to the official drudgery to which he devoted nine years of his life; although, while he was occupied with that, the ideal activities of his nature lay dormant. The two sets of faculties never could be exercised in equal measure at the same time: one or the other had to predominate. Yet in the conduct of his own affairs, so far as his pecuniary obligations were concerned, he was very prudent, and to the last degree scrupulous. One or two exceedingly small debts, which he was forced to contract, weighed upon him with a heaviness that to the ordinary commercial mind would be altogether inconceivable; and the relief he experienced when he was able to cancel them was inexpressible. His fault, in business, was that he attributed to other people a sense of honor equal to his own. This entailed upon him sundry losses which he was not well able to afford, through loans made to supposed friends. Notwithstanding the carefulness of his expenditure and a few moderately good receipts from the publication of his books in England, he died leaving a property of little more than twenty thousand dollars, besides his house at Concord and the copyright of his works.

In addition to the strong physical frame and tall stature several times noticed in the present sketch, Hawthorne's personal appearance was distinguished by his large and lustrous gray-blue eyes, luxuriant dark brown hair of remarkable fineness, and a delicacy of the skin that gave unusual softness to his complexion; a complexion subdued, but full of " healthy, living color," as Mrs. Hawthorne once described it. " After his Italian journey he altered much, his hair having begun to whiten, and a thick dark mustache being permitted to grow, so that a wit described him as looking like a ' boned pirate.' When it became imperative to shake off his reticence, he seems to have had the power of impressing as much by speech as he had before done by silence. It was the same abundant, ardent, but self-contained and perfectly balanced nature that informed either phase. How commanding was this nature may be judged by the fact related of him by an acquaintance, that rude people jostling him in a crowd would give way at once ' at the sound of his low almost irresolute voice.' . . . Something even of the eloquent gift of old Colonel Hathorne seemed to be locked within him, like a precious heirloom rarely shown ; for in England, where his position called for speech-making, he acquitted himself with brilliant honor. But the effort which this compelled was no doubt commensurate with the success. He never shrank, notwithstanding, from effort, when obligation to others put in a plea. A member of his family has told me that, when talking to any one not congenial to him, the effect of the contact was so strong as to cause an almost physical contraction of his whole stalwart frame, though so slight as to be perceptible only to eyes that knew his informal and habitual aspects; yet he would have sunk through the floor rather than betray his sensations to the person causing them. Mr. Curtis, too, records the amusement with which he watched Hawthorne paddling on the Concord River, with a friend whose want of skill caused the boat continually to veer the wrong way, and the silent generosity with which he put forth his whole strength to neutralize the error, rather than mortify his companion by explanation. His considerateness was always delicate and alert." [1] A niece of Horace Mann, who passed a part of the spring of 1852 with Mr. and Mrs. Hawthorne

[1] *A Study of Hawthorne:* Chapter, xi., 291, 292.

at West Newton, supplies one little instance of this, which shall be registered here. Mrs. Dean, the lady in question, was then under engagement to teach in Boston, but had an interval of time on her hands before the work should begin. She was invited by the Hawthornes to the West Newton house (at that time owned by Mr. Mann), where she was to occupy a room which had formerly been hers. She found that a fire was carefully laid in the stove every night, to warm the room in the morning, and, thinking that too much trouble was taken on her account, she begged to be allowed to attend to this detail herself. It was then she discovered that it was Hawthorne who made up the fire; and he insisted upon continuing his service. Mrs. Dean also recalls that he listened attentively to the incidental and ordinary chat between Mrs. Hawthorne and herself, seldom making any remark, but, when he did volunteer one, giving it a pungent and epigrammatic or humorous turn. Entering the room where she was constructing a raised map for schoolroom use, he watched her with close interest for a while, and then observed: " I would rather have had the making of the world itself, in the beginning."

Taking whatever happened in a spirit always very much the same; reflective, penetrating, quietly sportive — a spirit, likewise, of patience and impartiality — Hawthorne kept his power of appreciation fresh to the very last. He could endure the humdrum tasks of government office, but they did not dull his pleasure in the simplest incidents of home-life, nor his delight in nature. " Every year the recurrent changes of season filled him with untold pleasure ; and in the spring, Mrs. Hawthorne has been heard to say, he would walk with her in continuous silence, his heart full of the awe and delight with which the miracle of buds and new verdure inspired him." Taking everything in this spirit, we may repeat, mingling with the rough and the refined, and capable of extracting the utmost intellectual stimulus from the least of mundane phenomena, he maintained intact a true sense of relativity and a knowledge that the attainable best is, in the final analysis, incomplete. Contemplating a rose one day, he said : " On earth, only a flower is perfect." He cherished a deep, strong, and simple religious faith, but never approved of intellectual discussion concerning religion.

The slightness of the definite fact, or of the reminiscence vouchsafed by those who knew him, is continually impressed upon us in reviewing this career. Considered in its main outline, how very plain and unambitious is the history ! A sea-captain's son, born in Salem ; living obscurely ; sent up to the rude clearing where a new village was founding in Maine ; induced, against his preference, to go to college; writing timid stories and essays, which the world had no suspicion that it needed, and prompted to this by an impulse of which the origin is inexplicable ; next, the author coming into notice, but under eclipse now and then from disappearance behind a public office ; finally, the acknowledged romancer of indefinitely great endowment — the head of his order in America — sent abroad to an important post, where he is recognized and warmly greeted by every one who can discern clearly : such is the general course of the narrative. Afterwards, the now eminent man comes back to his native land, labors a little longer in comparative obscurity, suffers unmerited obloquy for his fidelity to a personal friend, while perfectly loyal to his government; then dies, and is mourned not alone by those devoted companions who felt him to be the one great fact to them in present human nature, but also by famous scholars and poets, and by a multitude of strangers, who gather around his bier with a stricken sense of loss ineffable. It is very simple; it is very democratic — the unnoticed American boy in humble circumstances becoming the centre of a circle of fame which is still extending its radius. Very simple it is, and yet inexplicable. But if we cannot tell precisely how the mind came into being, nor what were the fostering influences that most cogently aided its growth, we can, at least, pay our reverence to the overruling Power that brings genius to the flowering-point under circumstances seemingly the most unpropitious.

In 1863 — the last year of his life — Hawthorne wrote to Mr. Stoddard, who had sent him a copy of his poem, "The King's Bell." "I sincerely thank you," he said, "for your beautiful poem, which I have read with a great deal of pleasure. It is such as the public had a right to expect from what you gave us in years gone by; only I wish the idea had not been so sad. I think Felix might have rung the bell once in his lifetime, and again at the moment of death. Yet you may be right. I have been a happy man, and yet I do not remember any one moment of such happy conspiring circumstances that I could have rung a joy-bell for it."

Yes, he had been a happy man; one who had every qualification for a rich and satisfactory life, and was able to make such a life out of whatever material offered. He might not have been willing to sound the joy-bell for himself, but the world has rung it because of his birth. As for his death, it is better not to close our sketch with any glimpse of that, because, in virtue of his spirit's survival among those who read and think, he still lives.

G. P. L.

NEW YORK, *May* 20, 1883.

# ORDER OF ARRANGEMENT

## OF

# NATHANIEL HAWTHORNE'S WORKS,

*in this Edition,*

WITH LIST OF FRONTISPIECES AND VIGNETTES.

———◇———

## I.

TWICE-TOLD TALES.

*Frontispiece.* Lady Eleanore's Mantle. By WALTER SHIRLAW.

*Vignette.* The Maypole of Merrymount. By WALTER SHIRLAW.

## II.

MOSSES FROM AN OLD MANSE.

*Frontispiece.* The Old Manse. By ROSS TURNER.

*Vignette.* On the Concord River. By R. SWAIN GIFFORD.

## III.

THE HOUSE OF THE SEVEN GABLES.

THE SNOW-IMAGE AND OTHER TWICE-TOLD TALES.

*Frontispiece.* The Snow-Image. By FREDERIC S. CHURCH.

*Vignette.* The Puritan Girl. By FREDERIC S. CHURCH.

## IV.

A WONDER BOOK FOR GIRLS AND BOYS.

TANGLEWOOD TALES.

THE WHOLE HISTORY OF GRANDFATHER'S CHAIR.

*Frontispiece.* Pandora's Box. By FREDERIC S. CHURCH.

*Vignette.* Ideal Head. By FREDERIC S. CHURCH.

## V.

THE SCARLET LETTER.

THE BLITHEDALE ROMANCE.

*Frontispiece.* "Sooner or later he must needs be mine."
By FREDERIC DIELMAN.

*Vignette.* Pearl. By FREDERIC DIELMAN.

## VI.

THE MARBLE FAUN ; OR, THE ROMANCE OF MONTE BENI.

*Frontispiece.* Miriam and Donatello. By WALTER SHIR-
LAW.

*Vignette.* Hilda and the Doves. By WALTER SHIRLAW.

## VII.

OUR OLD HOME.

PASSAGES FROM THE ENGLISH NOTE-BOOKS. I.

*Frontispiece.* A London Suburb. By ROBERT BLUM.

*Vignette.* St. Botolph's Church. By ROBERT TURNER.

## VIII.

PASSAGES FROM THE ENGLISH NOTE-BOOKS. II.

*Frontispiece.* St. Paul's, London. By R. SWAIN GIFFORD.

*Vignette.* Traitor's Gate. By R. SWAIN GIFFORD.

## IX.

PASSAGES FROM THE AMERICAN NOTE-BOOKS.

*Frontispiece.* Along the Shore. By R. SWAIN GIFFORD.

*Vignette.* In the Maine Woods. By R. SWAIN GIFFORD.

## X.

PASSAGES FROM THE FRENCH AND ITALIAN NOTE-BOOKS.

*Frontispiece.* Roma. By ROSS TURNER.

*Vignette.* Florence. By ROSS TURNER.

## XI.

THE DOLLIVER ROMANCE.

FANSHAWE.

SEPTIMIUS FELTON ; OR, THE ELIXIR OF LIFE.

APPENDIX.

The Ancestral Footstep.

*Frontispiece.* The Grave on the Hill-Top. By FREDERIC
DIELMAN.

*Vignette.* The Draught of Immortality. By FREDERIC
DIELMAN.

## XII.

TALES AND SKETCHES.

BIOGRAPHICAL STORIES.

BIOGRAPHICAL SKETCHES.

ALICE DOANE'S APPEAL.

CHIEFLY ABOUT WAR MATTERS.

LIFE OF FRANKLIN PIERCE.

APPENDIX.

Biographical Sketch of Nathaniel Hawthorne. By GEORGE
PARSONS LATHROP.

Order of Arrangement, with List of Frontispieces and Vignettes.

Index of Titles.

*Frontispiece.* Portrait from a Photograph. By J. A. J.
WILCOX.

*Vignette.* The Wayside. By WILLIAM L. TAYLOR.

# INDEX TO TITLES

## IN THIS EDITION OF

## NATHANIEL HAWTHORNE'S WORKS.

———◆———

The titles in capitals are those of the separate volumes or of principal divisions ; those in Roman small letters are single short pieces.

|  | VOL. | PAGE |
|---|---|---|
| About Warwick | VII. | 85 |
| Acadian Exiles, The | IV. | 547 |
| Alice Doane's Appeal | XII. | 277 |
| Ambitious Guest, The | I. | 364 |
| AMERICAN NOTE-BOOKS, PASSAGES FROM THE | IX. | |
| ANCESTRAL FOOTSTEP, THE | XI. | 431 |
| Antique Ring, The | XI. | 51 |
| Artist of the Beautiful, The | II. | 504 |
| At Home | II. | 457 |
| Bell's Biography, A | III. | 499 |
| BIOGRAPHICAL SKETCHES | XII. | 215 |
| BIOGRAPHICAL STORIES | XII. | 137 |
| Birthmark, The | II. | 47 |
| BLITHEDALE ROMANCE, THE | V. | 313 |
| Book of Autographs, A | XII. | 88 |
| Boston Massacre, The | IV. | 589 |
| "Browne's Folly" | XII. | 131 |
| Buds and Bird Voices | II. | 170 |
| Burns, Some of the Haunts of | VII. | 231 |
| Canal Boat, The | II. | 484 |
| Canterbury Pilgrims, The | III. | 518 |
| Celestial Railroad, The | II. | 212 |
| Chiefly about War Matters | XII. | 297 |
| Chimæra, The | IV. | 168 |
| Chippings with a Chisel | I. | 455 |
| Christina, Queen | XII. | 203 |

|  | VOL. | PAGE |
|---|---|---|
| Christmas Banquet, The | II. | 322 |
| Cilley, Jonathan | XII. | 264 |
| Circe's Palace | IV. | 306 |
| Civic Banquets | VII. | 363 |
| Consular Experiences | VII. | 19 |
| CUSTOM HOUSE, THE | V. | 18 |
| David Swan | I. | 211 |
| Devil in Manuscript, The | III. | 574 |
| DOLLIVER ROMANCE, THE | XI. | 15 |
| Dr. Bullivant | XI. | 78 |
| Dr. Heidegger's Experiment | I. | 258 |
| Dragon's Teeth, The | IV. | 271 |
| Drowne's Wooden Image | II. | 347 |
| Earth's Holocaust | II. | 430 |
| Edward Fane's Rosebud | I. | 517 |
| Edward Randolph's Portrait | I. | 291 |
| Egotism, or the Bosom Serpent | II. | 303 |
| Endicott and the Red Cross | I. | 485 |
| ENGLISH NOTE-BOOKS, PASSAGES FROM THE | VII., VIII. | |
| Ethan Brand | III. | 477 |
| Fancy's Show-Box | I. | 250 |
| FANSHAWE | XI. | 73 |
| Feathertop | II. | 253 |
| Fellow Traveller, A | II. | 464 |
| Fessenden, Thomas Green | XII. | 246 |
| Fire Worship | II. | 159 |
| Flight in the Fog, A | II. | 461 |
| Footprints on the Sea-Shore | I. | 504 |
| Fragments from the Journal of a Solitary Man | XII. | 23 |
| Franklin, Benjamin | XII. | 189 |
| FRENCH AND ITALIAN NOTE-BOOKS, PASSAGES FROM THE | X. | |
| Gentle Boy, The | I. | 85 |
| Golden Fleece, The | IV. | 379 |
| Golden Touch, The | IV. | 55 |
| Gorgon's Head, The | IV. | 21 |
| GRANDFATHER'S CHAIR | IV. | 431 |
| Grandfather's Dream | IV. | 632 |
| Graves and Goblins | XII. | 68 |
| Gray Champion, The | I. | 21 |
| Great Carbuncle, The | I. | 173 |

|  | VOL. | PAGE |
|---|---|---|
| Great Stone Face, The | III. | 413 |
| Hall of Fantasy, The | II. | 196 |
| Haunted Mind, The | I. | 343 |
| Hollow of the Three Hills, The | I. | 228 |
| HOUSE OF THE SEVEN GABLES, THE | III. | |
| Howe's Masquerade | I. | 272 |
| Hutchinson Mob, The | IV. | 574 |
| | | |
| Indian Bible, The | IV. | 471 |
| Inland Port, The | XII. | 13 |
| Intelligence Office, The | II. | 363 |
| | | |
| John Inglefield's Thanksgiving | III. | 584 |
| Johnson, Samuel | XII. | 166 |
| | | |
| Lady Arbella, The | IV. | 436 |
| Lady Eleanore's Mantle | I. | 307 |
| Leamington Spa | VII. | 58 |
| LEGENDS OF THE PROVINCE HOUSE | I. | 272 |
| Lichfield and Uttoxeter | VII. | 148 |
| Lily's Quest, The | I. | 495 |
| Little Annie's Ramble | I. | 143 |
| Little Daffydowndilly | III. | 607 |
| London Suburb, A | VII. | 254 |
| | | |
| Main Street | III. | 439 |
| Man of Adamant, The | III. | 564 |
| MARBLE FAUN, THE | VI. | |
| Maypole of Merry Mount, The | I. | 70 |
| Minister's Black Veil, The | I. | 52 |
| Minotaur, The | IV. | 213 |
| Miraculous Pitcher, The | IV. | 140 |
| Monsieur du Miroir | II. | 182 |
| MOSSES FROM AN OLD MANSE | II. | |
| Mr. Higginbotham's Catastrophe | I. | 127 |
| Mrs. Bullfrog | II. | 149 |
| Mrs. Hutchinson | XII. | 217 |
| My Home Return | XII. | 35 |
| My Kinsman, Major Molyneux | III. | 616 |
| | | |
| New Adam and Eve, The | II. | 279 |
| Newton, Sir Isaac | XII. | 157 |
| Niagara, My Visit to | XII. | 42 |
| Night Scene, A | XII. | 21 |

|  | VOL. | PAGE |
|---|---|---|
| Night Sketches | I. | 477 |
| Notch of the White Mountains, The | II. | 476 |
|  |  |  |
| Old Apple-Dealer, The | II. | 495 |
| Old Esther Dudley | I. | 328 |
| Old-Fashioned School, The | IV. | 505 |
| Old French War, The | III. | 541 |
| Old Manse, The | II. | 11 |
| OLD NEWS | III. | 531 |
| Old Ticonderoga | III. | 591 |
| Old Tory, The | III. | 555 |
| Old Woman's Tale, An | XII. | 119 |
| Oliver Cromwell | XII. | 178 |
| Our Evening Party among the Mountains | II. | 479 |
| OUR OLD HOME | VII. |  |
| Outside Glimpses of English Poverty | VII. | 326 |
| Oxford, Near | VII. | 201 |
|  |  |  |
| Paradise of Children, The | IV. | 82 |
| PASSAGES FROM A RELINQUISHED WORK | II. | 457 |
| Pepperell, Sir William | XII. | 235 |
| Peter Goldthwaite's Treasure | I. | 428 |
| Phips, Sir William | XII. | 227 |
| PIERCE, FRANKLIN, LIFE OF | XII. | 347 |
| Pilgrimage to Old Boston | VII. | 169 |
| Pine-Tree Shillings, The | IV. | 459 |
| Pomegranate Seeds, The | IV. | 341 |
| Procession of Life, The | II. | 235 |
| Prophetic Pictures, The | I. | 192 |
| Provincial Muster, The | IV. | 535 |
| P.'s Correspondence | II. | 407 |
| Pygmies, The | IV. | 247 |
|  |  |  |
| Rappaccini's Daughter | II. | 107 |
| Recollections of a Gifted Woman | VII. | 113 |
| Red Cross, The | IV. | 445 |
| Rejected Blessing, The | IV. | 519 |
| Rill from the Town Pump, A | I. | 165 |
| Rochester | XII. | 17 |
| Roger Malvin's Burial | II. | 381 |
|  |  |  |
| SCARLET LETTER, THE | V. |  |
| Select Party, A | II. | 70 |
| SEPTIMIUS FELTON | XI. | 229 |

|  | VOL. | PAGE |
|---|---|---|
| Seven Vagabonds, The | I. | 392 |
| Shadow Brook | IV. | 51, 75 |
| Shaker Bridal, The | I. | 469 |
| Sights from a Steeple | I. | 219 |
| Sister Years, The | I. | 375 |
| SKETCHES FROM MEMORY | XII. | 13 |
| Snow-Flakes | I. | 385 |
| SNOW-IMAGE, AND OTHER TWICE-TOLD TALES, THE | III. | 379 |
| Snow-Image, The | III. | 391 |
| Some of the Haunts of Burns | VII. | 231 |
| Sunday at Home | I. | 32 |
| Sunken Treasure, The | IV. | 484 |
| Sylph Etheridge | III. | 508 |
| TALES AND SKETCHES | XII. | 11 |
| TANGLEWOOD TALES | IV. | 199 |
| Three Golden Apples, The | IV. | 110 |
| Threefold Destiny, The | I. | 527 |
| Time's Portraiture | XII. | 121 |
| Toll-Gatherer's Day, The | I. | 234 |
| Tory's Farewell, The | IV. | 617 |
| TRUE STORIES. (See GRANDFATHER'S CHAIR AND BIO-GRAPHICAL STORIES.) | | |
| TWICE-TOLD TALES | I. | |
| Up the Thames | VII. | 288 |
| Village Theatre, The | II. | 470 |
| Village Uncle, The | I. | 349 |
| Virtuoso's Collection, A | II. | 537 |
| Vision of the Fountain, The | I. | 242 |
| Wakefield | I. | 153 |
| Wedding Knell, The | I. | 41 |
| West, Benjamin | XII. | 144 |
| White Old Maid, The | I. | 414 |
| Wives of the Dead, The | III. | 598 |
| WONDER-BOOK, A | IV. | 7 |
| Young Goodman Brown | II. | 89 |